BATTLE HONOURS
of the
BRITISH ARMY

FROM TANGIER 1662, TO THE COMMENCEMENT OF THE REIGN OF KING EDWARD VII

by
C. B. NORMAN

 DAVID & CHARLES REPRINTS

ISBN 0 7153 5398 5

First published in 1911
This reprint published in 1971

Reproduced and Printed in Great Britain by
Redwood Press Limited, Trowbridge & London
for David & Charles (Publishers) Limited
Newton Abbot Devon

BATTLE HONOURS OF THE BRITISH ARMY

THE DUKE OF MARLBOROUGH.

Frontispiece.

BATTLE HONOURS OF THE BRITISH ARMY

FROM TANGIER, 1662, TO THE COMMENCEMENT
OF THE REIGN OF KING EDWARD VII

BY C. B. NORMAN

(LATE 90TH LIGHT INFANTRY AND INDIAN STAFF CORPS)

AUTHOR OF "ARMENIA AND THE CAMPAIGN OF 1877," "TONQUIN ; OR, FRANCE IN
THE FAR EAST," "COLONIAL FRANCE," "THE CORSAIRS OF FRANCE," ETC.

WITH MAPS AND ILLUSTRATIONS

LONDON

JOHN MURRAY, ALBEMARLE STREET, W.

1911

TO

THE HONOURED MEMORY

OF

THE OFFICERS AND MEN

WHO HAVE FALLEN IN DEFENCE OF

THEIR COUNTRY

ALPHABETICAL LIST OF BATTLE HONOURS

CHRONOLOGICAL LIST OF BATTLE HONOURS

1806. Cape of Good Hope.
,, Maida.
1808. Roleia.
,, Vimiera.
,, Sahagun.
1808-14. Peninsula.
1809. Arabia.
,, Corunna.
,, Cochin.
,, Douro.
,, Talavera.
,, Bourbon.
,, Martinique.
1810. Amboyna.
,, Guadeloupe.
,, Ternate.
,, Banda.
1811. Java.
,, Barrosa.
,, Fuentes d'Onor.
,, Albuera.
,, Almaraz.
,, Busaco.
,, Arroyos dos Molinos
,, Tarifa.
1812. Ciudad Rodrigo.
,, Badajos.
,, Detroit.
,, Salamanca.
1813. Vittoria.
,, Miami.
,, Pyrenees.
,, St. Sebastian.
,, Nivelle.
,, Nive.
,, Niagara.
1814. Orthes.
,, Toulouse.
,, Bladensburg.
1815. Waterloo.
1817. Kirkee.
1817. Seetabuldee.
,, Nagpore.
,, Maheidpore.
1818. Corygaum.

1819. Nowah.
,, Persian Gulf.
1821. Arabia.
1823. Beni Boo Alli.
1824. Ava.
,, Kemmendine.
1825. Arracan.
1826. Bhurtpore.
1835. South Africa.
1839-42. Afghanistan.
1839. Ghuznee.
,, Kelat.
,, Aden.
1840. Kahun.
1842. Jelalabad.
,, Khelat-i-Ghilzai.
,, Candahar.
,, Cabool.
,, Cutchee.
,, China.
1843. Scinde.
,, Meeanee.
,, Hyderabad.
,, Maharajpore.
,, Punniar.
1845. Moodkee.
,, Ferozeshah.
1846. Aliwal.
,, Sobraon.
1846-47. South Africa.
1846. New Zealand.
1849. Chillianwallah.
,, Mooltan.
,, Goojerat.
,, Punjaub.
1851-53. South Africa.
1852. Pegu.
1854. Alma.
,, Balaclava.
,, Inkerman.
,, Sevastopol.
1856. Reshire.
,, Bushire.
1856-57. Persia.
1857. Koosh-ab.

1857. Delhi.
,,   Lucknow.
,,   Central India.
,,   Defence of Arrah.
,,   Behar.
,,   Canton.
1858-60. China.
1860. Taku Forts.
,,   Pekin.
1861-65. New Zealand.
1867. Abyssinia.
1873-74. Ashantee.
1877-79. South Africa.
1878-80. Afghanistan.
1878. Ali Masjid.
,,   Peiwar Kotal.
,,   Charasia.
1879. Kabul.
,,   Ahmed Khel.
1880. Kandahar.
1882. Egypt.
,,   Tel-el-Kebir.
1884. Egypt.
1884-85. Nile.
1885. Abu Klea.
,,   Kirbekan.

1885. Suakin.
,,   Tofrek.
1885-87. Burmah.
1887. West Africa.
1892-1894. West Africa.
1895. Defence of Chitral.
,,   Chitral.
1897-98. Punjab Frontier.
1897. Malakand.
,,   Samana.
,,   Tirah.
,,   Hafir.
1898. Atbara.
,,   Khartoum.
,,   Sierra Leone.
1899-1902. South Africa.
1899. Modder River.
1900. China.
,,   Pekin.
,,   Ashanti.
,,   Defence of Kimberley.
,,   Relief of Kimberley.
,,   Paardeburg.
,,   Defence of Ladysmith.
,,   Relief of Ladysmith.

CONTENTS

CHAPTER 1

BATTLE HONOURS FOR SERVICES IN THE MEDITERRANEAN, 1662-1900

CHAPTER II

BATTLE HONOURS FOR SERVICES IN NORTHERN EUROPE, 1695-1709

CHAPTER III

BATTLE HONOURS FOR SERVICES IN NORTHERN EUROPE, 1743-1762

CHAPTER IV

BATTLE HONOURS FOR SERVICES IN NORTH AND SOUTH AMERICA

CONTENTS

b

CHAPTER XV

BATTLE HONOURS FOR SERVICES IN BURMAH, 1885-1887

CHAPTER XVI

BATTLE HONOURS FOR THE FIRST AFGHAN WAR, 1839-1842

CHAPTER XVII

BATTLE HONOURS FOR SERVICES IN INDIA, 1843

CHAPTER XVIII

BATTLE HONOURS FOR THE CONQUEST OF THE PUNJAB

CHAPTER XIX

BATTLE HONOURS FOR THE CRIMEAN WAR, 1854-55

CHAPTER XX

BATTLE HONOURS FOR THE INDIAN MUTINY, 1857-1859

CHAPTER XXI

BATTLE HONOURS FOR SERVICES IN CHINA, 1842-1900

CHAPTER XXII

BATTLE HONOURS FOR SERVICES IN SOUTH AFRICA, 1806-1879

CHAPTER XXIII

BATTLE HONOURS FOR MISCELLANEOUS ACTIONS

CHAPTER XXIV

BATTLE HONOURS FOR THE SECOND AFGHAN WAR

CHAPTER XXV

BATTLE [HONOURS FOR OPERATIONS ON THE NORTH-WEST INDIAN FRONTIER, 1895-1897

CHAPTER XXVI

BATTLE HONOURS FOR SOUTH AFRICA, 1899-1902

CHAPTER XXVII

MISSING BATTLE HONOURS

LIST OF ILLUSTRATIONS

MAPS

INTRODUCTION

In the following pages I have endeavoured to give a
brief description of the various actions the names of
which are emblazoned on the colours and appointments
of the regiments in the British army. So far as I have
been able, I have shown the part that each individual
corps has played in every engagement, by appending to
the account a return of the losses suffered. Unfortunately,
in some cases casualty rolls are not obtainable ; in others,
owing to the returns having been hurriedly prepared,
and later corrections neglected, the true losses of regiments
do not appear.

The whole question of the award of battle honours
abounds in anomalies. Paltry skirmishes have been immortalized, and many gallant fights have been left unrecorded. In some cases certain corps have been singled
out for honour ; others which bore an equal share in the
same day's doings have been denied the privilege of
assuming the battle honour. In some campaigns every
skirmish has been handed down to posterity ; in others
one word has covered long years of fighting. Mysore,
with its one honour, and Persia, with four, are cases in
point. In some instances honours have been refused on
the plea that the headquarters of the regiment was not
present in the action ; in others the honour has been
granted when but a single troop or company has shared
in the fight. There are regiments whose colours bear
the names of battles in which they did not lose a single
man ; others have suffered heavy losses in historic battles

xxiii

which are as yet unrecorded. At Schellenberg, for example, Marlborough's earliest victory, and one unaccountably absent from our colours, the losses of the fifteen regiments engaged exceeded the total casualties of the whole army in the campaign in Afghanistan from 1879 to 1881, for which no less than seven battle honours were granted.

Esprit de corps is the keystone of the discipline of the British army, and the regimental colours are the living symbol of that *esprit de corps*. It is to their colours that men look as the emblems of their regimental history, and on those colours are—or should be—emblazoned the names of all historic battles in which the regiment has been engaged. A soldier knows—or ought to know— the history of his own regiment, but the moment arrives when his curiosity is piqued, and he wishes to learn something about a corps which has fought side by side with his own. Perchance curiosity may be excited as to the reason why Copenhagen appears on the appointments of the Rifle Brigade, and Arabia on the colours of the York and Lancaster; or how it comes about that Dominica is alone borne by the Cornwalls and Pondicherry by the Dublin Fusiliers. I have made no attempt to deal exhaustively with the subject; that would be beyond my powers and would open up too wide a field. I have therefore touched but lightly on those campaigns, such as the Peninsular and Waterloo, which are familiar to everyone in the least conversant with the history of his country, and have dwelt in more detail with those wars which are less well known. Memories are short. Already the South African War has been effaced by that titanic struggle between Russia and Japan. How, then, can the ordinary man be expected to carry in his mind even the rough outline of the Defence of Chitral, an episode which rivals Arcot in the heroism of its few defenders, or of Mangalore and Corygaum, which were in no way inferior in point of steadfast gallantry. When I read of the efforts made to insure the regular supply of jam during the South African War, my mind turns to

Chitral, where the daily ration for six long weeks was one pound of flour a day, rice and meat being issued only on the doctors' orders, the one antiseptic available being carbolic tooth-powder! Or I think of Mangalore, which capitulated after Campbell had cut up his last horse and served out his last ration of flour. Yet I know that the men who defended Mangalore were in no way the superior of those who " muddled through " in South Africa, and that these were in no way inferior to the men who drove the French out of Spain. There were complaints of the stamp of recruits two centuries ago, as there are to-day. " The men you send me," wrote Grey from Martinique, " are not fit to bear arms." " I know not which are worse, officers or men," wrote Moore. " Send me men, not boys," wrote Sir Colin Campbell from India. Yet the boys who were not fit to bear arms captured the West Indies from the French ; the worthless officers and men traversed Spain and held Napoleon's veterans in check at Corunna while their leader lay dying ; and the boys in Sir Colin's regiments helped to restore peace in India.

Does the nation realize the calls it has made upon the army, or what oceans of blood have been shed owing to the vacillation and parsimony of successive Ministries ? Three times have we captured the West India Islands ; twice have our troops taken the Cape of Good Hope ; three times have our armies marched from sea to sea in Spain ; and there are few towns of importance in the Low Countries which have not been captured more than once by British troops. Conquests have been restored at the conclusion of a war in the full knowledge that on the outbreak of fresh hostilities those same conquests would have to be freshly undertaken and more lives sacrificed. Armies hastily reduced on the conclusion of a spurious peace had to be as hastily improvised on the renewal of war. Officers have been censured, broke, and shot if they have not performed prodigies with raw, untrained recruits. Uncomplainingly, all ranks went forth to die, eager only to uphold the honour of their Sovereign, of their regiments, and of their country.

I have not confined myself to the honours which appear only on the colours of British regiments, but have included all which have been granted to any corps which bears allegiance to our King. Some of the noblest feats of arms have been achieved by a few British officers at the head of a handful of Indian troops. At Mangalore and at Lucknow the sepoy regiments fought no less gallantly than the British corps which bear the same battle honour. The despatches of Colonel Campbell and of Sir John Inglis bear testimony to this fact; but at Seedaseer, Saugor, and Seetabuldee, at Corygaum, Arrah, and Kahun, and last, but by no means least, at Chitral, the sepoys had no British soldier to stiffen the defence. Yet there was no wavering. So long as the fighting races of India show the devotion to their officers and their loyalty to the Crown they have ever shown, we may smile at the frothy vapourings of the over-educated Bengalis, who have never furnished a single man for the defence of the country which they wish to emancipate from our rule. We read in the story of Chitral how the water-carrier, with his jaw smashed by a bullet, insisted as soon as his wound was dressed in taking more water to his Sikhs in the fighting-line. Is there not a story rife of a British regiment in the Mutiny which wished to recommend the regimental bheesti for a similar act of valour? There are few names amongst these battle honours around which stories of equal gallantry have not been woven. The memory of those deeds which men have dared, and in daring which they have gone forth to certain death, is the heritage not merely of those who serve under the colours, but of every man and woman of our race : Hardinge, rallying the men round the colours of the 57th at Albuera, with the now historic words, " Die hard, my men, die hard !"—a title that has clung to the regiment to this day. Luke O'Connor, then a colour-sergeant, holding high the colours of the Royal Welsh

Fusiliers at the Alma, under which ten young subalterns had fallen, and he with bullet through the breast, refusing to leave his sacred charge. Souter, of the 44th, tearing the colours from their staff and wrapping them under his sheepskin coat, and so saving them, when 667 officers and men fell under the fierce onslaughts of the Afghans in the dim defiles of the Khurd Kabul Pass, one solitary survivor reaching the shelter of the mud walls, held by the 13th, at Jelalabad. Or those two boy heroes, Melville and Coghill, whose dead bodies were found in the bed of the Tugela River, hard by the colours they had died to save. Or Quentin Battye, the first of three brothers to fall in the " Guides," dying with the old tag on his lips : " Dulce et decorum est pro patria mori."

These are the stories our colours have to tell, these the lessons the names upon them teach. Not merely gallantry in action—that is a small thing, and one inherent in our race. They teach of privations uncomplainingly borne, of difficulties nobly surmounted, of steadfast loyalty to the Crown, and of cheerful obedience to orders even when that obedience meant certain death. Such are the honours which have found an abiding-place on the colours of the British army.

I am aware that I possess few qualifications for the task I have undertaken, and I am also painfully aware that I have entirely failed to do justice to my theme. That failure would have been immeasurably greater had I not received the most valuable assistance from those far better qualified than I am to bring into relief the history of our army.

To these I would now venture to offer my most cordial thanks—to the Army Council, for some invaluable casualty returns, which I believe are now published for the first time ; to the ever-courteous officials at the Record Office and in the libraries of the British Museum, the India Office, and the Royal United Service Institution, for the patience with which they have suffered my many importunities; last, but by no means least, to the many officers of regiments, British and Indian, who have so kindly given me unrecorded details of their regimental histories.

For the reproduction of the colours of " The Queen's" and the Royal Dublin Fusiliers I am indebted to the courtesy of the commanding officers of those two distinguished regiments. A close relationship exists between them. When Tangier and Bombay passed into our possession as the dowry of Queen Catharine of Braganza two regiments were raised as garrisons for our new possessions. The one proceeded to Tangier, and after some years of hard fighting, returned to England, to be known as " The 2nd Queen's." The other went to Bombay, and for two long centuries nobly upheld the honour of our name under the title of " The Bombay Europeans." On the transfer of the East India Company to the Crown the regiment appeared in the Army List as the 103rd Royal Bombay Fusiliers. Twenty years later, when regimental numbers were thrown into the melting-pot and the nomenclature of historic regiments changed, the Bombay Regiment became the Royal Dublin Fusiliers, and as such worthily maintained its old reputation in South Africa. The Royal Scots and the Munster Fusiliers may claim seniority to the Queen's and the Dublins, but the battle honours on the colours I have selected cover the whole period with which I deal— from Tangier to Ladysmith, from Arcot to Lucknow.

I would, in conclusion, beg those—and they are many— whose knowledge of regimental history is far deeper than my own to deal gently with the many imperfections in this book—an unworthy tribute of homage to the incomparable heroism of the British soldier.

C. B. NORMAN.

January, 1911.

BATTLE HONOURS OF THE BRITISH ARMY

CHAPTER I

BATTLE HONOURS FOR SERVICES IN THE MEDITERRANEAN, 1662-1902

Tangier, 1662-1680—Gibraltar, 1704—Gibraltar, 1779-1783—
Maida, 1806—Mediterranean—Mediterranean, 1901-02.

TANGIER, 1662-1680.

IN the year 1910, just two centuries and a half after the event, the regiments which upheld British honour on the coast of Morocco were authorized to bear the above battle honour on their colours and appointments :

Royal Dragoons, 1662-1680.   Grenadier Guards, 1680.
Coldstream Guards, 1680.   Royal Scots, 1680.
      The Queen's, 1662-1680.

The King's Own Lancaster Regiment has been un-accountably omitted from this list ; but there is no doubt that the 4th (King's Own), under Colonel Kirke took part in the final series of actions with the Moors prior to our evacuating the fortress.

Tangier passed into our hands, together with Bombay, as a portion of the dowry of Catherine of Braganza on her marriage with Charles II. At that time there were many who considered it the more valuable of the two acquisitions, commanding as it did the entrance to the Mediterranean. Immense sums were spent in strengthening the fortifications and in improving the harbour. The inveterate hostilities of the Moors, however, only increased with time. The one regiment first raised for the garrison, then styled the " Regiment of Tangier " (now The Queen's

Royal West Surrey) was from the outset of its career engaged in a long series of engagements waged against desperate odds. Soon it was found necessary to raise a regiment of horse to supplement the task of the infantry in dealing with the Moorish horsemen. The Royal Dragoons then came into existence, and laid the foundations of that reputation for dash and discipline which has never left them. Later on, owing to the persistent hostility of the Moors, the Grenadier Guards, the Coldstreams, and the 2nd Tangier Regiment (now the 4th King's Own) were sent as reinforcements; and a reference to the Tangier Papers shows that men from the fleet were continually employed against the enemy. On one occasion Sir Cloudesley Shovel, with 600 seamen, took a leading part in the defence. Casualty returns were not so carefully prepared in the seventeenth as in the twentieth century, and I have found it impossible to discover the total losses incurred during our occupation. Between the years 1660 and 1664 there was scarcely a month in which our troops were not fighting for their lives, and on one occasion at any rate they were so hard pressed that the Governor applied, and successfully, to the Spaniards at Gibraltar for assistance. Thus it comes about that in the casualty list which has come down to us of the action on October 27, 1680, the Spanish Horse figures side by side with the Grenadier Guards.

CASUALTIES IN ACTION AT TANGIER, OCTOBER 27, 1680.

Regiments.	Officers.		Men.		Regiments.	Officers.		Men.	
	K.	W.	K.	W.		K.	W.	K.	W.
Royal Dragoons	—	2	11	35	The Queen's R. W. Surrey ..	2	10	34	120
Grenadier Gds.	—	1	7	51					
Royal Scots ..	4	15	36	100	Spanish Horse	5	4	12	22

A few weeks after this action the King's Own (Lancaster Regiment), then commanded by Colonel Kirke, arrived as

THE COLOURS OF THE TANGIER REGIMENT, 1684.

(Now The Queen's Royal West Surrey Regiment.)

To face page 2.

a reinforcement, and later in the year the Coldstream Guards. In 1684 the place was evacuated, having cost us many millions in money and many thousand valuable lives.

GIBRALTAR, 1704-05.

This battle honour, which commemorates the capture of Gibraltar by the fleet under Admiral Sir George Rooke, and the subsequent defence of the fortress under Prince George of Hesse, is borne by the following regiments :

Grenadier Guards.	Coldstream Guards.
King's Own (Lancaster).	Somerset Light Infantry.
East Lancashire.	East Surrey.
Cornwall Light Infantry.	Royal Sussex.

Queen Anne caused a medal to be struck in recognition of the services of the senior officers at the capture of this historic fortress, but it was left to King Edward VII. to sanction the grant of the battle honour to the regiments which added the Rock to the possession of Great Britain.

Owing to our having espoused the cause of Charles III. in the War of the Spanish Succession, a fleet of fifty sail was sent into the Mediterranean, under the command of Sir John Rooke, but it was practically placed at the disposal of King Charles. Embarked on the fleet under the command of Prince George of Hesse were the 4th (King's Own), 30th (East Lancashire), 31st (East Surrey), the 32nd (Cornwall Light Infantry), with Holt's and Shannon's Regiments, all acting as Marines. On July 22, 1704, the fleet anchored in Gibraltar Bay, and landed on what is now known as neutral ground. To a summons to surrender, the Governor sent a defiant answer. He, at all hazard, refused to recognize King Charles as his Sovereign, or our right to dictate to Spaniards in the choice of their monarch. On the following day Admiral Byng, with twenty-seven vessels, stood close in and silenced the batteries, when the bellicose Governor, in order to avoid the effusion of blood, accepted the terms offered. Rooke then landed the troops under Prince George, and sailed away to attack the allied fleets which were in the offing. In the course of the month of August he fought the Battle of Malaga, the effects of which were overshadowed by the glorious victory of Blenheim. The French and Spaniards were not prepared to sit down and see England established at the entrance of the Mediterranean, and at once took steps to recover possession of Gibraltar. We, on the other hand, took equally decisive measures to hold it. At that moment we had a considerable force in Portugal, acting in support of Charles III., and from this force reinforcements were immediately despatched to Gibraltar.

CASUALTIES AT THE CAPTURE OF AND SUBSEQUENT OPERATIONS AT GIBRALTAR, 1704-05.

Regiments.	Officers.		Men.		Regiments.	Officers.		Men.	
	K.	W.	K.	W.		K.	W.	K.	W.
Royal Artillery Grenadier Gds. Coldstream Gds. 4th K.O. (R. Lancaster Regt.) .. 13th Somerset L.I.					Roy. Engineers 30th East Lancashire .. 31st E. Surrey 32nd Cornwall L.I. .. .. 35th R. Sussex	1	—	—	—

NOTE.—I have been unable to ascertain the casualties of individual corps at Gibraltar. I leave this table in the hope that at some future day the omission may be repaired ; the total losses amounted to 3 officers and 57 men killed, 8 officers and 258 men wounded.

A combined battalion of the Grenadier and Coldstream Guards, the 13th (Somerset Light Infantry), and the 35th (Royal Sussex), some 1,800 of all ranks, embarked on transports. Narrowly escaping capture,[1] they succeeded in eluding the French fleet, and landed in Gibraltar Harbour on December 18. On the 23rd Prince George made a successful sortie at the head of his new troops, and destroyed a considerable portion of the siege-works ; but the allies, having the land side open to them, were

[1] Three companies of the 13th Regiment were captured and interned at Nantes until the conclusion of the war.

able to bring up supplies and fresh troops without difficulty, whereas we were dependent entirely on our fleet—
in fact, on our command of the sea.   In the early dawn of
February 7, 1705, the allies made a determined attempt
to carry the place by assault, but they were repulsed with
terrible loss by the Coldstream Guards and the 13th (Somersets) ; then, finding their efforts useless, they abandoned
the siege.   Seventy-five years later a fresh attempt to
dispossess us of the fortress led to a new battle honour
appearing on the colours, but the siege of 1727 has been
unaccountably lost sight of.

GIBRALTAR, 1727.

It is somewhat difficult to understand why the defence
of Gibraltar in the year 1727 has not been considered
worthy of being inscribed on the colours of the regiments
which fought so well under the veteran Lord Portmore.
From February 22 to June 23 the garrison, barely 6,000
strong, withstood a close siege, repelling many assaults
and suffering many casualties.   Famine as well as disease
stared them in the face.   I have been unable to ascertain
the complete details of the losses of individual regiments
engaged, but from the accounts of contemporary writers
who went through the siege it would appear that the
Grenadier Guards alone lost upwards of 100, of whom nineteen were killed in one day.   Surely " Gibraltar, 1727,"
might be added to the colours of the twelve regiments
which held the fortress for England under Lord Portmore.

The story of the siege is not pleasant reading.   It is an
early exemplification of the manner in which the warnings
of the " man on the spot " are almost invariably dis-
regarded by the authorities at home, and how our soldiers
are expected to make bricks without straw, and to undergo
perils which with a little exercise of forethought might be
avoided.   In the month of August, 1726, the Acting
Governor, Colonel Kane, reported the threatening attitude
of the Spaniards, and that Malaga was being converted
into a military base, where large quantities of war material
were being collected.   He further asked for the paltry

sum of £3,000, in order to place the fortress in a better
state of defence.   One of the most pressing questions
was the levelling of the earthworks constructed by the
Spaniards during the last siege, which were still left
standing, and which would afford shelter to the enemy
in the event of the outbreak of hostilities.   The troops
were lodged in houses in the town ; there were no barracks,
and no casemates to the various outworks.   His garrison
consisted of but four weak battalions.   On these representations one battalion was sent from Minorca.   In
December Kane reported the mobilization at Malaga of
5,000 Walloon Guards, of fourteen Spanish battalions, and
eight regiments of cavalry.   No doubt as to the intention
of the Spaniards now remained.   Orders had been published for the Governors of the four Andalusian provinces
to raise 8,000 men, and in reporting this circumstance
Kane drew attention to the fact that the artillery under
his command consisted of *three non-commissioned officers
and fifteen gunners*, whilst the infantry amounted to but
1,400 men.   His lines of defences were three miles in
extent, and the two works mounted no less than 150
guns, the large majority of which had long since been
condemned.   In the month of January the Spaniards
openly commenced their siege-works, throwing up
batteries within gunshot of the fortress ; but it was not
until the month of April that General Clayton arrived
with the first reinforcements, but with no siege material.
By the end of April the garrison had been increased to
a total of 6,000 men, two only of the regiments being
over 600 strong, whilst the reinforcements of artillery
brought up the strength of the Royal Regiment to 127
of all ranks ; and of these Lord Portmore wrote that
the gunners " are the worst that ever were employed." [1]
The want of fresh provisions told heavily on the men, and
all ranks and all arms were busily employed in throwing
up fresh defensive works.   Complaints were rife as to the

---

[1] So far back as the year 1710 Lord Portmore had addressed
strong remonstrances as to the condition of the defences and the
weakness of the garrison, begging for money and for engineer
officers to supervise the proposed works.

guns—large numbers burst—and the Governor reiterated his complaints that the Spanish guns were far superior in range and accuracy to our own. By the end of May the garrison was reduced to 4,427 effectives, the men rarely getting one night in three in bed. Still the stout old veteran answered shot for shot, warning the Government that the Spaniards were evidently determined on wresting the position from us, and that unless reinforcements were speedily sent the place was liable to be carried by assault, as his men were not sufficiently numerous to man the whole of the works. Fortunately for the garrison, diplomacy was at work, and by the end of July preliminaries of peace had been signed, and the safety of the fortress was assured.

When actual hostilities broke out, the garrison of Gibraltar, including the two regiments that had been sent from Ireland and Minorca, consisted of the 5th (Northumberland Fusiliers), 13th (Somerset Light Infantry), 18th (Royal Irish), 20th (Lancashire Fusiliers), and the 29th (Worcesters). Considerable delays occurred in despatching the reinforcements, and, as I have remarked, it was not until the month of April that these left England. The Governor, the veteran Lord Portmore, who was at home on leave, returned to his post, and at the same time a battalion of the Grenadier Guards, under Colonel Guise— a name which has ever been synonymous in the service with daring gallantry—the 14th (West Yorks), 25th (Scottish Borderers), 26th (Cameronians), 34th (Border Regiment), and 39th (Dorsets), were despatched under convoy of the fleet to Gibraltar.

There would appear to have been the same eagerness amongst the younger members of the House of Lords to see active service in those days as there was in the Crimea and in the Boer War. The Duke of Richmond, who was a Knight of the Garter and a member of the King's Household, applied for leave to join the army, and so did a son of the Duke of Devonshire. On the other hand, the Duke Wharton joined the Spanish forces, and was happily wounded very early in the siege, and so spared the shame of taking a prolonged share in the operations against his own fellow-countrymen.

I have experienced considerable difficulty in obtaining any records of the casualties, but the following list appears in a contemporary publication written by an officer who took part in the siege, and may, I think, be relied on as showing to a certain extent the losses incurred during a portion of the siege :

Regiments.	Officers.		Men.		Regiments.	Officers.		Men.	
	K.	W.	K.	W.		K.	W.	K.	W.
Royal Artillery	I	—	11	16	25th K.O. Scottish Borderers	I	—	3	13
Grenadier Gds.	—	—	2	19					
5th Fusiliers ..	—	—	4	18	26th Cameronians	—	—	6	28
13th Somerset L.I.	—	—	7	26	29th Worcesters	—	—	2	11
14th W. Yorks	—	—	6	22	30th E. Lancs	—	—	8	14
18th Roy. Irish	—	—	8	17	34th Border Reg.	—	—	2	16
20th Lanc. Fus.	I	—	8	12	39th Dorsets ..	I	—	6	13

GIBRALTAR, 1779-1783.

(With Castle and Key and motto, " Montis Insignia Calpe.")

The regiments permitted to bear these distinctions are the

Suffolk.	Dorset.
Northampton.	Essex.

Highland Light Infantry.

In the month of June, 1779, Spain declared war against England, France having done so in the preceding year. There was no doubt as to the object of the Spaniards— the recapture of Minorca, Gibraltar, and the American Colonies lost to us in the preceding wars. Fortunately, we had in Gibraltar a soldier who knew his work. Though the name of Eliott will ever be associated with the Rock, soldiers may also like to know that the gallant defender of Gibraltar raised and trained that distinguished regiment

the 15th Hussars.   From the moment that he took over
the command in 1777 Eliott set to work to strengthen
the defences.   On the declaration of war he had but 5,382
of all ranks in his garrison, including 458 gunners.   His
chief danger was starvation, for on the land side he was
completely hemmed in, whilst on the sea the Spaniards
instituted a close blockade, and brought pressure to bear
on His Shereefian Majesty to forbid the exportation of
fresh meat and vegetables to the garrison from Morocco.
In November of that year Rodney defeated the blockading
fleet, and threw in the 71st (Highland Light Infantry), a
welcome reinforcement, and also stores sufficient to
maintain the garrison for a year.   The Spaniards now
drew closer the blockade, and commenced to throw up
elaborate siege-works ; but it was not until April, 1781,
that the blockade was converted into a siege in earnest,
and it is said that between then and November upwards
of 100,000 shot and shell were poured into the place.   Our
casualties were by no means heavy, nor did the fortifications suffer much, though the town itself was utterly
destroyed.   On the 27th of that month (November) Eliott
attacked the Spaniards, destroyed and burnt their
batteries, spiking a large number of guns, but though his
losses in this sortie were slight, his men suffered much
from scurvy and the incessant duty which was imposed
on an all too scanty garrison.   From time to time a vessel
would elude the blockading fleet ; and on one occasion
Admiral Darby forced his way through with the 97th Regiment, and later still the King's Own Scottish Borderers and
the 59th (East Lancashires) were also thrown in.   In May,
1782, the Spaniards were reinforced by a strong French
division, and the siege was continued with renewed
vigour.   Floating batteries, with massive timber roofs
to protect the gunners, were built by the allies, and then
on September 14, 1782, convoyed by forty-seven sail of
the line, this formidable armada entered the bay,
and opened a fresh bombardment from the sea.   To this
Eliott responded with red-hot shot, and once more the

garrison was saved. In the following month Howe was enabled to convoy a fleet of transports under the Rock, and so relieved Eliott of his one dread—starvation. In February, 1783, peace was signed between Spain and England, and on the 6th of the month the gates of the fortress were thrown open, after a bombardment of thirteen months.

CASUALTIES AT THE DEFENCE OF GIBRALTAR, 1779-1783.

Regiments.	Officers.		Men.		Regiments.	Officers.		Men.	
	K.	W.	K.	W.		K.	W.	K.	W.
Royal Artillery	2	8	29	121	59th E. Lancs.	—	—	8	9
Roy. Engineers	—	—	—	—	71st Highland				
12th Suffolks..	1	3	27	110	L.I.	—	6	42	115
25th K. O. Scottish Borderers	—	—	2	8	72nd Seaforth Highlanders	—	3	55	148
39th Dorsets ..	2	3	27	60	73rd Regt. ..	—	6	44	115
56th Essex ..	—	3	27	67	97th Regt. ..	—	—	13	41
58th N'amptons	1	2	18	74					

MAIDA, JULY 4, 1806.

This distinction is borne on the colours of the

Lancashire Fusiliers.   Inniskilling Fusiliers.
Royal Sussex.   North Lancashire.
Northamptons.   Seaforth Highlanders.
                Gloucestershire Regiment.

It recognizes the gallant services of these regiments in the engagement fought in defence of our ally, the King of Naples, by the little force under the command of General Stuart against a superior body of French under General Regnier. In 1847, when the so-called Peninsular medal was issued, a special clasp, " Maida," was awarded to the survivors of the brilliant little action on the shores of the Straits of Messina. The Grenadier and Light Infantry battalions, which bulk so largely in the accompanying list of casualties, were composed of the flank companies of the five battalions engaged, supplemented by 250 men of the 35th (Royal Sussex) and a company of the 61st (Gloucesters), and so it comes about that, although the headquarters were not present, the old 35th and 61st were accorded the battle honour. The losses in this engagement were :

Regiments.	Officers.		Men.		Regiments.	Officers.		Men.	
	K.	W.	K.	W.		K.	W.	K.	W.
Grenadier batt.	o	1	4	26	Light Infantry battalion ..	1	3	7	42
Lancs Fusiliers	—	—	1	6	78th Seaforth Highlanders	—	7	4	74
27th Inniskillings	—	—	6	47	81st North Lancashire ..	—	2	19	63
58th Northamptons	—	—	—	2					

MEDITERRANEAN.

This distinction was awarded to the following regiments of Militia for their services during the Crimean War of 1854-55, when they volunteered to perform garrison duty in order to set free line regiments for service at the front :

3rd Batt. the Buffs.
5th Batt. Royal Fusiliers.
3rd Batt. South Stafford.
3rd Batt. Loyal North Lancashire.
3rd Batt. Royal Berkshire.
3rd Batt. the King's Own (Royal Lancaster).
3rd Batt. West Yorkshire.
3rd Batt. Oxford Light Infantry.
3rd Batt. Northamptons.
3rd Batt. Wiltshire.

MEDITERRANEAN, 1901-02.

The above honour is borne on the colours of the following regiments, in recognition of their services in performing garrison duty in the Mediterranean during the South African War of 1899-1902. For these services they were also granted a medal.

3rd Batt. Northumberland Fusiliers.
3rd Batt. West Yorkshire.
3rd Royal West Kent.
3rd Batt. Seaforth Highlanders.
5th Batt. Royal Fusiliers.
3rd Loyal North Lancashire.
3rd Batt. King's Own Yorkshire Light Infantry.
5th Batt. Royal Munster Fusiliers.

CHAPTER II

BATTLE HONOURS FOR SERVICES IN NORTHERN EUROPE, 1695-1709

Namur, 1695—Blenheim, 1704—Ramillies, 1706—
Oudenarde, 1708—Malplaquet, 1709.

NAMUR, 1695.

IN the month of February, 1910, an Army Order was published announcing that His Majesty King Edward VII. had been graciously pleased to approve of the following regiments being permitted to bear the honorary distinction " Namur, 1695 " upon their colours, in recognition of services rendered during the siege and capture of that city, 215 years previously :

Grenadier Guards.	Coldstream Guards.
Scots Guards.	Royal Scots.
Queen's (Royal West Surrey).	King's Own (Lancasters).
Royal Warwicks.	Royal Fusiliers.
West Yorkshire.	Bedfords.
Leicesters.	Royal Irish.
Royal Welsh Fusiliers.	King's Own Scottish Borderers.

Previously to this date the only regiment which in any way commemorated its association with the siege of Namur was the 18th (Royal Irish), which was entitled to bear on its colours the words " Virtutis Namurcensis præmium," and which had received the title of the " Royal Regiment of Ireland " from King William himself for its conduct at the storming of that fortress. There was no good reason why the Royal Irish should have been honoured above its fellows. The details of the operations at Namur were open to all the world, and the casualties suffered by other corps showed that they too had borne their fair share of the fighting.

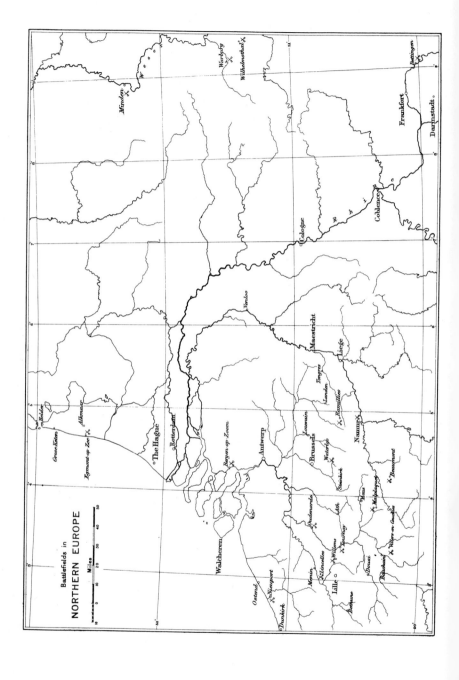

Battlefields in
NORTHERN EUROPE

Miles
0   10   20   30   40   50

Minden

Weser

Warburg
Wilhelmsthal

Frankfort

Hettingen

Darmstadt

Coblenz

Cologne

Rhine

Venloo

Maestricht

Liège

Tongres
Landen
X Ramilies

Namur

Louvain

Brussels
Waterloo
X Genappe

X Beaumont

Alkmaar
Egmont-op-Zee
Groot-Keten

The Hague
Rotterdam

Bergen-op-Zoom

Antwerp

Oudenarde

Lath
Tournay

X Fleurus
X Malplaquet
X Villers-en-Couchie

Walcheren

Ostend
Nieuport

Menin
Courtray

Lille
Williers

Braine
Bavaisme

Bethune

Dunkirk

Namur was one of the many fortified towns in Flanders which had fallen into the hands of the French during our struggles with that nation in the closing years of the seventeenth century. King William's military operations had not been attended with any marked degree of success. His troops, despite the gallantry of the English regiments, had been worsted at Steenkirk, Landen, and many other fights, and in the ranks of our own regiments there was a very decided feeling that our friends the Dutch were prone to throw the brunt of the hard work on us, and were not too eager to afford us that assistance in action which we had a right to expect. A glance at the casualty lists which follow the various actions—the names of which are inscribed on our colours—proves the truth of this statement. Whether at Namur, Dettingen, Emsdorff, in Flanders or in Spain, the British regiments were invariably expected to pull the chestnuts out of the fire for their allies.

The Siege of Namur commenced on July 3, 1695, and three days later King William determined to carry the outworks by assault. The Guards attacked on the right, the Royal Scots and Royal Fusiliers on the left. The assault was perfectly successful, but the loss was enormous, the Brigade of Guards losing thirty-two officers, the Royal Scots and Royal Fusiliers ten. A few days later, after the fire of the batteries had opened a practicable breach in the walls near the St. Nicholas Gateway, the British were again called upon to carry this work. This they did with a loss of 800 killed and wounded. Then came the final assault on the citadel, for which the Leicesters, the Royal Irish, and Mackay's and Buchan's Highlanders were told off. These two last are no longer with us. These four battalions lost 63 officers and 925 men killed and wounded. But the day was ours, and with the fall of the citadel Namur once more passed into the possession of the House of Orange.

Although the Army Order of February, 1910, only grants the distinction to infantry regiments, there were a number of British cavalry regiments employed in covering operations during the siege. There were the 1st and 2nd Life and the Royal Horse Guards, all seven regiments of Dragoon Guards, the Royal Dragoons, Scots Greys, 4th Hussars, 5th Lancers, and 7th Hussars. I regret I have not been able to ascertain the losses they suffered. Those of the infantry were as follows :

CASUALTIES AT THE SIEGE AND ASSAULT OF NAMUR, 1695.

Regiments.	Officers.		Men.		Regiments.	Officers.		Men.	
	K.	W.	K.	W.		K.	W.	K.	W.
Grenadier Gds.	6	12	152	298	19th Yorkshire	—	—	8	11
Coldstream Gds.	4	9	101	193	23rd Roy. Welsh				
Scots Guards	3	4	51	60	Fusiliers ..	6	15	92	123
Royal Scots ..	6	5	62	109	25th K.O. Scot-				
2nd Queens ..	2	4	54	46	tish Borderers	7	4	79	95
3rd Buffs ..	—	1	8	47	27th R. Innis.	—	3	44	25
4th K.O. (Lan-					Mackay's Regt.	2	15	73	126
caster Regt.)	3	4	46	59	Buchan's Regt.	4	9	65	140
6th R. Warwick	2	3	66	40	Collingwood's				
7th R. Fusiliers	1	3	33	58	Regt. ..	1	5	77	36
14th W. Yorks	5	5	47	82	Saunderson's				
16th Bedfords	2	2	56	77	Regt. ..	—	8	80	128
17th Leicesters	4	8	101	149	Seymour's Regt.	—	—	49	71
18th Roy. Irish	12	13	86	185	Lauder's Regt.	4	2	70	99

NOTE.—I am indebted to the courtesy of the Army Council for the figures relating to the Grenadier and Coldstream Guards, as well as for the casualties amongst the commissioned ranks of a regiments. I am bound to observe that the figures given by the Army Council do not correspond with a return which I have seen at the Record Office, entitled "Liste des Soldats Morts et blessés devant Namur depuis le Commencement jusqu'à la fin du Siege," which may have been overlooked by the War Office.

THE WAR OF THE SPANISH SUCCESSION.

In the month of May, 1701, just two months after the death of William III., we found ourselves involved in war with France, in consequence of the quarrel as to the right of succession in Spain. One hundred and thirty years later a similar cause led to the Franco-German War. In those far-off days England was a Continental Power, and whatever affected the Low Countries affected also the United Kingdom. The Dutch provinces of

Flanders lent themselves to attack, and as in the wars under William, so now once more they formed the theatre of war. We had no King to assume the command, and to Marlborough was confided the task of commanding our armies. The Spaniards were no longer our allies, and Spanish Flanders was in the hands of our enemies, adding considerably to the military difficulties. The Dutch, too, showed themselves no more favourably disposed to us than when William of Orange was on the throne, and the whole year of 1701 was wasted in fruitless wrangling. There was infinite jealousy between ourselves and the Prussians and Dutch as to Marlborough's position, and both nations seemed to forget that their troops were but mercenaries, maintained in the field to a very great extent by the subsidies voted by the English Parliament. In 1702 Marlborough found himself in nominal command of about 60,000 men, of whom 12,000 were British soldiers. His freedom of action was much hampered by Dutch Deputies and Prussian jealousies. That year, however, saw him victorious on three occasions : at Venloo, which, after a short siege, was carried by assault in the most gallant manner by the English, led by the noted fire-eater Cutts ; at Maestricht, in August, where we lost 4 officers and 132 men killed, 7 officers and 134 men wounded ; and at Liége, which was captured with a loss to us of 11 officers and 143 men killed, 20 officers and 360 men wounded. As was the custom in those days, the army went into winter-quarters, whilst the Commander-in-Chief returned to England to face Parliament and secure funds and reinforcements for the coming year.

In 1704 Marlborough determined to carry the war into his enemies' country, and by a masterly movement, worthy of Napoleon in his best days, transferred the scene of operations from the Valley of the Meuse to that of the Danube, and on June 21, 1704, gained a brilliant victory at Schellenberg, on the banks of that river— a name that might well be borne on the colours and appointments of the sixteen regiments which bore such a distinguished part in the fight. I append the casualty lists of the losses incurred in this now almost forgotten battle, which surely deserves recognition.

CASUALTIES AT SCHELLENBERG, JUNE 21, 1704.

Regiments.	Officers.		Men.		Regiments.	Officers.		Men.	
	K.	W.	K.	W.		K.	W.	K.	W.
Scots Greys ..	1	2	7	17	Royal Irish ..	—	4	12	36
5th Lancers ..	—	2	4	19	Royal Scots				
Grenadier Gds.	4	8	82	135	Fusiliers ..	—	3	—	—
Royal Scots ..	5	25	115	302	Royal Welsh				
Buffs	2	—	3	37	Fusiliers ..	5	11	66	162
King's Liver-					24th S. Wales				
pool Regt. ..	1	2	5	33	Borderers ..	1	4	29	44
Lincolns ..	1	—	13	39	26th Cameron-				
East Yorkshire	—	3	10	22	ians	—	2	19	60
Bedfords ..	2	3	30	34	37th Hampshire	4	10	17	61

Marlborough, in conjunction with the Prince Eugène of Savoy, now pushed up to the vicinity of Munich, and there is little doubt, had he been in possession of a sufficient artillery force, that the capital of Bavaria would have fallen into his hands. He had with him but thirty-five guns of the Royal Artillery, and he felt compelled to relinquish the attempt. Falling back, he attacked the Allies at Blenheim, where again the British troops covered themselves with glory.

BLENHEIM, AUGUST 2, 1704.

This battle honour has been conferred on the

King's Dragoon Guards.
5th Dragoon Guards.
7th Dragoon Guards.
Royal Scots Greys.
Grenadier Guards.
Buffs.
Lincolns.
Bedfords.
Royal Welsh Fusiliers.
Cameronians.

3rd Dragoon Guards.
Carabiniers.
5th Lancers.
Royal Scots.
King's Liverpool Regiment.
East Yorkshire.
Royal Irish.
South Wales Borderers.
Hampshire.

A medal to commemorate this victory was struck by order of Queen Anne, but, unfortunately, no lists of the losses suffered by regiments as regards the rank and file have been preserved, or, if preserved, they have been lost sight of. We know from contemporary journals that there were eighteen squadrons and fourteen battalions of British troops engaged, and that the total casualties amounted to 51 officers and 625 men killed, 147 officers and 1,381 men wounded, the casualties amongst the officers being—

CASUALTIES AT BLENHEIM.

Regiments.	Officers.		Men.		Regiments.	Officers.		Men.	
	K.	W.	K.	W.		K.	W.	K.	W.
King's Dragoon Guards	—	—			Buffs	3	9	—	—
3rd Dragoon Guards	3	5			King's Liverpool	1	3	—	—
5th Dragoon Guards	3	5			Lincolns	8	9	—	—
Carabiniers	1	—	93	156	East Yorkshire	5	13	—	—
7th Dragoon Guards	5	5			Bedfords	4	12	—	—
Royal Dragoons	3	3			Royal Irish	4	10	57	96
Scots Greys	—	—			Royal Scots Fusiliers	5	12	—	—
5th Lancers	—	—	10	22	Royal Welsh Fusiliers	—	9	—	—
Grenadier Gds.	1	5			South Wales Borderers	3	9	84	—
Royal Scots	3	8			Cameronians	5	13	—	—
					Hampshire	—	3	—	—

Seldom has there been a victory more complete. Twenty-four battalions surrendered *en bloc*, the total number of prisoners aggregating upwards of 11,000, amongst them being two General officers; 124 guns and 109 stand of colours also fell into our hands. Ireland is now an integral portion of the British Empire, and Irish soldiers have in all our campaigns fought with stubborn determination on our side. So, too, the Royal Irish covered itself with glory on this day, as it has ever done when fighting for us. At the same time, it is worthy of note that the fiercest of our opponents at Blenheim were the regiments of the Irish Brigade in the pay of the King of France.

Marlborough now retraced his steps to the Low Countries, and once more prepared to oppose the French in the field and the Dutch in the Council. The whole of the following year was spent in futile attempts to organize a successful series of military movements in face of the persistent antagonism of our Dutch colleagues.

RAMILLIES, MAY 12, 1706.

A medal was struck to commemorate this victory, which is inscribed on the colours and appointments of the following regiments :

1st King's Dragoon Guards.	3rd Dragoon Guards.
5th Dragoon Guards.	6th Carabiniers.
7th Dragoon Guards.	5th R.I. Lancers.
Royal Scots Greys.	Grenadier Guards.
Royal Scots.	Buffs.
Liverpool Regiment.	Lincolns.
East Yorkshire.	Bedfords.
Royal Irish.	Royal Scots Fusiliers.
Royal Welsh Fusiliers.	South Wales Borderers.
Cameronians.	Gloucesters.
Worcester.	Hampshire.

Though inscribed on our colours, there were but few British troops actually under fire at the Battle of Ramillies. On the cavalry fell the task of converting a victory into a rout, and to this end the six regiments of British dragoons enumerated above were worthily employed, their trophies being 56 guns, 80 stand of colours, and 2,000 prisoners. No regimental lists of casualties have been preserved, but it would appear that the Cameronians lost two officers killed, and that the cavalry in the pursuit lost 384 of all ranks killed and wounded.

Ramillies was not the only success that attended our arms in Flanders during the year 1706, and it is difficult to understand why it alone should have been selected for recognition. The whole of Flanders in those days was studded with fortresses, under cover of which the French lay secure. To capture these was a necessity, and one by one they fell into our hands. In the months of August, Menin, after a siege of six weeks, was carried by assault, our loss being 32 officers and 551 men killed, 80 officers and 1,944 men wounded ; the regiments which took part in the siege and assault being the Scots Greys, the 3rd and 5th Dragoon Guards, the King's, Liverpool Regiment, the Lincolns, the Royal Irish, and the Royal Welsh Fusiliers, the latter losing fifteen officers killed and wounded.

CASUALTIES AT THE BATTLE OF RAMILLIES.

Regiments.	Officers.		Men.		Regiments.	Officers.		Men.	
	K.	W.	K.	W.		K.	W.	K.	W.
King's Dragoon Guards ..					Lincolns				
3rd Dragoon Guards ..					East Yorkshire				
5th Dragoon Guards ..					Bedfords.. ..				
Carabiniers ..					Royal Irish ..	—	—	4	6
7th Dragoon Guards ..					Royal Scots Fusiliers ..				
Grenadier Gds.					Royal Welsh Fusiliers ..				
Coldstream Gds.					24th S. Wales Borderers ..				
Royal Scots ..					26th Cameronians	2	—	—	—
Buffs					28th Gloucester				
King's Liverpool Regt. ..					29th Worcester				
					37th Hampshire				

NOTE.—I have left the tables of casualties blank in the hope that some more diligent searcher after truth may be fortunate enough to find the missing details.

OUDENARDE, JUNE 30, 1708.

This, again, was one of those victories to commemorate which a medal was struck by order of Her Majesty Queen Anne, whilst a century and three-quarters later the name " Oudenarde " was inscribed on the colours and appointments of the following regiments, by order of Her Majesty Queen Victoria :

1st King's Dragoon Guards.	3rd Dragoon Guards.
5th Dragoon Guards.	Carabiniers.
7th Dragoon Guards.	Scots Greys.
5th Lancers.	Grenadier Guards.
Coldstream Guards.	Royal Scots.
King's Liverpool Regiment.	Buffs.
Lincolns.	East Yorkshire.
Bedfords.	Royal Irish.
Royal Scots Fusiliers.	Royal Welsh Fusiliers.
Cameronians.	South Wales Borderers.

Hampshire Regiment.

The year 1707 was wasted, owing to the opposition of the Dutch and the treachery of the Austrians. The French were accordingly enabled by the early spring of 1708 to mass an army of 100,000 men in Flanders. To face them the Allies could bring but 80,000 ; but the weight of Marlborough's name and the few thousand British veteran troops in his army made up for this deficiency ; and when, after a series of the most brilliant manœuvres, the Duke at last met the French at Oudenarde, he at any rate had no doubt as to the result.

At Oudenarde, as at Ramillies, the British troops were not heavily engaged, their losses numbering 4 officers and 41 men killed, 17 officers and 160 men wounded.

Lille, the capital of French Flanders, was Marlborough's next objective. The difficulties attendant on the siege were enormous, owing to the swampy nature of the neighbourhood and the strength of the fortifications. In spite of being some 10,000 men inferior to the French mobile army, Marlborough determined to essay the task, and from the month of August to October there were five British battalions actively employed in the siege, the rest of the army being engaged in covering the operations and holding in check 96,000 French who were endeavouring to find an opening to save the fortress. On October 11 the place was carried by assault, our losses during the operations having been 17 officers and 447 men killed, 82 officers and 1,093 men wounded. The Bedfords, Royal Irish, Royal Scots Fusiliers, Royal Welsh Fusiliers, and the South Wales Borderers, were the regiments which would be entitled to this distinction.

To commemorate the capture of Lille, Queen Anne caused a medal to be struck, but the name is not on our colours.

CASUALTIES AT THE BATTLE OF OUDENARDE, JUNE 30, 1708.

Regiments.	Officers.		Men.		Regiments.	Officers.		Men.	
	K.	W.	K.	W.		K.	W.	K.	W.
1st King's Dragoon Guards					8th Roy. Liverpool Regt...				
3rd Dragoon Guards ..					10th Lincoln ..				
5th Dragoon Guards ..					15th E. Yorkshire				
6th Carabiniers					16th Bedford..				
7th Dragoon Guards					18th Roy. Irish	1	—	8	12
Scots Greys ..					21st Roy. Scots Fusiliers ..				
5th Lancers ..					23rd Roy.Welsh Fusiliers ..				
Grenadier Gds.	2	—	---	—	24th S. Wales Borderers ..				
Coldstream Gds.					26th Cameronians				
Royal Artillery					37th Hampshire				
Royal Scots ..									
3rd Buffs ..									

NOTE.—According to the published Diary of Private Deane, the Grenadier Guards lost 2 officers killed at Oudenarde, but no detailed list of casualties is forthcoming.

MALPLAQUET, SEPTEMBER 11, 1709.

A medal was struck by Queen Anne to commemorate this victory, and in the reign of Queen Victoria the regiments which were present were permitted to add the name " Malplaquet " to the other distinctions won in more recent battles :

1st King's Dragoon Guards.	3rd Dragoon Guards.
5th Dragoon Guards.	Carabiniers.
7th Dragoon Guards.	Royal Scots Greys.
5th Lancers.	Grenadier Guards.
Coldstream Guards.	Royal Scots.
Buffs.	King's Liverpool Regiment.
Lincolns.	East Yorkshire.
Bedfords.	Royal Irish.
Yorkshire Regiment.	Royal Scots Fusiliers.
Royal Welsh Fusiliers.	South Wales Borderers.
Cameronians.	Hampshire Regiment.

Prior to the Battle of Malplaquet, the Royal Scots, the Buffs, and the Hampshires had been actively employed at the siege and capture of the Fortress of Tournay, in which they suffered heavily; but no distinction was awarded for this siege, save a medal struck by Queen Anne, the word " Tournay " borne by the West Yorkshire, the Hampshire, and the Shropshire, being granted for the action, which took place in the same neighbourhood in 1794, and which I have dealt with on page 94.

Leaving a force to level the fortifications of Tournay, which was looked upon as one of the masterpieces of the great master, Vauban, Marlborough moved towards Mons, where the French, under Marshal Villars, lay with 95,000 men. Their position was a most formidable one. From the forest of Laignieres to the wood of Blangier (a distance of three miles) a series of entrenchments had been thrown up, following the sinuosities of the ground. In advance of this position a number of formidable redans had been constructed, in some of which as many as twenty guns were placed. Fortune, however, favoured the allies in many ways. In front of the position, but out of cannon shot, were the woods of Sart, which enabled Marlborough to conceal his intended movements from the French; whilst the nature of the ground in rear of the French entrenchment prevented Marshal Villars from making any use of his cavalry in the early stages of the fight. On this occasion at any rate we had no reason to complain of the conduct of our allies. The Dutch, under the Duke of Orange, fought with unaccustomed gallantry, whilst the Germans showed that they were not disposed to allow the English to carry off all the honours of the day. Of the details of the battle but little is known, except that it was one of the bloodiest ever fought, scarcely exceeded even by the passage of the Beresina. Although we were the victors, there is no doubt that our losses were greater than those of the French. Sixteen guns and twenty colours remained in our hands.

The twenty British battalions engaged lost 36 officers and 571 men killed, 66 officers and 1,281 men wounded.

There were many more occasions in which we crossed swords with the French in Flanders before peace was declared. At Douai, Bethune, and Bouchain, our troops suffered severely, but no honorary distinctions were granted for any of these fights, so they do not fall within the scope of this chapter.

Unfortunately, the lists of regimental losses of non-commissioned officers and men have not been preserved, and all it is possible to give, with any degree of accuracy, are the number of officers killed, and, to a certain extent, of men wounded at Malplaquet.

CASUALTIES AT THE BATTLE OF MALPLAQUET,
SEPTEMBER 11, 1709.

Regiments.	Officers.		Men.		Regiments.	Officers.		Men.	
	K.	W.	K.	W.		K.	W.	K.	W.
1st King's Dragoon Guards	I	—	—	—	King's Liverpool	I	8	—	—
					10th Lincoln ..	—	2	—	—
3rd Dragoon Guards ..	—	—	—	—	15th East Yorks	3	—	2	62
					16th Bedford..	—	4	—	50
5th Dragoon Guards ..	—	—	—	—	18th Roy. Irish	—	—	—	—
6th Carabiniers	—	—	—	—	19th Yorkshire Regiment ..	—	—	—	—
7th Dragoon Guards ..	—	—	—	—	21st Roy. Scots Fusiliers ..	5	3	—	—
Scots Greys ..	—	—	—	—	23rd Roy. Welsh Fusiliers ..	3	7	—	—
5th Lancers ..	—	—	—	—	24th S. Wales Borderers ..	—	—	—	—
Grenadier Gds.	I	2	—	—	26th Cameronians	4	3	—	—
Coldstream Guards ..	5	2	—	—	37th Hampshire	I	—	—	—
Royal Scots ..	I	3	—	—					
3rd Buffs ..	6	9	—	—					

CHAPTER III

BATTLE HONOURS FOR SERVICES IN NORTHERN EUROPE, 1743-1762

Dettingen—Minden—Emsdorff—Warburg—Wilhelmstahl.

DETTINGEN, JUNE 27, 1743.

THIS battle honour is now borne by the following regiments :

1st Life Guards.	2nd Life Guards.
Royal Horse Guards.	1st King's Dragoon Guards.
7th Dragoon Guards.	1st Royal Dragoons.
Scots Greys.	3rd Hussars.
4th Hussars.	6th Inniskillings.
7th Hussars.	Grenadier Guards.
Coldstream Guards.	Scots Guards.
Buffs.	King's Liverpool Regiment.
Devons.	Suffolk.
Somerset Light Infantry.	Lancashire Fusiliers.
Royal Scots Fusiliers.	Royal Welsh Fusiliers.
East Surrey.	Cornwall Light Infantry.
West Riding Regiment.	Hampshire.

It commemorates the last battle in which a King of England was present in person, the last in which the Order of Knighthood was conferred on the field. The actual command was in the hands of the veteran Earl of Stair, a soldier who had learned the art of war under Marlborough. He had commanded a brigade at Ramillies, and served on the great commander's staff at Blenheim, Oudenarde, and Malplaquet.

We were fighting in support of the claims of Maria Theresa to the throne of Austria. France, on the other hand, was supporting those of the House of Bavaria.

24

Side by side with our own men fought the armies of Austria and Hanover. The field of battle was on the banks of the Main, midway between Darmstadt and Frankfort, hard by the village of Aschaffenburg, where, in the " Seven Weeks' War," the Prussians gained one of their many successes over the Germans of the Southern States. At Dettingen the brunt of the fighting fell on the British, whose losses far exceeded the combined casualties of the allies, the principal sufferers being the 3rd Dragoons, all their officers but two, and more than half their men, being killed or wounded. The heroism of Trooper Brown of this regiment has been handed down to this day, and King George, recognizing his valour, dubbed him Knight-Banneret at the close of the fight, the Commander-in-Chief (the Earl of Stair), and the Honourable J. Campbell, Colonel of the Scots Greys, being similarly honoured. Brown's deed is recorded in the regimental history, but it is little known outside the ranks of what is now the 3rd King's Own Hussars. Three times did this gallant regiment charge into the French massed infantry, outnumbering them four to one ; thrice did they overthrow the enemy's horse. Their standards had been torn to ribbons, the staves shot through and riddled. At the close of one charge a colour fell from a dead Cornet's hand and lay abandoned on the ground. Trooper Brown dismounted to recover it, and, as he regained the saddle, a French trooper with a sabre-cut disabled his bridle-hand. His horse bolted with him into the midst of the French army, when the colour was torn from his grasp and borne away by a gendarme. Wounded and faint, but with the lust of battle strong upon him, the dragoon rallied to his flag, cut down the triumphant captor, then, gripping the broken staff between knee and saddle, bore it in safety to the skeleton squadrons of his own corps. Historians ridicule the part played by King George on the field of Dettingen, but we may rely upon it that the British army appreciated the kingly action when, at the close of the day, veteran Field-

Marshal and wounded dragoon alike received from their Sovereign the accolade of honour. In these prosaic days the prosperous tradesman receives the knighthood, the wounded dragoon is relegated to the workhouse.

CASUALTIES AT THE BATTLE OF DETTINGEN, JUNE 27, 1743.

Regiments.	Officers.		Men.		Regiments.	Officers.		Men.	
	K.	W.	K.	W.		K.	W.	K.	W.
1st Life Guards	—	3	3	4	3rd Buffs ..	—	—	3	3
2nd Life Guards	—	1	2	1	8th King's Liverpool Regt. ...	1	2	6	30
Royal Horse Guards ..	—	1	8	11	11th Devons ..	—	2	11	28
1st King's Dragoon Guards	3	4	8	30	12th Suffolk ..	2	3	27	65
7th Dragoon Guards ..	—	5	22	31	13th Somerset L.I.	—	2	21	30
1st Royal Dragoons ..	—	—	3	3	20th Lancashire Fusiliers ..	—	—	1	2
Scots Greys ..	—	1	—	—	21st Roy. Scots Fusiliers ..	1	1	36	55
3rd Hussars ..	1	6	41	100	23rd Roy. Welsh Fusiliers ..	1	1	15	27
4th Hussars ..	—	—	4	5	31st E. Surrey	—	—	—	1
6th Inniskillings	—	—	2	1	32nd Cornwall L.I.	—	1	—	3
7th Hussars ..	2	2	2	15	33rd W. Riding Regt.	4	—	26	50
Royal Artillery	1	—	4	8	37th Hampshire	—	1	4	14
Grenadier Gds.	—	—	—	—					
Coldstream Gds.	—	—	—	—					
Scots Guards..	—	—	—	—					

The Brigade of Guards, though bearing the honour, were not actually engaged at Dettingen.

NOTE.—Lieutenant Shaw of the Royal Welsh Fusiliers was promoted to a lieutenant-colonelcy in the Marines for gallantry at Dettingen.

MINDEN, AUGUST 1, 1759.

The following six regiments bear this honour :

Suffolks.
Royal Welsh Fusiliers.
Hampshire.

Lancashire Fusiliers.
King's Own Scottish Borderers.
King's Own Yorkshire L.I.

As at Dettingen, so at Minden, the British troops were acting in support of foreign allies. At the former we were supporting the cause of Austria against France, at the latter we were assisting Frederick the Great in his campaign against the combined forces of France and Austria. Our troops were under the command of Prince Ferdinand of Brunswick, whose rôle it was to prevent Hanover (then an appanage of the British Crown) from being overrun by the French. In addition to the above regiments, there were present fifteen squadrons of English cavalry under Lord George Sackville, and four batteries of artillery under Captains Foy, Phillips, Drummond, and MacBean. The fruits of the victory and the glory of the day were marred by the inaction of the British cavalry, due to the supineness or something worse of Lord George Sackville. The feature was the majestic advance of the British infantry under Brigadiers Waldegrave and Kingsley, and the magnificent manner in which the four batteries of artillery followed the retreating French, converting an orderly retirement into a disorderly rout.

CASUALTIES AT MINDEN.

Regiments.	Officers.		Men.		Regiments.	Officers.		Men.	
	K.	W.	K.	W.		K.	W.	K.	W.
Royal Artillery	1	2	2	9	K.O. Scottish				
Suffolk	3	14	82	190	Borderers ..	—	7	19	119
Lancs Fusiliers	6	11	80	224	37th Hampshire	3	12	43	188
Royal Welsh					51st K.O. York-				
Fusiliers ..	—	10	35	161	shire L.I. ..	1	9	20	78

On the morning after the battle Prince Ferdinand addressed a personal letter to Captain MacBean of the " Royal British Artillery," in which he said : " It is to you and your brigade that I am indebted for having silenced the fire of a battery of the enemy, which extremely galled the troops."

Still further to show his appreciation of the services of the Royal Artillery, the Prince ordered the Paymaster-

General to hand 1,000 crowns to Captain Phillips, and 500 each to Captain MacBean, Drummond, Williams, and Foy, for distribution amongst their men.

Concerning the Marquis of Granby, he wrote : " Had he (Lord Granby) been at the head of the cavalry of the Royal King, his presence would, I am persuaded, have greatly contributed to have made our success more complete and more brilliant."

EMSDORFF, JULY 16, 1760.

This distinction is borne only by the
15th Hussars,
and commemorates their association with a body of German troops in Prince Ferdinand's campaign against the French, the opening action of which was Minden. A French division, consisting of six battalions with a regiment of hussars, was surprised by a force of similar strength under Prince Ferdinand, and by sundown the " King's " Hussars had gained for the Allies a glorious victory. It was to the 15th, and to the 15th alone, that the credit of the day was due. It was their *baptême de feu*, and well may they pride themselves on their conduct at Emsdorff. Their gallantry was the theme of the whole army, and the recollection of it has stood them in good stead on many a hard-fought field. As Fortescue so generously writes : " The traditions of charging home remained with the regiment, and doubtless remains with it to this day."

In his official despatch Prince Ferdinand bears high testimony to the very distinguished services rendered by the 15th. After describing the action and the conduct of the troops generally, the Prince wrote : " Particularly to Eliott's regiment, which was allowed by everybody present to have done wonders.

" H.S.H. the Prince could not enough commend to the Duke the bravery, good conduct, and good countenance, with which that regiment fought."

In addition to the 15th, a regiment of Hanoverian cavalry and five battalions of Hanoverian infantry were engaged at Emsdorff, their total casualties being 8 men killed, 2 officers and 52 men wounded.   The total losses of the French were never ascertained, but that evening the prisoners numbered 2 Generals and 177 other officers, with ·2,482 non-commissioned officers and men, whilst 9 stand of colours and 5 guns remained in our hands. The 15th have good reason to be proud of the battle honour " Emsdorff." Their casualties were 2 officers and 73 non-commissioned officers and men killed, 2 officers and 48 of other ranks wounded, their casualties in horses being 168 killed and wounded.

WARBURG, JULY 31, 1760.

It was not until the close of the year 1909, just 150 years after the battle, that the cavalry regiments which took part in this brilliant action were authorized to bear on their colours and appointments the battle honour " Warburg." Why the infantry regiments which bore the brunt of the fighting should be denied this distinction is not for me to tell.   The regiments now honoured are the

Royal Horse Guards.	King's Dragoon Guards.
Queen's Bays.	3rd Dragoon Guards.
Carabiniers.	7th Dragoon Guards.
1st Royal Dragoons.	Scots Greys.
Inniskillings.	7th Hussars.
10th Hussars.	11th Hussars.

At Emsdorff, just a fortnight previously, the 15th Hussars had nobly retrieved the slur which had been cast on the British cavalry owing to the unfortunate behaviour of Lord George Sackville at Minden. At Warburg the mass of the cavalry under Lord Granby had an opportunity of showing that they were by no means behind the 15th in dash or steadiness.   De Muy, the French Commander, occupied a very strong position in a bend of the River Diemel.   His right resting on the village of Warburg. The British infantry, consisting of one brigade of four battalions under the command of Colonel Beckwith of Kingsley's Regiment (now the Lancashire Fusiliers) attacked in two columns. The right, under Major Maxwell of the Lancashire Fusiliers, consisted of the Grenadier companies of the Suffolks, Lancashire Fusiliers, Royal Welsh Fusiliers, Scottish Borderers, 37th (Hampshire), and 51st (King's Own Yorkshire Light Infantry). On its outer flank was the Heavy Cavalry Brigade under Lord Granby. The left infantry column was under Major Daulhat of the West Riding Regiment; this comprised the flank companies of the Northumberland Fusiliers, the King's Liverpool Regiment, the Devons, the South Wales Borderers, the 33rd (West Riding Regiment), and the 50th (West Kent). On Daulhat's left were the light cavalry under General Mostyn, the 7th Hussars leading. In support came the two regiments of Highlanders, Keith's and Campbell's.[1] Between the two infantry columns were three troops of Horse Artillery, under Captains Phillips, Macbean, and Stephens; these earned Prince Ferdinand's highest praise for their dash and the accuracy of their fire. Some delay occurred in supporting the attack of the British infantry, who alone sustained the early stages of the action; and the Prince ordered Lord Granby to move round the rear of the columns and press home an attack on the French right rear. Granby was a different stamp of leader to Lord George Sackville. Two hours at the trot brought him within striking distance of the French. Then, forming his six regiments of heavy cavalry in two brigades, and supporting them with Mostyn's Light Dragoons, charged straight home. The French never waited the attack, save three squadrons which stood firm and which were cut to pieces. The main portion of the French cavalry turned and fled. Ordering Mostyn to follow these up, Granby (always well to the front) wheeled the heavies to the right, and threw himself

[1] Then numbered the 87th and 88th Regiments.

on the right rear of De Muy's infantry. These, like the cavalry, broke, throwing down their arms and making for the ford across the Diemel in their rear. Our artillery now came up at the gallop, and effectually prevented any attempt at reforming on the part of the beaten foe. The loss in our cavalry was trifling. That of the French amounted to nearly 8,000 killed, wounded, and prisoners, whilst 12 guns remained in our hands as trophies of war at Warburg.

CASUALTIES AT WARBURG.

Regiments.	Officers. K.	Officers. W.	Men. K.	Men. W.	Regiments.	Officers. K.	Officers. W.	Men. K.	Men. W.
Royal Horse Guards ..	—	1	2	6	King's Liverpool Regt. ...	—	1	4	13
King's Dragoon Guards ..	—	1	7	28	Devons	—	—	12	21
Queen's Bays..	—	3	12	11	Suffolks	1	1	15	35
3rd Dragoon G.	—	—	1	5	Lancs. Fusiliers	—	1	15	38
Carabiniers ..	—	—	3	3	Royal Welsh Fusiliers ..	—	2	12	19
7th Dragoon G.	—	2	4	3	24th S. Wales Borderers ..	1	1	—	—
Royal Dragoons	—	—	8	12	K.O. Scottish Borderers ..	—	1	8	25
Scots Greys ..	—	—	1	—	W. Kent Riding Regt. ..	—	—	5	33
Inniskillings ..	—	—	2	3	Hampshire ..	—	2	10	20
7th Hussars ..	—	—	1	—	Royal W. Kent	—	—	4	14
10th Hussars..	2	—	2	10	K.O. Yorkshire L.I.	—	1	9	23
11th Hussars..	—	—	3	2					
Royal Artillery	—	—	2	7					
Northumberland Fusiliers	—	2	4	26					

For his services at Minden, Major Daulhat was given the Lieutenant-Colonelcy of the 51st (King's Own Yorkshire Light Infantry), and his battalion of Grenadiers was placed under Major Welsh, of the 11th (Devons), who commanded it at Wilhelmstahl.

In his official report of the action to King George, Prince Ferdinand wrote :

" The English artillery got up at a gallop and seconded

the attack in the most spirited mannei. All the troops
have done well, and particularly the English."

      *   *   *   *   *

" The loss on our side is very numerous, and falls
chiefly upon the brave battalions of Maxwell's Grenadiers,
which did wonders. Colonel Beckwith, who commanded
the Brigade of English Grenadiers and Scotch Highlanders, distinguished himself greatly, and is badly
wounded in the head. My Lord Granby with the
English cavalry contributed extremely to the success of
the day."

This casualty return exemplifies the lack of system
in the method of distributing battle honours. The losses
in the cavalry amounted to 129 killed and wounded, in
the infantry to 376, yet the latter have no " distinction "
to show the part they played at Warburg.

WILHELMSTAHL, JUNE 24, 1762.

The Northumberland Fusiliers

is the only regiment authorized to bear this honour ; but
here, as in so many other instances, it is difficult to
understand why one regiment should be singled out for
a battle honour to the exclusion of others which have
borne an equally meritorious part in the same engagement.

Wilhelmstahl was one of the closing actions in Prince
Ferdinand's campaigns. As at Warburg, the Valley of
the Diemel was the scene of the fight, and, as at Warburg,
the honours of the day rested with the English. The
French, some 70,000 strong, had their right resting on
the forest of Rheinhardswald, with their headquarters
at the village of Wilhelmstahl. Ferdinand detached
Generals Luckner and Sporcke to attack the flank of the
enemy, whilst he with the ten battalions of English
infantry—some Brunswickers and Hessians—supported
by Lord Granby's cavalry, made a direct attack on their

front. With the other columns I have no concern. That under the personal command of the Prince consisted of the three battalions of the Brigade of Guards—one of Grenadiers, one of the Coldstreams, and one of the Scots Guards; a brigade under Colonel Beckwith, of the 20th (Lancashire Fusiliers), comprising a composite battalion, made up of the flank companies of the Brigade of Guards, a second battalion of the grenadier companies of the Northumberland Fusiliers, the 8th (King's), 11th (Devons), 24th (South Wales Borderers), the 33rd (West Riding Regiment), and the 50th (Royal West Kent), commanded by Major Welsh, of the Devons. The third battalion in Beckwith's brigade was under Major Maxwell, of the Lancashire Fusiliers, and was made up of the flank companies of the Suffolks, Lancashire Fusiliers, Royal Welsh Fusiliers, King's Own Scottish Borderers, 37th (Hampshire Regiment), and the 51st (King's Own Yorkshire Light Infantry). The 5th (Northumberland Fusiliers), 8th (King's Liverpool Regiment), and the two Highland regiments of Keith and Campbell (then the 87th and 88th), completed the English portion of Prince Ferdinand's column.

The combined movement was well executed. The central column was in presence of the enemy before they had the least apprehension of being attacked. Finding themselves threatened in front, flank, and rear, they struck their tents and fell back in some confusion. Prince Ferdinand, to quote an officer who was present, " pursued and pressed upon them as close as possible. They would have been entirely routed had not Monsieur de Stainville thrown himself forward with the Grenadiers of France, the Royal Grenadiers, and the Regiment of Aquitaine (the flower of the French infantry), to cover their retreat. His resolution cost him dear, his whole infantry having been either killed or dispersed after a very gallant defence. Two battalions only succeeded in escaping. Some of these troops surrendered to Lord Granby's cavalry, and when the infantry came up, the remainder, after one fire, laid down their arms to the

3

5th Fusiliers, having been driven out of the forest at the point of the bayonet by Beckwith's Grenadiers." Amongst the prisoners taken were 58 officers of the Grenadiers of France, 38 of the Royal Grenadiers, and 22 of the Regiment of Aquitaine, " the flower of the French army." In all 162 officers and 2,570 men.

In his official despatch Prince Ferdinand wrote :

" All the troops behaved exceedingly well, and showed great zeal and willingness, but particularly the battalions of Grenadiers belonging to Colonel Beckwith's brigade, which distinguished themselves exceedingly."

CASUALTIES AT WILHELMSTAHL.

Regiments.	Officers.		Men.		Regiments.	Officers.		Men.	
	K.	W.	K.	W.		K.	W.	K.	W.
Royal Horse Guards	—	—	1	5	Northumberland Fusiliers	1	—	1	11
15th Hussars	—	—	2	3	Welsh's Gren.	—	—	3	41
Royal Artillery	1	—	2	5	Maxwell's Gren.	2	—	3	58
Grenadier Gds.	1	—	8	28	Keith's Highlanders (87th)	—	—	9	23
Coldstream Gds.	—	—	9	11	Campbell's Highlanders (88th)	—	—	5	22
Scots Guards	—	—	11	17	Fraser's Chasseurs	—	—	1	12
Grenadier Batt. of the Guards	—	1	8	25					
King's Liverpool	—	—	—	1					

An artillery officer who was present wrote of the battle :

" They [the French] were fairly surprised, and our troops behaved with a bravery not to be paralleled in history, especially our Grenadiers and Highlanders, who sent prisoners, I dare say, more than double their own numbers out of the forest. The 5th Regiment behaved nobly, and took prisoners about twice their own number. We had the misfortune to lose Lieutenant Cock (an officer of our regiment, and as pretty an officer as any in the army) by a cannon - shot, which took off his head."

The casualties in the British regiments amounted to 54 killed and 249 wounded ; those of the allies, only to 144 killed and wounded.

The surrender of the French Grenadiers to the old " Fighting Fifth " is commemorated by the Fusilier or, rather Grenadier, cap, which at one time was worn only by the Northumberland Fusiliers. Now, however, all Fusilier regiments share this honour with the Northumberlands.

Studying the above list in conjunction with Prince Ferdinand's despatch gives rise to the question, Why should the Northumberland Fusiliers alone bear the battle honour " Wilhelmstahl " ?

NOTE.—During the years 1756-1762 the annual subsidies voted by the English Parliament to enable the Prussian armies to keep the field amounted to £670,000, aggregating £3,350,000. During the same period England paid for the upkeep of the armies of Hesse-Cassel £2,631,438.

CHAPTER IV

BATTLE HONOURS FOR SERVICES IN NORTH AND SOUTH AMERICA, 1758-1814

Louisburg, 1758—Quebec, 1759—Monte Video, 1807—Detroit, August 12, 1812—Miami, April 23, 1813—Niagara, July 25, 1814—Bladensburg. October 24, 1814.

LOUISBURG, JULY 25, 1758.

THE following regiments are authorized to bear this honour :

Royal Scots.	East Yorkshire.	Leicester.
Cheshire.	Gloucester.	Royal Sussex.
South Lancashire.	Sherwood Foresters.	North Lancashire.
Northampton.	King's Royal Rifles.	Wiltshire.

It commemorates the siege and capture of the fortress of Louisburg (Cape Breton's Island, North America) from the French in July, 1758. The army, which was under the command of General the Lord Amherst, numbered 12,000 of all ranks, and was distributed as follows :

First Brigade—Brigadier Whitmore : 1st Royal Scots, 22nd (Cheshires), 40th (South Lancashire), 48th (Northampton), and 3rd Batt. 60th (King's Royal Rifles).

Second Brigade—Brigadier James Wolfe : 17th (Leicester), 35th (Royal Sussex), 47th (Loyal North Lancashire), and 2nd Batt. 60th (King's Royal Rifles).

Third Brigade—Brigadier Lawrence : 15th (East Yorkshire), 28th (Gloucester), 45th (Sherwood Foresters), and 58th (North-ampton).

The grenadiers and light companies of the various regiments were, as was customary in those days, organized into separate battalions. The force, which was convoyed by twenty-three ships of the line, under Admiral Boscawen, on which the 62nd (Wiltshires) were serving as marines,

36

arrived at Jabarus Bay, a little to the westward of the fortress, on June 8, 1758. The country was well known, for Commodore Sir R. Warren, with some colonial troops, had wrested it from the French in 1745. A reconnaissance revealed three possible landing-places, and, to make assurance trebly sure, Amherst determined to threaten all three, whilst the true attack should be made by Wolfe's brigade, with the grenadier and light infantry battalions, at Freshwater Cove, about three miles from the city.

CASUALTIES AT THE SIEGE AND CAPTURE OF LOUISBERG, JULY 25, 1758.

Regiments.	Officers.		Men.		Regiments.	Officers.		Men.	
	K.	W.	K.	W.		K.	W.	K.	W.
Royal Artillery	—	1	4	5	45th Sherwood Foresters ..	—	—	10	14
Royal Scots ..	2	4	13	27	47th N. Lancs	—	—	9	30
15th E. Yorks..	2	3	27	26	48th N'hampton	1	1	8	17
17th Leicester	1	3	11	33	58th N'hampton	—	1	2	11
22nd Cheshire	—	3	7	15	60th King's Royal Rifles	1	1	24	57
28th Gloucester	—	1	12	25	78th[1]	4	3	17	41
35th R. Sussex	—	4	?	?					
40th S. Lancs	—	1	8	21					

The landing was stubbornly contested by the French, but, thanks to the gallantry of Major Scott, at the head of the light infantry battalion, Wolfe was enabled to effect his object with a loss of about 100 killed and wounded.   Lawrence's brigade was immediately thrown ashore, and by nightfall Amherst had pitched his camp to the westward, and just out of the range of the guns of the fortress.   The task of disembarking the siege material was exceedingly arduous, and Amherst, owing to the nature of the ground, was compelled to restrict the siege operations to the western face of the fortress. Wolfe, however, was detached to move round the city,

[1] The existing 2nd Batt. Seaforths has not been awarded this battle honour.

and seize some works on the northern side of the harbour.
This he effected with but slight loss, and was enabled
by a daring *coup de main* to occupy a commanding position
some 300 yards distant from the northernmost bastion.
Thanks to the powerful and cordial co-operation of the
fleet, Amherst carried on the bombardment with ceaseless vigour.   By the end of July the walls were so battered
that they could barely withstand the shock of their own
guns, and on the 27th of that month the French General
surrendered unconditionally, with 5,600 men.

QUEBEC, SEPTEMBER 12, 1759.

The following regiments are authorized to bear this
honour :

Oxford Light Infantry.		North Lancashire.
Northampton.		King's Royal Rifles.
East Yorkshire.	Gloucester.	Royal Sussex.

It commemorates that glorious eleven weeks' campaign
which culminated in the capture of Quebec and established British supremacy in Canada. It is doubly
memorable owing to the fact that the two opposing
commanders, Wolfe and Montcalm, fell in the hour of
victory, and that vanquished as well as victor are held
in veneration by friend and foe alike.

The capture of Louisburg and the successes over the
French in West Africa, as well as on the continent of
North America, determined Pitt to carry out the scheme
formulated in the preceding year for the capture of
Quebec. Wolfe, who had so distinguished himself at
Louisburg, was, to the surprise of the army, nominated
to the command, having under him three Brigadiers—
Monckton, Townsend, and Murray. The former had as
a regimental commander shown himself possessed of every
capacity for high command.   The force, which numbered
about 8,000 men, was composed of ten battalions of the
line : two of grenadiers, made up from the flank companies of all regiments in North America ; two of light
infantry ; and a corps of local troops styled " Roger's

Rangers," men inured to war and of proved capacity. The distribution of the force was as under :

First Brigade—Brigadier Murray : 35th (Royal Sussex), 48th (Northampton), and 3rd Battalion King's Royal Rifles.
Second Brigade—Brigadier Townsend : 28th (Gloucester), 47th (North Lancashire), and 2nd Battalion King's Royal Rifles.
Third Brigade—Brigadier Monckton : 15th (East Yorkshire), 43rd (Oxford Light Infantry), 58th (Northampton), and Fraser's Highlanders.

It was not until June 27 that Wolfe landed, without resistance, on the Island of Orleans, just below Quebec, and on the following day Monckton's brigade, with some heavy guns, was thrown across to the right bank of the St. Lawrence. Emboldened by the passive attitude of the French Commander, who seemed averse to adopt any offensive measures, Wolfe moved the brigades of Murray and Townsend to the left bank of the St. Lawrence, below the French entrenched camp, whilst he himself, still holding on to the Isle of Orleans, threw up batteries on the left bank *below* the city. This dissemination of his forces constituted a grave danger, but Montcalm took no advantage of such a palpable error. On July 31 a determined attempt to assault the city was repulsed, our loss being upwards of 500 killed and wounded, and the spirits of the besiegers sank to zero. The British Admiral pointed out to Wolfe that the proper course to pursue was to transfer his main force to a position on the right bank of the St. Lawrence, above Quebec, so as to prevent Montcalm from obtaining supplies or reinforcements from Montreal. This proposition was concurred in warmly by the General, and early in September Townsend and Murray took up their new position to the west of the citadel. On September 13 Wolfe, by a most daring midnight movement, scaled the Heights of Abraham, and so encompassed the fall of what was considered an impregnable city. Shot in the wrist early in the fight, the heroic young commander still led on his men, until, just as the French were falling back, he received a second ball in the groin, and finally fell at the head of the 28th (Gloucesters), at the moment of victory. The command now devolved on Townsend (Monckton having been disabled by a severe wound), and he pressed forward the siege with vigour. On September 18 General Ramesay, who had succeeded Montcalm in command of the French, signed the capitulation of a city which was little better than a mass of shapeless ruins. The praise for the capture of Quebec is due to Wolfe; but Quebec was but an incident in the long-drawn-out campaign which resulted in transferring Canada from the Bourbon to British rule, and the credit for this belongs to a General little remembered in these days—General the Lord Amherst.

CASUALTIES DURING THE OPERATIONS AT QUEBEC, 1759.

Regiments.	Officers.		Men.		Regiments.	Officers.		Men.	
	K.	W.	K.	W.		K.	W.	K.	W.
Staff	1	5	—	—	60th King's Royal Rifles (3rd Batt.)..	4	13	22	176
Royal Artillery	—	—	1	14					
15th E. Yorks	1	11	13	107					
28th Gloucesters	1	7	18	100	60th King's Royal Rifles (4th Batt.) ..	—	1	2	30
35th R. Sussex	3	10	29	69					
40th S. Lancashire	1	7	1	29	78th Seaforth Highlanders	3	11	35	138
43rd Oxford L.I.	—	3	12	33	Grenadiers of Louisburg ..	1	7	13	112
47th L.N. Lancashire ..	1	3	16	49					
48th N'hampton	1	4	13	47	Roger's Rangers	2	2	21	26
58th N'hampton	1	8	17	129	Royal Marines	—	—	8	22

MONTE VIDEO, 1807.

A battle honour borne by the

South Staffords.	South Lancashire.
Royal Irish Fusiliers.	Rifle Brigade.

The expedition to South America redounds little to the credit of our arms, and, as is well known, ended in disaster. A few words are necessary as to its inception. Prior to the expedition to the Cape of Good Hope in 1806, the Admiral, Sir Home Popham, who was in command of the naval forces in the South Atlantic, had been at some pains to impress upon Pitt, the Prime Minister, the immense advantages that would accrue to our trade by the conquest of the Spanish possessions in South America ; and though it would appear that Popham was not entrusted with any mission in furtherance of his design, there is no doubt that Pitt did look with considerable favour on his proposals, and a force under General Crawford was actually despatched to make a descent on the western shore of the continent, and to occupy Chili or Peru. Popham, however, did not lose sight of his own scheme, which was the conquest of Buenos Ayres ; and no sooner were we in possession of the Cape than he persuaded Sir David Baird to place General Beresford, with the 38th (South Staffords) and the 71st (Highland Light Infantry) at his disposal. With these and the St. Helena Regiment, which consisted of an infantry battalion and a company of artillery, Popham sailed across the Atlantic, and early in June appeared off the coast near Monte Video. After reconnoitring Mondanado, Popham decided that an attack on Monte Video was impracticable, and, overcoming the scruples of Beresford, proceeded to Buenos Ayres. The troops were landed a short distance from the city, and, after a short skirmish, the Spaniards, completely surprised, surrendered. The troops engaged at the first capture of Buenos Ayres were the 71st (Highland Light Infantry), a naval brigade, consisting of seamen and marines, and the St. Helena Regiment, the casualties only amounting to 4 men killed, an officer and 15 men wounded.

The Spaniards soon recovered from their surprise, and, realizing the weakness of our force, took measures for the recapture of the city. On August 12 a body of some 12,000 men appeared before Buenos Ayres, and at the end of the day, our men being entangled in the streets, and the 71st having lost 165 killed and wounded, Beresford felt himself obliged to surrender.

When the news of the disaster reached England, reinforcements were at once despatched to the coast, and Baird was ordered to send all troops he could spare from the Cape. The command of the new expedition was entrusted to Sir Samuel Auchmuty, whilst the naval forces were placed under Admiral Sterling, Popham being recalled for the purpose of undergoing trial by court-martial. On arriving at Mondanado, Auchmuty found the troops from the Cape. These were unprovided with artillery, and there was much difficulty in securing the necessary provisions. Meat there was in plenty, but for flour and other food-stuffs the troops were dependent on England. After consultation with the Admiral, it was decided to make an attack on Monte Video as a necessary preliminary to the recapture of Buenos Ayres, and the release of the troops in the hands of the Spaniards (close on 1,500 in number). On January 18, 1807, the force was successfully disembarked at Carretas, some seven miles to the eastward of Monte Video. A reconnaissance proved that the defences of the city were far more formidable than had been reported, and on the 19th the Spaniards made a sortie, in which they displayed a gallantry which our men had by no means anticipated. Heavy guns were landed from the fleet, and breaching batteries erected within 1,000 yards of the citadel. The Admiral also landed upwards of 1,400 seamen and marines to assist the troops. The General did not possess the means for a regular siege, and, risky though the experiment was, he determined to carry the place by storm so soon as a practicable breach was effected. On the night of January 24 Sir Samuel made the preparations for the assault. The storming column was composed of the Rifle Brigade, the light and grenadier companies of all the regiments of the force, with the 38th (South Staffords). The 40th (South Lancashire) and the 87th (Royal Irish Fusiliers) were in immediate support, whilst the General held in reserve the 47th (North Lancashire), a company of the 71st (Highland Light Infantry), 700 seamen and marines, and the details of the 17th Lancers, 20th and 21st Light Dragoons. The night was very dark, and it was found that the Spaniards had repaired the breach with timber faced with damp hides, to avoid the contingency of their being set on fire; but the Rifle Brigade and light infantry battalion forced their way over all obstacles in the face of a very determined resistance, and by daybreak we were in possession of the town. The conduct of our men during the actual assault and during the occupation called forth the warmest praise of the General.

CASUALTIES DURING THE OPERATIONS AT MONTE VIDEO.

Regiments.	Officers.		Men.		Regiments.	Officers.		Men.	
	K.	W.	K.	W.		K.	W.	K.	W.
Royal Navy ..	—	2	6	32	47th Loyal N. Lancashires	—	—	3	16
17th Lancers (dismt. troop	—	—	—	4	72nd Seaforths	—	1	—	—
20th Light Dragoons ..	—	—	1	3	83rd R. Irish Rifles ..	—	1	—	—
21st Light Dragoons ..	—	—	—	4	87th R. Irish Fusiliers ..	3	3	60	80
Royal Artillery	—	1	1	4	95th Rifle Brig.	1	3	15	45
38th S. Staffs	2	10	29	98	Light Infantry				
40th S. Lancs	4	5	18	76	Battalion ..	1	6	66	99

In the month of March the troops, under General Crawford, which had been destined for the Chilian coast arrived at Monte Video, and General Whitelock assumed command. An advance was now made on Buenos Ayres, which resulted in the capitulation of our force and the trial of the Commander-in-Chief. This disaster cast no reflections either on the gallantry of our troops or the skill of Auchmuty. At the same time, it is impossible to think of this battle honour without recalling the unfortunate circumstances connected with the two attacks on Buenos Ayres.

NORTH AMERICA, 1812-1814.

The war in North America in the early years of the nineteenth century gave rise to much hard fighting, and though at the close of the campaign in the Iberian Peninsula we were enabled to send a number of our seasoned regiments as reinforcements, the operations were by no means creditable to our arms.

On the institution of the Land General Service Medal in 1847 (commonly called the Peninsular Medal), a certain number of engagements which had taken place in North America were included in the list of those for which the medal was granted, and clasps were issued for the following actions :

> Fort Detroit, August, 1812.
> Châteaugay, October 26, 1813.
> Christler's Farm, November 11, 1813.

But in the distribution of battle honours the two last names were not authorized to be borne on the colours of the regiments engaged. In the case of Christler's Farm an application for permission to bear this honour on behalf of the 89th Regiment (now the 2nd Royal Irish Fusiliers) met with a decided refusal. On the other hand, four battle honours were granted to regiments to commemorate engagements for which the medal was not issued—namely, Queenstown, Miami, Niagara, and Bladensburg.

DETROIT

is borne only on the colours of the Welsh Regiment, and commemorates the services of the old 41st Regiment at the affair which took place in the vicinity of Fort Detroit, on August 16, 1812, when its casualties amounted to 1 officer and 3 men killed, 1 officer and 10 men wounded.

QUEENSTOWN

records the services of the Welsh Regiment and the Berkshires in the affair of October 26, 1813, in which their casualties were—

Regiments.	Officers.		Men.		Regiments.	Officers.		Men.	
	K.	W.	K.	W.		K.	W.	K.	W.
41st Welsh ..	—	—	2	18	49th Berkshire	—	2	8	30

MIAMI

This, again, is an honour which was granted alone to the Welsh Regiment as a recognition of its services in the affair of April 23, 1813, when the casualties were 11 men killed, 1 officer and 38 men wounded.

NIAGARA

is borne on the colours and appointments of the

19th Hussars.	Royal Scots.
Royal Warwick.	Welsh Regiment.
King's Liverpool Regiment.	Royal Canadians.
Royal Irish Fusiliers.	South Lancashire.

In the *London Gazette* of July 25, 1814, the above regiments, as well as the 103rd Regiment, were authorized to add this battle honour to their other distinctions. In November, 1815, the 104th Regiment were also awarded the honour.[1] The casualties at this engagement were—

LOSSES AT NIAGARA.

Regiments.	Officers.		Men.		Regiments.	Officers.		Men.	
	K.	W.	K.	W.		K.	W.	K.	W.
19th Hussars	—	—	—	2	89th R. Irish Fusiliers ..	2	11	27	177
Royal Artillery	—	—	—	15	100th Royal Canadians ..	—	—	—	—
Royal Scots ..	1	3	15	112					
8th King's Liverpool ..	—	3	12	57	103rd Regiment	—	1	6	46
41st Welsh Regiment ..	—	—	3	34	104th Regiment	—	—	1	5

[1] Neither the Royal Munster nor Royal Dublin Fusiliers, which for many years bore the numbers 103rd and 104th, have availed themselves of the privilege accorded to the 19th Hussars and 100th Royal Canadians.

BLADENSBURG, AUGUST 24, 1814.

This honour is borne on the colours of the following regiments :

King's Own (Royal Lancaster).   Royal Scots Fusiliers.
Essex.   Shropshire Light Infantry.

The campaign on the Canadian frontier had been waged with varying fortune : sometimes success attended our arms, at others we suffered considerable reverses. We were fighting, however, under many disadvantages. The bulk of our forces were employed in Spain, or in the abortive expedition to the Low Countries. The abdication of Napoleon, however, set free a portion of our troops, and a brigade was despatched, under the command of Major-General John Ross, from the South of France to North America. It consisted of the 4th (King's Own), the 41st (Welsh), and the 44th (Essex). On arrival at Bermuda it was met by the 21st (Royal Scots Fusiliers), and by Admiral Cochrane, commanding the naval forces on the station. The Admiral had been in the habit whilst blockading the coast of landing at the mouth of the Potomac River, and making incursions into the country, accompanied only by a few Marines. He pointed out to the General the feasibility of an attack on Washington, the young capital of the United States. On August 15 the General, accompanied by the Admiral, landed and made a lengthy reconnaissance up the Patuxent River, which runs parallel to the Potomac, and a short distance to the east. The landing presented no difficulties, and on the 20th the whole of the brigade, having arrived, were disembarked without opposition at a place called Benedict, on the right bank of the Patuxent, only fifty miles from Washington. On the following day the force moved to Nottingham in three columns. The right, under Colonel Brooke, of the 44th, consisted of the 4th (King's Own) and the 44th (Essex) ; the centre, commanded by Colonel Patterson, of the 21st (Royal Scots Fusiliers), comprised that corps and a strong naval brigade ;

whilst the left column, which was under Colonel Thornton, of the 85th (King's Light Infantry), was made up of that regiment and the light companies of the other three battalions, and was accompanied by the little artillery force, which consisted of but a couple of 3-pounders and a howitzer. On August 22 the brigade reached Marlborough, a small town sixteen miles from the capital, and here Ross learnt that a body of American troops, about 6,000 strong, was drawn up for the defence of Washington at Bladensburg, to the north of the city. Leaving some marines to guard his lines of communication at Marlborough, Ross pushed on, the left column, under his own personal command, leading, and on the morning of the 24th he found the enemy. The action was soon over, and by nightfall Ross entered Washington, having captured ten of the enemy's guns. Whether the subsequent burning of the Capitol was justified or not is a question that everyone will decide for himself. Suffice to say that public property to the extent of close on half a million sterling was destroyed, in addition to several ships on the stocks, and that we carried away 206 guns. Our losses were by no means heavy. In justice to the memory of the General, it should be put on record that a perfectly orderly entry into the city was effected, and that all firing had long since ceased when, as he and the Admiral were passing through the city, some shots were fired from a private house, and that by his orders that house was set on fire. The flames spread to neighbouring buildings, and before they could be stopped the Capitol was in flames.

The raid—for raid it was—was looked upon as a decided success, and Ross, who had succeeded in carrying off the greater part of the guns found in Washington, determined to carry out a similar raid on Baltimore. This, too, was successful, but it was achieved at the loss of the gallant General, who was one of the four officers who fell in the engagement outside Baltimore on September 12. The action of Bladensburg is com-

memorated not only on the colours of the four regiments
which were present, but the family of the General were
authorized by royal licence to add the word " Bladensburg " to their own name of Ross.

CASUALTIES AT BLADENSBURG.

Regiments.	Officers.		Men.		Regiments.	Officers.		Men.	
	K.	W.	K.	W.		K.	W.	K.	W.
Royal Artillery	—	—	—	6	44th Essex ..	—	—	14	35
R. Engineers ..	—	—	2	—	85th K. Shrop-				
4th King's Own	1	7	23	56	shire L.I. ..	2	11	12	53
21st R. Scots					Royal Marines	—	—	6	1
Fusiliers ..	—	2	2	11	6th West India	—	—	1	—

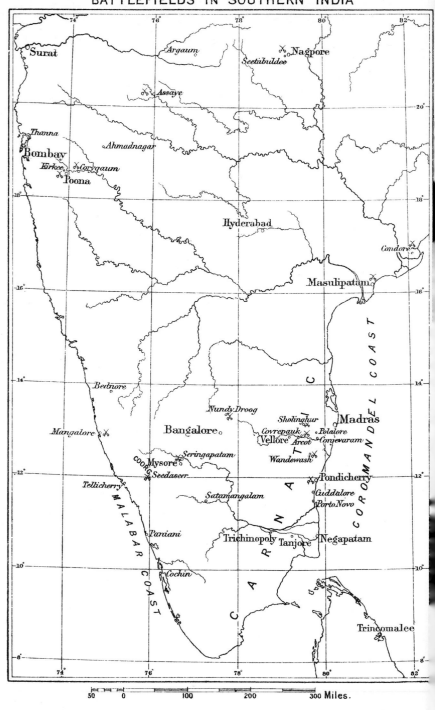

BATTLEFIELDS IN SOUTHERN INDIA

Surat

Argaum

Nagpore

Seetabuldee

Assaye

Thanna

Ahmadnagar

Bombay

Kirkee   Coregaum

Poona

Hyderabad

Condore

Masulipatam

Bednore

Nundy Droog

Madras

Sholinghur

Mangalore

Bangalore

Covrepauk   Polalore

Vellore   Arcot   Conjevaram

Seringapatam

Mysore   Wandewash

COORG

Seedaseer

Tellicherry

Satyamangalam

Pondicherry

Cuddalore

Porto Novo

Paniani

Trichinopoly   Tanjore   Negapatam

Cochin

CARNATIC

MALABAR COAST

COROMANDEL COAST

Trincomalee

50   0   100   200   300 Miles.

CHAPTER V

INDIA, 1751-1764

Arcot — Plassey — Condore — Masulipatam — Badara — Wande-wash—Pondicherry—Buxar.

THE names at the head of the chapter commemorate a number of long-forgotten Indian campaigns, waged against desperate odds and extending over many years. The Colar Goldfields, Dindigul Cigars, and the Nundy Droog Mine are names of pleasant memories to the fortunate shareholders in those concerns. Little did soldier or sepoy think that those fields on which he shed his blood in order to maintain British supremacy in India would thus become familiarized to British speculators. For us, their successors, it is humiliating to feel that the heroic forging of the link which connects them with the military history of our Empire should have been long since forgotten. A few words in retrospect are necessary.

In the year 1600 a charter was granted by Parliament to the East India Company, and within ten years factories had been established at Surat, to the north of Bombay, and Petapolam, to the north of Madras. We were not the first-comers in the field, for both Dutch and Portuguese had been for many years engaged in commerce with the East. In 1612 our first troubles arose with the Portuguese, whom we defeated at Surat, and since then no question of their supremacy has arisen. Fifty years later the French had firmly established themselves at Masulipatam and Pondicherry, on the south-east coast,

49

as well as at Chandernagore, a few miles above Calcutta, and for the next 150 years the rivalry between France and England was the cause of much strife. The policy of the French was to stand well in with the native rulers, to organize their armies on a European model, and so, with their aid, to drive the English out of India.

At the commencement of the eighteenth century Calcutta, Bombay, and Madras were our chief centres, the former with factories stretching to Patna, in the north-west. The influence of the Governor of Bombay extended from the settlement at Ahmedabad, in the north, to Calicut, on the west or Malabar coast, whilst Madras had under its rule all factories on the eastern coast from Vizagapatam to Cuddalore. The British East India Company of those days boasted of but little Government support ; the French company was fast becoming a military rather than a commercial force. In 1750 the French had driven us out of Madras, and were virtually rulers of Southern India, and the bulk of our forces were besieged in Trichinopoly. Fortunately for England, even in her darkest hour a man has arisen to cope with and surmount her difficulties. Amongst the writers or clerks in the employ of the factory at Madras was one Robert Clive. He, with rare prescience, argued that, as the bulk of the French forces, aided by their ally, the ruler of the Carnatic, were employed in the reduction of Trichinopoly, therefore Arcot, the capital of the Carnatic, in all probability lay unguarded. Mr. Saunders, the Governor of Madras, cordially supported the plan advocated by the young writer, which was to carry the war into the enemy's country, and to seize Arcot, the capital, by a *coup de main*.

ARCOT, AUGUST 31, 1751.

This honour is alone borne by the Royal Dublin Fusiliers, the lineal descendants of the gallant band of Englishmen in the service of the East India Company at Madras, who

ROBERT, LORD CLIVE.

To face page 50.

in the year 1751, under the incomparable Clive, laid the foundation of our Indian Empire. In those days Arcot, the capital of the Carnatic, was a city of about 100,000 inhabitants, dominated by a fort almost in ruins. It lies some sixty miles south-west of Madras, and Clive determined not only to effect the relief of Trichinopoly, then besieged by the French, but also to strike at French supremacy by seizing the capital of their most powerful ally, the Sovereign of the Carnatic. He left Madras on September 6, 1751, in command of a small force of 200 Englishmen and 300 sepoys, with but three field-guns. Of his officers, eight in number, four, like him, were " writers " in the Company's factory. Five days later Clive had thrown himself into the half-ruined fort of Arcot, which had been hastily evacuated by its garrison, mounted the guns, which had been abandoned, repaired the defences, and made every preparation for a siege. A month later the siege commenced in earnest, 10,000 trained troops of the Nawab, aided by 300 French, drawing a close cordon round the fort, whilst a siege-train directed by Frenchmen opened fire on its walls. Macaulay, in his brilliant essay on Lord Clive, has borne eloquent testimony to the heroism both of the leader and the led (I have not the space to dwell on the details of the siege) —how the sepoys, with starvation staring them in the face, brought their rations of rice to their English comrades, with the remark that the water in which it was boiled was sustenance enough for them ; and how, after being beleaguered for fifty days, in which he had lost one-third of his force, Clive repelled a final assault, and was enabled to assume the offensive against his disheartened and discomfited foes.

Arcot was a prelude to a campaign in which many gallant actions were fought—actions long since forgotten, and which are unrecorded on our colours. Trichinopoly and Covrepauk are no less worthy of emblazonment than Reshire or Koosh-ab. But, alas ! no connection can now be traced between the sepoys who fought under Clive and the regiments of our native army, whilst the identity of the First Madras Europeans has for a whole generation been hidden under the title of " Royal Dublin Fusiliers."

Little by little public interest was now being centred on India. The desperate efforts of France to gain an ascendancy in the Peninsula of Hindoostan, and the gallant endeavour of the servants of the East India Company to thwart those efforts, had at last aroused our Ministers to the value of Indian commerce, and to the necessity of affording military assistance in the shape of trained regiments to the " Honourable Company of Merchants trading to the East." In 1754 a first step was made in this direction, and in that year the 39th Regiment (now the 1st Dorsets) landed in Madras, and, in memory of their connection with our early struggles in India, have been permitted to bear on their colours the legend "Primus in Indis." The following year a truce was signed between France and England, thus putting an end to active hostilities. No steps, however, were neglected by either party in order to secure a paramount influence with native rulers. In this, however, we were less successful than our rivals.

PLASSEY, JUNE 23, 1757.

The following regiments are entitled to bear this battle honour :

The Dorsetshire Regiment.   Royal Munster Fusiliers.
                    Royal Dublin Fusiliers.

Just as in the South of India the rulers of the Carnatic and of Mysore were the bitter foes of the English settlement at Madras, so at Calcutta we had against us Surajah Dowlah, the ruler of Bengal, Behar, and Orissa—a nominal Viceroy of the Mogul Emperor—straining every nerve to wrest from us the territories on which our factories were built. The tragedy of the Black Hole of Calcutta is familiar to every schoolboy. Fortunate indeed for England was it that, when the news of the fall of Calcutta reached Fort St. George an English fleet, under Admiral Watson, was lying in Madras Roads, and that men of action sat in the Madras Council. Two hundred Europeans were at once despatched to the Hooghly, and a force of 2,500 men hastily organized, consisting of 250 men of the 39th Regiment (1st Dorsets), 700 Madras Europeans, and 1,500 sepoys, for their support. This force was under the joint command of Admiral Watson and Robert Clive. Calcutta was relieved ; and as war with France had again broken out, it was determined—now that all pressure on the part of Surajah Dowlah was removed—to attack the French settlement at Chandernagore. The fleet sailed up the Hooghly, and on March 23 the British flag was flying over the French fortress. I have been unable to ascertain the losses of Clive's troops on this occasion. Those of the Royal Navy amounted to 4 officers and 46 men killed, 9 officers and 156 men wounded. In the burial-ground of St. John's Church, Calcutta, may yet be seen two monuments recording this daring feat of arms and of superb seamanship—the one raised in memory of the Admiral, the other of a midshipman. The former reads :

HERE LIES INTERRED THE BODY OF

CHARLES WATSON, ESQ.,

VICE-ADMIRAL OF THE WHITE,

COMMANDER-IN-CHIEF OF HIS MAJESTY'S

NAVAL FORCES IN THE EAST INDIES,

WHO DEPARTED THIS LIFE THE 16TH DAY OF AUGUST, 1757,

IN THE 44TH YEAR OF HIS AGE.

Gheria taken, February 13th, 1756.
Calcutta freed, January 11th, 1757.
Chandernagore taken, March 23rd, 1757.

Exegit monumentum ore perennius.

On the boy's tomb is inscribed :

HERE LYES THE BODY OF

WILLIAM SPEKE,

AGED 16, SON OF HENRY SPEKE, ESQ.,

CAPTAIN OF HIS MAJESTY'S SHIP *KENT*.

HE LOST HIS LEG AND LIFE IN THAT SHIP

AT THE CAPTURE OF FORT ORLEANS,

THE 24TH MARCH, ANNO 1757.

Having punished the French for their refusal to afford assistance to our beleaguered countrymen and country-women in Calcutta, Clive now determined to march against the Nawab Surajah Dowlah. On June 13, having received fresh reinforcements on this occasion from Bombay, he left Chandernagore at the head of 3,000 men, with ten guns. Of these about 1,000 were English—the 39th Foot, under Major Eyre Coote, some gunners of the Royal Artillery who had accompanied the 39th from England, and detachments of the Bengal, Madras, and Bombay European regiments. The Englishmen were conveyed in boats up the Hooghly ; the sepoys marched along the banks. On June 23 Clive found himself face to face with Surajah Dowlah's army at Plassey, a town on the River Hooghly, about 100 miles due north of Calcutta. The odds were hopelessly unequal—Clive with 3,000 men and ten light field-guns on the one side ; Surajah Dowlah with 55,000 men, of whom 15,000 were cavalry, and fifty guns of all calibres on the other. Had Englishmen ever been in the habit of counting the odds, the Indian Empire would never have been ours. Neither Clive nor Coote were men to quail before difficulties. From eight until eleven our infantry lay motionless, the field-guns only maintaining an unequal duel with the more numerous artillery of the enemy, which were being served—and very badly served—by some Frenchmen in the service of the Nawab. Plassey was the foundation-stone of British

supremacy in Bengal, as Arcot was in Madras ; yet the
fight was, from the soldier's standpoint, a very hollow
one.   Dawn broke with the odds immeasurably in favour
of the Mogul host.   At sunset that host was in full
retreat, and yet our total losses were but 11 English
and 13 sepoys killed, the wounded being 22 and 21
respectively. Such was the price we paid for the establishment of British rule over what is known as the Province
of Bengal.

CASUALTIES AT PLASSEY.

Regiments.	Officers.		Men.		Regiments.	Officers.		Men.	
	K.	W.	K.	W.		K.	W.	K.	W.
Royal Navy ..	—	1	—	2	1st R. Dublin Fusiliers ..	—	—	1	3
Royal Artillery	1	2	6	10	2nd R. Dublins	—	—	—	1
39th Dorset ..	1	—	1	4	Bengal sepoys	—	—	9	11
Royal Munster Fusiliers ..	—	1	1	2	Madras sepoys	—	—	4	10

CONDORE, DECEMBER 9, 1758.

Royal Munster Fusiliers.   Royal Dublin Fusiliers.

In the course of this year there was incessant fighting
between our troops in Madras and the French and their
allies ; but the value of India was now becoming more
thoroughly appreciated by the Cabinet, and a second
regiment, then numbered the 79th, was sent out to
Madras, under Colonel William Draper. The French,
on their part, were not behindhand. The Count Lally
and Admiral d'Ache arrived, with close on 3,000 French
troops, and the British forts at Cuddalore and St. David
were captured.   Matters were looking serious indeed in
Southern India, when Clive, still in Calcutta, determined
to make a diversion.   Eyre Coote, the Major of the 39th,
who had shown such gallantry at Plassey, was in England
busily employed in raising a regiment for service in India,

and so was not available ; but Clive detached Major
Forde, of the 39th, with detachments of his own regiment
and of the 1st Bengal Europeans (now the Munster
Fusiliers), barely numbering 600 men, and some 2,000
sepoys, down the coast to Vizagapatam, which was being
threatened by a French force, under Conflans. Despite
the odds against him—for the French army outnumbered
his by at least three to one—Forde pushed on, finally
meeting Conflans near the mouth of the Godavery River.

CASUALTIES AT CONDORE.

Regiment.	Officers.		Men.	
	K.	W.	K.	W.
Royal Munster Fusiliers (1st Bengal Europeans)	1	4	15	29

There has been a long-standing dispute as to whether
this honour can be rightly claimed by the Dublin Fusiliers
as the representatives of the Madras and Bombay regiments which were sent to assist Clive in 1757. It appears
certain that the men from Madras and Bombay were
incorporated with the Bengal European Regiment in
April, 1758, and that none but Bengal troops accompanied
Forde to Vizagapatam. The India Office has therefore
given its decision in favour of the Munsters for both
Condore and Masulipatam.

MASULIPATAM, APRIL 8, 1759.

This honour is borne by the Royal Munster Fusiliers
alone. In spite of many obstacles thrown in his way after
the action of Condore by our native allies, Forde determined to follow up Conflans. It was not until March 6
that he arrived before Masulipatam, behind the fortifications of which the French were awaiting him. A fortnight was taken up in landing siege-guns from the fleet,
which had followed the army down the coast, and a small

number of bluejackets were disembarked to aid in the siege. On April 6 Forde learnt that a force of 40,000 natives, under Salabad Jung, was advancing to the relief of Conflans, and he determined on storming at once. His position was full of difficulty : in front a formidable work, with a garrison exceeding his own force in number, his land communications threatened by a Franco-native army 40,000 strong, and an empty treasure-chest. A weaker man would have taken advantage of the presence of the fleet, contented himself with his own marvellous success at Condore, and embarked his little army for Bengal. Not of such stuff was Forde, and fortunate for him and for England that he had with him men of like metal to himself. On April 8 Forde ordered the assault, and by nightfall Conflans, with 3,000 men, had unconditionally surrendered. Salabad Jung, the Viceroy of the Circars Province, now realizing that all power did not belong to the French, entered into a treaty with Forde, by which he ceded to the English eighty miles of coast-line, and entered into an agreement, not merely to dismiss all the French then in his service, but also never again to employ French troops or instructors. Forde was now free to return to Bengal, where his services were soon to be urgently needed.

CASUALTIES INCURRED DURING THE OPERATIONS AT MASULIPATAM, ENDING WITH THE ACTION OF APRIL 8, 1759.

Regiment.	Officers.		Men.	
	K.	W.	K.	W.
Royal Munster Fusiliers	2	—	22	62

BADARA, NOVEMBER 25, 1759.

An honour borne by the Royal Munster Fusiliers only. The crushing defeats inflicted by Forde on Conflans had the effect of restoring our prestige in Madras. But

in Bengal Clive was in no very enviable position. The
Dutch, who had a settlement at Chinsura, on the Hooghly,
had commenced open hostilities, and a Dutch fleet,
with a considerable force on board, entered that river.
Clive had at his disposal about 300 of the 1st Bengal
Europeans, and until the return of Forde from Masulipatam matters at Calcutta were serious. As soon as
Forde arrived, Clive, who believed only in the offensive,
ordered the victor of Condore to attack the land force,
whilst he determined to destroy the Dutch fleet with some
armed East Indiamen at his disposal. On November 20
Forde marched to Chandernagore (the French settlement
on the Hooghly, some miles above Calcutta), and on the
following day moved on to Chinsura—only a few miles
distant—where a small detachment of the Dutch were
encamped. He was joined here by Knox (a Company's
officer who had been under Forde at Condore), with a
body of eighty volunteer cavalry, raised from the English
residents in Calcutta, and a strong battalion of sepoys.
He now learnt that the Dutch force was moving to attack
him. Confident of victory, Forde wrote to Clive, asking
for permission to forestall them. The story runs that
Clive was playing cards when Forde's letter reached him.
Laying down his hand, Clive scribbled on the back of
the letter : " Dear Forde,—Fight them. I will send you
the Order in Council to-morrow." Then, taking up his
cards, went on with the game. On November 25 the two
forces came into collision. Forde's handful of cavalry
converted the check, which the steady fire of Knox's
guns had inflicted on the Dutch, into a rout. Practically
the entire Dutch force was either killed, wounded, or
taken. The Government in Holland repudiated the action
of the Governor of their Indian settlements, and paid
compensation to the East India Company. But Forde's
little fight at Badara is deserving of recognition, not merely
because it was a gallant action fought against serious odds,
but more especially because it put an end once and for all
to all pretensions of the Dutch to supremacy in the East.

Unfortunately, no records exist showing the casualties we suffered at the action of Badara.

WANDEWASH, JANUARY 22, 1760.

An honour borne only by the Royal Dublin Fusiliers.

The operations in Southern India had not been characterized by the same degree of success which had marked Forde's campaign against Conflans and the Dutch, but in the very month that we won the action of Badara Eyre Coote disembarked at Madras at the head of his newly-raised regiment, then numbered the 84th. At the same time some 300 recruits arrived for the Company's battalions, bringing the total force at the disposal of the Government of Madras to four battalions of infantry, 100 English troopers, and eighteen field-guns. With these Coote determined to resume the offensive, and on January 22 the two armies met at Wandewash, about 100 miles south-west of Madras. The forces were fairly equally matched. Hyder Ali, with his allies, the French, however, had a considerable preponderance in cavalry. When we reflect on the momentous issue decided by this and the preceding actions between the French and ourselves in India, and compare the number of the troops engaged with those we now mobilize for an Indian frontier campaign, it seems little short of marvellous that our Indian Empire should have been built up with such slender means.

The troops engaged, under the command of Eyre Coote, consisted of Draper's Regiment (then the 79th), his own (the 84th), and two English battalions in the Company's employ (now the Munster Fusiliers), 2,000 sepoys, 1,200 Indian cavalry, and one squadron of English horse, with sixteen guns. The brunt of the fighting fell on the British regiments, Draper's suffering the most heavily ; but our total casualties — 63 killed and 124 wounded — was a small price to pay for a victory which cost the French 600 killed and wounded and 24 guns.

Step by step Coote now undertook the reduction of all

the French ports in Southern India. Arcot, Trincomalee, and finally Pondicherry, all fell into our hands, only to be restored, as was Chandernagore, to the French at the conclusion of peace in 1763—an act of generous imbecility which necessitated their recapture on the renewal of the war fifteen years later, at the cost of many hundred valuable British soldiers.

CASUALTIES AT WANDEWASH.

Regiments.	Officers.		Men.	
	K.	W.	K.	W.
Draper's Regiment (79th)	3	4	17	66
Coote's Regiment (84th)	1	3	13	36
Royal Dublin Fusiliers	1	1	3	29

PONDICHERRY, 1761, 1778, 1793.

This battle honour is borne only by the Royal Dublin Fusiliers (at that time the 1st Madras European Regiment), and was conferred upon it by the Governor of Madras in recognition of its services at the three sieges of that fortress in the years 1761, 1778, and 1793. The operations were conducted by Sir Eyre Coote, an officer who had received his early training in the 39th (Dorsets), and who, on that regiment being recalled to England, undertook, as I have shown, to raise a battalion for service in India.

This corps, which was numbered the 84th, and which we have already seen at Wandewash, played an all-important part in the early campaigns waged in India ; but as it was disbanded in the year 1788, the battle honours it gained are not to be found on the colours of any existing regiment. Coote laid siege to Pondicherry in the month of September, 1760, but it was not until the January following that the Governor surrendered. In accordance with our invariable custom, the fortress and neighbouring colony were restored to the French on the conclusion of peace in 1763. The regiments asso-

ciated with the Dublin Fusiliers in the Siege of Pondicherry in 1760 were the 79th (Draper's Regiment), the
84th (Coote's), the 89th (Highlanders), under Major Hector
Munro, and the 96th, under the Hon. G. Monson.   None
of these corps survive to bear the battle honour.

In the year 1778, on the renewal of the war with
France, the reduction of Pondicherry once more became
a matter of urgent necessity.   On this occasion the
Dublin Fusiliers were again to the fore in their capacity
as the 1st Madras European Regiment (two of its battalions being present).   With them were no less than
ten battalions of sepoys.   Many of these are still borne
on the rolls of the Madras army.   The distinction has
not been conferred on the Indian corps for the operations
in 1778 ; but if the losses suffered during a successful campaign constitute a claim to a battle honour, the words
" Pondicherry, 1778," may well be accorded to the regiments who figure in the subjoined list of casualties.

CASUALTIES AT PONDICHERRY, 1778.

Regiments.	Officers.		Men.		Regiments.	Officers.		Men.	
	K.	W.	K.	W.		K.	W.	K.	W.
Dublin Fus. (two battalions) ..	1	8	45	92	73rd Carnatic Inf. (Natives)	1	—	6	14
Bengal Recruits	1	1	4	12	74th Punjabis (Natives) ..	—	—	21	34
62nd Punjabis (Natives) ..	—	2	17	57	75th Carnatic Inf. (British)	1	—	—	—
67th Punjabis (Natives) ..	—	2	10	37	Do. (Natives)	—	—	23	44
69th Punjabis (British) ..	1	—	—	—	76th Punjabis (Natives) ..	—	—	8	29
Do. (Natives)	—	2	7	36	79th Carnatic Inf. (British)	1	1	—	—
72nd Punjabis (British) ..	1	1	—	—	Do. (Natives)	—	1	5	12
Do. (Natives)	—	1	6	43	80th Carnatic Inf. (British)	1	1	—	—
73rd Carnatic Inf. (British)	—	1	1	—	Do. (Natives)	—	2	8	35

NOTE.—The total losses of the Company's troops at Pondicherry in 1778 were 148 sepoys killed and 482 wounded.   For
this success Hector Munro, who commanded, was made a K.B.

The Bengal Recruits alluded to above were a party of recruits on their way out to join what is now known as the Munster Fusiliers. They were detained by the Governor of Madras to swell the British element at the siege, and they well sustained the honour of the regiment now known as the Royal Munster Fusiliers.

In the year 1793 the reduction of Pondicherry became once more necessary. The fortress had been captured by Sir Eyre Coote and its works demolished in 1761. On its restoration to the French, the place was converted into an exceptionally strong fortification, and its capture by Sir Hector Munro in 1778 entailed a loss of upwards of 600 killed and wounded. In 1793 we found that our friends the French had once more—and very rightly, too—done their utmost to render the place impregnable, and that a very considerable force would be necessary for its reduction. Colonel Braithwaite, of the Madras army, was entrusted with its capture. The force at his disposal consisted of the following troops :

Cavalry Brigade—Colonel Floyd : 19th Hussars and 4th Madras Cavalry.

First Infantry Brigade—Colonel Nesbitt : 36th (Worcesters), 52nd (Oxford Light Infantry), and the battalion companies of the Dublin Fusiliers.

Second Infantry Brigade—Colonel David Baird : 71st (Highland Light Infantry), 73rd (Royal Highlanders), and the flank companies of the two battalions of the Madras European Regiment (Dublin Fusiliers), under Majors Petrie and Vigors.

Third Infantry Brigade—Colonel Bilcliffe : 61st Pioneers, 62nd Punjabis, and 63rd Light Infantry.

Fourth Brigade—Colonel Campbell : 66th Punjabis, 67th Punjabis, and the 8th Madras Infantry, which has ceased to exist.

Fifth Infantry Brigade—Colonel Trent : 69th Pioneers, and the old 17th and 19th Regiments of Madras Infantry, which have been merged in other corps.

Sixth Infantry Brigade—Colonel Cuppage : 23rd, 24th, and 25th Regiments of Madras Infantry.

The artillery consisted of 117 men of the Royal and 731 of the Madras Artillery, and there were 75 English sappers, together with that well-tried regiment which has fought so bravely on so many fields—the Madras Sappers and Miners.

I regret that I have been unable to trace the losses of all the native regiments ; their total casualties amounted to 4 British officers and 135 native ranks killed and wounded.

CASUALTIES AT PONDICHERRY, 1793.

Regiments.	Officers.		Men.		Regiments.	Officers.		Men.	
	K.	W.	K.	W.		K.	W.	K.	W.
Royal Artillery	—	2	12	17	Petrie's batt. . .	—	1	2	6
Roy. Engineers	1	4	5	18	Vigor's batt. . .	—	1	1	3
36th Worcesters	—	—	5	9	61st Pioneers	—	—	2	8
52nd Oxford L.I.	1	—	2	5	62nd Punjabis	1	—	6	12
71st Highl. L.I.	—	1	8	14	66th Punjabis	—	—	3	5
73rd R. Highl.	3	—	7	13	67th Punjabis	1	—	9	16

Although no battle honours have been awarded to the Indian regiments which took part in the operations against Pondicherry in the years 1778 and 1793, I have been at some pains to give a brief account of the operations, both of which, with their accompanying loss of life, might have been avoided had the Home Government either insisted on the retention of the conquests we had made in the East, or, were that impracticable, refused to allow the rebuilding of fortifications in the French settlements in India. "Pondicherry, 1778 and 1793," might be added with propriety to the battle honours of regiments which took part in the sieges of those years.

BUXAR, OCTOBER 23, 1764.

Royal Munster Fusiliers.   Royal Dublin Fusiliers.

In the interval between Eyre Coote's victory at Wande-wash in January, 1760, and the Battle of Buxar in October, 1764, our troops in India had been continuously at war ; yet the colours even of those regiments which still survive, and which were then in the service of the Company, bear no record of the many stubborn fights, the by no means inglorious victories achieved over our gallant foes. In the South, the Government of Madras had been carrying on campaign after campaign against the trained troops of France and the scarcely less formidable army of Mysore. In the North, Clive and his successor had found foemen no less worthy of their steel in the armies of the Emperor of Delhi and those of the ruler of Oude, under Surajah Doolah. History—even Greek history—affords no more striking episodes than those early struggles of our countrymen in India ; and though the names of Beerpore, Sooty, and Oondna Nullah are forgotten, they deserve to stand side by side with other well-remembered names that are emblazoned on the colours of the old Company's regiments. The Battle of Buxar was the final episode in the long-fought campaign with the ruler of Oude.

Now that the two senior battalions of the old Company's army have been converted into the Royal Munster and Royal Dublin Fusiliers, they are the only regiments which bear on their colours a memento of one of the finest actions ever fought in India. The British force numbered between 6,000 and 7,000 men, with twenty-eight guns. It included, besides the two European regiments in the Company's employ, a composite battalion, just 167 strong, made up of detachments of the 84th, or Coote's Regiment, and volunteers from the disbanded 89th Regiment and 90th (Light Infantry) ; two companies of Royal Marines, under Captain Wemyss ; a handful of seamen, with a midshipman, working some guns side by side with the Bengal Artillery ; and a small troop of cavalry, the total being about 1,200 Englishmen. To these must be added 900 Mogul horse and 5,000 sepoys. This little army was under the command of Colonel Sir Hector Munro, of the 89th Regiment. The two Company's battalions were inured to Indian warfare, and the men of the 90th (then the only Light Infantry regiment in the British army), had learned their lesson at the capture of Belleisle, Martinique, and Havana, under their brave Colonel, James

Stuart, who was destined to add to the laurels gained at the Moro a great reputation in Southern India.

The force opposed to Munro was a formidable one. It included eight battalions trained and commanded by French officers, two batteries of artillery manned by Europeans, 5,000 Afghan horse, and 40,000 men of Shah Shujah Daulah's own fairly trained army. The battle was stubbornly contested, but the victoy was complete. Our weakness in cavalry, however, prevented Munro reaping the full benefits of his success. In addition to the losses of the British contingent, the sepoy battalions lost 257 killed and 435 wounded. Our trophies included 137 guns, whilst the enemy left upwards of 2,000 dead on the field.

CASUALTIES AT BUXAR.

Regiments.	Officers.		Men.		Regiments.	Officers.		Men.	
	K.	W.	K.	W.		K.	W.	K.	W.
R. Munster Fus.	—	3	37	58	Royal Dublin Fusiliers	—	—	2	3
Composite batt.	1	1	2	13					
Royal Artillery	1	1	2	3	British cavalry	—	1	2	4

Broome, in his admirable "History of the Bengal Army," states that the two officers who figure in the list of casualties in the composite battalion both belonged to the 90th Light Infantry. This is an error. On comparing the names of the officers with the Army Lists, I am convinced that they belonged to the 96th Regiment, and that the error has arisen in the transcription by a clerk at the War or India Office. I have come across many such errors. Perhaps the most amusing is in the *Gazette* recording the capture of Havana in 1762, where the 42nd is referred to in the casualty rolls as the "42nd Royal Hunters"!

5

CHAPTER VI

INDIA, 1774-1799

ROHILCUND, 1774.

THIS honorary distinction was awarded to the 2nd European Regiment of the Bengal army for its services in the campaign undertaken in that year to defend our ally, the King of Oude, against the incursions of the Mahrattas. It is now borne by the Royal Munster Fusiliers.

The campaign of 1774 was under the personal command of Colonel Champion, the Commander-in-Chief in Bengal. There was a good deal of hard work, of privations little to be understood by the soldier who serves in India in these days, and more than one sharp skirmish. The principal engagement was that fought at Kutra, in the near neighbourhood of Bareilly, on St. George's Day (April 23), 1774, long known in India as St. George's Battle. Colonel Champion had with him the 2nd Bengal European Regiment (now the 2nd Battalion Royal Munster Fusiliers) and six battalions of native infantry. Unfortunately, no representatives of these remain to bear the honour on their standards.

Our casualties amounted to 2 officers and 37 men killed, 7 officers and 93 men wounded. Immense booty was captured, and in the distribution of this, officers and men benefited largely, the respective shares being : Colonels, £1,900 ; Lieutenant-Colonels, £1,600 ; Major, £1,300 ; Captains, £685 ; subalterns, £343 ; cadets, £100 ; sergeants, £6 ; privates, £4 ; Subadars, 131 rupees ; Jemidars, 65 rupees ; havildars, 40 rupees ; sepoys, 35 rupees.

THE CARNATIC.

This honour has been awarded to the following regiments :

Highland Light Infantry.	Royal Munster Fusiliers.
Seaforth Highlanders.	Royal Dublin Fusiliers.
27th Light Cavalry.	2nd Queen's Own Sappers
61st Pioneers.	and Miners.
62nd Punjabis.	72nd Punjabis.
63rd Light Infantry.	73rd Carnatic Infantry.
64th Pioneers.	74th Punjabis.
66th Punjabis.	75th Carnatic Infantry.
67th Punjabis.	76th Punjabis.
69th Punjabis.	79th Carnatic Infantry.

80th Carnatic Infantry.

It records their services in repelling the invasion of the Carnatic by Hyder Ali, the ruler of Mysore, and covers all the operations undertaken against him up to the invasion of Mysore by the army under Lord Cornwallis in 1791.

The renewal of the war with France in 1788 found Sir Hector Munro, the victor of Buxar, Commander-in-Chief at Madras. It now became necessary to reoccupy the fortified positions which we had captured during the previous war with the expenditure of many lives, and which had been restored to France on the conclusion of peace. Although subsequent to the battle at Wande-wash Hyder Ali, the ruler of Mysore, had entered into a treaty with us, it was well known that he had a striking predilection for the French ; and on the resumption of the war between France and England he openly espoused the cause of our enemies, and prepared to invade the Carnatic at the head of his troops. The Mysorean army was by no means contemptible. It was partly trained on the European model, and numbered little short of

100,000 men, of whom 25,000 were cavalry, and it included a battalion of French troops. Munro's first care was to prevent Hyder Ali receiving assistance from France, and he at once took measures to seize the seaports of Mahé and Pondicherry. In the defence of the former some of Hyder Ali's troops took an active part, and the place made a gallant defence before it surrendered. Sir Hector Munro undertook the reduction of Pondicherry in person, but the garrison, anticipating the arrival of a French fleet, made a most stubborn defence ; and it was not until the middle of October, after a siege lasting over two months, that the British flag flew over its walls, our losses during these operations amounting to upwards of 800 of all ranks, British as well as native, killed and wounded.[1]

When Hyder Ali, in June, 1779, actually crossed the frontier, our forces were much dispersed. Braithwaite, with 1,500 men, held Pondicherry ; Colonel Baillie, with 3,000, was at Guntoor, on the Kistnah River ; Colonel Cosby, with 2,000 native troops, was at Trichinopoly ; and Munro, with barely 5,000 men, at Madras. Braithwaite and Baillie were immediately called in to strengthen the Commander-in-Chief, whilst Colonel Cosby was ordered to threaten Hyder Ali's line of communication. Wandewash, an important strategical point on the Mysorean line of advance, was held by a gallant young subaltern, Lieutenant Flint, with 200 sepoys, aided by one single sergeant of the line. From August 11, 1780, until January 22, 1781, this little band of heroes withstood assault after assault, holding Hyder Ali's besieging force at bay until relieved by Eyre Coote. The story of that siege has yet to be written. Flint improvised his own artillery, made his own powder, infused his own cheerful daring into the breasts of his sepoys, and died unhonoured and unsung. There were, unfortunately, grievous disasters to counterbalance this gallant achievement. Hyder Ali threw himself on Baillie's force before it effected its junction with Munro, practically annihilating it, the sur-

---

[1] For details of casualties at Pondicherry, see p. 61.

vivors, including fifty English officers (amongst them Captain, afterwards Sir David, Baird, of the 71st), being sent as prisoners to Seringapatam.

Whenever our fortunes in India have been at their lowest ebb we have, fortunately, had men at hand to retrieve them. The " man on the spot," unhampered from " home," has rarely failed us. In 1781 Warren Hastings was Governor-General, Eyre Coote Commander-in-Chief at Calcutta. On hearing of Baillie's disaster and of Munro's indecision, Warren Hastings despatched Eyre Coote to Madras armed with full powers (suspending both Munro, the Commander-in-Chief, and Whitehill, the Governor, from their functions). Coote had at his disposal barely 8,000 men—the 71st (Highland Light Infantry), 1st Bengal, and 1st Madras European Regiments, some 1,600 men in all, with six sepoy battalions and three regiments of native cavalry. Munro, a gallant leader of men, but no General, at once put himself under Coote's orders, and was entrusted with the command of a brigade composed of the three British regiments. James Stuart, who had commanded the 90th Light Infantry at Martinique and Havana, and who had subsequently entered the Company's service, being placed in command of the sepoy battalions. On July 1, 1781, Coote inflicted his first defeat on Hyder Ali at the Battle of Porto Novo, a fortified position on the sea-coast about 100 miles south of Madras. On September 27 the two armies again met at Sholinghur, about fifty miles west of Madras, when Coote, with 11,000 men and thirty guns, signally defeated Hyder Ali's army, 70,000 strong, killing, it is said, 5,000 of the enemy.

GUZERAT, 1778-1782.

This distinction is borne by the Royal Munster Fusiliers and the Royal Dublin Fusiliers. There is, however, considerable doubt as to the propriety of the Munsters bearing the honour. Colonel P. R. Innes, the painstaking and accurate historian of that regiment, maintains that the old 1st Bengal European Regiment has no right to it, and if the honour was granted, as it undoubtedly was, for the operations conducted by General Goddard in Guzerat in the years 1778-1782, it is very certain that the 1st Bengal Europeans never were with Goddard. The early part of the year 1778 found the army of the Bombay Presidency hard pressed, and help was solicited from Bengal, where all for the moment was quiet. Warren Hastings at once despatched a force consisting of six battalions of sepoys (none of which are now remaining), a couple of batteries of artillery, and 500 Afghan horsemen, to Bombay. The march was an arduous undertaking—to cross India from east to west, with a possible and very probable combination of Mahratta chieftains to bar its progress. The officer originally nominated to the command was soon superseded by Brigadier - General Goddard, an officer who had received his early training in the 84th under Coote, and who, on that regiment being ordered to England, had been offered increased rank in the army of the East India Company. Goddard marched via Cawnpore and Kalpee, which he stepped aside to capture, to Hoshungabad, finally co-operating with a column sent up from Bombay, which included the 1st Bombay European Regiment, now the Royal Munster Fusiliers, as well as some battalions of native infantry. Later the Madras Presidency was also called upon to assist, and 500 men of the Madras Europeans, now the 1st Battalion of the Dublins, with a battery of artillery and a sepoy battalion, was sent round by sea to Surat, to which place Goddard had advanced. For close on two years the little army was constantly engaged. It captured Bassein on December 11, 1780, Ahmadabad in the following month, and in the space of a little more than a year after the arrival of the Madras troops Goddard had reduced the provinces of Guzerat and the Concan. The Bengal troops were now allowed to return, and once more they marched across India, reaching Cawnpore in April, 1784.

To commemorate their services the supreme Government struck a medal, which was distributed to all ranks, officers receiving gold and the sepoys silver, medals. According to Mayo, this was the first occasion in which a medal was granted to the private soldiers of our army.

I regret that I have been unable to ascertain the casualties of all the forces engaged. Stubbs, in his invaluable history of the Bengal Artillery, gives the names of the officers of his corps who were killed, but Begbie ignores the fact that Madras artillery were employed. Colonel Harcourt does not allude to the losses of the Madras European Regiment in his history of the old "Blue Caps." The Royal Dublin Fusiliers, then the 1st Bombay Regiment, lost 3 officers and 19 men killed, and 14 officers and 41 men wounded, in the course of these operations, and there is no doubt that the campaign in Guzerat was attended with considerable loss.

SHOLINGHUR, SEPTEMBER 27, 1781.

This battle honour, which commemorates the defeat of the Mysorean Army of Hyder Ali and its expulsion from the Carnatic by Sir Eyre Coote, is borne by the following regiments :

Highland Light Infantry.	66th Punjabis.
Royal Dublin Fusiliers.	69th Punjabis.
Royal Munster Fusiliers.	72nd Punjabis.
27th Light Cavalry.	73rd Carnatic Infantry.
2nd Queen's Own Sappers	74th Punjabis.
and Miners.	75th Carnatic Infantry.
63rd Light Infantry.	76th Punjabis.
64th Pioneers.	79th Carnatic Infantry.
80th Carnatic Infantry.	

The total casualties in the action were by no means heavy. They fell principally on the British troops. Unfortunately, although Sir Eyre Coote alludes to a casualty return in his despatch announcing the battle, all trace of this has disappeared, so that the losses sustained by individual regiments must, in the case of Sholinghur, as in those of Marlborough's earlier battles, always remain unrecorded.

Early in the following year welcome reinforcements
arrived from England, the 73rd (then the 2nd Battalion
of the 42nd) Highlanders, the 98th and 100th Regiments
disembarking on the Malabar coast, the 72nd coming to
Madras to reinforce Coote.   These reinforcements came
none too early.   Tippoo Sultan (Hyder Ali's son, his most
able Lieutenant and his successor) had surprised and
annihilated a British force under Colonel Braithwaite,
all the officers save one being either killed or carried
prisoners to Seringapatam.   A few months later fresh
reinforcements arrived in the 23rd Light Dragoons (now
the 19th Hussars), the 101st and 102nd Regiments (long
since disbanded, and not to be confused with the 101st
Royal Bengal and 102nd Royal Madras Fusiliers), with
two Hanoverian battalions.   With these forces Stuart inflicted a severe defeat on Tippoo Sultan at Cuddalore,
taking from him thirteen guns.   For this fine action
no battle honour was granted, though there are many
names on many colours less hardly earned.

CASUALTIES AT CUDDALORE.

Regiments.	Officers.		Men.		Regiments.	Officers.		Men.	
	K.	W.	K.	W.		K.	W.	K.	W.
Royal Artillery	—	2	19	67	72nd Seaforths	1	—	23	47
71st H.L.I. ..	2	6	84	112	Dublin Fus. ..	—	2	8	29
101st Regiment	4	6	42	55	72nd Punjabis	—	3	6	39
Hanoverians	4	12	62	144	18th Madras In.	—	3	4	50
64th Pioneers	—	—	6	16	20th M.N.I. ..	1	1	6	14
67th Punjabis	—	—	—	8	Bengal Infantry	7	5	12	90

On the opposite or Malabar coast Colonel McLeod,
with the 2nd Battalion of the 42nd, details of the 98th,
100th, and 102nd Regiments, and the 8th Battalion of
Bombay Sepoys, won a decisive victory at Paniani on
November 27, 1782, the 42nd losing 3 officers and
57 men in the action ; but the chief honours were
reserved for the 42nd at Mangalore.

Mangalore, 1783.

The Royal Highlanders and 101st Grenadiers alone bear this battle honour, and surely in the many names inscribed on the colours and appointments of the Black Watch, there is not one which redounds more to the glory of the regiment than this little-known achievement, one of the brightest in the military history of our own or of any other country.

A glance at the map of India will show Mangalore on the west or Malabar coast of the peninsula. During our operations against Hyder Ali, and subsequently against his son, the redoubted Tippoo Sultan, its possession was of vital importance to both ourselves and to the Mysoreans. Tippoo Sultan was in direct communication with Napoleon, and through the Malabar ports reinforcements and supplies reached him from France. When, in 1783, General Matthews, the Commander-in-Chief in Bombay, led a column to reduce the fortress of Bednore, in which Tippoo's treasure was stored, he left garrisons at Mangalore and Onore to keep open his communication with the sea. At first successful, Matthews was in the end compelled to capitulate, and he, with the bulk of his army, were done to death by the Mysoreans. Mangalore was held by a force of about 1,800 men, under Colonel Campbell, of the 42nd ; Onore by an officer of the Bombay Army named Torriano, with whom at present I have nothing to do.

Early in May Colonel Campbell learned of the disaster to General Matthews, and at the same time he received a summons from Tippoo Sultan demanding the surrender of the fort and town of Mangalore in virtue of the terms of the capitulation arranged with the Commander-in-Chief. Now, it is necessary for me here to interpolate that General Matthews and the officers of the King's regiments had not been on the best of terms. He, a servant of the East India Company, refused to recognize their superior rank, and two of the Colonels of the King's regiments (McLeod, of the 42nd, and Humberston, of the 100th) had left his camp and formulated complaints against the Commander-in-Chief to the Governor-General. Campbell therefore replied to Tippoo Sultan's envoy that he refused to recognize any arrangements which might have been made by the Commander-in-Chief, and that he intended to defend the fort to the last.

On May 9 the siege commenced on the land side, and for the next six months Campbell was hemmed closely in by some 60,000 men. It is true that communication by sea was still precariously maintained. On May 23 the Indiaman *Fairford* appeared off the port, and threw ashore a small party of English recruits destined for the Bombay European Regiment, which had been practically annihilated with Matthews.[1] That day, May 23, Colonel Campbell made a vigorous sortie, and destroyed a portion of the enemy's siege-works and batteries ; but in the retirement three companies of native troops were cut off, and three British officers with 225 sepoys fell into Tippoo Sultan's hands. On the morrow Campbell prepared for a determined resistance. The women of the 42nd were told off to the hospitals, and a stern code of orders published. The men were forbidden to fire without explicit orders, and officers were enjoined to remember that the bayonet, and the bayonet alone, was the weapon of the British soldier. " Englishmen must recollect," runs the order, " that the bayonet is the service required of them, and that they demean themselves by firing at such a dastardly foe."

A return, dated May 24, showed the garrison to consist of 70 British and 67 native officers, with 315 British and 1,394 native soldiers. Attached to and included in the total of the 42nd were a few of the then 98th and 101st Regiments (not to be confused with the present Royal Munster Fusiliers), both of which were · with General Matthews at Bednore. The native troops included the headquarters of the 8th Battalion (now the 101st Grenadiers), some companies of the 15th Bombay

---

[1] These recruits were attached to the Artillery, and did excellent work throughout the siege, losing 65 per cent. of their number killed.

Battalion, and details of other regiments which were with the Commander-in-Chief at Bednore. Amongst the officers was Lieutenant MacKay, of the Royal Navy, who volunteered to act as a gunner during the siege. He did right good and gallant service, and was twice wounded in the course of the operations. Another name appears prominently in the despatches—a name which has since become a household word in the British Army. Campbell's Brigade-Major was a certain Captain Wolseley, of the 98th Regiment, and much of the credit of the defence was due to the gallantry and unwearied exertions of this officer.

Between the Highlanders and the 8th Battalion of Bombay Grenadiers a strong *camaraderie* existed ; they had fought side by side at Panianee, when Colonel Macleod had drawn attention to the dash and steady gallantry of the regiment. Campbell, in his despatches from Mangalore, bore frequent testimony to the unselfish devotion of the native officers, and the uncomplaining heroism of the men.

Into the details of the siege it is not my intention to enter. Suffice to say that from May 23 until July 27, when news arrived of peace between France and England, there was only one day in which the garrison did not suffer some casualties, and that from June 12 the men were on half-rations of flour ; of meat they had from the first been deprived. Desertions amongst the sepoys were frequent, and this was not to be wondered at. Life within the walls was not a bed of roses, whereas Tippoo Sultan offered golden inducements to those who would enter his service. On August 2 an armistice was arranged, a French officer attached to Tippoo Sultan's army acting as intermediary, Campbell declining to surrender the fortress until he had received specific instructions on this head from Bombay. The Mysorean Prince promised to furnish supplies on condition that no attempts were made to strengthen the works or to communicate with the outside world, except with the consent of the Tippoo

Sultan himself. On several occasions vessels came close
enough for Campbell to send an officer on board (indeed,
Colonel McLeod, the acting Commander-in-Chief, landed
at Mangalore, and had an interview with Tippoo Sultan).
Campbell's pitiable condition was well known to the authorities in Bombay ;[1] but no well-sustained effort appears to
have been made to relieve him, and at last, on January 30,
his men reduced to skeletons with fatigue and sickness,
and his garrison reduced in numbers to one-half of their
original strength, he was compelled to capitulate ; but he
marched out with all the honours of war, and even Tippoo
Sultan kept honourably to the terms of the capitulation,
and gave the garrison a safe conduct to Bombay.
Colonel Campbell arrived there on March 13, and ten
days later he was laid to rest in the cathedral in
that city. The Bombay Government, at last recognizing his work, erected a monument to commemorate his
heroic defence of the little fort committed to his charge.

The actual siege of Mangalore lasted from May 23 to
July 27, 1783, when hostilities ceased ; but from that date
until January 30, 1784, the garrison suffered from the
want of food and the exposure necessitated by being ever
on the alert in case of treachery.

The losses of the garrison between those dates amounted
to—

British Troops.	Officers.		Men.		Native Troops.	Officers.		Men.	
	K.	W.	K.	W.		K.	W.	K.	W.
Total of British troops .. 42nd R. High-landers ..	12	15	45	127	Total of Native troops ..	5	16	121	438
	5	4	34	96					

[1] The men were glad to eat the frogs, rats, and water-snakes,
which were caught in the ditch of the works. Officers' chargers
had been salted down for the sick, and it was not until the last
joint of " salt horse " had been served out to the hospital, and the
last barrel of flour broached, that the gallant Campbell capitulated.

On p. 74 I have given the strength of the garrison on May 24, the actual date of the commencement of the siege. The " marching-out " state on January 27, 1784, shows the true extent of the sufferings of the garrison of Mangalore :

Regiments.	May 24, 1783.		Jan. 27, 1784.	
	Officers.	Men.	Officers.	Men.
BRITISH :				
42nd and details	28	245	16	119
Bombay Artillery	4	15	3	9
Bombay Fusiliers	6	55	4	19
Officers of Sepoy Corps ..	32	—	23	—
NATIVES :				
Bombay Artillery	4	133	3	83
8th Grenadiers and details ..	63	1,261	53	490

MYSORE.

This honour is now borne by the following regiments :

19th Hussars.
West Riding.
Middlesex.
Seaforth Highlanders.
Royal Dublin Fusiliers.
27th Light Cavalry.
2nd Queen's Own Sappers and Miners.
63rd Light Infantry.
66th Punjabis.
68th Punjabis.
74th Punjabis.
76th Punjabis.
80th Carnatic Infantry.
82nd Punjabis.
103rd Light Infantry.
105th Light Infantry.
108th Infantry.

Worcester.
Oxford Light Infantry.
Highland Light Infantry.
Gordon Highlanders.
26th Light Cavalry.
28th Light Cavalry.
61st P.W.O. Pioneers.
62nd Punjabis.
64th Pioneers.
67th Punjabis.
73rd Carnatic Infantry.
75th Carnatic Infantry.
79th Carnatic Infantry.
81st Pioneers.
101st Grenadiers.
104th Rifles.
107th Pioneers.
109th Infantry.

The aggressive action of Tippoo Sultan, who had been recognized as ruler of Mysore on the death of Hyder Ali, and the cruelties perpetrated on the English prisoners in Seringapatam, rendered fresh hostilities with Mysore inevitable. The Home Government therefore agreed to raise four more regiments, to be paid by, and held at the disposal of the East India Company. These were numbered 74th and 75th Highlanders, and 76th and 77th of the line. All four arrived in India in the course of the year 1788. It was known that Tippoo Sultan had sent emissaries to France in the hope of securing French aid in his efforts to drive us out of India, and in 1789 he threw down the glove by invading the territory of our ally, the Maharajah of Travancore. The Commander-in-Chief at Madras, General Meadows, was a most gallant officer, who had distinguished himself in the West Indies, but who was new to the East, and, brave man that he was, was quite prepared to recognize that as yet he had not sufficient experience of Eastern life to warrant his assuming command of a large army operating under entirely novel conditions. Lord Cornwallis, the Governor-General in India, therefore determined to come down from Calcutta and take command of the army destined for the subjugation of Tippoo Sultan. The task was no easy one. Circumstances arose which delayed the Governor-General, and the year 1790 was wasted in an abortive campaign under Meadows.

The year 1791 opened more auspiciously. The Commander-in-Chief at Bombay, General Robert Abercromby, who was to co-operate with the Governor-General, had by a well-executed movement seized Cannanore, and made himself master of the province of Malabar.

Tippoo was now threatened from both sea-coasts, and seems to have been utterly unprepared for the daring stroke so brilliantly carried out by Cornwallis, who, leaving Madras early in February, and passing through the famous Colar Goldfields, arrived before Bangalore on March 5, and two days later had carried the fortifications of that city by assault, and so secured a base of operations for his projected advance on Seringapatam.

In May, after an unsuccessful attempt to carry that fortress by storm, Cornwallis was compelled to fall back on Bangalore, where he passed the hot weather.

CASUALTIES AT THE CAPTURE OF BANGALORE, MARCH, 1791.

Regiments.	Officers.		Men.		Regiments.	Officers.		Men.	
	K.	W.	K.	W.		K.	W.	K.	W.
19th Hussars..	—	1	3	7	74th Highl. L.I.	—	2	1	7
36th Worcester	1	4	9	54	76th W. Riding				
52nd Oxfd. L.I.	1	2	4	12	Regiment ..	—	1	8	45
71st Highl. L.I.	—	1	6	14	2nd Q.O. Sap-				
72nd Seaforths	—	—	5	18	pers	—	3	24	25

NOTE.—The Indian regiments present at the capture of Bangalore were the 61st Pioneers, 62nd Punjabis, 63rd Palamcottah L.I., 64th Pioneers, and 80th Carnatic Infantry; their total losses were 62 killed and 123 wounded.

NUNDY DROOG, OCTOBER 19, 1791.

This honour is borne by the Royal Dublin Fusiliers alone, and records the capture of what was considered by the Mysoreans an impregnable stronghold by the force under Cornwallis prior to the capture of Seringapatam in 1792. Nundy Droog lies some thirty miles north of Bangalore, and threatened the communications between Cornwallis's army and that of our ally, the Nizam of Hyderabad. It became necessary then to possess it. It bore a great reputation, and for three years had defied the whole strength of Hyder Ali's army, and then only fell into his hands through starvation. Early in September, 1791, Cornwallis detached Major Gowdie, with the 1st Madras European Regiment (now the Dublin Fusiliers) and six battalions of sepoys, to effect its reduction. The fort is on the summit of a granite mountain, its walls being three miles in circumference, the hill itself being inaccessible except on one side. With much diffi-

culty heavy guns were dragged up the cliffs, and the siege
begun in due form. Cornwallis, chafing at the delay,
moved out from Bangalore with his whole army, thinking
to overawe the defenders ; but on the night of October 18
he determined to carry the place by assault. This was
performed in the most dashing manner, and with but
slight loss, by the flank companies of the 36th (Worcester)
and 71st (Highland Light Infantry), with the 1st Madras
European (Dublins) in support.

Abercromby was now approaching from the Malabar
coast, and Lord Cornwallis was preparing for the final
advance on Tippoo Sultan's famed stronghold.

In January, 1792, Cornwallis, apprised that Abercromby, with the Bombay division, was within striking
distance, commenced his advance on Seringapatam.
His force consisted of the 19th Light Dragoons, two regiments of Madras cavalry, and the Governor-General's
Bodyguard, which he had brought down from Calcutta,
the 36th (Worcester), 52nd (Oxford Light Infantry), 72nd
(Seaforths), 74th (Highland Light Infantry), 76th (West
Riding), 1st Madras Europeans (Royal Dublin Fusiliers),
and sixteen battalions of sepoys, with forty-six field and
forty siege guns.

Abercromby's force comprised the 73rd (Royal Highlanders), 75th (Gordons), 77th (Middlesex), 1st Bombay
Europeans (2nd Battalion of the Dublins), and eight
battalions of sepoys, with twenty field and sixteen siege
guns, giving a total of about 9,000 British and 22,000
native troops.

On February 7 Seringapatam was carried by assault,
our casualties numbering about 535 of all ranks, and our
trophies amounting to eighty guns. On March 19 Tippoo
Sultan signed a definitive treaty of peace, ceding to
England Malabar and Coorg on the west, Baramahal and
Dindigul on the Carnatic frontier, besides restoring to
the Nizam the territories wrested from Hyderabad by
Hyder Ali.

The distribution of prize-money afforded Lord Corn-

wallis and General Meadows, the second in command, an
opportunity of giving an example of noble generosity,
these two commanders placing their shares, amounting
to £47,000 and £15,000, into the common fund. The
following were the shares for each rank : Colonels, £1,160 ;
Lieutenant-Colonels, £958 ; Majors, £734 ; Captains, £308 ;
Lieutenants, £205 ; Ensigns, £159 ; sergeants, £29 ; and
privates, £14 10s. In the native army Subadars received
275 rupees ; Jemidars, 132 rupees ; havildars, 110 rupees ;
and sepoys, 51 rupees.

CASUALTIES AT THE SIEGE AND CAPTURE OF
SERINGAPATAM, 1792.

Regiments.	Officers.		Men.		Regiments.	Officers.		Men.	
	K.	W.	K.	W.		K.	W.	K.	W.
19th Hussars	—	—	—	—	76th W. Riding				
Royal Artillery	1	9	9	20	Regiment ..	1	4	1	8
36th Worcesters	2	3	6	33	Royal Dublin				
52nd Oxfd. L.I.	1	5	9	25	Fusiliers ..	—	1	2	32
71st Highl. L.I.	2	1	25	54	61st P.W.O.				
72nd Seaforth					Pioneers ..	0	1	5	18
Highlanders	1	4	15	43	62nd Punjabis	—	—	1	3
73rd R. High-					66th Punjabis	—	1	9	14
landers ..	—	—	—	3	76th Punjabis	—	—	3	12
74th Highl. L.I.	—	2	2	18	79th Carnatic I.	—	2	5	9
75th Gordon					80th Carnatic I.	1	2	6	25
Highlanders	—	—	3	12					

ROHILCUND, 1794.

This distinction is borne only by the Royal Munster
Fusiliers.

The campaign was necessitated owing to a serious
rising in the independent State of Rampur, and Lord
Cornwallis, the Governor-General, deemed the occasion
so grave that he took the field in person. The troops
employed were the 2nd Regiment of Bengal Europeans
(now the 2nd Battalion Royal Munster Fusiliers), with
ten regiments of sepoys, none of which are now borne

on the Army List. The force was divided into three brigades of infantry, commanded respectively by Colonel Ware, who afterwards lost his life at the Battle of Laswarree, Colonel MacGowan, and Colonel Burrington. One brigade of two regiments of native light cavalry and four batteries of artillery made up the army. The only action of importance was that of Betourah, which took place some nine miles north of Bareilly. The enemy fought with great gallantry, and charged home on our native cavalry, who do not appear to have been well led—indeed, they fell back in disorder, breaking through the ranks of the 13th Bengal Infantry. This regiment suffered very heavily, all its officers being either killed or wounded, and the Brigadier of the Third Brigade, Colonel Burrington, was cut down in endeavouring to rally the cavalry. The officer commanding that arm disappeared in the course of the action, and so escaped court-martial. It was reported that he entered the service of the French, and was given a commission by Napoleon.

Our casualties were heavy, fourteen officers falling on the field. A monument was erected by Lord Cornwallis to mark the site of their interment, and may yet be seen by the roadside near the village of Betourah. The action, though costly, was decisive as to its results. The recalcitrant leaders of the insurrection made their submission to the Governor-General, and the army was immediately demobilized.

CASUALTIES AT BETOURAH.

Regiments.	Officers.		Men.		Regiments.	Officers.		Men.	
	K.	W.	K.	W.		K.	W.	K.	W.
Staff	3	—	—	—	13th Bengal I.	5	4	—	—
Artillery.. ..	2	—	—	—	18th Bengal I.	2	—	—	—
Munster Fuslrs.	2	—	—	—					

Here again it would appear that no record of the losses of the men has been kept.

SEEDASEER, MARCH 6, 1799.

This distinction is borne on the colours of the

103rd Mahratta L.I.   105th Mahratta L.I.   107th **Pioneers**.

It commemorates a brilliant engagement with the army of Tippoo Sultan, in which these three regiments of Bombay sepoys held at bay for eight long hours some 18,000 of the flower of the Mysorean army.

As in 1792, so now in 1799, the armies of all three presidencies were employed in a last endeavour to crush the power of the Mysorean usurper. The Bombay column, under the command of Major-General James Stuart, moving from the coast at Cannanore, consisted of three brigades. The Centre Brigade, under Colonel Dunlop, comprised the 75th (Gordon Highlanders), 77th (Middlesex), and the 1st Bombay Europeans (now the 2nd Dublin Fusiliers) ; the Right Brigade, under Colonel Montresor, was made up of the 1st Battalions of the 2nd, 3rd, and 4th Bombay Infantry (now the 103rd, 105th, and 107th Regiments of the Indian army) ; the Third or Left Brigade, under Colonel Wiseman, comprised the 2nd Battalion of the 2nd, 2nd Battalion of the 3rd, and 1st Battalion of the 5th Regiment of Bombay Infantry. For convenience of supplies, and also owing to the bad state of the roads, the army was marching in three columns, the Right Brigade, under Colonel Montresor, leading.

On March 5 the Right Brigade had reached Seedaseer, on the frontiers of Coorg, the British Brigade being about eight miles in its rear, and the Left Brigade some four miles farther off. Tippoo Sultan was well informed of all our movements, and he endeavoured to put into effect one of the great Napoleon's maxims—namely, to beat your enemy in detail. With the bulk of his army, amounting to some 20,000 men, he cut in between Montresor's brigade and the British General, never doubting of an easy victory over the three sepoy battalions. Montresor, however, had been warned of his approach, and at once commenced to strengthen his position. Stuart, too, had learnt of the near approach of the Mysoreans, and he sent forward the 1st Battalion of the 5th Bombay N.I. to support Montresor, and later in the day hurried up with the flank companies of the 75th (Gordon Highlanders) and the whole of the 77th (Middlesex). In the meantime Montresor had fought out the battle unaided. The 1st Battalion of the 5th N.I. had never been able to reach him, and the British troops only arrived in time to relieve the pressure and to follow up the defeated enemy. The result of the fight augured well for the future, and showed the Bombay sepoy that he was more than a match even for Tippoo Sultan's men.

The casualty returns prove that the name of Seedaseer was worthily earned by the three regiments which have been allowed to place that battle honour on their colours ; but it may reasonably be asked why the same honour has not been conferred on the 109th Infantry, which in those days was the 1st Battalion of the 5th Bombay Regiment, and which contributed in some measure to the success of the day. The Gordon Highlanders and the Middlesex content themselves with the battle honours " Mysore " and " Seringapatam."

CASUALTIES AT THE ACTION OF SEEDASEER.

Regiments.	Officers.		Men.		Regiments.	Officers.		Men.	
	K.	W.	K.	W.		K.	W.	K.	W.
Royal Artillery	—	I	6	18	105th Mahratta L.I. (Natives)	—	—	4	33
75th Gordon Highlanders	—	—	3	9	107th Pioneers (British) ..	—	—	—	—
77th Middlesex	—	—	2	6	Do. (Natives) ..	—	—	3	48
103rd Mahratta L.I. (British)	I	3	—	—	109th Infantry (British) ..	—	I	—	—
Do. (Natives)	—	2	11	25	Do. (Natives)	—	—	I	26
105th Mahratta L.I. (British)	—	I	—	—					

SERINGAPATAM, MAY 4, 1799.

The regiments authorized to bear this battle honour are the

Suffolks.
Royal Highlanders.
Highland Light Infantry.
Connaught Rangers.
26th Light Cavalry.
28th Light Cavalry.
61st Pioneers.
66th Punjabis.
76th Punjabis.
80th Carnatic Infantry.
82nd Punjabis.
84th Punjabis.
104th Wellesley's Rifles.
107th Pioneers.

West Riding.
Middlesex.
Gordon Highlanders.
Royal Dublin Fusiliers.
27th Light Cavalry.
2nd Queen's Own Sappers and Miners.
73rd Carnatic Infantry.
79th Carnatic Infantry.
81st Pioneers.
83rd Light Infantry.
103rd Light Infantry.
105th Light Infantry.
109th Infantry.

The troops destined for the final capture of Seringapatam were placed under the command of General Harris, the Commander-in-Chief at Madras. All three Presidencies were represented.

The cavalry division was under Major-General Floyd (an officer well versed in Indian warfare), who had commanded the 19th Hussars in the previous capture of the fortress in 1792. It consisted of the 19th and 25th Light Dragoons and four regiments of Madras cavalry, organized in two brigades, each consisting of one British and two native regiments.

The Madras Column was distributed in three brigades, one composed entirely of British regiments—the 12th (Suffolks), 74th (Highland Light Infantry), and the Scots Brigade (now 2nd Connaught Rangers). Major-General David Baird was in command of this brigade. The six regiments of Madras sepoys were formed in two brigades, under Colonels Gowdie and Roberts, of the Company's service, the Madras Division being under Major-General Bridges, an officer of the Company's service.

The Bengal Column was commanded by Major-General Popham, a Company's officer, and consisted of three brigades. The First, under Colonel Sherbrooke, comprised the 73rd (Royal Highlanders) and a regiment of Swiss mercenaries (de Meurons) ; the Second Brigade was made up of three battalions of Bengal sepoys, under Colonel Gardiner ; and the Third Brigade was composed of three battalions of Madras sepoys, under Colonel Scott, of the Scots Brigade.

The Bombay Column was commanded by General J. Stuart, and consisted of the 75th (Gordon Highlanders), the 77th (Middlesex), and the 1st Bombay Europeans (now the Royal Dublin Fusiliers), under Colonel Dunlop, with six battalions of Bombay sepoys in two brigades, under Colonels Montresor and Wiseman. A fourth column was under the command of Colonel Arthur Wellesley, and comprised two regiments of Bengal and four of Madras infantry, with his own regiment, the 33rd Foot (West Riding Regiment), to stiffen the whole. Wellesley also was given the supervision of the Nizam's troops, numbering some 6,000 irregular cavalry and 3,000 infantry, trained and organized by French officers. In round numbers, the force at General Harris's disposal numbered 7,000 British and 27,000 native troops, with a well-equipped siege-train of forty-seven pieces of heavy ordnance.

Early in February the Commander-in-Chief received his final orders to advance from Madras, and on April 14 he joined hands with Stuart's column in the immediate vicinity of Seringapatam. Three days afterwards the siege commenced, and on May 3 the breach was declared practicable. Baird claimed the privilege of leading the stormers (a privilege his by right). He had been a prisoner in the fortress for over four years as a young Captain, and he had been present in command of a brigade of Madras sepoys at Cornwallis's capture of the fortress seven years before. Taking into consideration the strength of the work and the immense numerical superiority of the enemy, the fortress was carried with marvellously slight loss, the killed numbering 69 English and but 12 sepoys, the wounded 248 and 32 respectively, that of the Mysoreans being estimated at 1,000 killed alone. The total casualties during the siege, however, testified to the stubborn stand made prior to the assault, as the following figures show :

CASUALTIES AT THE SIEGE AND CAPTURE OF SERINGAPATAM
IN MAY, 1799.

British Troops.	Officers.		Men.		Native Troops.	Officers.		Men.	
	K.	W.	K.	W.		K.	W.	K.	W.
19th Light Dragoons	2	6	17	49	25th Light Cavalry	—	—	—	—
22nd Light Dragoons	—	—	—	—	27th Light Cavalry	—	—	—	—
Royal Artillery	2	2	35	85	28th Light Cavalry	—	—	—	—
12th Foot (Suffolks)	—	—	17	49	61st Pioneers	1	—	3	14
33rd W. Riding Regiment	—	—	6	28	66th Punjabis	—	—	5	13
73rd Royal Highlanders	1	4	21	99	73rd Carnatic I.	1	2	12	47
74th Highland L.I.	4	—	45	111	76th Punjabis	—	—	11	33
75th Gordon Highlanders	1	3	16	64	79th Carnatic I.	—	—	4	16
77th Middlesex	1	2	10	51	80th Carnatic I.	—	—	4	10
94th Connaught Rangers	—	—	14	86	81st Pioneers	—	—	3	11
1st Royal Dublin Fusiliers	—	1	5	17	82nd Punjabis	—	—	1	4
2nd Royal Dublin Fusiliers	—	1	9	25	84th Punjabis	—	—	4	7
					83rd L.I.	1	3	8	46
					103rd L.I.	1	1	4	10
					104th Wellesley's Rifles	—	2	2	10
					105th L.I.	—	1	6	21
					107th Pioneers	—	—	3	14
					109th Infantry	—	1	2	25
					2nd Q.O. Sappers and Miners	—	—	2	26

NOTE.—The prize-money at the second capture of Seringapatam was unusually satisfactory, the share of the Commander-in-Chief being upwards of £100,000. General officers received in round figures £10,000, other ranks having as their share :

Colonels	..	..	£4,320	Lieutenants	..	..	£432
Lieutenant-Colonels		£2,590		Warrant Officers		..	£108
Majors	..	..	£1,720	Sergeants	..	..	£14
Captains	..	..	£864	Privates	..	..	£7

CHAPTER VII

BATTLE HONOURS FOR SERVICES IN FLANDERS, 1793-1799

Lincelles — Nieuport — Villers - en - Couches — Beaumont — Willems—Tournay—Egmont-op-Zee.

THESE seven names record engagements between the allied forces of Prussia, Austria, and Great Britain, with the French at the outbreak of the Revolutionary War in 1793 and 1794. Our army, which was composed of British, Hanoverians, and Hessians, was under the command of the Duke of York. His Royal Highness, who was but eight-and-twenty, had studied his profession in Berlin, and was a thorough partisan of the red-tape and pipe-clay system of the Prussian army. He possessed undeniable courage, with but little experience; and as all his movements were controlled, on the one hand, by the Cabinet at home, and on the other by the Austrian Commander-in-Chief, it is a matter for small wonder that the results of the campaign were something less than negative. At the opening of the operations the British troops at the disposal of the Duke consisted of three cavalry brigades, composed of the Blues; the 1st, 2nd, 3rd, 5th, and 6th Dragoon Guards; the Royal Scots Greys and Inniskilling Dragoons, with the 7th, 11th, 15th, and 16th Light Dragoons. His infantry was made up of three battalions of the Guards, the 14th (West Yorks), 37th (Hampshire), and 53rd (Shropshire) Regiments—the three latter brigaded under Sir Ralph Abercromby, an officer of very considerable experience.

In 1794 it became necessary to strengthen the army
very largely, and by the month of July of that year the
Duke of York had under his command some 26,000
British troops, distributed as under :

First Cavalry Brigade : 2nd and 6th Dragoon Guards, the Scots
    Greys, and the Inniskilling Dragoons.
Second Cavalry Brigade : The Blues, 3rd and 5th Dragoon
    Guards, and the Royal Dragoons.
Third Cavalry Brigade : 7th, 11th, 15th, and 16th Light Dragoons.
Fourth Cavalry Brigade : 1st Dragoon Guards, the 8th and
    14th Light Dragoons.
Brigade of Guards : 1st Battalion of the Grenadiers, the Cold-
    stream and the Scots Guards.
First Infantry Brigade : The Buffs, 63rd (Manchesters), and
    88th (Connaught Rangers).
Second Infantry Brigade : 8th (King's Liverpool Regiment),
    33rd (West Riding Regiment), and 44th (Essex).
Third Infantry Brigade : 12th (Suffolks), 36th (Worcesters), and
    55th (Border Regiment).
Fourth Infantry Brigade : 14th (West Yorkshire), 37th (Hamp-
    shire), and 53rd (Shropshire).
Fifth Infantry Brigade : 19th (Yorkshire), 42nd (Black Watch), and
    54th (Dorsetshire).
Sixth Infantry Brigade : 27th (Inniskilling Fusiliers—two bat-
    talions).
Seventh Infantry Brigade : 40th (South Lancashire), 57th (Middle-
    sex), 67th (Hampshire), and 87th (Royal Irish Fusiliers).

There is ample evidence to show that all these regiments were actually under fire during the campaign in
Flanders, yet of the twenty-two infantry regiments employed, only ten bear on their colours any record of the
share they took in the operations undertaken against
revolutionary France.   All regiments that served under
Wellington in Spain and Portugal bear the word " Peninsula " on their colours and appointments ; all which
served under Cornwallis in India, the honour " Mysore ";
all which landed in the Crimea bear the honour " Sebas-
topol "; whilst the distinction " South Africa " was conferred on every battalion of Volunteers which sent a
company to guard Boer prisoners.   Surely, then, the
regiments which fought and bled under the Duke of
York have a claim to some recognition of their
services.

LINCELLES, AUGUST 18, 1793.

This battle honour is peculiar to the three senior regiments of the Brigade of Guards—

Grenadier Guards.   Coldstream Guards.   Scots Guards.

—and commemorates one of the many actions fought in Flanders at the outset of the Revolutionary War with France. The Brigade, under Lord Lake, had just arrived at Menin, *en route* to the Siege of Dunkirk. When the sound of firing was heard, and information reached the Duke of York that the Prince of Orange had met with a sharp rebuff at the hands of the French, he immediately ordered the Brigade of Guards to march to the assistance of the Prince. Although the men had but just arrived from a long, hot, and tiring march, Lake at once marched to the sound of the guns, covering the six miles in a little over the hour ; but on reaching Lincelles, which was supposed to be in possession of the Duke of Orange, he was met with a " whiff of grape-shot." The Guards, with their usual dash, at once stormed the French redoubts, which they carried at the point of the bayonet, capturing twelve guns, one stand of colours, and close on 100 prisoners. The action was one of those isolated affairs which had no bearing on the campaign, but merely serve to show the superior stamina and discipline of the Brigade of Guards. Taking into consideration the strength of the force engaged, the casualties were undoubtedly heavy.

PRESENT AT LINCELLES.

Grenadier Guards	..	..	..	378 of all ranks.
Coldstream Guards	..	..	..	346 ,,
Scots Guards	..	..	..	398 ,,

CASUALTIES AT LINCELLES, AUGUST 18, 1793.

Regiments.	Officers.		Men.		Regiments.	Officers.		Men.	
	K.	W.	K.	W.		K.	W.	K.	W.
Grenadier Gds.	—	5	21	44	Scots Guards ..	—	2	8	45
Coldstream Gds.	1	2	8	47	Royal Artillery	1	—	1	3

NIEUPORT, OCTOBER, 1793.

This battle honour is borne by the Shropshire Light Infantry, and commemorates the gallant defence of this town by the old 53rd Foot, when besieged for ten days by a force of 12,000 French troops, under Vandamme, who later became one of Napoleon's most famous Marshals. With the 53rd were associated some artillery, a half-company of the Black Watch, and two Hessian battalions—all told, some 1,300 men ; but the honours of the defence rested with a regiment which throughout its career has ever borne the highest reputation for steady gallantry.

CASUALTIES.

Regiment.	Officers.		Men.		Regiment.	Officers.		Men.	
	K.	W.	K.	W.		K.	W.	K.	W.
42nd Black Watch ..	—	—	—	3	53rd Shropshire L.I.	I	I	12	32

VILLERS-EN-COUCHES, APRIL 24, 1794.

This is one of the four honours which the 15th Hussars has alone the privilege of wearing. It records the gallantry of the regiment practically under the eyes of the Austrian Emperor, when two squadrons of the 15th charged side by side with the Austrian Leopold Hussars, overthrowing a vastly superior body of the French, taking three guns, and sabring, it is claimed, some 1,200 of the enemy. The eight officers of the regiment were awarded the coveted distinction of the Maria Theresa Order.

CASUALTIES AT VILLERS-EN-COUCHES.

Regiments.	Officers.		Men.		Regiments.	Officers.		Men.	
	K.	W.	K.	W.		K.	W.	K.	W.
3rd Drag. Gds.	—	—	38	2	11th Hussars	—	—	I	—
1st R. Dragoons	—	—	I	2	15th Hussars	—	I	17	12

BEAUMONT, APRIL 26, 1794.

This honour, which was not conferred until the year 1909, is borne by the

Royal Horse Guards.
1st King's Dragoon Guards.
3rd Dragoon Guards.
5th Dragoon Guards.

1st Royal Dragoons.
7th Hussars.
11th Hussars.
16th Lancers.

There had been rumours after the fight at Villers-en-Couches that General Mansel's brigade of cavalry, consisting of the Blues, Royals, and 3rd Dragoon Guards, had not supported the 15th with sufficient promptitude in the affair on April 22.[1] It was Minden and Warburg over again. So when, on April 25, at Beaumont, General Otto, the Austrian officer in command of the allied cavalry, led his division against 20,000 unbroken French infantry, British Dragoons and Austrian Hussars cheerfully essayed what seemed a mad undertaking. The total loss of the allied cavalry amounted to 15 officers and 284 men killed and wounded, amongst the former being General Mansel, who commanded the British heavies, two of his sons figuring amongst the wounded. Forty-one guns and 750 prisoners were taken, whilst the French casualties, it is said, numbered over 7,000, 1,200 being killed by the sabre alone.

CASUALTIES AT THE ACTION OF BEAUMONT, APRIL 26, 1794.

Regiments.	Officers.		Men.		Regiments.	Officers.		Men.	
	K.	W.	K.	W.		K.	W.	K.	W.
R. Horse Gds.	1	—	15	20	1st Royal Dragoons ..	—	1	6	13
1st King's Dragoon Guards	—	—	6	13	7th Hussars ..	—	—	1	19
3rd Drag. Gds.	2	2	15	8	11th Hussars	—	—	—	—
5th Drag. Gds.	—	1	9	9	16th Lancers ..	—	—	1	14

[1] The casualties given on the preceding page show that the 3rd Dragoon Guards at any rate suffered heavily at Villers-en-Couches.

WILLEMS, MAY 10, 1794.

In the month of January, 1910, an Army Order was published authorizing the following regiments to assume this battle honour :

Royal Horse Guards.	1st Royal Dragoons.
2nd Queen's Bays.	Scots Greys.
3rd Dragoon Guards.	6th Inniskilling Dragoons.
6th Carabiniers.	11th Hussars.
15th Hussars.	16th Lancers.

As at Beaumont a fortnight earlier, so here at Willems, our cavalry showed themselves able to break the French infantry formation, even when not pounded by artillery. Thirteen guns and 450 prisoners were the trophies of the day, and fully 2,000 of the enemy fell under the sabres of the British horse.

CASUALTIES AT THE ACTION OF WILLEMS, MAY 10, 1794.

Regiments.	Officers.		Men.		Regiments.	Officers.		Men.	
	K.	W.	K.	W.		K.	W.	K.	W.
Royal Horse Guards ..	—	1	2	8	2nd Scots Greys	—	1	6	11
					6th Inniskill.	—	—	3	7
2nd Drag. Gds.	—	—	2	2	7th Hussars ..	—	—	—	1
3rd Drag. Gds.	—	—	—	3	11th Hussars	—	—	7	3
6th Carabiniers	—	1	7	19	15th Hussars	—	—	—	14
1st Roy. Drag.	—	—	—	1	16th Lancers	—	2	13	7

TOURNAY, MAY 22, 1794.

An honour borne by the

West Yorkshire.   Hampshire.   Shropshire Light Infantry.

Just four days previously to the fight, the allied army, under Field-Marshal Otto, had received a handsome beating at the hands of the French. It is true we were hopelessly outnumbered, being able to oppose but 18,000 to 64,000. Though beaten, we were not disgraced. Fox's brigade, consisting of the three regiments above, losing 520 of all ranks, whilst in the retirement the 7th and 15th Hussars showed persistent gallantry. Nevertheless, it was a defeat, for nineteen guns were left in the hands of the victors. We were soon to learn that the failure on the part of the Archduke Charles to support Otto and the Duke of York was a deliberate design to discredit the British, and was due to jealousy of the Royal Duke, who, if not a brilliant strategist, was at any rate a brave commander, and ever solicitous for the comfort of his men.

On May 19 the Allies were concentrated in the immediate neighbourhood of Tournay. The French were attempting to press home their success of the preceding day. In the early morning of the 22nd Pichegru, who had hastened to assume command, attacked in four columns. After some hours his superior numbers told, and the Allies were gradually forced back. Then, late in the day, four brigades were moved up to recapture the position of Pont-à-chin, which practically commanded the Valley of the Scheldt. Fox's brigade, having lost very heavily on the 18th, had been held in reserve, and now numbered barely 600 men. At last, even they were pushed forward into the fight, and, though entirely unsupported, these three fine regiments, nobly responding to the Brigadier's call, dashed forward, sweeping the French out of their hard-won vantage-ground and capturing seven guns. This timely action turned the fortunes of the day, and by nightfall the French had been beaten back, with a loss of 6,000 men. So ended Tournay.

CASUALTIES AT THE BATTLE OF TOURNAY, MAY 22, 1794.

Regiments.	Officers.		Men.		Regiments.	Officers.		Men.	
	K.	W.	K.	W.		K.	W.	K.	W.
14th W. Yorks	—	1	5	29	37th Hampsh.	—	3	1	30
53rd Shrops. L.I.	—	3	6	29	Royal Artillery	—	—	1	2

EGMONT-OP-ZEE, OCTOBER 2, 1799.

In 1799 a fresh attempt was made to wrest Holland from the French, and Sir Ralph Abercromby was despatched to the Low Countries at the head of a division to co-operate with the Russians. His force consisted of a Brigade of Guards (one battalion from each of the three regiments, with a composite battalion of the grenadier companies of the whole Brigade) and two brigades of infantry, under Generals Coote and John Moore. On April 17 a landing was effected at Grote Keten, in face of the determined opposition of a brigade of French troops, our total loss being 27 officers and 440 men killed and wounded. Before the end of the month Abercromby had been reinforced by seven more battalions, and by September 20 the British forces had been brought up to a total of 30,000, with H.R.H. the Duke of York once more in chief command, the whole being distributed as follows :

Cavalry Brigade : 7th, 11th, and one squadron of the 18th Light Dragoons.

First Brigade—Major-General D'Oyley : 1st Battalion Grenadier Guards, and a composite battalion of the grenadier companies of the whole Brigade.

Second Brigade of Guards—Major-General Burrard : 1st Battalion Coldstreams, 1st Battalion Scots Guards.

Third Brigade—Major-General Coote : 2nd (Queen's), 27th (Inniskillings), 29th (Worcesters), and 85th (Shropshire Light Infantry).

Fourth Brigade—Major-General Sir John Moore : 1st (Royal Scots), 25th (King's Own Scottish Borderers), 49th (Berkshires), 79th (Cameron Highlanders), and the 92nd (Gordon Highlanders).

Fifth Brigade—Major-General Don : 17th (Leicesters—two battalions), 40th (South Lancashires—two battalions).

Sixth Brigade—Lord Cavan : 20th (Lancashire Fusiliers—two battalions), and the 63rd (Manchesters).

Seventh Brigade—Lord Chatham : Three battalions of the 4th (King's Own) and the 31st (East Surrey).

Eighth Brigade—H.R.H. Prince William : Two battalions of the Northumberland Fusiliers and the 35th (Royal Sussex).

Ninth Brigade—Major-General Manners : Two battalions of the 9th (Norfolks) and the 56th (Essex).

Reserve Brigade—Colonel Macdonald : The Royal Welsh Fusiliers and the 55th (Border Regiment).

In garrison at the Helder were a battalion of the 35th (Royal Sussex) and the 69th (Welsh).

After an indecisive action on September 19, the Duke of York attacked the French on October 2 at Egmont-op-Zee, inflicting on them a severe defeat. The brunt of the fighting fell on the Fourth and Sixth Brigades, under Sir John Moore and Lord Cavan, Sir Ralph Abercromby being present and exercising supreme command. Our losses were very heavy, amounting to no less than 1,348 of all ranks killed and wounded.

The following regiments alone have been authorized to bear the honour " Egmont-op-Zee ":

15th Hussars.	Royal Scots.
Lancashire Fusiliers.	King's Own Scottish Borderers.
Berkshire.	Manchester.
Cameron Highlanders.	Gordon Highlanders.

But the casualty rolls published in the Duke of York's despatch show that many other regiments were engaged.

Regiments.	Officers.		Men.		Regiments.	Officers.		Men.	
	K.	W.	K.	W.		K.	W.	K.	W.
7th Hussars ..	—	—	2	11	27th Inniskilling Fusiliers ..	—	4	4	41
11th Hussars	—	—	1	4	29th Worcester	—	—	8	35
15th Hussars	—	1	2	2	40th S. Lancs	—	—	—	3
Royal Artillery	—	1	9	65	55th Border R.	—	1	2	18
Grenadier Gds.	—	3	6	52	49th Berkshire	2	5	31	50
Royal Scots ..	—	7	7	65	63rd Manchest.	—	1	1	36
The Queen's ..	—	—	2	16	79th Cameron Highlanders	1	4	13	58
K.O. Lanc. Reg.	—	1	3	9	85th King's Own Shrop. L.I.	—	4	7	67
Leicestershire	—	2	2	5	92nd Gordon Highlanders	3	11	57	182
Lancs. Fus. ..	—	1	3	40					
R. Welsh Fus.	—	2	7	52					
K.O. Scottish Borderers ..	2	8	34	67					

CHAPTER VIII

BATTLE HONOURS FOR SERVICES IN THE WEST INDIES, 1759-1810

West Indies, 1759-1810—Guadeloupe, 1759—Martinique, 1762—Havana — St. Lucia, 1778 — Martinique, 1794 — St. Lucia, 1796—St. Lucia, 1803—Surinam—Dominica—Martinique, 1809—Guadeloupe, 1810.

THE battle honours conferred for services in the West Indies cover the half - century from the capture of Guadeloupe in 1759 to the third capture of the same island in the year 1810. The appended tables of casualties show that our losses in action were by no means contemptible, but these did not represent one-tenth of those we suffered from disease or from neglect of the most elementary precautions against the effects of the climate on our troops. In the event of our being at war with those nations which had possessions in the West Indies, the islands formed convenient bases for operations against our North American Colonies, as well as harbours of refuge for the innumerable privateers which preyed upon our commerce. When war unhappily broke out between our Colonies and the Mother-Country, it became more than ever a matter of paramount necessity that no Power but ourselves should hold possession of these islands. Unfortunately, at the end of each successive war England, as has ever been her custom, restored her conquests to their original holders, with the inevitable result that our soldiers and sailors were called upon to sacrifice their lives in the recapture of the islands in pursuance of the time-worn policy of English Cabinets. In the course of fifty years St. Lucia, Guadeloupe, and Martinique were thrice wrested from the French, and the two last-named islands thrice restored. Up to the year 1909 the battle honours " Martinique " and " Guadeloupe," which figured on the colours and appointments of some of our regiments, had been granted only for the capture of those islands by Sir George Beckwith in the years 1809 and 1810. Last year it was determined (and very rightly) that the previous expeditions, which dated back to 1759, were also worthy of being recorded, and an Army Order was issued in the month of November, 1909, announcing that the King had been graciously pleased to approve of the undermentioned honorary distinctions being borne on the colours and appointments of a certain number of regiments present in the following expeditions : " Havana "; " Guadeloupe, 1759 "; " Guadeloupe, 1810 "; " Martinique, 1762 "; " Martinique, 1794 and 1809 "; " St. Lucia, 1778, 1793, and 1803."

In any case where a regiment had been awarded the same distinction, but with different dates, it was to bear on its colours or appointments one distinction only, with the dates. Thus, so far as Martinique is concerned, the East Yorkshire Regiment will have on its colours " Martinique, 1762, 1794, 1809."

The services performed by our troops in the many expeditions for the reduction of the Island of Guadeloupe have been scantily recognized. So far as I have been able to ascertain, the first capture of the Island of Guadeloupe took place in the year 1702, when the Yorkshire Regiment lost 2 officers killed and 3 wounded ; the 20th (Lancashire Fusiliers) 3 officers killed and 5 wounded ; and the 35th (Royal Sussex), 2 killed, 3 wounded, and no less than 16 by disease.

Then came the expedition of 1759, with which I deal at length, and for which a battle honour was granted.

In the year 1794 we once more captured the island, the losses being :

Regiments.	Officers.		Men.		Regiments.	Officers.		Men.	
	K.	W.	K.	W.		K.	W.	K.	W.
Royal Artillery	2	—	3	57	35th R. Sussex	—	4	9	47
Roy. Engineers	—	1	1	3	39th Dorsets ..	—	—	3	18
E. Yorkshire ..	—	1	3	31	56th Essex ..	—	2	6	35
R. Scots Fus.	—	4	6	97	60th K.R.R. ..	2	—	6	107

For this expedition no battle honour was granted.

In the year 1814 Guadeloupe was handed over to the French, but on Napoleon's escape from Elba in 1815 it declared for him, and a fresh expedition became necessary for which no distinction has yet been awarded. Possibly, in due course of time, the dates 1702, 1794, and 1815 may be added to the name " Guadeloupe " on the colours of the regiments which participated in those long-forgotten, but by no means bloodless, expeditions.

Late in the year 1758 it was determined by the Cabinet to effect the reduction of the colonial possessions of France. With the capture of the Settlements on the West Coast of Africa I have nothing to do. For their reduction no battle honour was granted. The campaigns, which resulted in the reduction of Louisburg and Quebec are narrated on pp. 37 and 38. I now propose to deal with the expeditions which led to the honour " Guadeloupe, 1759 "; " Martinique, 1762 "; and " Havana " being inscribed on the colours and appointments of our regiments.

GUADELOUPE, 1759.

By the Army Order of November, 1909, the above battle honour was conferred on the following regiments :

Buffs.	King's Own (Lancaster).
Gloucester.	South Staffords.
Royal Highlanders.	North Staffords.
Manchester.	York and Lancaster.

Thus, a century and a half after the event, the services of our troops at the second capture of the Island of Guadeloupe received a tardy recognition.

In November, 1758, the Buffs, King's Own, Gloucester, North Stafford, Manchester, and York and Lancaster Regiments embarked at Spithead for Barbados, where they were joined by the South Staffords and the Royal Highlanders, Lieutenant-General Peregrine Hopson assuming the command. The force was divided into four brigades, under Colonels Robert Armiger, George Haldane, Cyrus Trapaud, and John Clavering, whilst Major-General the Hon. John Barrington joined as second in command. It was also strengthened by a detachment of 500 artillerymen, under Major S. Cleveland, R.A., and a battalion of Marines, under Colonel Rycaut, making a total of about 6,800 men. On January 13, 1759, the expeditionary force sailed for Martinique, where the French were well prepared for defence, and no landing was attempted. Three days afterwards the armament stood on to Fort Royal Bay, Martinique, and, under cover of the guns of the fleet, the troops disembarked. On the following morning a sharp skirmish took place, in which the French were driven out of some entrenched buildings, our casualties amounting to 100 killed and wounded ; but it was found impossible to follow up the enemy owing to the denseness of the jungle and the absence of roads.

General Hopson, who was suffering from a mortal disease, appears to have formulated no plan of operations for the reduction of Martinique, and on the following morning the troops re-embarked without opposition, and the fleet stood on to Guadeloupe, arriving before that island on January 22. Basse Terre, the capital of the southern island (for Guadeloupe practically consists of the two islands, Guadeloupe, or Basse Terre and Grande Terre), was bombarded by the fleet and utterly destroyed, the Governor withdrawing his troops to a well-entrenched and most formidable position some miles distant. The disembarkation of the troops was consequently unopposed, but our outposts were much worried day and night by incessant firing and desultory attacks from the French, who had taken refuge in the surrounding jungle. The General again seemed to have no definite plan of operations, and contented himself with strengthening his position on the inland side of the capital. Our troops suffered terribly from the climate. By the end of January 600 men had been invalided to Antigua, and 1,500 were on the sick-list.

The Commodore was a man of action, as also, indeed, was General Barrington ; but the former was independent of General Hopson, the latter was not. About the middle of February Commodore Moore sailed round to Port Louis, on the northern island, where he found a good harbour. He at once bombarded its defences, forced the garrison to surrender, and disembarked a battalion of Marines, thus securing for Hopson a second base.

On February 16 the Commander-in-Chief died, and Barrington determined to put an end to the inaction which was demoralizing the troops. Leaving the 63rd (Manchester) Regiment to hold Basse Terre (the defences of which on the land side had been considerably strengthened), Barrington embarked the rest of his troops and occupied Port Louis, whence he despatched Colonel Crump, of the 4th (King's Own), who had succeeded to the command of Haldane's brigade, to effect the reduction of the French settlements in the northern island. Early in April Brigadier Clavering was detached with his brigade (reduced to 1,300 men) to destroy the French position at Arnouville, in Guadeloupe itself. In this attack the 4th (King's Own) and the 42nd (Royal Highlanders) particularly distinguished themselves, and in the middle of the month Clavering was able to join hands with Crump, who had been withdrawn from the Grande Terre, and to march southwards along the coast. Position after position was carried until Clavering finally drove the French from their entrenchments at Capesterre, in the south-west of the mainland, where the inhabitants compelled the French commander to sue for terms ; and on May 1 the possession of Guadeloupe passed into our hands.

CASUALTIES DURING EXPEDITION TO GUADELOUPE, 1759.

Regiments.	Officers.			Men.	
	Killed.	Wounded.	Died of Disease.	Killed.	Wounded.
Royal Artillery	1	4	1	3	7
Royal Navy	1	1	—	30	68
3rd Buffs (East Kent Regiment)	1	1	2	9	19
4th King's Own (Lancaster Regt.)	2	2	3	8	5
38th Regt. (South Staffords)	1	3	1	11	37
42nd (R. Highlanders) ..	1	5	2	11	32
61st (2nd Gloucesters) ..	1	1	1	3	16
63rd (1st Manchesters) ..	3	2	2	4	18
64th (1st N. Staffords) ..	0	2	6	1	4
65th (1st York and Lancasters)	1	3	3	5	9

NOTE.—I am indebted to the courtesy of the Army Council for this hitherto unpublished return of the rank and file killed and wounded at Guadeloupe.

MARTINIQUE, 1762.

This distinction was conferred on the following regiments by an Army Order in November, 1909 :

East Yorkshire.　　　　Leicester.
Cheshire.　　　　　　　Royal Inniskilling Fusiliers.
Gloucester.　　　　　　Royal Sussex.
South Stafford.　　　　South Lancashire.
Welsh.　　　　　　　　Royal Highlanders.
Oxford Light Infantry.　Northampton.
　　　　King's Royal Rifles.

The employment of our troops on the Continent of Europe and in Canada had prevented the Cabinet from carrying out the designs for the capture of the Islands of Dominica, Martinique, and St. Lucia ; but the fall of Louisburg and Quebec set sufficient forces at liberty to enable Pitt in the early part of 1762 to carry out the long-deferred expedition. Its command was entrusted to General the Hon. Robert Monckton, an officer of considerable experience, who had more recently distinguished himself in command of a brigade under Wolfe at Quebec. Carlisle Bay (Barbados) was the point selected for the mobilization of the expeditionary force, and there, at Christmas, 1761, the Commander-in-Chief arrived with eleven battalions from North America. He was joined shortly by Lord Rollo with five more battalions from Canada, and by General Ruffane with four seasoned regiments fresh from the capture of Belleisle; a couple of regiments from Guadeloupe, and two from Antigua, brought the force at Monckton's disposal to some 12,000 men, distributed in five brigades, under Brigadier W. Havilland, W. Rufane, F. Grant, Lord Rollo, and Hunt Walsh.

On January 5, 1762, escorted by a powerful fleet under Lord Rodney, the expeditionary force left Barbados, and on the 7th had arrived at St. Ann's Bay, the southernmost harbour in Martinique. Our knowledge of the island was very defective. More than one attempt at disembarkation proved ineffective, owing to the want of roads by which the troops might advance, and it was not until the 16th of the month that the entire force was landed at Case Navire, a little to the north of the capital, Port Royal. A series of works, dominated by powerful entrenchments on the hills, Morne Tortenson and Morne Grenier, had been thrown up for the defence of Port Royal. On January 24 the first-named position was carried by Brigadiers Havilland and Walsh, with a loss of 33 officers and 357 men killed and wounded, and three days later the Morne Grenier was taken, with a loss of about 100 of all ranks. On February 12, finding further resistance useless, the French commander capitulated, and Monckton, in conjunction with Lord Rodney, who was in command of the fleet, despatched detachments for the capture of St. Lucia, Grenada, and St. Vincent, which fell into our hands without offering any resistance. Our casualties during the operations in Martinique were as follows :

Regiments.	Officers.		Men.		Regiments.	Officers.		Men.	
	K.	W.	K.	W.		K.	W.	K.	W.
4th K.'s Own	1	1	8	23	48th N'hampton	—	2	9	15
15th E. Yorks	—	—	4	15	60th K.R.R. ..	—	3	12	42
17th Leicesters	—	—	4	17	65th York and				
22nd Cheshires	1	1	2	3	Lancaster ..	—	—	—	3
27th Inniskil-					69th Welsh ..	—	—	2	6
ling Fusiliers	—	2	4	19	75th W. Riding				
28th Gloucs. ..	—	2	5	9	Regiment ..	—	—	—	3
35th R. Sussex	—	2	4	19	77th Middlesex	1	1	4	21
38th S. Staffs	—	—	2	13	90th Scot. R.	—	—	3	17
41st Welsh ..	—	1	1	6	91st Argyll				
42nd Royal					Highlanders	—	—	—	—
Highlanders	2	11	12	76	98th N. Staffs	—	—	2	5
43rd Oxford					100th Royal				
L.I.	—	—	—	—	Canadians ..	—	1	4	8

It will be seen from the above list, copied from the *London Gazette* (in which the 42nd are styled " Royal Hunters "!), that many regiments suffered casualties which have not been authorized to assume the honour " Martinique, 1762."

HAVANA.

The regiments authorized by the Army Order of November, 1909, to bear this battle honour are :

Royal Scots.
East Yorkshire.
Cheshire.
Gloucester.
Royal Sussex.
Royal Highlanders.
Essex.

Norfolk.
Leicester.
Royal Inniskilling Fusiliers.
Border.
South Lancashire.
Oxford Light Infantry.
Northampton.

King's Royal Rifles.

A perusal of the following brief account of the campaign will show that, if the ruling holds good under which the 5th Lancers, 18th, 19th, and 20th Hussars, together with many infantry regiments, are permitted to bear the battle honours won by their predecessors, there are other regiments equally entitled to inscribe " Havana " on their colours and appointments than the fifteen above mentioned, and three at least which have more claim to the battle honour " Moro " than the Essex.

The campaign was decided on by the Ministry in the early spring of 1762, General the Earl of Albemarle being nominated to the chief command, with orders to co-operate with Admiral of the Blue, Sir George Pocock, who was at the time commanding the fleet in the West Indies.   The troops were composed of 4,000 men despatched from England with the Commander-in-Chief ; 8,000 were furnished by the large forces then garrisoning the West India Islands, and 4,000 were detached by Sir Jeffrey Amherst from the forces in North America.   For transport service on shore, the Governor of Jamaica raised a body of 1,500 negroes.   These were augmented on the arrival in Martinique of Lord Albemarle by the *purchase* of 500 more !   A small force of cavalry was improvised by the Commander-in-Chief, and placed under the orders of Captain Suttie, of the 9th Foot.   The whole force assembled at Martinique on May 5, 1762.   It would appear that Lord Albemarle, following the custom of the day, formed a couple of Light Infantry Battalions from the light companies, and a couple of Grenadier battalions from the grenadier companies of the regiments under his command, the Light Infantry being placed at the disposal of Colonel Guy Carleton, afterwards Lord Dorchester. The entire force was brigaded as under :

First Brigade—Brigadier-General W. Havilland : Royal Scots, 56th (Essex), and the 60th (King's Royal Rifles).
Second Brigade—Brigadier-General H. Walsh : 9th (Norfolks), 27th (Inniskilling Fusiliers), and the 48th (Northamptons).
Third Brigade—Brigadier-General John Reid : 34th (Border Regiment), 35th (Royal Sussex), 43rd (Oxford Light Infantry), and the 75th (Gordon Highlanders).

Fourth Brigade—Brigadier-General F. Grant : 17th (Leicesters), 42nd (Royal Highlanders)—two battalions, two companies of the 65th (York and Lancaster), and three companies of the 4th (King's Own), and four of the 77th (Middlesex).

Fifth Brigade—Brigadier-General the Lord Rollo : 22nd (Cheshires), 40th (South Lancashires), 72nd (Seaforths), and the 90th (Scottish Rifles).

Colonel Leith : Royal Artillery, 357 men.

Of these, Brigadiers Havilland, Hunt Walsh, and Lord Rollo had been employed in the reduction of the Island of Martinique, and it will be noticed that a large proportion of the regiments had fought under Wolfe at Quebec, or Studholme Hodgson at the capture of Belleisle, or under Monckton at Martinique. Owing to the nature of the ground, considerable difficulty was experienced in constructing the siege batteries, which were armed with heavy guns from the fleet, the stores and ammunition being conveyed to the front by the corps of negroes purchased in Martinique by the General. In consequence of the scarcity and badness of the water, the troops suffered terribly. The seamen and Marines escaped the sickness which more than decimated the army, and the Admiral landed a body of 800 Marines to lighten the labours of the army.

On July 1 a heavy bombardment commenced, the fleet standing in to aid. In this the *Dragon, Cambridge,* and *Marlborough* suffered severely. For a time the fire of the defence slackened, only to be renewed with increased vigour in a couple of days. On the 21st the garrison made a gallant sortie, which was repelled with equal gallantry by the 90th Light Infantry, under Colonel Stuart. From this date the defence gradually slackened, and on July 30 the General determined to assault the Moro, which was the key of the situation. The storming-party, which was under the command of Colonel Stuart, of the 90th, was composed as follows :

1st Royal Scots	.. ..	6 officers, 107	N.C.O.'s and men.
90th Light Infantry	..	8 ,, 53	,,
Marksmen	..	8 ,, 129	,,

the 35th Regiment in support. The assault was admirably planned, and carried out with dashing gallantry.

CASUALTIES DURING THE EXPEDITION TO HAVANA, FROM DATE OF LANDING TO CAPITULATION ON AUGUST 13, 1762.

Regiments.	Officers.			N.C.O.'s and Men.		
	Killed.	Wounded.	Died of Disease.	Killed.	Wounded.	Died of Disease.
Royal Artillery ..	2	—	2	25	49	25
Engineers	—	2	—	—	—	—
1st Royal Scots ..	2	3	—	34	78	12
4th (K.O. Lancs.)	2	1	1	2	1	—
9th Foot (Norfolk)	1	1	3	24	31	28
15th Foot (E. Yorks)	1	1	2	12	20	10
17th Foot (Leics.)	1	2	—	3	2	26
22nd Foot (Cheshire Regiment) ..	1	1	2	7	13	28
27th Foot (1st Inniskilling Fusiliers)	1	1	1	15	23	13
28th Foot (1st Gloucester Regt.)	—	—	—	11	17	7
34th Foot (1st Border Regiment) ..	1	1	2	32	70	85
35th Foot (1st Roy. Sussex Regt.) ..	1	2	—	19	26	17
40th Foot (1st South Lancashire) ..	—	—	1	9	13	10
42nd (Royal Highlanders) ..	—	—	9	3	8	73
43rd Foot (1st Oxford L.I.) ..	—	1	—	10	15	13
46th Foot (2nd Cornwall L.I.) ..	—	—	—	—	—	1
48th Foot (1st Northamptonshire)	—	—	3	8	30	10
56th Foot (2nd Essex)	—	—	2	36	83	85
60th Foot (King's Royal Rifles) ..	2	2	1	24	63	13
65th Foot (1st York and Lancaster)	—	—	—	—	1	—
72nd Foot (1st Seaforth Highlanders)	1	1	2	20	27	85
77th Foot (2nd Middlesex) ..	1	3	—	3	8	16
90th Foot (2nd Scottish Rifles) ..	1	1	2	11	35	49
98th Foot (2nd N. Staffords) ..	—	1	1	6	3	32
Totals.. ..	15	19	—	284	586	—

In addition to the losses in action, it will be noticed that 39 officers and 641 N.C.O.'s and men died of disease.

With the Moro in our possession, the capitulation of the island was a mere matter of time, and on August 14 the Captain-General signed the articles of surrender of the Island of Cuba to the British forces. Ninety-one officers and 29,700 of other ranks surrendered as prisoners of war, and Admiral Pocock had the satisfaction of takng possession of thirteen Spanish line-of-battle ships.

Our losses during the forty-four days' campaign had been considerable, as the table of casualties on page 107 proves.

Hitherto the old 56th Regiment (now the Essex) has been the only regiment entitled to carry the battle honour " Moro." The Royal Scots have always, but as yet unsuccessfully, advanced their claim to this distinction. The above facts show that the Scottish Rifles and the Royal Sussex have an equal claim with the Royals to the double distinction.

In conformity with our usual custom, the island was restored to the Spaniards on the conclusion of the war, to be conquered by our American cousins 130 years subsequently.

In those days the ardour of our sailors and soldiers was whetted by the prospects of prize-money, and the capture of Havana, whilst it brought wealth to the senior officers, brought consolation also to all ranks in the shape of a rich distribution of doubloons.

DISTRIBUTION OF PRIZE-MONEY FOR THE CAPTURE OF HAVANA.

NAVY.	£	s.	d.	ARMY.	£	s.	d.
Commander-in-Chief	122,697	0	0	Commander-in-Chief	122,697	0	0
Commodore ..	24,539	0	0	Lieut.-General	24,539	0	0
Captain	1,600	0	0	Major-General	6,816	0	0
Lieutenants ..	234	0	0	Field Officers ..	564	0	0
Warrant officers	118	0	0	Captains	184	0	0
Petty officers..	17	5	0	Subalterns ..	116	0	0
Seamen	3	14	9	Sergeants ..	8	18	8
				Corporals ..	6	16	6
				Privates and drummers ..	4	1	8

St. Lucia, 1778.

This honour was awarded in 1909 to the following regiments—

King's Own (Lancaster).   Northumberland Fusiliers.
East Yorkshire.   Inniskilling Fusiliers.
Gloucester.   Cornwall Light Infantry.
Border Regiment.   Royal Sussex.
South Lancashire.   Royal Berkshire.

—for their services at the capture of the island from the French, and for its gallant defence a few days later against a vastly superior force.

On the outbreak of war between France and England in 1778 the French at once assumed the offensive in the West Indies by the capture of Dominica on September 8, that island, with a garrison of barely 500 men, being compelled to surrender to the Marquis de Bouillé, who landed some 8,000 troops, drawn from the large forces massed in Martinique and Guadeloupe, which, in pursuance of our time-honoured custom, had been restored to France at the end of the previous war in 1763. In the month of November a combined naval and military expedition under Admiral Barrington and Major-General James Grant left Barbados for the reduction of St. Lucia. It numbered some 6,000 men, composed as under :

First Brigade—Brigadier Robert Prescott : 15th (East Yorkshire), 28th (Gloucester), 46th (Cornwall Light Infantry), and 54th (Border Regiment).
Second Brigade—Brigadier Sir H. Calder : 27th (Inniskilling Fusiliers, 35th (Sussex), 40th (South Lancashire), and 49th (Royal Berkshire).
Third Brigade—Brigadier W. Meadows : 5th (Northumberland Fusiliers), Grenadier Battalion and Light Infantry Battalion, made up of the flank companies of all regiments present.

In addition, there were two companies of Royal Artillery and a troop of Dragoons. Knowing that Admiral d'Estaing, with a fleet outnumbering his own three to one, had already left Boston to oppose him, Admiral Barrington set sail from Barbados on December 10, and the following day entered in Cul de Sac Bay, on the western coast of the island. Two brigades were at once

disembarked, and they, carrying the French entrenchments, made themselves masters of a strong position
overlooking the main works of the enemy at Castries.
On December 12 the remainder of the troops were landed,
and an attack on the French entrenchments at the Morne
Fortunée was successfully carried out, and by evening
we were in possession of all the forts and batteries defend-
ing Castries Bay.   Two days later the French fleet,
carrying 9,000 troops, appeared in the offing, and d'Estaing
at once attacked Barrington's squadron, which was
anchored across Cul de Sac Bay.   Foiled there, he stood
to the northward, with the intention of turning General
Grant's position at Castries, and, under cover of the guns
of the fleet, several thousand French were landed.   Here,
however, they met with stout opposition. Meadows, at
the head of the Northumberland Fusiliers and the Light
Infantry Battalion, repulsing several most determined
attacks, in which the French lost 400 dead left on the
field, with some 1,200 wounded, our casualties in killed
and wounded barely reaching 175.   D'Estaing re-
embarked his men on the 28th, and withdrew his fleet to
Martinique, whereupon the French commandant had no
option but to surrender.

CASUALTIES AT THE CAPTURE OF THE ISLAND OF ST. LUCIA
IN 1778.

Regiments.	Officers.		Men.		Regiments.	Officers.		Men.	
	K.	W.	K.	W.		K.	W.	K.	W.
Royal Artillery	—	—	1	2	35th R. Sussex	—	1	—	1
4th King's Own	—	—	—	—	40th S. Lancs	—	1	1	1
5th North. Fus.	—	2	2	20	46th Corn. L.I.	—	1	3	9
15th E. Yorks	—	1	—	1	49th Berks ..	—	—	—	—
27th Innis. Fus.	—	—	—	—	55th Border				
28th Gloucester	1	1	1	2	Regiment ..	—	1	—	2
L.I. Battalion	—	—	6	48	Grenadier Batt.	—	—	3	76

NOTE.—I am indebted to the courtesy of the Army Council for
the above casualty list.

MARTINIQUE, 1794.

This distinction, awarded in 1909, is borne by the following regiments—

Royal Warwick.   Norfolk.   East Yorkshire.
Royal Scots Fusiliers.   East Surrey.   North Stafford.
Northampton.   Dorset.   York and Lancaster.

—and commemorates the second capture of the island from the French. Considerable care had been bestowed on the preparation of this expedition. Its command was entrusted to capable hands, Sir John Jervis—afterwards Lord St. Vincent—having charge of the naval, and General Sir Charles Grey of the military forces. These last were divided into five brigades :

First Brigade—Brigadier Sir C. Gordon : 15th (East Yorkshire), 39th (Dorset), and 43rd (Oxford Light Infantry).
Second Brigade—Brigadier Thomas Dunbar : 56th (2nd Essex), 63rd (1st Manchester), and 64th (1st North Staffords).
Third Brigade—Brigadier J. Whyte : 6th (Royal Warwick), 58th (2nd Northampton), and 70th (2nd East Surrey).
Fourth Brigade—Brigadier Campbell (subsequently replaced by H.R.H. Duke of Kent) : Three battalions, composed of the grenadier companies of all regiments in Ireland and Flanders.
Fifth Brigade—Colonel Myers : Three battalions, composed of the light companies of the same regiments.

Profiting by the experience of the expedition in 1762, a number of gunboats—flat-bottomed craft, to assist in the disembarkation of the troops—had been sent out from England in sections, and a number of negroes purchased for the formation of a transport corps. On February 3 the expedition set sail from Carlisle Bay, Barbados, and two days later appeared off the island of Martinique in three divisions, the Commander-in-Chief with the Third and Grenadier Brigades, landing at Trois Rivières, in the extreme south ; Dundas, with his own and the Light Infantry Brigade, near Trinité, on the east coast ; and Gordon at Casé de Navire, a little to the north of Port Royal, the capital. By February 12 Grey and Gordon, greatly assisted by the guns of the fleet, had gradually converged on Port Royal, driving the French before them, whilst Dunbar was steadily pushing his way across the island from east to west. On February 17 St. Pierre (the commercial capital) surrendered to Dunbar, and on March 8 Grey commenced to throw up siege batteries for the reduction of the fortifications at Fort Royal ; fourteen days later Fort Louis fell to a combined assault of seamen and soldiers, and on the 23rd General Rochambean surrendered.

Leaving six battalions in the island, Grey, who had been reinforced by the Buffs and Norfolks, embarked with these two regiments, the Warwicks, 43rd (Oxford Light Infantry), 63rd (Manchester), and the Grenadier and Light Infantry Brigades, for St. Lucia, which was captured on April 2 ; then, proceeding to Guadeloupe, he effected the reduction of that island by the end of May, not, however, without very sharp fighting. The casualties we incurred at the capture of Guadeloupe are given on p. 99. At the capture of St. Lucia our losses were trifling ; those at the capture of Martinique are given below.

No less than 122 officers of the garrison died of disease before the end of the year :

Regiments.	Officers.		Men.		Regiments.	Officers.		Men.	
	K.	W.	K.	W.		K.	W.	K.	W.
Royal Artillery	—	3	10	18	Roy. Engineers	—	1	1	3
6th R. Warwick	1	—	1	2	38th S. Stafford	—	—	—	—
8th King's Liverpool ..	2	—	—	—	39th Dorsets ..	1	—	1	4
9th Norfolks ..	1	—	—	1	40th Loyal N. Lancashires	1	—	—	—
12th Suffolks	2	—	—	—	43rd Oxford L.I.	2	—	—	3
15th E. Yorks	2	—	3	4	44th Essex ..	—	—	—	—
17th Leicesters	1	—	—	—	58th N'ampton	2	—	—	—
21st Roy. Scots Fusiliers ..	3	—	—	—	60th K.R.R. ...	1	—	—	—
34th Border Regiment ..	1	—	—	—	64th N. Staffs	—	—	—	—
35th R. Sussex	1	—	—	—	63rd Manchesters	—	—	2	11
Royal Navy ..	2	4	19	65	70th E. Surrey	—	—	—	2
Three L.I. Battalions ..	—	2	20	62	Three Grenadier Battalions ..	1	4	30	74

St. Lucia, 1794.

No battle honour was conferred for the capture of the island on this occasion.

Immediately after the capture of Martinique, on March 25, 1794, General Sir George Grey, with Admiral Sir John Jervis, sailed for St. Lucia with a force composed as under :

First Brigade—H.R.H. Prince Edward (afterwards Duke of Kent, father of Queen Victoria) : Comprising three battalions, made up of the grenadier companies of the whole force in Martinique.

Second Brigade—Major-General Dundas : Comprising three light infantry battalions.

Third Brigade—Colonel Sir C. Gordon : 6th (Warwick), 9th (Norfolk), and 43rd (Oxford Light Infantry) Regiments.

On April 1 the squadron arrived off the island, and the Second Brigade was at once disembarked under the guns of the *Winchelsea*, the operation being executed, to use Sir John Jervis's words, " with neatness and despatch, under the direction of Lord Viscount Garlies." Colonels Blundell and Coote, at the head of their battalions, advanced rapidly on the fortified position on the Morne Fortunée, which was evacuated by the enemy, when the French commander hoisted the white flag, and the island for the second time in its history passed into the possession of the English. Leaving Sir C. Gordon in command with the 6th and 9th Regiments as garrison, Sir G. Grey returned to Martinique.

Owing to the exigencies of the service, and the inability of the Ministry at home to realize the necessity of maintaining the troops in the West Indies at a proper strength, Grey from time to time was compelled to reduce the garrison, so that when, in the spring of the following year, the negroes of St. Lucia, in common with their fellows in the neighbouring islands, rose in revolt, the then Governor, Colonel Stuart, had only some 400 men to make headway against the revolt. In June the island was evacuated.

St. Lucia, 1796.

The only regiments authorized to bear the battle honour are the Royal Inniskilling Fusiliers and the Shropshires.

Early in the year 1796 it became necessary to re-conquer practically the whole of the French West India Islands—not, indeed, from the armies of the French Republic, but from the hordes of negroes, whose passions had been inflamed by revolutionary agents, and whose ambitions had been fired by the pernicious doctrines of "the rights of man." The command of the expeditionary force was entrusted to Sir Ralph Abercromby, with whom was associated the ever-to-be-remembered Sir John Moore. The total force numbered some 18,000 men, distributed as under, and was mobilized in Carlisle Bay, Barbados, in March, 1796 :

Cavalry : 27th Light Dragoons and Royal Irish Artillery.
First Brigade : 14th, 27th, 28th, and 57th Regiments.
Second Brigade : 3rd, 19th, 31st, and 35th Regiments.
Third Brigade : 8th, 37th, 44th, and 55th Regiments.
Fourth Brigade : 38th, 48th, 53rd, and 63rd Regiments.
Fifth Brigade : 2nd, 10th, 25th, 29th, and 88th Regiments.
Sixth Brigade : 42nd (Highlanders), and two battalions composed of the grenadier companies of all the regiments present.

Abercromby's first care was to throw reinforcements into Grenada, which was still holding out, and on April 21 the convoy left Carlisle Bay for St. Lucia. On the 26th Moore landed with the 14th and 42nd, and on the following day he was reinforced by the 53rd, 57th, and the 2nd West India Regiment, under Brigadier Hope. By the 28th the whole of the force was ashore, but the operations dragged on until May 15, when the whole island was in our hands. On the 17th of that month there had been a sharp engagement, in which the 31st (East Surrey) lost heavily. Moore complained bitterly of the troops, writing as follows : "It is hard to say whether the officers or men are the worst." Moore was left in command at St. Lucia, whilst Abercromby undertook the reduction of Grenada and St. Vincent. Although the only regiments authorized to carry the distinction "St. Lucia, 1796" are the Inniskilling Fusiliers (27th), and Shropshire Light Infantry (53rd), reference to the casualty lists shows that this selection casts an unnecessary slur on the other corps which bore their fair share of fighting in the reconquest of the island.

Regiments.	Officers.		Men.		Regiments.	Officers.		Men.	
	K.	W.	K.	W.		K.	W.	K.	W.
14th W. Yorks	—	1	1	4	42nd H'landers	—	1	—	4
27th Inniskil-					44th Essex ..	—	3	4	17
lings	1	6	22	65	48th N'ampton	—	1	2	15
28th Gloucester	—	3	3	18	53rd Shropshire				
31st E. Surrey	2	6	61	107	L.I.	—	3	13	46

By the close of the year 1796, Moore had buried 1,500 of his garrison. So terrible were the losses we incurred from sickness—losses due to the neglect of the home authorities to provide for the sick—that it was with a sense of relief the army learnt the welcome news that, under the terms of the Treaty of Amiens, St. Lucia was restored to the French. This retrocession, however, necessitated its recapture in 1803.

NOTE.—The battle honour " St. Lucia, 1803," has been granted to the Royal Scots and North Staffords for their services in the expedition under General Grinfield, in which the 68th Durham Light Infantry and 3rd West India Regiment also shared.

CASUALTIES.

Regiments.	Officers.		Men.		Regiments.	Officers.		Men.	
	K.	W.	K.	W.		K.	W.	K.	W.
Royal Scots ..	—	2	9	45	64th North Staf-				
3rd W. India R.	—	2	4	23	fords ..	—	4	6	33

SURINAM, 1804.

The regiments authorized to bear this distinction are the Bedfordshire and the North Staffords.

It commemorates the capture of this colony from the Dutch by a combined naval and military expedition on the resumption of hostilities with Holland after the Treaty of Amiens. The colony had been captured in

1799 by Admiral Lord Hugh Seymour and General Trigge, but had been restored to the Dutch in 1802.

Carlisle Bay (Barbados) was the rendezvous, the squadron being under the command of Commodore Samuel Hood, whilst the troops were commanded by Major-General Sir Charles Green. These consisted of the 16th (Bedfords), 64th (North Staffords), and the 6th West India Regiment. Leaving Barbados on April 6, 1804, the squadron, delayed by adverse and light winds, did not arrive off the mouth of the Surinam River until the 25th, when the Dutch commander was invited to surrender. To the summons he returned a truculent reply ; and the troops, divided into two brigades, under Colonels Maitland and Hughes, were thrown ashore, reinforced by a naval brigade 600 strong. The defence was feeble, and in three days the place fell into our hands. Our loss was trifling, falling on the naval brigade and the North Staffords, neither the Bedfords nor the West India Regiment suffering any casualties.

CASUALTIES AT THE CAPTURE OF SURINAM, 1804.

Regiments.	Officers.		Men.		Regiments.	Officers.		Men.	
	K.	W.	K.	W.		K.	W.	K.	W.
Naval Brigade	2	2	1	5	Bedfords ..	—	—	—	—
N. Staffords ..	—	2	2	8	6th West India				
Naval Brigade	2	3	3	8	Regiment ..	—	—	—	—

DOMINICA, 1805.

The only regiments authorized to bear this distinction are the Duke of Cornwall's Light Infantry and the West India Regiment.

Our connection with the island dates back to the year 1762, when, on June 11, it was captured by a joint naval and military expedition under Colonel Lord Rollo and Commodore Sir James Douglas, R.N., with the *Belliqueux, Dublin, Montague,* and *Sutherland.* The troops concerned

in this first capture were detachments of the King's Own
(Lancaster Regiment), the Cheshires, and the Black
Watch. The brunt of the fighting fell on the Highlanders,
who lost 2 officers and 19 men killed, 10 officers and
74 men wounded. The possession of the island was
confirmed to us by the Treaty of Paris in the following
year. In 1778 it was taken from us by the French.
Prior to the outbreak of hostilities, the Governor, Major-
General the Hon. W. Stewart, had reported the precarious
position of the island. His total force amounted to
98 men of the 48th (Northamptons) and 28 gunners ; of
these but 41 were fit for duty. On September 7 a French
force of four frigates, convoying 3,000 troops, appeared
before the island, and the Governor was perforce compelled to surrender to De Bouillé. By the peace of 1783
the island was restored to us, but in 1805, mindful of their
former success, the French made a fresh attempt at its
capture. Five line-of-battleships, headed by the *Majes-
tueux*, of 120 guns, stood into the harbour and overwhelmed the town of Roseau with their fire. The Governor,
General Prevost, withdrew to a second position, and refused all summons for surrender, when the French, baffled,
left him undisturbed. The garrison consisted of the
46th Foot (now the 2nd Battalion of the Cornwall Light
Infantry), the 1st West India Regiment, and some local
militia. The casualties of the defenders were slight, but
their services were considered sufficiently meritorious for
the following notification in the *Gazette* :

" As a distinguished mark of the good conduct and
exemplary valour displayed by that regiment in the
defence of the Island of Dominica against a very
superior French force on February 22, 1805, the 46th
Regiment is permitted to bear on its colours and appointments the nam e' Dominica.' " For many long years
this was the only distinction borne by that regiment.

The casualties were—

Cornwall Light Infantry : 11 men killed, 1 officer and 7 men
wounded.
The West India Regiment : 9 men killed, 2 officers and 8 men
wounded.

MARTINIQUE, 1809.

This distinction is borne by the

Royal Fusiliers.   King's Liverpool Regiment.
Somerset Light Infantry. East Yorkshires.
Royal Welsh Fusiliers.   King's Own Scottish Borderers.
King's Own Royal Rifles. Manchesters.
Scottish Rifles.   West India Regiment.

Under the terms of the Treaty of Amiens, Martinique, amongst our many other conquests from France, was restored, thus necessitating its recapture on the resumption of hostilities. Had it not been for the fact that it was made a port of call and refit for all the privateers in the Western Atlantic, the island might have been left in peace ; but in the interests of our commerce, as well as for military reasons, its recapture was decided on, and General Sir George Beckwith was entrusted with the command of the operations.   His divisional commanders were Lieutenant-General Sir George Prevost and Major-General Maitland. The Commander-in-Chief himself accompanied the First Division, which comprised the

First Brigade—Brigadier-General Hoghton : Royal Fusiliers, Royal Welsh Fusiliers, and a wing of the 3rd West India Regiment.
Second Brigade—Brigadier-General Colville : 8th (King's Liverpool Regiment), 13th (Somerset Light Infantry), and a wing of the 1st West India Regiment.
Reserve Brigade : The 3rd and 4th Battalions of the King's Royal Rifles and the 4th West India Regiment.

This force disembarked on January 30 at St. Luce Bay, on the western coast of the island, and on the following day took possession of the town of Trinité without opposition.

First Brigade—Colonel Riall : 63rd (Manchesters) and the York Rangers (a colonial corps which did most excellent service in our West India campaigns).
Second Brigade—Major-General Maitland : 15th (East Yorkshire), the flank companies of the 46th (Cornwall Light Infantry), the 8th West India Regiment, and a body of local volunteers, known as the York Light Infantry.
Reserve Brigade—Colonel Macnair (90th) : 90th (Scottish Rifles) and the 3rd West India Regiment.

This force disembarked on the south of the island, near the Three Rivers—a spot at which considerable fighting had taken place in our previous descents on the island—and here again Maitland encountered some resistance. But his brigades, working over the hills to the left, effected a junction with the Commander-in-Chief, and by February 4, thanks to the effective co-operation of the fleet, the French Governor surrendered.

Amongst the trophies were the colours, or rather the eagles, of the 62nd and 80th Regiments of the French line. One of these fell to the Royal Fusiliers, the other to the 90th, and the Commander-in-Chief selected Captain Wilby, of the 90th, to carry these trophies to England and depose them at the feet of the King. These were the first eagles to be received in England, and His Majesty was pleased to command that they should be escorted in state by the regiments of the Household Brigade to St. Paul's Cathedral, where they were received with all due solemnity. In the early days of the reign of Queen Victoria these eagles were removed to the chapel of the Royal Hospital at Chelsea, where they may be seen to this day.

CASUALTIES AT THE CAPTURE OF MARTINIQUE, 1809.

Regiments.	Officers.		Men.		Regiments.	Officers.		Men.	
	K.	W.	K.	W.		K.	W.	K.	W.
Roy. Fusiliers	1	2	36	119	90th Scot. Rifles	—	2	8	31
8th K. Liverp.	1	0	4	13	W. India Regt.	—	—	2	19
R. Welsh Fus.	0	1	19	101	L.I. Battalion	1	5	26	71

In the year 1847, when the late Queen Victoria granted a medal to the survivors of the wars against France, Martinique was included in the list of campaigns for which the medal was to be conferred, and a special clasp "Martinique" was issued with both the military and naval General Service Medal.

By the Treaty of Amiens Martinique was handed over to the French, but on Napoleon's escape from Elba it declared for the Emperor, and General Leith was despatched with a strong force to recapture the island. Fortunately, the Governor, recognizing the hopelessness of resistance, surrendered without attempting a useless defence, and so for a few months Martinique again became a British possession, only to be handed back when Napoleon was safe under restraint.

GUADELOUPE, 1810.

The regiments which are authorized to bear this honour are the

East Yorkshire.	Scottish Rifles.
East Surrey.	Manchester.
West India.	

The island on three previous occasions had been captured, and thrice restored to the French. Once again it became necessary to take measures for its reduction. Sir George Beckwith, who had so successfully carried out the conquest of Martinique in the previous year, was selected for the command of the expedition, with Generals Hyslop and Harcourt as Divisional Generals under him. The force was distributed as under :

First Division : Major-General Hyslop.
Third Brigade—Brigadier-General McLean : 90th Light Infantry (2nd Scottish Rifles), 8th West India Regiment, and a battalion composed of the light companies of all the regiments present in the West Indies.
Fourth Brigade—Brigadier-General Skinner : 13th (Somerset Light Infantry), 63rd (Manchesters), and the York Rangers (a colonial corps).
Second Division : Major-General Harcourt, who also commanded the Third Brigade, which consisted of the 15th (East Yorkshire), 3rd West India Regiment, and a second light infantry battalion.
Third Brigade—Brigadier-General Barrow : 25th (King's Own Scottish Borderers), 2nd West India Regiment, and a battalion composed of the grenadier companies of the regiments present.
Reserve Brigade — Brigadier-General Wale, under whom were placed a battalion composed of the grenadier companies of the regiments in the West Indies, a detachment of the York Rangers, and 300 artillerymen.

CASUALTIES AT THE CAPTURE OF GUADELOUPE, 1810.

Regiments.	Officers.		Men.		Regiments.	Officers.		Men.	
	K.	W.	K.	W.		K.	W.	K.	W.
Staff	—	2	—	—	King's Roy. R.	—	2	4	11
Royal Artillery	—	—	1	3	63rd M'chesters	—	—	—	1
13th Somerset L.I.	—	—	1	5	90th Scottish Rifles	—	1	3	9
East Yorkshire	—	1	—	—	West India Regiments	—	4	7	84
40th Cornwall L.I.	—	—	3	8	York Rangers	4	5	28	102

In the year 1847 the General Service Medal was granted to the survivors of this expedition, with a special clasp inscribed " Guadeloupe."

In the year 1814, on the conclusion of the war with France, Guadeloupe was once more restored; but on the escape of Napoleon from Elba it threw off its allegiance to Louis XVIII., and declared for the Emperor. Once more an expedition was organized for its reduction, and though the futility of resistance was pointed out, the garrison, by its unnecessary loyalty to a dead cause, compelled the General to resort to force. The command of the 1815 expedition was entrusted to Major-General Leith, the regiments selected being the East Yorkshires, who have participated in every expedition to the West Indies since the year 1759; the King's Own Scottish Borderers; the 63rd (Manchesters); and the local West India Regiments. The only casualties were—

Regiment.	Officers.		Men.		Regiment.	Officers.		Men.	
	K.	W.	K.	W.		K.	W.	K.	W.
63rd M'chesters	—	2	3	20	W. India Regt.	—	2	13	31

CHAPTER IX

BATTLE HONOURS FOR SERVICES IN EGYPT AND THE SOUDAN, 1802-1898

Egypt (with the Sphinx)—Mandora, 1801—Marabout, 1801—Egypt, 1882—Tel-el-Kebir, 1882—The Nile, 1884-85—Abu Klea, 1885—Kirbekan, 1885—Suakin, 1885—Tofrek, 1885—Hafir, 1896—Atbara, 1898—Khartoum, 1898.

EGYPT (WITH THE SPHINX).

ON July 6, 1802, this distinction was conferred by King George III. on the regiments named below, " as a distinguished mark of His Majesty's royal approbation, and as a lasting memorial of the glory acquired to His Majesty's arms by the zeal, discipline, and intrepidity of his troops in that arduous and important campaign." So ran the *Gazette*.

Five-and-forty years later, after much discussion and not a little opposition, the grant of the Peninsular medal was extended to the survivors of the campaign. The regiments that bear this battle honour are the

11th Hussars.	12th Lancers.
Coldstream Guards.	Scots Guards.
Royal Scots.	Queen's.
King's Liverpool Regiment.	Lincolns.
Somerset Light Infantry.	Royal Irish.
Lancashire Fusiliers.	Royal Welsh Fusiliers.
South Wales Borderers.	Cameronians.
Inniskilling Fusiliers.	Gloucesters.
East Lancashire.	Dorsets.
South Stafford.	Royal Highlanders.
South Lancashire.	Northamptons.
Essex.	Royal West Kent.
Manchesters.	Cameron Highlanders
Royal Irish Rifles.	Gordon Highlanders.
Connaught Rangers.	Royal Irish Fusiliers.
102nd King Edward's Own Grenadiers.	2nd Queen's Own Sappers and Miners.

113th Infantry.

122

The only regiments of the Indian Army now left which accompanied the army under Sir David Baird in that memorable march across the desert from Kosseir to the Nile are the 102nd King Edward's Own Grenadiers, the 113th Infantry, and the 2nd Queen's Own Sappers and Miners, a grand offshoot of the Royal Engineers. This distinguished corps, known in olden days as the Madras Sappers and Miners, has no less than thirty-one battle honours on its appointments, all won between the Nile and the Peiho Rivers.

The object of the expedition to Egypt was to drive the French out of the country, to restore it to its rightful owners, the Turks, and to safeguard our Indian possessions, which were then threatened by attempts on the part of Bonaparte to enter into alliances with the independent Princes in Hindoostan. The command of the army was entrusted to Sir Ralph Abercromby, an officer who possessed the confidence of the army and of the country. He had recently effected the conquest of the West India Islands, and was one of the few Generals who had emerged from the late campaign in Flanders with an enhanced reputation. His army of 17,000 men was brigaded as under :

Cavalry Brigade : One troop of the 11th and the whole of the 12th and 26th Light Dragoons.
Guards' Brigade—Major-General Ludlow : 1st Coldstream and 1st Scots Guards.
First Brigade—Major-General Coote : Royal Scots, 54th (Dorsets—two battalions), and 92nd (Gordon Highlanders).
Second Brigade—Major-General Craddock : 8th (King's Liverpools), 13th (Somerset Light Infantry), 18th Royal Irish, and the 90th (Scottish Rifles).
Third Brigade—Major-General Lord Cavan : 50th (West Kent) and 79th (Cameron Highlanders).
Fourth Brigade—Major-General Doyle : 2nd (Queen's), 30th (East Lancashire), 44th (Essex), and 89th (Royal Irish Fusiliers).
Fifth Brigade—Major-General John Stuart : Minorca, De Rolles', and Dillon's Regiments.
Reserve—Major-General Sir John Moore : 23rd (Royal Welsh Fusiliers), 28th (Gloucesters), 42nd (Royal Highlanders), 58th (Northamptons), and a wing of the 40th (South Lancashires).

The artillery consisted of four batteries of 6-pounders, three batteries of 12 pounders, with a small siege-train. Only one battery was horsed, and although officers had been despatched many months before to purchase horses in Syria, the obstacles thrown in their way by the Turkish authorities had effectually prevented either artillery or cavalry taking the field properly equipped. When the army disembarked, the Cavalry Brigade consisted of 320 mounted men—

Regiment.	Officers.	N.C.O.'s and Men.	Horses.
Troop of 11th Light Dragoons (now 11th Hussars), C.-in-C.'s escort	4	55	61
12th Light Dragoons	23	527	128
26th Light Dragoons	19	473	131

—whilst for the artillery there were but sixty-four horses, and this despite the promises of the Turkish Government that all horses necessary for the army should be delivered in Marmorice Bay before the army left for Egypt.

The disembarkation of the army on March 8, 1801, was effected under a heavy fire, there being 31 officers and 642 of all ranks killed and wounded. It was carried out by the Reserve, under Sir John Moore, and the Brigade of Guards with a gallantry that compelled the admiration of the whole army. The point selected had been decided on by the Commander-in-Chief in conjunction with the Admiral. By nightfall the whole of the army, with the exception of the horses, was on shore, and on the morning of the 13th Abercromby commenced his advance on Alexandria. The troops moved in three columns, Moore's brigade being on the right, marching parallel to the sea. The centre division was composed of the brigades of Craddock, Coote, and the Brigade of Guards. It was led by the 90th (Scottish Rifles). The left column consisted of Lord Cavan's brigade, a battalion of Marines, and the three foreign regiments ; the 92nd (Gordon Highlanders)

GENERAL SIR RALPH ABERCROMBY.

To face page 124.

was in front.   In the course of the march the French made a most determined attack, their cavalry charging down on the leading companies of the 90th.   This corps and the 92nd, which bore the brunt of the fighting, behaved with the utmost steadiness, thus giving the regiments in rear time to deploy, when the French were driven back on their own position, from which they were driven with loss.

MANDORA, MARCH 13, 1801.

This battle honour is borne by the Scottish Rifles and the Gordon Highlanders, and was conferred upon these two young regiments in recognition of the gallantry with which they met and repelled the attack of a vastly superior body of French, as related above.   The total loss of the army on March 13 amounted to 6 officers and 153 men killed, 66 officers and 1,936 men wounded, the heaviest casualties being those of the two regiments who bear " Mandora " on their colours.   The 13th (Somerset Light Infantry), which was in the immediate rear of the 90th, at once moved up to its support, and also suffered very heavily.   The 90th (Scottish Rifles) were under the command of their junior Lieutenant-Colonel, afterwards better known as General Viscount Hill, the Commander-in-Chief of the Army.   He was badly wounded at Mandora, when the command of the regiment devolved on the next senior officer, Major Moncrieff, who a few days subsequently was given the command of the 44th (Essex), on its Colonel being killed.   Thence he was moved, at Sir John Moore's request, to the 52nd, in order to train that distinguished corps as a light infantry regiment.   Although the 90th at that time had not the designation of light infantry, its founder, Colonel Graham, afterwards Lord Lynedoch had from its earliest days trained it as a light infantry corps, impelled thereto because its predecessor, which had fought so well at the capture of Belleisle, Martinique, and Havana, was at that time (1759-1764) the only light infantry regiment in the British army, and the stout old

Scotsman never rested until he had secured the same title for the new 90th.

CASUALTIES OF THE 90TH AND 92ND AT MANDORA.

Regiment.	Officers.		Men.		Regiment.	Officers.		Men.	
	K.	W.	K.	W.		K.	W.	K.	W.
90th Scottish Rifles ..	I	7	29	242	92nd Gordon Highlanders	—	11	19	110

On March 21 the French made a third and final attack on Abercromby's army, now in the immediate vicinity of Alexandria. This again was repulsed, but our casualties were very heavy, amounting to 75 officers and 1,400 of all ranks killed and wounded, the heaviest loss falling on the 42nd (Royal Highlanders), a corps which in all three actions had shown the most consummate gallantry, its casualties in the three engagements being 506 killed and wounded. In the course of this action Sir Ralph Abercromby received a mortal wound, and the command of the army devolved upon General Hutchinson. Leaving a sufficient force to cover Alexandria, the new Commander-in-Chief at once commenced an advance on Cairo, and on June 13 he had the satisfaction of receiving the surrender of 13,000 French soldiers, who were massed at the capital. Of these, some 8,000 were effectives, and the task of guarding them on the return march to the sea was one that required much acumen, for the total number of British troops at this time at Cairo was barely 4,000. The army at Alexandria had, however, been reinforced by a strong brigade from the Mediterranean, made up of the 20th (Lancashire Fusiliers), 24th (South Wales Borderers), 25th (King's Own Scottish Borderers), 26th (Cameronians), and the 27th (Royal Inniskilling Fusiliers).

A further addition to the British army was now made in the shape of a division which had been despatched from India under the command of a tried and gallant officer, Sir David Baird. It comprised a squadron of the 8th Hussars, the 10th (Lincolns), 86th (Royal Irish Rifles), 87th (Royal Irish Fusiliers), 88th (Connaught Rangers), four battalions of sepoys, some English gunners in the Company's service, and some native sappers. The 8th Hussars and 86th (Royal Irish Rifles) had landed at Suez, and marched direct across the desert to Cairo. The other regiments were disembarked at Kosseir, whence they marched to Keneh, on the Nile, a distance of 100 miles ; then, taking native boats, they dropped down stream to Cairo. As soon as the convoy of prisoners had embarked to France, General Hutchinson was enabled to turn his attention to Alexandria, in which a considerable garrison was closely besieged.

MARABOUT, AUGUST 17, 1801.

This battle honour is borne by the Dorsetshires, and commemorates the service of the 54th Regiment in the operations outside Alexandria in the summer of 1801. The old 54th had been entrusted with the task of keeping watch and ward over the French garrison in Fort Marabout, and it was their successful capture of the redoubt at the tomb of a Moslem saint which brought home to General Menou the futility of further resistance. He hoisted the white flag, when he and his army were permitted a safe conduct to France, on giving an undertaking that they would not serve against England during the continuance of the war. The Treaty of Amiens followed soon after the surrender of Alexandria, and on the renewal of hostilities in 1803 the army of Egypt was once more free to act against us.

Before quitting the subject of the Egyptian campaign of 1801, it appears pertinent to remark that there seems to exist no valid reason why the 8th Hussars should not be accorded this distinction. It may be urged that the headquarters of the regiment was not present. The 11th Hussars bear the honour, and but one troop was

CASUALTIES IN THE THREE PRINCIPAL ENGAGEMENTS IN EGYPT.

Regiments	MARCH 8.				MARCH 13 (MANDORA).				MARCH 21 (ALEXANDRIA).				AUGUST 23 (MARABOUT).			
	Off. K	Off. W	Men K	Men W	Off. K	Off. W	Men K	Men W	Off. K	Off. W	Men K	Men W	Off. K	Off. W	Men K	Men W
11th Hussars	—	—	—	—	—	—	—	—	—	—	—	3	—	—	—	—
12th Hussars	—	—	—	—	—	1	1	15	—	—	—	6	—	—	—	—
Royal Artillery	—	—	—	—	—	—	—	—	—	—	14	40	—	—	—	—
Royal Engineers	—	—	—	—	—	—	—	—	—	5	—	—	—	—	—	—
Coldstream Guards	1	5	17	69	—	—	2	4	—	—	7	53	—	—	—	—
Scots Guards	—	—	5	40	—	—	2	14	—	—	41	153	—	—	—	—
1st Royal Scots	—	4	12	43	—	2	4	21	—	3	9	69	—	—	—	—
2nd Queen's	—	—	—	—	—	1	4	14	1	4	1	10	—	—	—	—
8th King's Liverpool Regt.	—	—	—	—	1	6	11	65	—	1	—	2	—	—	—	—
13th Somerset Light Infantry	—	—	—	—	1	9	16	100	—	—	—	1	—	—	—	—
18th Royal Irish	—	—	—	—	1	3	2	45	—	—	—	1	—	—	—	—
23rd Royal Welsh Fusiliers	—	—	6	38	—	—	1	4	—	1	—	—	—	—	—	—
28th Gloucesters	—	2	5	34	—	1	9	23	—	4	5	14	—	—	—	—
30th East Lancashire	—	—	—	—	—	2	2	6	—	2	20	50	—	—	—	—
40th South Lancashire	1	2	15	31	—	—	—	—	—	1	4	24	—	—	—	—
42nd Black Watch	—	8	21	148	—	—	1	12	4	8	48	253	—	—	—	—
44th Essex	—	—	—	—	—	—	2	22	—	1	1	15	—	—	—	—
50th West Kent	—	—	—	—	—	3	5	39	—	4	1	37	—	—	—	—
54th Dorsetshire	1	2	4	17	—	3	13	37	—	2	4	48	—	—	—	—
58th Northampton	1	2	10	45	—	—	2	9	—	2	2	19	—	—	—	—
79th Cameron Highlanders	—	—	—	—	1	7	8	58	—	—	1	20	—	2	2	14
89th Royal Irish Fusiliers	—	—	—	—	—	3	—	7	—	—	2	10	—	—	—	—
90th Scottish Rifles	—	—	—	—	1	7	29	214	—	2	—	1	—	—	—	—
92nd Gordon Highlanders	—	—	—	—	—	11	19	110	—	2	3	37	—	—	—	—

in Egypt, so that this contention does not hold good. Again, it may be urged that they were not engaged. This would bear with equal force against the infantry regiments which formed a portion of Sir David Baird's force. All these have been authorized to bear the distinction of " Egypt " (with the Sphinx). Why the 8th Hussars have been denied this privilege is one of the many anomalies which surround the question of battle honours.[1]

EGYPT, 1882.

The following regiments have been authorized to add the above honour to their colours and appointments :

1st Life Guards.	2nd Life Guards.
Royal Horse Guards.	4th Dragoon Guards.
7th Dragoon Guards.	19th Hussars.
Grenadier Guards.	Coldstream Guards.
Scots Guards.	Royal Irish.
South Stafford.	Cornwall Light Infantry.
Royal Highlanders.	Royal Sussex.
Sherwood Foresters.	Royal Berkshire.
Royal West Kent.	Shropshire Light Infantry.
King's Royal Rifles.	Manchesters.
York and Lancaster.	Highland Light Infantry.
Seaforth Highlanders.	Gordon Highlanders.
Cameron Highlanders.	Royal Irish Fusiliers.
2nd (Gardner's Horse).	6th King Edward's Own
2nd Queen's Own Sappers	Light Cavalry.
and Miners.	13th (Watson's Horse).
7th Rajputs.	20th (Brownlow's Punjabis).
129th Baluchis.	Royal Malta Artillery.

In the year 1882 the chronic misgovernment in Egypt led to serious disturbances, which culminated in the assumption of power by the military party, and an organized attack on all Christians. So critical was the situation, that it was considered necessary to send the fleets of the allied Powers to Alexandria ; and after an Arab mob had wreaked its vengeance on the city, the British fleet bombarded the forts and sent ashore landing parties to restore order. The British Government now determined to employ armed force to uphold the authority of the Khedive, and an Expeditionary Force, under the com-

[1] The Sultan of Turkey bestowed gold medals on all officers present in the campaign, and permission to wear these was accorded by the King.

mand of General Sir Garnet Wolseley, was organized for this purpose.

The Egyptian army, which had thrown off all allegiance to the Khedive, had taken up a strong position at Tel-el-Kebir astride of the railway, barring the advance on the capital. Sir Garnet, on landing at Alexandria, took steps to secure the safe passage of the Suez Canal, and on August 21 he was able to land the bulk of his troops at Ismailia, the halfway station between Port Said, the Mediterranean terminus, and Suez, the Red Sea terminus of the canal. After one or two minor actions at Kassassin and Tel-el-Mahuta, Sir Garnet advanced on Tel-el-Kebir.

The casualties sustained by the troops at the few engagements that took place during the operations (apart from those at Tel-el-Kebir) were insignificant :

	Officers.		Men.			Officers.		Men.	
Regiments.	K.	W.	K.	W.	Regiments.	K.	W.	K.	W.
1st Life Guards	—	—	6	8	46th Corn. L.I.	—	4	—	14
2nd Life Guards	—	1	1	6	R. Marine L.I.	—	—	—	25
Royal Horse Guards ..	—	—	1	9	3rd Batt. 60th Royal Rifles	—	—	2	28
4th Drag. Gds.	—	—	—	1	84th York and Lancaster ..	—	—	1	21
7th Drag. Gds.	1	1	1	8					
Royal Artillery	—	—	3	12					
Royal Marine Artillery ..	—	3	6	21	2nd Gardner's Horse ..	—	—	—	2
2nd Batt. Roy. Irish	—	—	—	2	13th Watson's Horse.. ..	—	—	1	1

TEL-EL-KEBIR, SEPTEMBER 12, 1882.

The regiments named below are authorized to bear this battle honour :

1st Life Guards.
Royal Horse Guards.
7th Dragoon Guards.
Grenadier Guards.
Scots Guards.
Cornwall Light Infantry.

2nd Life Guards.
4th Dragoon Guards.
19th Hussars.
Coldstream Guards.
Royal Irish.
Royal Highlanders.

King's Royal Rifles.	York and Lancaster.
Highland Light Infantry.	Seaforth Highlanders.
Gordon Highlanders.	Royal Irish Fusiliers.
Cameron Highlanders.	13th (Watson's Horse).
2nd (Gardner's Horse).	2nd Queen's Own Sappers
6th King Edward's Own	and Miners.
Cavalry.	20th (Brownlow's Punjabis).
7th Rajputs.	129th Baluchis.

This battle honour commemorates the first action in which the Household Cavalry were engaged since Waterloo. The hypercritical may claim that the composite regiment, under Brigadier Ewart, took part in the midnight charge on September 28, and this is strictly true ; but Kassassin does not figure on the standards or appointments of the Household Cavalry, whereas Tel-el-Kebir does.

The Egyptian position at Tel-el-Kebir lay at right angles to the railway and the Sweet Water Canal. It was covered by a long line of trenches, flanked with powerful redoubts, and was held by some 30,000 men, with 60 guns. Sir Garnet's force barely numbered 15,000. To attempt the attack of such a formidable position in daylight would have been to court serious loss, and Sir Garnet, with a firm faith in his men, essayed the hazardous task of a long night's march, as a prelude to an attack on the entrenched position at dawn. At 11 p.m. the advance commenced, the First Division, under Lieutenant-General Willis on the right ; the Second, under Lieutenant-General Hamley, on the left. Dawn was just breaking when the Highland Brigade reached the Egyptian trenches, and, with a mighty cheer, dashed over the parapet. Within a few minutes the first division attacked also, and the cavalry, sweeping round the rear, cut in on the flying enemy. An immediate pursuit was ordered, and on the evening of September 14 the citadel of Cairo was in our hands, the Cavalry Brigade having covered sixty-five miles in twenty-four hours. The promptitude with which Sir Garnet Wolseley followed up the victory of Tel-el-Kebir brought the rebellion to an end, but it was clear that the continuance of the Khedivial authority must henceforth rest on the protection that might be afforded him by the English army of occupation. For this purpose Sir Archibald Alison, who had commanded the Highland Brigade with conspicuous success during the course of the operations, was left in command of a British force, numbering some 10,000 men, whilst Major-General Sir Evelyn Wood was entrusted with the re-organization of the Egyptian army.

As will be seen from a perusal of the following list of casualties, the brunt of the fighting at Tel-el-Kebir fell on the Highland Brigade, which suffered more heavily here than it did at the historic Battle of the Alma.

CASUALTIES AT TEL-EL-KEBIR, SEPTEMBER 12, 1882.

Regiments.	Officers.		Men.		Regiments.	Officers.		Men.	
	K.	W.	K.	W.		K.	W.	K.	W.
Grenadier Gds.	—	1	1	9	75th Gordon Highlanders	1	1	5	29
Coldstream Gds.	—	1	—	7	79th Cameron Highlanders	—	3	13	45
Scots Guards	—	—	—	4	87th Roy. Irish Fusiliers ..	—	—	2	34
2nd Batt. Royal Irish	1	2	1	17					
46th Corn. L.I.	—	1	—	5	2nd Gardner's Horse.. ..	—	1	—	1
42nd Royal Highlanders	1	6	7	37	6th K. E. O. Cavalry ..	—	—	—	—
3rd Batt. K. Roy. Rifles	—	—	—	20	13th Watson's Horse.. ..	—	—	—	2
84th York and Lancaster ..	—	—	—	12	7th Rajputs ..	—	—	—	1
72nd Seaforth Highlanders	—	—	1	3	20th Brownlow's Punjabis ..	—	—	—	—
74th Highland L.I.	3	5	14	52					

Following the precedent of the Crimean War, when British officers and soldiers were authorized to receive and to wear decorations and medals bestowed by our allies, the Queen sanctioned the acceptance of a very generous bestowal of orders of the Osmanieh and Medjidieh, whilst every officer and man received a bronze star commemorative of the campaign at the hands of the Khedive.

TURKISH DECORATIONS BESTOWED FOR THE CAMPAIGN OF 1882.

Regiments.	Osma-nieh.	Medji-dieh.	Regiments.	Osma-nieh.	Medji-dieh.
General officers	4	6	60th King's		
Staff officers ..	51	94	Royal Rifles	3	1
1st Life Guards			72nd Seaforth		
(one squadron)	1	—	Highlanders	3	1
2nd Life Guards			74th High. L.I.	2	2
(one squadron)	1	1	79th Cameron		
Roy. Horse Gds.			Highlanders	3	1
(one squadron)	—	1	84th York and		
4th Drag. Gds.	—	3	Lancaster ..	3	1
7th Drag. Gds.	2	1	87th Roy. Irish		
19th Hussars ..	2	1	Fusiliers ..	3	1
Royal Artillery	3	18			
Roy. Engineers	1	4	2nd Gardner's		
Grenadier Gds.	2	2	Horse ..	1	2
Coldstream Gds.	3	1	6th K. E. O. Ca-		
Scots Guards ..	3	1	valry ..	1	2
Royal Irish ..	3	1	13th Watson's		
38th South Staf-			Horse ..	1	1
fords	2	2	2nd Q.O. Sappers		
42nd Roy. High-			and Miners ..	1	1
landers ..	3	1	7th Rajputs ..	1	2
46th Cornwall			20th Brownlow's		
L.I.	3	1	Punjabis ..	1	2
50th West Kent	3	1	129th Baluchis	1	2

NILE, 1884-85.

This distinction was conferred on the regiments which, under Generals Earle and Sir Herbert Stewart, essayed to save General C. Gordon, R.E., then hemmed in by fanatical Moslems at Khartoum. The regiments entitled to bear the honour are the

19th Hussars.
Cornwall Light Infantry.
South Staffordshire.
Essex.
Gordon Highlanders.

Royal Irish.
Royal Sussex.
Royal Highlanders.
Royal West Kent.
Cameron Highlanders.

Looking back after the event, it is clear that the British Government did not appreciate the responsibilities they had assumed when they left Sir Archibald Alison in command of the army of occupation after the victory of Tel-el-Kebir. Not only was the authority of the Khedive gone in Egypt proper, but it had vanished in the far-off regions of the Soudan, which were now in the hands of a fanatical Moslem false prophet, who styled himself the Mahdi. At one time, in the days of the Khedive Ismail, the Soudan had been administered by General Charles Gordon, of the Royal Engineers. One of the most remarkable men of his generation, General Gordon was the type of the earlier Christian martyrs, and as a Christian martyr he died. At the request of the Khedive, and with the consent of the British Government, General Gordon assumed the Governorship of the Soudan, and set out for his post early in 1884. Into the history of Gordon's gallant defence of Khartoum it is no part of my province to enter. Towards the end of the year he was hard pressed, and, though ordered to abandon the Soudan, he declined to do so. It became necessary to organize a force, not merely to effect his rescue, but also to restore the authority of the Khedive in the Soudan and the Equatorial provinces of Egypt, where only the writ of the Mahdi was allowed to run.

Once more Sir Garnet Wolseley was selected for the chief command, and two expeditionary forces were organized, the one operating by the River Nile, the other from the Red Sea port of Suakin. The Commander-in-Chief accompanied the river column, which numbered some 5,500 men. On reaching Korti, about the end of November, Sir Herbert Stewart, with the camel corps, was detached to push across the desert and occupy the Jakdul Wells. This was successfully accomplished, and on December 8 he commenced another stage on the march to Khartoum ; but on nearing the wells of Abu Klea, these were found to be in possession of the enemy, when was fought the action which is inscribed on the colours and appointments of but two regiments in the British army.

ABU KLEA, JANUARY 28, 1885.

This battle honour was conferred on the 19th Hussars and the Royal Sussex Regiment for their services in the sharp action of January 28, 1885, when the commander of the force, Major-General Sir Herbert Stewart, received a mortal wound, dying a few days after the fight. Although the distinction was only granted to the two regiments above mentioned, the brigade under General Stewart's command comprised a naval brigade, under Captain Lord Charles Beresford, and a camel corps, made up of regiments of heavy and of light cavalry of the Household Cavalry and of the Brigade of Guards, and a force of Mounted Infantry : no less than twenty-two regiments were represented in the camel corps which fought so well at Abu Klea.

CASUALTIES AT ABU KLEA.

Regiments.	Officers.		Men.		Regiments.	Officers.		Men.	
	K.	W.	K.	W.		K.	W.	K.	W.
19th Hussars	—	—	2	4	35th R. Sussex	—	—	5	25
Naval Brigade	2	2	6	9	Light Cavalry				
Royal Artillery	—	2	—	2	Camel Corps	1	3	8	9
Heavy Cavalry					Mounted In-				
Camel Corps	6	—	48	28	fantry　..	—	1	5	35

KIRBEKAN, FEBRUARY 10, 1885.

This battle honour, which is borne by the South Staffordshires and the Royal Highlanders, commemorates the only action fought by what was known as the River Column in the advance up the Nile for the relief of General Gordon in the Soudan Campaign of 1885.

Whilst Sir Herbert Stewart with the camel corps was endeavouring to force his way to Khartoum by the desert route, Major-General Earle, a guardsman at the head of the River Column, was slowly moving south from

Korti. On February 10 an indecisive action was fought with a small body of the enemy. Our losses were numerically insignificant, but they included the General in command, Major-General W. Earle, late of the Grenadier Guards, and the commanding officers of the two line regiments present.

The news of the death of General Gordon and the occupation of Khartoum by the Mahdi caused the Home Government to order the withdrawal of the British troops from the Nile, and the task of conducting the retirement was entrusted to Major-General Sir Redvers Buller.

CASUALTIES AT THE ACTION OF KIRBEKAN.

Regiment.	Officers.		Men.		Regiment.	Officers.		Men.	
	K.	W.	K.	W.		K.	W.	K.	W.
General Staff ..	I	—	—	—	42nd Royal				
38th S. Staffs	I	2	5	22	Highlanders	I	2	4	21

SUAKIN, 1885.[1]

This honour, which commemorates a short campaign in the Eastern Soudan, is borne by the

5th Lancers.
Grenadier Guards.
Scots Guards.
Shropshire Light Infantry.
2nd Queen's Own Sappers
  and Miners.

20th Hussars.
Coldstream Guards.
Royal Berkshires.
9th Hodson's Horse.
15th Ludhiana Sikhs.
17th (Loyal Regiment).

128th Pioneers.

Whilst the Mahdi himself was conducting his successful campaign against General Gordon at Khartoum, one of his Lieutenants, Osman Digna, a slave merchant of Suakin, was pursuing a no less successful career at Suakin, on the coast of the Red Sea. On two occasions

[1] The battle honour "Egypt, 1884," was granted to the 10th and 19th Hussars, Royal Highlanders, King's Royal Rifles, York and Lancaster Regiment, and Gordon Highlanders, for an expedition in the vicinity of Suakin in the spring of this year. See Appendix I.

Egyptian armies had been worsted by him, and in the month of December, 1883, a British officer, Colonel Valentine Baker, was routed by an inferior body of tribesmen in an endeavour to relieve the Egyptian fort at Tokar.   Of his force of 3,700 men, no less than 2,375 were killed, including 11 British officers.   In the spring of 1884 Major-General Sir Gerald Graham was despatched to Suakin to teach Osman Digna a much-needed lesson, and in the month of February Sir Gerald inflicted two severe defeats on the tribesmen at El-Teb and Tamai. A medal and clasp were granted for these services, but they have not been recorded on the list of battle honours of the army.

When the withdrawal from the Nile was decided on, instructions were despatched to Sir Gerald Graham at Suakin to prepare for an advance on Berber from Suakin. His force was brought up to a strength of 13,000 men, including a contingent from New South Wales and a brigade from India.   This force was distributed as under :

Commander - in - Chief : Lieutenant-General Sir Gerald Graham, V.C., K.C.B.

Cavalry Brigade—Major-General Sir Henry Ewart, K.C.B. : The 5th Lancers, 20th Hussars, and 9th (Hodson's Horse).

Brigade of Guards—Major-General Lyon Fremantle : A battalion of each of the three regiments—the Grenadiers, the Coldstream and the Scots Guards—and the Australian contingent.

Second Brigade—Major-General Sir John MacNeill, V.C., K.C.B. : The 49th (Royal Berkshire Regiment), 53rd (Shropshire Light Infantry), and a battalion of the Royal Marine Light Infantry.

Indian Brigade—Brigadier-General J. Hudson, C.B. : The 15th Ludhiana Sikhs, 17th (Loyal Regiment), and the 128th Pioneers.

To these must be added a battery of horse and two of field artillery, with a well-horsed, but only partially trained, battery of Australians.   Sir Gerald's orders were to press on the construction of the railway to Berber, a feat which did not receive much encouragement on the spot, as it was felt that the nature of the country and the want of water on the route selected somewhat militated against success.   The troops were much harassed by continuous night attacks, whilst the superior mobility of the enemy, who invariably shirked attack, prevented the General from inflicting any serious damage to the causes of the Mahdi. One action in this expedition has been rescued from oblivion, but it is open to question whether at the time it was considered a victory.

TOFREK, MARCH 22, 1885.

This battle honour records the services of the undermentioned regiments in a sharp little fight outside the town of Suakin, on the Red Sea, in the campaign of the Eastern Soudan, in 1885. It is borne on the colours of the

Royal Berkshire.
17th (Loyal Regiment).
15th Ludhiana Sikhs.

Queen's Own Sappers
and Miners.
128th Pioneers.

In the early morn of March 22 Sir John MacNeill, a gallant and experienced soldier, was sent out from Suakin with orders to form a halfway camp on the route to Tamai. The road lay through a dense thorn-bush, and the reconnoitring was unfortunately confided to the 5th Lancers, a young regiment with no experience of Eastern warfare. They were all unused to the glare of

CASUALTIES AT THE ACTION OF TOFREK.

Regiments.	Officers.		Men.		Regiments.	Officers.		Men.	
	K.	W.	K.	W.		K.	W.	K.	W.
Naval Brigade	1	1	6	5	Madras Sappers				
5th Lancers ..	1	—	—	5	and Miners	2	1	12	20
Royal Artillery	—	1	—	4	15th Sikhs ..	—	—	9	11
Roy. Engineers	2	1	13	3	17th Loyal				
49th Berkshires	1	—	22	30	Regiment ..	1	1	20	33
Royal Marines	—	—	7	16	128th Pioneers	1	1	5	9

the Egyptian desert, and gave no timely warning of the proximity of the enemy. The brigade was attacked when half the men were busy cutting the jungle to form a breastwork, but there was no confusion until the camels,

terrified by the onrush of the Soudanese, who commenced
ham-stringing the animals, broke the line of the rear face
of the hastily-formed square. The commanding officer of
the regiment fell in rallying his men. In twenty minutes
the rush of the tribesmen was repulsed, and though our
losses were severe, those of the enemy were enormous.
Over 2,000 were buried by our men. Such a lesson was
taught them that from that day until the withdrawal
of Sir Gerald Graham's force no further attacks were
made on his camp.

HAFIR.

This battle honour is borne only by the Prince of
Wales's (North Staffordshire) Regiment, and was awarded
to them in recognition of their conduct during the operation leading to the action of Hafir, in the month of
September, 1896.

Eleven years had elapsed since the engagements on the
Nile and at Tofrek, and during those eleven years the
process of reorganizing the Egyptian army had been
ceaselessly carried on under the direction of the British
officers lent to the Khedive. Sir Evelyn Wood had been
succeeded by General Grenfell, and Grenfell by General
Kitchener. Our Consul-General at Cairo occupied a
unique position, for he was the virtual ruler of Egypt.
A soldier by profession, and one of the earliest of the
Staff College graduates, Sir Evelyn Baring had profited
by his experience in many appointments, in all of which
he had acquired ripe stores of priceless knowledge.
Soldier, financier, diplomatist, he was *facile princeps* in
all; and though Sir Herbert Kitchener was the General
who broke the back of Mahdiism, the brain which
devised and the hand which guided the machinery
were those of Sir Evelyn Baring. During those eleven
years the Egyptian army had on more than one occasion
been pitted against the Mahdi's troops. The men had
learnt self-reliance, and possessed the most boundless
faith in their British officers. Step by step the army
was converted into a battle machine. The battalions

of fellaheen were stiffened with battalions of blacks
from the Soudan.   No better fighting material exists in
Africa.   And as it improved in value, so were the necessary
measures taken to break the power of the Mahdi.   The
railway was pushed farther south up the Nile, a strong
brigade of native troops was despatched from India to
Suakin, and the Egyptian army, stiffened with but one
British regiment, taught that it was now able to face the
Mahdi's men.   At Firket, in May, 1896, the first of these
combats took place, and in September, at Hafir, a decisive
success was gained, which opened the road to Dongola.
The 64th (North Staffordshire) Regiment—the only corps
which bears the honour on its colours—was not actually
engaged, and suffered no casualties at the hands of the
enemy ; but it lost heavily by disease in the operation
leading up to the action, and so has been authorized to
assume the battle honour.

In the meantime the Khalifa was not idle.   He recalled
Osman Digna from Suakin, and personally superintended
the organization of his troops at Omdurman, opposite
Khartoum.   Kitchener's force was gradually strengthened.
No less than thirteen gunboats had been brought up the
Nile in sections, and, being of shallow draft, were able
to co-operate with the troops on the banks.   The time
had now come for the final attempt to reconquer the
Soudan.   In January, 1898, Kitchener's force was further
reinforced by a brigade of British troops under Major-
General Gatacre, an officer who had shown himself
possessed of the highest attributes of a soldier in our
Indian frontier wars.   The army that now faced the
Khalifa on the Atbara River comprised Gatacre's brigade
(the Warwicks, Lincolns, Seaforth, and Cameron Highlanders), three brigades of Egyptian troops, with a brigade
of Egyptian cavalry and the camel corps.   On April 5
the Sirdar made a careful reconnaissance of the Khalifa's
position, and on the early morning of the 8th commenced
a · severe bombardment of the entrenchments behind
which the Khalifa's forces lay.

ATBARA, APRIL 8, 1898.

This battle honour is borne by the

Royal Warwicks.　　　　　　Lincolns.
Seaforth Highlanders.　　　　Cameron Highlanders.

It commemorates the action fought by the army
under Sir Herbert Kitchener, prior to the capture
of Khartoum and the overthrow of Mahdiism.　In
our earlier dealings with the forces of Mahdiism, even
when they were opposed to British troops, we had
always found the enemy ready to meet us.　At
El Teb and Abu Klea, at Tamai and Tofrek, they
had never hesitated to charge our squares.　Now a
different system of tactics was inaugurated, showing
that they had learnt a bitter lesson.　The fact that the
Mahdists awaited them behind entrenchments, instead
of charging down sword or spear in hand, naturally
infused courage into our own black troops, and when,
after an hour's bombardment, Kitchener stormed the
enemy's position, Egyptian fellaheen vied with kilted
Highlander as to who should lead the way to the front.
Our success was complete : over 3,000 of the enemy
were killed, our losses totalling 88 killed and 472 wounded,
in both British and Egyptian forces.

Regiments.	Officers.		Men.		Regiments.	Officers.		Men.	
	K.	W.	K.	W.		K.	W.	K.	W.
1st Batt. 6th R. Warwicks	—	1	2	11	72nd Seaforth Highlanders	2	4	5	22
1st Batt. 10th Lincolns ..	—	3	1	13	79th Cameron Highlanders	3	1	13	44

KHARTOUM, 1898.

This battle honour, which records the services of the
army commanded by Sir Herbert Kitchener at the

capture of the stronghold of Mahdiism, is borne by the

21st Lancers.	Grenadier Guards.
Northumberland Fusiliers.	Royal Warwicks.
Lincolnshire.	Lancashire Fusiliers.
Seaforth Highlanders.	Cameron Highlanders.

The decisive success achieved at the Atbara on April 8, 1898, opened the road to Khartoum. The railway was now pushed on to the Atbara River, and fresh reinforcements sent out from home, bringing up Sir Herbert Kitchener's force to nearly 26,000 men, thus distributed :

British Division : Major-General Gatacre.
First Brigade—Brigadier-General A. Wauchope : 1st Warwicks, 1st Lincolns, 72nd (Seaforth Highlanders), and the 79th (Cameron Highlanders).
Second Brigade—Brigadier-General Hon. N. Lyttleton : 1st Grenadier Guards, 1st Northumberland Fusiliers, 2nd Lancashire Fusiliers, and the 1st Rifle Brigade.
Egyptian Division—Major-General Hunter : Consisted of four strong brigades.

In addition, there were 2 batteries of Royal Artillery, 5 Egyptian batteries, 20 machine guns, a flotilla of 10 gunboats, under Commander Keppel, R.N., the 21st Lancers, with a brigade of Egyptian cavalry and the camel corps, making a total force of 8,200 British and 17,600 Egyptian troops, with 44 field, 12 mountain, and 22 machine guns. The flotilla of armoured gunboats mounted 36 guns in addition, and these in the final action contributed not a little to the success of the day.

Late in August the whole force was concentrated at Metemneh, the site of one of the actions between the little force under Sir Herbert Stewart and the Mahdi's troops in January, 1885. On the left bank of the river lay the British force, on the opposite bank a large levy of friendly tribes eager to throw off the despotism and tyranny of the Khalifa. On September 4 the British force encamped four miles from Khartoum, and Sir Herbert Kitchener, who was not the man to leave anything to chance, threw up a strong breastwork, and bivouacked for the night. On the morrow the gunboats bombarded the fort of Omdurman. The Khalifa, stung into action, delivered a fierce attack on the zareba, but was repulsed with heavy loss. Kitchener then left its shelter, and advanced towards Omdurman ; but the spirit of the Mahdiists was by no means broken. Twice did they attack the British troops, but all was of no avail. The training of the British officer now bore good fruit. Under its incomparable leader, Brigadier Hector Macdonald, his brigade of black troops manœuvred with all the coolness of veterans, and the 21st Lancers, seizing their chance, charged into the struggling mass of the enemy, who met them with the utmost gallantry. The day was well won, and ere nightfall the British flag was flying over the walls of the Khalifa's capital. His black flag was amongst our trophies, and 10,000 of his misguided followers lay dead on the sand-hills outside the accursed city. The results of the battle, in which we lost some 500 of all ranks, killed and wounded, were the destruction of the Khalifa's army, and the restoration to the Khedivial Government of those provinces which had thrown off his rule in the great upheaval of 1884.

CASUALTIES AT THE BATTLE OF KHARTOUM.

Regiments.	Officers.		Men.		Regiments.	Officers.		Men.	
	K.	W.	K.	W.		K.	W.	K.	W.
21st Lancers ..	1	4	20	46	2nd Batt. 20th Lancs Fus.	—	—	—	6
1st Batt. Grenadier Guards	—	1	—	4	72nd Seaforth Highlanders	—	1	—	17
1st Batt. 5th Northum. F.	—	—	—	2	79th Cameron Highlanders	—	2	2	27
1st Batt. 6th R. Warwicks	1	1	—	6	2nd Batt. Rifle Brigade ..	—	—	—	8
1st Batt. 10th Lincolns ..	—	1	—	17	Egyptian Army	2	8	18	273

CHAPTER X

BATTLE HONOURS FOR SERVICES IN INDIA, 1803-1809

Ally-Ghur, 1803—Delhi, 1803-04—Assaye, 1803—Laswarree, 1803
—Deig, 1803-04—Cochin, 1809.

FIRST MAHRATTA WAR, 1803-04.

In the *London Gazette* of February 28, 1851, appeared
a notification that Her Majesty the Queen had been
graciously pleased to sanction the bestowal of a medal
on the survivors of the First Mahratta War of 1803-04.
The following clasps were issued with this medal, now
generally known as the First Indian General Service
Medal. It was also bestowed on the survivors—few, indeed,
in numbers—of (1) the siege and capture of Seringapatam,
by the force under Lord Harris; (2) the Second Mahratta
War, 1817-18 ; (3) the campaign in Nepaul ; (4) and that
in Burmah, as well as on (5) the troops who took Bhurtpore, under Lord Combermere, in 1826.

The following clasps were issued with the medal in
connection with the First Mahratta War :

1. Ally-Ghur.	5. Laswarree.
2. Delhi.[1]	6. Argaum.
3. Assaye.	7. Gawilghur.
4. Asseerghur.	8. Deig.[2]

The growing power of the Mahrattas and the insolence
of the Mahrajah Scindia rendered it necessary for us
to strengthen and rectify our frontiers in the North-West
of India. Delhi, which for centuries had been the capital

[1] This clasp covered the operations in September, 1803, and
October, 1804.
[2] The one clasp covered the battle on November 15 and the
assault on December 23, 1804.

144

of the Mogul Empire, had fallen into the hands of the Mahrattas, and the aged King had been treated with barbarous cruelty. Our own territory, as well as that of our allies, had been invaded. At last Lord Lake, the brilliant leader at Lincelles, who had become Commander-in-Chief in India, determined on action. Scindia was a formidable foe, and it was a matter of doubt as to which of the other Ruling Chiefs would follow him in the field ; his troops had been organized and drilled by Frenchmen, many of whom he entrusted with high command, and it was computed that his army numbered 100,000 men, the greater part cavalry. India was a country in which we could take no risks ; we were always fighting, as it were, with our backs to the wall, for there was no Suez Canal, nor were there fast steamships to pour reinforcements into the country when necessary. Lord Lake therefore assembled practically the whole of his available army, and advanced simultaneously from the north, south, east, and west.

I. The main army, under his own command in the north, was the most powerful in point of numbers, but it contained only one regiment of British infantry (the 76th, long knc vn as the Hindoostan Regiment). It was composed as ι nder :

CAVALRY DIVISION : COLONEL VANDELEUR, AND ALSO COMMANDING THE FIRST BRIGADE.
First Brigade : 8th Light Dragoons, 1st and 3rd Bengal Cavalry.
Second Brigade—Colonel St. Leger : 27th Light Dragoons, 2nd and 6th Bengal Cavalry.
Third Brigade—Colonel Macan : 29th Light Dragoons, and the 4th Bengal Cavalry.

FIRST INFANTRY DIVISION : MAJOR-GENERAL WARE.
First Brigade—Colonel the Hon. G. Monson : 76th Foot, 4th (two battalions) and 17th Bengal Infantry.
Third Brigade—Colonel Macdonald : 1st Batt. 12th and 15th Bengal Infantry.

SECOND DIVISION : MAJOR-GENERAL ST. JOHN.
Second Brigade—Colonel Clarke : 8th, 9th, 1st Batt. 12th, and 16th Bengal Infantry.
Fourth Brigade—Colonel Powell : 2nd and 14th Bengal Infantry.
Artillery—Colonel Horsford : One horse and three field batteries.

10

It must be borne in mind that at this time each regiment of cavalry and battalion of infantry had two galloper guns. There was also a powerful siege-train attached to the army. This army was to advance westward on Agra and Delhi.

II. The division under Sir A. Wellesley :

Sir Arthur Wellesley was entrusted with the army of the south, and had under his orders, not only his own division, but also the one in Guzerat and the Hyderabad subsidiary force, commanded respectively by Colonels Stevenson and Murray. A fourth army was assembled in Cuttack, on the coast of Bengal, under Colonel Harcourt. These forces were composed as follows :

19th Light Dragoons, 4th, 5th, and 7th Regiments of Madras Cavalry ; the 74th and 78th (Highlanders) ; and eight regiments of Madras sepoys, of which only three now survive. This force amounted to 3,000 British and 5,000 native troops, and it was subsequently strengthened by 2,500 Mysorean horse and a considerable body of cavalry sent by the Peishwa.

The Hyderabad subsidiary force, also under Wellesley's orders, comprised 120 English gunners, the Scots Brigade (now the 2nd Connaught Rangers), 900 native cavalry, and 6,000 native infantry. It was commanded by Colonel Murray.

III. The division in Guzerat, which was to insure the safety of Cambay, and then to operate from the west, was under Colonel Stevenson, and comprised the 65th (York and Lancasters), 75th (Gordon Highlanders), the 86th (Royal Irish Rifles), and detachments of the 61st (Gloucesters), 84th (York and Lancasters), and 88th (Connaught Rangers), with 200 English artillerymen.

The most difficult task was that assigned to Wellesley, for he had to arrange for the security of an enormous tract of country, ruled over by chiefs whose friendship was more than doubtful. After providing for the defence of Guzerat, he left 2,000 men, including the 86th (Irish Rifles), near Baroda, a force of similar strength with the 65th (York and Lancaster) on the Taptee, and retained the rest for active operations under himself and Stevenson.

IV. Harcourt had with him for the advance through Cuttack the 80th Foot, two companies of the 22nd, and the 25th Light Dragoons, two regiments of Bengal cavalry, including a squadron of the Governor-General's Bodyguard, and four regiments of Bengal infantry.

The campaign opened with a simultaneous advance of all four armies, Lake moving on Ally-Ghur, Wellesley on Ahmadnagar, Stevenson on Broach, and Harcourt on Balasore.

On September 3 Lake stormed and carried the fortress of Ally-Ghur.

ALLY-GHUR, SEPTEMBER 3, 1803.

This battle honour is borne on the colours of the West Riding Regiment alone ; no other corps which shared in that decisive victory being now existent ; the two native regiments which bore such a gallant part in the storming of the fortress having been swept away during the Mutiny of 1857.

On the issue of the India General Service Medal in 1851 the survivors of this action were granted that medal, with a clasp inscribed " Ally-Ghur."

Ally-Ghur was held by a powerful force under the command of the Frenchman Perron, and it made a gallant defence. The troops selected for the assault were the 76th Foot, the 1st Battalion of the 4th and the 17th Native Infantry, under Colonel the Hon. G. Monson, the casualties being :

Regiments.	Officers.		Men.		Regiments.	Officers.		Men.	
	K.	W.	K.	W.		K.	W.	K.	W.
27th Lt. Drag.	—	—	—	6	4th Bengal Infantry ..	1	4	20	84
Royal Artillery	—	1	2	7					
76th West Ridings	6	4	19	62	17th Bengal Infantry ..	—	2	8	36

In the fortress were 280 guns, which, with a large number of prisoners, fell into our hands; Scindia's French Commander-in-Chief, Monsieur Perron, a man of unusual ability, also threw himself on the generosity of Lord Lake.

Leaving a garrison in Ally-Ghur, the Governor-General now pushed on to Delhi, where a large force had been assembled, under Monsieur Bourquieu. On the 11th of the same month (September) was fought the first action in which British troops were ever engaged on this historic spot.

DELHI, SEPTEMBER 11, 1803.

This distinction is borne only by the West Riding Regiment and the 2nd Queen's Own Rajput Light Infantry, the latter one of the most distinguished regiments in the Bengal army. The India General Service Medal of 1851 was issued to the few survivors, with a clasp inscribed " Delhi." Our total losses in this action amounted to 463 killed and wounded.

Regiments.	Officers.		Men.		Regiments.	Officers.		Men.	
	K.	W.	K.	W.		K.	W.	K.	W.
27th Light Dragoons	1	1	11	18	3rd Bengal Cav.	1	6	6	11
					2nd Bengal Inf.	—	3	9	34
Royal Artillery	—	1	4	27	4th Bengal Inf.	—	3	12	76
76th W. Riding					12th Bengal Inf.	2	1	16	36
Regiment	—	1	33	97	14th Bengal Inf.	—	—	—	13
2nd Bengal Cav.	—	2	—	15	15th Bengal Inf.	1	3	10	34

The last regiment in the above return, the 15th Bengal Infantry, now being the 2nd Queen's Own Rajput Light Infantry, is the only regiment of the Bengal army still existing; the others, alas! disappeared in the rebellion of 1857.

ASSAYE, SEPTEMBER 23, 1803.

This battle honour, the first won by Wellington as an independent commander, is borne by the

19th Hussars.	Highland Light Infantry.
Seaforth Highlanders.	2nd Queen's Own Sappers
62nd Punjabis.	and Miners.
64th Pioneers.	84th Punjabis.

On the issue of the India Medal of 1851 the survivors were awarded the medal, with clasp " Assaye."

Wellington's force did not amount to more than 4,500 men, of whom only 1,300 were British, and he was further handicapped, as, owing to the nature of the ground, he was compelled to leave his heavy field-guns in the rear. Opposed to him were some of Scindia's finest troops, including two brigades commanded by the Frenchmen Pohlman and Dupont, with a well-equipped brigade belonging to the Begum Somroo. In all, the enemy were estimated at 30,000, with 100 guns. That they were well handled during the fight was self-evident, for when Wellesley's turning movement was discovered, the Mahrattas changed position with all the accuracy of veterans. The fight was one of the most stubbornly contested of any that we have fought even in India. Our casualties amounted to 23 officers and 381 men killed, 30 officers and 1,035 men wounded. Those of the enemy were estimated at upwards of 6,000 whilst of the 100 guns with which they commenced the action, no less than 98 remained in our hands. The losses suffered by the regiments at Assaye which still figure in the Army List were as follows :

Regiments.	Officers.		Men.		Regiments.	Officers.		Men.	
	K.	W.	K.	W.		K.	W.	K.	W.
19th Light Dragoons	2	4	15	36	2nd Q.O. Sappers and Miners ..	1	5	19	46
Royal Artillery	4	4	22	31	62nd Punjabis	1	—	20	22
74th Highld.L.I.	11	6	113	231	64th Pioneers	2	2	26	89
78th Seaforth H.	1	4	23	71	84th Punjabis	1	12	43	178

On November 28 Sir Arthur Wellesley captured Argaum, where we lost 346 officers and men killed and wounded. No battle honour was awarded for this action, but on the issue of the India Medal the survivors received the medal, with clasp " Argaum."

On December 14 the hill-fortress of Gawilghur was carried by assault, the Scots Brigade, now the 2nd Connaught Rangers, being the stormers. Here we lost 126 killed and wounded. No battle honour was granted for Gawilghur, but it was included in the list of actions for which the India Medal was granted, and a special clasp, with the word " Gawilghur," was added to the decoration.

LASWARREE, NOVEMBER 1, 1803.

This battle honour has been awarded to the

8th Hussars.	West Riding Regiment.
1st Brahmins.	2nd Queen's Own Light
4th Rajputs.	Infantry.

On the issue of the India General Service Medal in 1851, it, with a clasp inscribed " Laswarree," was issued to the survivors.

This was the hardest-fought action in Lord Lake's campaign, our total casualties amounting to 267 killed and 682 wounded, amongst the former being General Ware, commanding the First Division of the army, and Brigadier-General Vandeleur, commanding the Cavalry Division. The Commander-in-Chief was, as usual, in the thick of the fight, having no less than three horses killed under him, three of his staff being killed. The victory, however, was complete. It is noticeable for the fact that our infantry came into action after a forced march of sixty-five miles in forty-eight hours, a feat which rivals that so extolled by Napier at Talavera. Unfortunately, the Indian army had no historian to paint with stirring language the deeds of the giants who lived in those days.

Regiments.	*Officers.*		*Men.*		Regiments.	*Officers.*		*Men.*	
	K.	W.	K.	W.		K.	W.	K.	W.
8th Light Drag.	2	2	16	34	1st Brahmins	—	—	4	12
Bengal Artillery	—	—	7	6	2nd Q. O. Light				
76th West Rid-					Infantry ..	1	1	11	26
ing Regiment	2	4	41	165	4th Rajputs ..	—	1	17	69

In the meantime Agra had fallen into our hands,
despite a very gallant defence by the Mahrattas under
their French commanders, our losses amounting to the
respectable total of 228 killed and wounded, amongst
them being 5 British officers.

The other columns had not been idle. Colonel Harcourt,
advancing through Cuttack, had added that province to
our fast-increasing Indian possessions, and at the capture
of the fort of Barabuttee had given the 22nd Foot (the
Cheshires) an opportunity of distinguishing themselves.
He then pushed on to the westward, to co-operate with
the army of Sir Arthur Wellesley.

Sir Arthur, moving from the west, had carried the
fortress of Ahmadnagar by storm, with a loss of but
141 killed and wounded, the 74th (Highland Light
Infantry) and the 78th (Seaforths) being the principal
sufferers. On September 22 he came across the main
army of the Mahrattas, some 30,000 strong, under their
French leaders, and as we have seen on p. 249, defeated
them at Assaye.

DEIG, NOVEMBER 13 TO DECEMBER 23, 1804.

The battle honour " Deig " is borne by the

West Riding Regiment.   Royal Munster Fusiliers.
2nd Queen's Own Light Infantry.

It recognizes the services of those regiments at the
battle with Holkar's troops on November 13, and the
subsequent siege operations, which ended with the

capture of that city by assault on December 23 following. The attitude of Holkar during Lord Lake's campaign in the year 1803 had given us good cause to doubt his loyalty. Why he did not throw in his lot with Scindia in 1803 can only be ascribed to the immemorial jealousy between the two Princes. No sooner was a truce patched up between Scindia and ourselves than Holkar embarked on a series of operations which were evidently intended to provoke hostilities. Lord Lake spent the hot weather of 1803 on the frontier, and in September be took up the challenge. Lord Lake's army was massed in the vicinity of Agra, and consisted of an infantry division of three brigades, commanded by Major-General Fraser, a cavalry division under Brigadier Macan, and a reserve infantry division of two brigades under Brigadier Don. The infantry division included the 76th (West Riding Regiment), the 1st Bengal European Regiment (now the 1st Munster Fusiliers), and six regiments of Bengal infantry, of which only the 2nd Queen's Own Rajput Light Infantry now remains. The cavalry division included the 8th and 27th regiments of Light Dragoons, and four regiments of native cavalry. Brigadier-General Don's brigade consisted of four battalions of Bengal infantry. On October 14, 1803, Holkar, throwing off the mask, made a sudden attack upon Delhi, which was held by a garrison of Bengal troops under Colonel Ochterlony. He was beaten off, with heavy loss, and on learning that Lord Lake was moving on Delhi, Holkar precipitately retreated. His infantry retired on Deig, he himself towards Furracakabad. Lake ordered Fraser, with his division, to march at once to Deig, whilst he, with the cavalry and Don's brigade, followed up the Mahratta Prince. On November 13 Fraser found the Mahratta army drawn up outside the fortress of Deig. They held a very strong position, with one flank resting on a morass and the other on a large tank. After a sharp fight, in which our little force lost 148 killed and 479 wounded, the Mahrattas broke, and took refuge

behind the walls of the fortress. In the engagement
General Fraser lost his leg from a round shot, and he sank
beneath the effects of the wound. Lake, following up
the Maharajah, overtook him, and cut up his army, with
a loss to the 8th Hussars of but 2 killed and 13 wounded,
those of the enemy being estimated at 2,000. Lake
now made his way to Deig, ordering up the siege-train
from Agra, and he also called up reinforcements in the
shape of a column from Bombay, and the flank companies
of the 22nd (Cheshires) from Cuttack. On the morning
of December 23 the breach was declared practicable,
and the orders for the assault given. Three columns
were told off, under Colonel Macrae, of the West Riding
Regiment. The centre or main column was led by Macrae
in person. It consisted of two companies of the 76th
(West Riding), two of the 22nd (Cheshires), and two of
the 1st Bengal European Regiment.[1] The right and
left columns were each composed of two companies of
the Bengal European Regiment, and five of the 12th
Bengal Infantry, a regiment no longer with us. Considerable opposition was experienced, especially from
a body of Afghan mercenaries in Holkar's pay ; but
Christmas morning found the British flag flying over the
walls of Holkar's stronghold, our total loss amounting to
no more than 43 killed and 184 wounded.

The Regimental History of the 22nd (Cheshires)
gives the casualties of the regiment as 2 men killed and
4 wounded ; but as Lord Lake's despatch gives the names
of four officers of that regiment as among the wounded,
I conclude the History is wrong. I have compared the
names of the wounded officers with the official Army List
for the year in question, and as these stand in the official
records it would appear that the *Gazette* is right, and the
Regimental History wrong. Three out of the four officers
were again wounded in the attacks on Bhurtpore in the
following month, when Sergeant Shipp of the 22nd covered
himself with glory, and obtained a commission in the 65th
for repeated acts of gallantry.

[1] Now the Royal Munster Fusiliers.

Casualties at the Battle of Deig.					Casualties at the Siege and Assault.				
Regiments.	Officers.		Men.		Regiments.	Officers.		Men.	
	K.	W.	K.	W.		K.	W.	K.	W.
76th W. Ridings	I	3	31	120	8th Hussars ..	—	—	2	12
2nd Batt. N.I.	I	I	25	66	Royal Artillery	—	I	—	—
4th Batt. N.I.	2	2	22	28	22nd Cheshires	—	4	2	13
Royal Dublins	—	5	12	52	76th W. Ridings	—	2	5	17
8th Batt. N.I.	—	—	4	2	Royal Dublins	—	I	?	?
2nd Q.O. Light					8th Bom. N.I.	I	4	?	?
Infantry ..	I	6	19	143	12th Bom. N.I.	I	—	?	?
Royal Artillery	—	—	16	47	Pioneers ..	—	2	?	?

COCHIN, 1809.

On September 30, 1840, the Governor of Madras in Council conferred the above distinction on the 17th Madras Infantry (the predecessors of the 93rd Burmah Infantry), for their gallant conduct at the defence of the Residency of Cochin during the rebellion in Travancore in the year 1809.

Under the terms of various treaties the Maharajah of Travancore was bound to maintain a Subsidiary Force of native troops, officered by Englishmen of our own army, such force to be at the disposal of the East India Company, under certain conditions. Differences arose with the Maharajah, and an attempt to murder the British Resident unmasked a plot for the expulsion of the British garrisons in Southern India. The General commanding the Malabar coast, on learning of the threatening condition of affairs, at once ordered the 12th (Suffolks) and the 17th Madras Infantry to reinforce the troops of the subsidiary force at Cochin, these were permeated with discontent, having been seduced from their allegiance by the Prime Minister of the State. A very determined attack on the Residency at Cochin was repulsed by the small garrison, which consisted of a detachment of the Suffolks and a wing of the 17th Madras Infantry. Further operations became necessary, and a general movement of troops from all the stations in Southern India was ordered. The 19th (Yorkshires), 59th (East Lancashires), 69th (Welsh), and 80th (North Staffords), with a certain number of regiments of Madras sepoys, advanced on Travancore. At Palamcottah the 69th (Welsh) and the 3rd Regiment of Madras Infantry had a sharp brush with the Travancoreans, in which the Madras regiment showed considerable dash, and earned for itself the title, which its successor now bears, of Palamcottah Light Infantry. The 12th (Suffolks) and the 17th Madras Infantry were on another occasion compelled to submit to an attack on the part of the misguided Travancoreans, but the advent of such a large force had a sobering influence on the Maharajah: the obnoxious Prime Minister was removed and disgraced, the arrears of subsidy paid, and the independence of the Maharajah became a mere figment. The distinction " India " on their colours serves to remind the Suffolks that in their long tour of service in the early years of the last century they had some sharp fighting, irrespective of the campaign in Mysore. The casualties in Cochin show that it was not a mere summer picnic.

Regiments.	Officers.		Men.	
	K.	W.	K.	W.
Suffolks	0	4	9	67
93rd Burmah Infantry	—	1	10	45

NOTE.—On the renumbering of the regiments of the Indian Army in 1903, the 93rd Infantry renounced their claim to these battle honours, to which, as the direct representation of the old 17th Madras Infantry, they are legitimately entitled.

CHAPTER XI

BATTLE HONOURS FOR SERVICES IN THE
PENINSULAR WAR, 1808-1814

Roleia — Vimiera — Sahagun — Corunna — The Douro — Talavera—Busaco — Barrosa — Fuentes d'Onor — Albuera — Almaraz — Arroyos dos Molinos—Tarifa—Ciudad Rodrigo — Badajos — Salamanca — Vittoria — Pyrenees — San Sebastian—Nivelle—Nive—Orthes—Toulouse.

THE campaign was entered upon with a view of preventing the Iberian Peninsula from falling under the domination of Napoleon, who, prior to the landing of our troops in Portugal in August, 1808, had brought about the abdication of the King of Spain, and placed his brother Joseph on the throne of Madrid. Portugal had been invaded also by the French. The King, taking refuge on an English squadron, had sailed to Brazil, and Lisbon was at the moment in possession of the French Army, commanded by Marshal Junot.

The honour " Peninsula " was granted to all regiments which served under the Duke of Wellington from the date of his first landing in Figueras Bay in August, 1808, to the Battle of Toulouse, in April, 1804. Regiments which served under Sir John Moore and were present at Corunna in January, 1809, but were not fortunate enough to return to Spain, were debarred from this " distinction," the 14th Foot (now the West Yorks) and the 26th Cameronians being cases in point.[1] Gold medals and crosses were conferred on field and general

---

[1] The 26th did, indeed, return to the Peninsula, but they were employed in the thankless task of performing garrison duty at Lisbon, and not having been actively engaged, have not received the battle honour.

officers during the operations, but it was not until the year 1847 that the Duke of Richmond was enabled to carry out the project of inducing Her Majesty Queen Victoria to grant to the few remaining survivors a silver medal with clasps for the various actions, as below :

Roleia.	Ciudad Rodrigo.
Vimiera.	Badajoz.
Sahagun.	Salamanca.
Benevente.	Vittoria.
Corunna.	Pyrenees.
Talavera.	San Sebastian.
Busaco.	Nivelle.
Barrosa.	Nive.
Fuentes d'Onor.	Orthes.
Albuera.	Toulouse.

ROLEIA, AUGUST 17, 1808.

This was the opening action of the Peninsular War, which, commencing with Roleia in August, 1808, lasted until the final defeat of Soult by the Duke of Wellington at Toulouse in March, 1814.

The following regiments have been authorized at different times to carry the word " Roleia " on their colours and appointments, and the Land General Service Medal, with clasp " Roleia," was granted to all survivors on June 1, 1847 :

Northumberland Fusiliers.	Royal Warwick.
Norfolk.	Worcester.
Cornwall Light Infantry.	South Stafford.
South Lancashire.	Sherwood Foresters.
King's Royal Rifles.	Highland Light Infantry.
Argyll Highlanders.	Rifle Brigade.

They were brigaded as under, the chief command being held by Lieutenant-General the Honourable Sir Arthur Wellesley :

First Brigade—Hill :

5th (Northumberland Fusiliers) ..	..	..	990	
1st Batt. 9th (Norfolk) ..	..	..	833	
38th (South Staffords) ..	..	..	957	
				2,780

Second Brigade—Fergusson :

36th (Worcester) ..	..	..	591	
40th (South Lancashire) ..	..	..	926	
71st (Highland Light Infantry) ..	..	..	903	
				2,420

Third Brigade—Nightingale :
    29th (Worcester) 806
    82nd (South Lancashire) 929
                                  1,735

Fourth Brigade—Bowes :
    6th (Royal Warwick) 946
    32nd (Cornwall Light Infantry) 874
                                  1,820

Fifth Brigade—C. Crawford :
    50th (West Kent) 948
    91st (Argyll Highlanders) 917
                                  1,865

Sixth Brigade—Fane :
    45th (Sherwood Foresters) 670
    5th Batt. King's Royal Rifles 936
    2nd Batt. Rifle Brigade 400
                                  2,060

                                  12,626
    20th Light Dragoons 240
    Royal Artillery 226

Opposed to these, the French had, under General Delaborde, not more than 6,000 men. The odds, therefore, were considerably in our favour ; but the opposition was nowhere very determined, and our casualties were slight. Three regiments, it will be seen from the accompanying return, suffered no loss.

CASUALTIES AT ROLEIA.

Regiments.	Officers.		Men.		Regiments.	Officers.		Men.	
	K.	W.	K.	W.		K.	W.	K.	W.
20th Hussars	—	—	—	3	40th S. Lancs	—	—	1	2
Royal Artillery	1	—	1	—	45th Sherwood				
Roy. Engineers	—	1	—	—	Foresters ..	1	1	—	9
5th Northumberland Fus.	—	2	3	41	50th West Kent	—	—	2	1
					60th K.R.R. ..	—	2	8	39
6th R. Warwick	—	1	—	2	71st Highland				
29th Worcester	—	7	33	111	L.I.	—	—	1	1
32nd Cornwall					82nd S. Lancs	—	1	6	18
L.I.	—	—	1	3	91st Argyll				
36th Worcester	—	—	—	—	Highlanders	—	—	—	—
38th S. Stafford	—	—	4	—	95th Rifle Brig.	—	2	17	30

NOTE.—The riflemen of the 60th and 95th (Rifle Brigade) had been engaged on August 15, when the latter regiment lost one officer killed and another wounded.

VIMIERA, AUGUST 21, 1808.

Four days after Roleia, Sir Arthur Wellesley, at the head of the following regiments, inflicted a second defeat on the French army under Junot, capturing three guns and many prisoners. The following regiments bear the honour :

20th Hussars.	Queen's.
Northumberland Fusiliers.	Royal Warwicks.
Norfolk.	Lancashire Fusiliers.
Worcesters.	Cornwall Light Infantry.
South Stafford.	South Lancashire.
Oxford Light Infantry.	Sherwood Foresters.
West Kent.	King's Royal Rifles.
Highland Light Infantry.	Argyll Highlanders.
Rifle Brigade.	

The casualties incurred were as follows :

CASUALTIES AT VIMIERA.

Regiments.	Officers.		Men.		Regiments.	Officers.		Men.	
	K.	W.	K.	W.		K.	W.	K.	W.
20th Hussars..	1	—	19	24	40th S. Lancs	—	2	6	30
Royal Artillery	—	2	—	2	43rd Oxford				
2nd Queen's ..	—	—	—	7	L.I. ..	—	3	27	51
5th Northumberland Fus.	—	—	—	—	45th Sherwood Foresters ..	—	—	—	—
6th Royal Warwicks	—	—	—	—	50th West Kent	1	4	19	63
9th Norfolk (2nd Batt.)	—	—	—	—	52nd Oxford L.I. ..	—	2	5	33
20th Lancs Fus.	1	1	—	5	50th K.R.R. ..	—	2	14	22
29th Worcester	—	1	2	11	71st Highland L.I. ..	—	7	12	92
32nd Cornwall L.I.	—	—	—	—	82nd S. Lancs	1	—	7	53
36th Worcester	—	5	7	36	91st Argyll Highlanders	—	—	—	—
38th S. Staffs	—	—	—	—	95th Rifle Brig.	—	4	37	43

Immediately after the action negotiations were entered into with the French to secure their evacuation of Portugal. The Convention of Cintra, the result of these negotiations, raised a storm of indignation in

England. The three Generals—Harry Burrard, Sir Howard Dalrymple, and Sir Arthur Wellesley—were recalled, and their conduct submitted to a Court of Inquiry held at the Royal Hospital, Chelsea, under the presidency of Sir Henry Dundas. The *Times* took a strong line against Wellesley, but the Court of Inquiry to a great extent exonerated him. Subsequently he returned to Portugal, as we know, to carry the war to a successful conclusion, thus belying his detractors.

The troops engaged at Vimiera were brigaded as under :

20th Light Dragoons	240
Royal Artillery (three batteries)	226

First Brigade—Hill :

5th (Northumberland Fusiliers)	944	
1st Batt. 9th (Norfolk)	761	
38th (South Staffords)	953	
		2,658

Second Brigade—Fergusson :

36th (Worcester)	591	
40th (South Lancashire)	923	
71st (Highland Light Infantry)	935	
		2,449

Third Brigade—Nightingale :

29th (Worcester)	616	
82nd (South Lancashire)	904	
		1,520

Fourth Brigade—Bowes :

6th (Royal Warwick)	943	
32nd (Cornwall Light Infantry)	870	
		1,813

Fifth Brigade—C. Crawford :

45th (Sherwood Foresters)	915	
91st (Argyll Highlanders)	917	
		1,832

Sixth Brigade—Fane :

50th (West Kent)	945	
5th Batt. 60th (King's Royal Rifles)	604	
2nd Batt. Rifle Brigade	456	
		2,005

Seventh Brigade—Anstruther :

2nd Batt. 9th (Norfolk)	633	
43rd (Oxford Light Infantry)	721	
52nd (Oxford Light Infantry)	654	
97th (West Kent)	695	
		2,703

Eighth Brigade—Acland :

2nd (Queen's)	..	..	..	..	.. 731
20th (Lancashire Fusiliers)		..	..	..	401
1st Batt. Rifle Brigade	..	..	..	..	200

$$1,332$$

Total British .. 16,712

To which must be added about 2,000 Portuguese troops. Of the French forces it is not so easy to speak. Wellesley estimated their strength at 14,000, inclusive of 1,500 cavalry, with 23 guns. Professor Oman's figures are 13,056, including 1,850 cavalry. Whatever their strength may have been, they made but a poor stand against Sir Arthur's troops.

MOORE'S CAMPAIGN IN SPAIN.

When the three Generals responsible for the Convention of Cintra were recalled to England, Sir John Moore was nominated to the chief command in Spain. The appointment was a popular one, for Moore had greatly distinguished himself in command of a brigade at the capture of the Island of St. Lucia, and later still at the Battle of Egmont-op-Zee and in Egypt. His masterly advance from Lisbon to the relief of Madrid, and his still more masterly retreat from Salamanca to Corunna, are ably recounted in Professor Oman's monumental work on the Peninsular War, and by General Maurice in his Life of Moore. With not more than 30,000 men Moore held at bay five times that number, and finally, at Corunna, covered the embarkation of his worn-out army in the face of 25,000 French, commanded by Marshal Soult. The one episode during that famous retreat which is emblazoned on the colours and appointments of our army is the brilliant cavalry action of Sahagun, for which, as well as for the cavalry action of Benevente a few days afterwards, the medal and clasps were granted.

SAHAGUN, DECEMBER 21, 1808.

This honour has been awarded to the 15th Hussars only, and commemorates a brilliant little engagement, when the 15th attacked and routed a far superior body

11

of French cavalry. With the trifling loss of 2 Hussars killed and 18 wounded, they captured 13 officers and 150 men of the enemy. Sahagun and Benevente—a similar action which took place a few days subsequently, in which the 10th and 18th Hussars bore their share, but for which no battle honour was granted, though a clasp " Benevente " was added to the Peninsular medal— bore testimony to the admirable manner in which our light cavalry was handled during Moore's retreat to Corunna.

CORUNNA, JANUARY 16, 1809.

Authority to assume this battle honour was given in April, 1823, and the medal and clasp were granted June 1, 1847.

This honour has been conferred on the following regiments :

Grenadier Guards.	Royal Scots.
Queen's R.W. Surrey	King's Own.
Northumberland Fusiliers.	Royal Warwicks.
Norfolks.	West Yorkshires.
Lancashire Fusiliers.	Royal Welsh Fusiliers.
Cameronians.	Gloucesters.
Worcesters.	East Lancashire.
Cornwall Light Infantry.	West Riding.
South Staffords.	South Lancashire.
Black Watch.	K.O. (Yorkshire Light Infantry).
Oxford Light Infantry.	North Lancashire.
Royal West Kent.	Highland Light Infantry.
Gordon Highlanders.	Cameron Highlanders.
Argyll and Suth. Highlanders.	Rifle Brigade.

The following table gives the strength of Sir John Moore's army at the commencement of the retreat. Unfortunately, no complete list of casualties exists to show the exact losses at the Battle of Corunna, but we know that on that day we had forty French guns opposed to nine English, and that the losses inflicted on the enemy were little short of 1,500, ours being about 800 only.

CAVALRY DIVISION : LORD PAGET.

7th Hussars	..	..	..	..	..	497
10th Hussars	..	..	..	..	..	514
15th Hussars	..	..	..	..	..	527
18th Hussars	..	..	..	..	..	565
						———
						2,103
Royal Artillery	..	..	..	..	..	1,297

FIRST DIVISION : SIR DAVID BAIRD.

Brigade of Guards—Ward :
  1st Batt. Grenadiers   1,300
  2nd Batt. Grenadiers   1,027
                  ————— 2,327

First Brigade—Bentinck :
  1st Batt. 4th (King's Own)   754
  1st Batt. 42nd (Royal Highlanders)   ..   880
  1st Batt. 50th (Royal West Kent)   ..   794
                  ————— 2,428

Third Brigade—Manningham :
  3rd Batt. Royal Scots. 597
  1st Batt. 26th (Cameronians)   745
  2nd Batt. 81st (North Lancashire)   ..   615
                  ————— 1,957

SECOND DIVISION : SIR JAMES HOPE.

Third Brigade—Leith :
  51st King's Own (Yorkshire Light Infantry) ..   516
  2nd Batt. 59th (East Lancashire)   ..   557
  2nd Batt. 76th (West Riding Regiment)   ..   654
                  ————— 1,727

Fourth Brigade—Hill :
  2nd (Queen's)   616
  1st Batt. 5th (Northumberland Fusiliers)   ..   835
  2nd Batt. 14th (West Yorkshire)   ..   550
  1st Batt. 32nd (Cornwall Light Infantry)   ..   756
                  ————— 2,757

Fifth Brigade—C. Crawford :
  1st Batt. 36th (Worcester)   736
  1st Batt. 71st (Highland Light Infantry)   ..   724
  1st Batt. 92nd (Gordon Highlanders)   900
                  ————— 2,360

THIRD DIVISION : LIEUTENANT-GENERAL FRASER.

Sixth Brigade —Beresford :
  1st Batt. 6th (Royal Warwicks)   783
  1st Batt. 9th (Norfolk)   607
  2nd Batt. 23rd (Royal Welsh Fusiliers)   ..   496
  2nd Batt. 45th (Oxford Light Infantry)   ..   411
                  ————— 2,297

Seventh Brigade—Fane :
  1st Batt. 38th (South Stafford)   823
  1st Batt. 79th (Cameron Highlanders)   ..   838
  1st Batt. 82nd (South Lancashire)   ..   812
                  ————— 2,473

RESERVE DIVISION : MAJOR-GENERAL E. PAGET.

Eighth Brigade—Anstruther :
  20th (Lancashire Fusiliers)   499
  1st Batt. 52nd (Oxford Light Infantry)   ..   828
  1st Batt. Rifle Brigade   820
                  ————— 2,147

Ninth Brigade—Disney :
 1st Batt. 28th (Gloucester) 750
 1st Batt. 91st (Argyll Highlanders) 698
 ———— 1,448
Light Brigade—R. Crawford :
 1st Batt. 43rd (Oxford Light Infantry) .. 817
 2nd Batt. 52nd (Oxford Light Infantry) .. 381
 2nd Batt. Rifle Brigade 702
 ———— 1,900

Total British .. 27,221

Casualties at Corunna.

Regiments.	Officers.		Men.		Regiments.	Officers.		Men.	
	K.	W.	K.	W.		K.	W.	K.	W.
General Staff	1	—	—	—	42nd Royal Highlanders	—	6	39	105
7th Hussars ..	—	—	—	—	43rd Oxfd. L.I. (two batts.)	—	—	—	—
10th Hussars	—	—	—	—	50th Royal West Kent	2	3	—	—
15th Hussars	—	—	—	—	51st K. O. Yorks L.I.	—	—	5	20
18th Hussars	—	—	—	—	52nd Oxf. L.I. (1st and 2nd Batts.) ..	—	2	5	33
Royal Artillery	—	—	—	—	59th E. Lancs	—	—	—	—
Grenadier Gds. (2nd Batt.)	—	—	13	40	71st Highld. L.I.	—	—	—	—
1st Royal Scots	—	—	—	—	76th West Riding Regiment	—	—	1	6
2nd Queen's ..	—	—	—	—	79th Cameronian Highdrs.	—	—	—	—
4th K.O. Lancaster Regt.	1	3	—	—	81st L. North Lancashire	3	11	27	113
5th Northumberland Fus.	—	—	—	—	82nd S. Lancs	—	—	—	—
6th Royal Warwicks ..	—	—	—	—	91st Argyll Highlanders	—	—	—	—
9th Norfolk ..	—	—	—	—	92nd Gordon Highlanders	1	1	3	15
14th W. Yorks	—	—	10	30	Rifle Brigade (1st and 2nd Batts.) ..	—	—	12	33
20th Lancs F.	—	—	—	—					
23rd Royal Welsh Fus.	—	—	—	—					
26th Cameronians ..	—	—	—	—					
28th Gloucester	—	—	—	—					
32nd Corn. L.I.	—	—	—	—					
36th Worcester	—	—	—	—					
38th S. Stafford	—	—	—	—					

It is useless disguising the fact that the French claim Corunna as a victory. Moore, who fell during the action, and who, with General Anstruther, was buried within the precincts of the work, had been compelled to destroy the greater number of his horses and to bury some of his guns prior to giving the order for embarkation, and a large number of his sick were left behind.   Nothing, however, can detract from the magnificent manner in which he conducted the retirement in the face of enormous odds, nor from the gallant way in which his men pulled themselves together after the hardships endured during the retreat, and stood at bay outside Corunna.   It was not a victory in the fullest sense of the word, but Corunna was a grand military achievement.

THE PENINSULAR WAR (SECOND PHASE), 1809-1814.

To give even a summary of the campaign would be beyond the limits of this work.   It is the campaign which more than any other has formed the theme for countless books, and is more or less known to every schoolboy. My scheme is merely to bring before the regimental officer and those interested in the " price of blood " the losses sustained by each corps in each action, and so to bring home to the army the anomalies that exist in the system under which battle honours have been awarded.

We have seen that the Convention of Cintra, which was the closing act of the successful campaign of Vimiera, had been received with a storm of indignation in England. When it became known that Sir Arthur Wellesley, one of the Signatories of that Convention, had been appointed to succeed the late Sir John Moore in command of the troops in Portugal, the attacks broke out afresh.   The result, however, gave the lie to the arm-chair critics, for the " Sepoy General " proved a consummate master of the art of war.   Landing at Lisbon on April 22, Sir Arthur struck at once.   There was one French army still in Portugal, at Oporto, where Soult lay with a considerable force. Leaving a portion of his army under Beresford to watch the French main army, who were near Talavera, Wellesley moved swiftly to the north.   By a masterly stroke, he threw one brigade across the Douro, and, with the loss of but 190 killed and wounded drove Soult out of Oporto.

DOURO.

is inscribed on the colours and appointments of the

14th Hussars.	Buffs.
Northamptons.	Royal Berkshires.

and commemorates this, Wellington's first victory after he had been entrusted with the supreme command in the Peninsula. In addition to the regiments which are entitled to bear this battle honour, there was a battalion of detachments engaged made up of the light companies of the 29th (Worcesters), 38th (South Staffords), 43rd and 52nd (Oxford Light Infantry), and the Rifle Brigade. The 16th Lancers, who were generally to the fore when fighting was expected, also suffered some casualties. Soult was not only surprised; he was, despite the smallness of our losses, badly beaten, and it was only Wellesley's want of cavalry which prevented his being overwhelmed with disaster. As it was, Soult only succeeded in effecting a junction with Ney by burning his baggage, throwing his guns over the mountain-side, and, by following goat-tracks, he at last escaped the English pursuit.

CASUALTIES AT THE PASSAGE OF THE DOURO, MAY 10, 11, AND 12, 1809.

Regiments.	Officers.		Men.		Regiments.	Officers.		Men.	
	K.	W.	K.	W.		K.	W.	K.	W.
14th Hussars	—	4	13	19	38th S. Staffs				
16th Lancers	—	3	—	—	(detachment)	—	1	—	—
20th Hussars	—	—	1	—	48th N'ampton	—	1	—	—
Royal Artillery	—	—	—	—	52nd Oxf. L.I.				
3rd Buffs ..	—	1	—	—	(detachment)	—	1	—	—
29th Worcester	—	—	2	7	66th Berkshire	—	3	9	26

NOTE.—No detailed list of the casualties in the three days' skirmishing on the Douro is appended to Sir Arthur Wellesley's despatch. On May 11 we lost 19 men killed and 62 wounded, and on the 12th 23 killed and 86 wounded. The despatch alludes to the conduct of the 20th Hussars, and of the light companies of the 29th, 43rd, and 52nd, and the riflemen of the 95th Regiment. None of these regiments have been awarded the honour. A detachment of the 83rd (Royal Irish Rifles) was present, and lost 14 men wounded.

TALAVERA, JULY 27, 1808.

Returning south after the success at the Douro, Wellesley at once took steps to attack the main French army, which, under Marshal Victor, with King Joseph himself as nominal leader, lay at Talavera, to the north-east of Lisbon, across the Spanish frontier.

This battle honour is borne by the

3rd Dragoon Guards.	4th Hussars.
14th Hussars.	16th Lancers.
Coldstream Guards.	Scots Guards.
Buffs.	Royal Fusiliers.
South Wales Borderers.	Gloucesters.
Worcesters.	East Surrey.
South Lancashire.	Sherwood Foresters.
Nórthamptons.	Royal Berkshires.
Shropshire Light Infantry.	King's Royal Rifles.
Royal Irish Rifles.	Royal Irish Fusiliers.

Connaught Rangers.

Talavera was a very different stamp of fight to anything in which our troops had been previously engaged in the Peninsula. We had but 20,000 men present, and our losses amounted to 4,000 killed and wounded, those of the French to over 7,000. The full fruits of the victory were lost owing to the failure of our Spanish allies to afford us proper support, and the British army was compelled to retire on the following day, leaving its wounded in the hands of the French. It is true that we captured 17 guns, but the fact of our retreat, coupled with the abandonment of the sick and wounded, have induced the French to claim Talavera as a French victory. Marshal Victor was created Duke of Talavera by King Joseph, while Sir Arthur Wellesley was raised to the peerage under the title of Lord Wellington,—of Wellington, in the county of Somerset, and of Talavera. The fighting was exceedingly severe, and on more than one occasion matters looked very doubtful. Sir Arthur, however, had every reason to be proud of the manner in which his men faced the tried veterans of France.

CASUALTIES AT THE BATTLE OF TALAVERA, JULY 27 AND 28, 1809.

Regiments.	Officers.		Men.		Regiments.	Officers.		Men.	
	K.	W.	K.	W.		K.	W.	K.	W.
3rd Drag. Gds.	1	1	—	—	40th S. Lancs	—	1	17	90
4th Hussars ..	—	3	—	9	45th Sherwood				
14th Hussars	—	6	3	7	Foresters ..	—	3	13	147
16th Lancers	—	1	6	5	48th N'ampton	—	12	34	280
23rd Lt. Drag.	2	4	47	46	53rd Shropshire				
Royal Artillery	1	3	7	23	L.I. ..	—	2	6	36
Roy. Engineers	—	2	—	—	60th K.R.R.	—	7	10	29
Coldstream Gds.	2	9	33	253	61st Gloucesters	3	11	46	196
Scots Guards	5	6	49	261	66th R. Berks	—	11	16	88
3rd Buffs ..	—	2	6	107	83rd Royal				
7th Royal Fus.	1	3	6	53	Irish Rifles	4	11	38	282
24th S. Wales					87th R.Irish Fus.	1	13	35	170
Borderers ..	—	10	45	274	88th Connaught				
29th Worcesters	—	7	36	140	Rangers ..	3	3	19	85
31st E. Surrey	1	7	34	190	97th West Kent	—	—	6	25

NOTE.—There were two battalions of detachments at Talavera. The one composed of the flank companies of the 52nd, 79th, and 91st lost an officer, and 74 men killed and wounded. The other, made up from the 28th, 35th, 38th, 42nd, and 43rd, had 194 casualties.

The Cameron Highlanders lost 9 killed and 28 wounded at Talavera.

BUSACO, SEPTEMBER 27, 1810.

At Talavera Wellington realized that he was too weak to cope in the field with the immense forces that France had poured into the Peninsula. His plan of campaign now was to wear the enemy down until he should have organized the Portuguese and Spanish armies. He therefore retired once more into Portugal, and commenced that systematic defence of the kingdom which ultimately led to the destruction of French pretensions in the Iberian Peninsula. By the summer of 1810 Napoleon had 300,000 men in Spain. By that time Wellington had thrown up the famous lines of Torres Vedras, behind the shelter of which the task of reorganizing the Portuguese army proceeded apace. The winter of 1809-10 was passed without any open conflict.

It was not until the end of September, 1810, that the next great fight was fought, when Wellington, with 50,000 men, barred Massena's advance at the Ridge of Busaco. This battle honour has been conferred on the

Royal Scots.	Northumberland Fusiliers.
Royal Fusiliers.	Norfolks.
South Wales Borderers.	Gloucesters.
Royal Highlanders.	South Staffords.
Oxford Light Infantry.	Sherwood Foresters.
King's Royal Rifles.	Highland Light Infantry.
Cameron Highlanders.	Connaught Rangers.
Royal Irish Rifles.	Rifle Brigade.

Our losses are tabulated below. Those of the French amounted to 4,400 killed and wounded, including 5 General Officers.

Casualties at the Battle of Busaco, September 27, 1810.

Regiments.	Officers.		Men.		Regiments.	Officers.		Men.	
	K.	W.	K.	W.		K.	W.	K.	W.
Royal Artillery	—	—	1	7	45th Sherwood Foresters ..	3	4	25	109
14th Hussars	—	—	—	3	50th Royal W. Kent ..	—	1	—	—
16th Lancers	—	1	—	—	52nd Oxf. L.I.	—	2	3	10
1st Royal Scots	—	—	—	2	60th K.R.R.	—	5	3	16
5th Northumberland Fus.	—	—	1	7	74th Highl. L.I.	1	1	6	21
7th Royal Fus.	—	1	1	22	79th Cameron Highlanders	1	2	11	41
9th Norfolk ..	—	1	5	18	83rd Royal Irish Rifles ..	—	1	—	4
24th S. Wales Borderers ..	—	1	—	—	88th Connaught Rangers ..	1	7	29	95
38th S. Stafford	—	1	5	17	95th Rifle Brig.	—	—	9	22
42nd Black Watch ..	—	—	—	7					
43rd Oxf. L.I.	—	—	—	7					

Wellington had once more shown his men that they were more than a match for the French in the field, but he still clung to his old plan of campaign, and, retiring behind the lines of Torres Vedras, prepared to wear the enemy down. The winter was passed with the English secure within their formidable entrenchments at Torres Vedras, the French starving outside. We held the command of the sea, and, with the Tagus in his rear, Wellington was able to feed his men without difficulty, to replenish supplies, and to continue the reorganization and training of the Portuguese army. In the South of Spain the French were showing renewed activity and Wellington detached a division under General Graham to afford support to the garrison of Cadiz. This the stout old Scotsman did most effectually by attacking Victor at Barrosa.

BARROSA, MARCH 4, 1811.

This distinction is borne on the colours of the

Grenadier Guards.	Coldstream Guards.
Scots Guards.	Gloucesters.
Hampshires.	Royal Irish Fusiliers.

Rifle Brigade.

Here a little British division not 4,000 strong over-threw double the number of Frenchmen, capturing six guns and two eagles. The subjoined list of casualties shows that others besides the regiments which are authorized to emblazon this battle honour on their colours did their duty as Englishmen on that March day. There seems no valid reason why the Norfolks, North Lancashires, South Lancashires, and the Rifle Brigade should not be permitted to assume this honour, albeit the headquarters of those regiments were not present in the engagement.

CASUALTIES AT THE BATTLE OF BARROSA, MARCH 4, 1811.

Regiments.	Officers.		Men.		Regiments.	Officers.		Men.	
	K.	W.	K.	W.		K.	W.	K.	W.
Grenadier Gds.	2	8	33	177	87th R. Irish F.	1	4	44	124
Coldstream Guards ..	1	2	8	46	9th Norfolk (flank cos.)	—	4	8	56
Scots Guards ..	1	1	14	85	47th N. Lancs				
Royal Artillery	—	8	6	40	(flank cos.)	1	1	20	49
Roy. Engineers	—	—	1	2	82nd S. Lancs				
28th Gloucester	—	8	16	135	(flank cos.)	—	2	8	89
67th Hampshire	—	4	10	30	95th Rifle Brig.	1	3	14	48

NOTE.—A battalion composed of the flank companies of the 9th (Norfolk), 28th (Gloucester), and 82nd (South Lancashire) went into action 475 bayonets ; its losses were 225 non-commissioned officers and men killed and wounded. A fellow battalion of the flank companies of the 47th and three companies of the 95th (Rifle Brigade) lost 130 men out of 594.

FUENTES D'ONOR, MAY 5, 1811.

In March, 1811, Massena, with his army much worn with the hard winter blockade outside Torres Vedras, fell back into Spain, closely followed by Wellington. Then ensued a number of rearguard actions which are not inscribed on our colours, but which brought out, on the one hand, the capacity of Ney as a rearguard commander, and, on the other, the admirable handling of our own Light Division of immortal fame. Pressing Massena back, Wellington endeavoured to relieve the beleaguered garrison of Ciudad Rodrigo with his own army, and detached Beresford to perform the same action with regard to Badajoz, and so it came about that within a few days of each other two general actions were fought.

Fuentes d'Onor is borne on the colours or appointments of the

1st Royal Dragoons.
14th Hussars.
Coldstream Guards.
Oxford Light Infantry.
King's Own (Yorkshire Light Infantry).
Highland Light Infantry.
Cameron Highlanders.
Connaught Rangers.

16th Lancers.
Scots Guards.
Royal Highlanders.
South Wales Borderers.
Sherwood Foresters.
Shropshire Light Infantry.
King's Royal Rifles.
Gordon Highlanders.
Royal Irish Rifles.

Rifle Brigade.

CASUALTIES AT THE BATTLE OF FUENTES D'ONOR,
MAY 3-5, 1811.

Regiments.	Officers.		Men.		Regiments.	Officers.		Men.	
	K.	W.	K.	W.		K.	W.	K.	W.
1st Roy. Drag.	—	4	1	36	King's Roy. R.	—	4	3	21
14th Hussars	—	5	4	28	71st Highl. L.I.	3	8	28	105
16th Lancers ..	—	2	7	16	74th Highl. L.I.	1	3	3	63
Royal Artillery	—	3	6	22	79th Cameron				
Roy. Engineers	—	—	—	—	Highlanders	3	11	58	166
Coldstream Gds.	—	1	4	49	85th Shropshire				
Scots Guards	1	1	5	52	L.I. ..	1	3	12	37
24th S.Wales B.	1	—	6	21	83rd R. Irish R.	1	1	6	36
42nd Black Wat.	—	1	3	29	88th Connaught				
45th Sherwood					Rangers ..	1	2	12	53
Foresters ..	—	—	3	1	92nd Gordon				
51st K. O.					Highlanders	—	3	7	43
Yorks L.I. . .	—	—	—	5	95th Rifle Brig.	1	1	3	19

The feature of the action was the marvellous gallantry of a troop of horse artillery under Norman Ramsay, which, though surrounded by the French, cut its way through the hostile hosts, and, amidst the tumultuous applause of the whole army, rejoined Wellington, with guns intact, but with the loss of half its men.

The following regiments appear in the casualty returns published in the *London Gazette*, but do not yet bear the battle honour :

Regiments.	Officers.		Men.		Regiments.	Officers.		Men.	
	K.	W.	K.	W.		K.	W.	K.	W.
Royal Scots ..	—	—	—	9	30th E. Lancs	—	—	—	4
5th Northumberland Fus.	—	—	—	7	50th West Kent	—	2	3	24
9th Norfolk ..	—	—	—	4	94th Connaught Rangers ..	—	—	—	7

ALBUERA, MAY 16, 1811.

Ten days after Wellington had defeated Massena at Fuentes d'Onor, Beresford, at the head of 32,000 men, of whom only 8,000 were English, repulsed a determined attack on the part of Soult at Albuera. This battle, which was one of the most severe ever fought by British troops, is recorded on the colours of the

3rd Dragoon Guards.
13th Hussars.
Royal Fusiliers.
Gloucester.
East Surrey.
Dorsets.
Royal Berkshire.
4th Hussars.
Buffs.
Royal Welsh Fusiliers.
Worcesters.
Border Regiment.
Northamptons.
Middlesex.
King's Royal Rifles.

The Allies were undoubtedly superior in numbers, but the brunt of the fighting fell on the British division, which lost 3,500 out of 8,000 engaged. The French losses amounted to upwards of 8,000 killed and wounded.

The following table, published in the *London Gazette*,

shows once more that battle honours are bestowed in a
very capricious fashion :

CASUALTIES AT THE BATTLE OF ALBUERA.

Regiments.	Officers.		Men.		Regiments.	Officers.		Men.	
	K.	W.	K.	W.		K.	W.	K.	W.
3rd Drag. Gds.	I	—	9	9	29th Worcesters	5	12	75	232
4th Hussars ..	—	2	3	17	31st E. Surrey	—	7	29	119
13th Hussars	—	—	—	I	34th Border				
Royal Artillery	—	I	3	10	Regiment ..	3	4	30	91
Roy. Engineers	2	2	—	3	39th Dorsets ..	I	4	14	77
Buffs　.. ..	4	14	212	234	48th N'ampton				
2nd Batt. Royal					(2nd Batt.)	7	23	116	276
Fusiliers　..	2	28	112	563	57th Middlesex	2	21	87	318
Royal Welsh					King's Roy. R.	—	I	2	18
Fusiliers　..	2	11	74	245	66th R. Berks	3	12	52	104

NOTE.—In the casualties for Albuera I have included the losses
on May 15, the previous day.

The following regiments figure in the official casualty
returns, but they have not as yet been authorized to
assume the battle honour :

Regiments.	Officers.		Men.		Regiments.	Officers.		Men.	
	K.	W.	K.	W.		K.	W.	K.	W.
27th Inniskillgs.	—	3	8	66	40th S. Lancs	—	3	10	18
28th Gloucester	—	6	27	131	97th R.W. Kent	—	—	7	21

It will be remarked that, whereas the 13th Hussars,
with the loss of one man wounded, has been awarded the
distinction, the Gloucesters, which lost a total of 164
killed and wounded, has been denied it.

ALMARAZ, MAY 19, 1811.

Royal West Kent.　　　　Highland Light Infantry.
Gordon Highlanders.

This battle honour is borne on the colours and appointments of the above regiments for their conduct in one of
the many sharp little engagements under that brilliant

tactician General, afterwards Viscount, Hill, who in his despatch calling special attention to the services of the 50th (West Kent) and 71st (Highland Light Infantry), added : " Nor can I avoid mentioning the steadiness of the 6th Portuguese Regiment and two companies of the 60th Rifles." Particular stress also was laid on the conduct of the 13th Hussars in capturing some of the enemy's guns. Neither the 13th Hussars nor the King's Royal Rifles have as yet been permitted to assume this distinction.

CASUALTIES AT THE ACTION OF ALMARAZ, MAY 19, 1811.

Regiments.	Officers.		Men.		Regiments.	Officers.		Men.	
	K.	W.	K.	W.		K.	W.	K.	W.
Royal Artillery	—	—	—	3	71st Hig'land				
Roy. Engineers	—	1	—	—	L.I.	—	4	8	28
28th Gloucesters	—	—	—	2	92nd Gordon				
50th West Kent	1	7	27	93	Highlanders	—	—	—	2

NOTE.—Our trophies at Almaraz included the Standard of the 4th Battalion of the " Corps Etrangères," taken by the 71st, and eighteen guns.

ARROYOS DOS MOLINOS, OCTOBER 28, 1811.

This distinction is only to be found on the colours of the Border Regiment.

Like Almaraz, it was one of the many engagements fought by Hill's division single-handed, and it has always been a matter of keen jealousy—if such a word can be used—on the part of the other regiments present that they have been denied the privilege of inscribing this battle honour on their colours. Lord Hill in his despatch laid no especial stress on the conduct of the 34th ; indeed, his highest praise was reserved for the two Highland regiments, the 71st and the 92nd. Hill's division consisted of :

Howard's Brigade : The 50th (West Kent), 71st (Highland Light Infantry), and the 92nd (Gordon Highlanders).
Wilson's Brigade : The 28th (Gloucesters), 34th (Border Regiment), 39th (Dorsets), and a Portuguese battalion.
Erskine's Brigade of Cavalry : The 9th and 16th Lancers, with a couple of batteries of artillery.

The French occupied the town of Arroyos dos Molinos, when, to use Hill's own words, " The 71st and 92nd charged into the town with cheers, and drove the enemy out at the point of the bayonet." Wilson's brigade had been sent round to attack the enemy in the rear, and the 50th (West Kent) supporting the Highlanders, secured the prisoners, whilst the 28th (Gloucesters) and the 34th (Borderers) pursued the flying French until the arrival of the cavalry enabled them to follow up the enemy. One general and 35 other officers, with upwards of 1,000 men, were taken, our total casualties being but 65 of all ranks killed and wounded. On more than one occasion the Gordon Highlanders have applied to be permitted to assume this distinction, but whilst conceding the valuable part they played at Arroyos dos Molinos, the War Office have declined to accede to their request on the plea that the battle honour was conferred on the 34th in lieu of a particoloured pom-pom to their shako. As the present generation of soldiers apply the term " pom-pom " to a man-destroying weapon, and not to the ornament of infantry headgear, and as shakos have been relegated to museums, it might be fitting to reopen the vexed question of this battle honour.

CASUALTIES OF THE ACTION OF ARROYOS DOS MOLINOS, OCTOBER 28, 1811.

Regiments.	Officers.		Men.		Regiments.	Officers.		Men.	
	K.	W.	K.	W.		K.	W.	K.	W.
9th Lancers ..	—	—	—	—	60th King's Roy. Rifles	—	—	—	—
13th Hussars	—	—	—	—					
Royal Artillery	—	—	—	—	71st Highland L.I.	—	—	—	—
28th Gloucesters	—	—	—	—					
34th Border ..	—	—	—	—	92nd Gordon Highlanders	—	4	3	7
50th West Kent	—	—	—	—					

NOTE.—I have been unable to trace any record of the losses of individual regiments, except in the case of the 92nd.

Tarifa, December, 1811.

This distinction is borne on the colours of the North Lancashire Regiment and the Royal Irish Fusiliers, in recognition of their services in the gallant defence of the fortress of Tarifa in the month of December, 1811. General Skerrett in his despatch drew particular attention to the conduct of the companies of the Rifle Brigade which were also present. The casualty list which I append shows that this battle honour was earned without a great effusion of blood.

Casualties at Tarifa, December, 1811.

Regiments.	Officers.		Men.		Regiments.	Officers.		Men.	
	K.	W.	K.	W.		K.	W.	K.	W.
Royal Engineers	—	—	—	1	Royal Artillery	—	—	—	2
47th Loyal N. Lancashires	1	2	—	5	87th Roy. Irish Fusiliers ..	—	2	5	21
					95th Rifle Brig.	—	—	3	17

Ciudad Rodrigo, January, 1812.

This hardly-earned battle honour has been awarded to the

Northumberland Fusiliers. Oxford Light Infantry.
Sherwood Foresters. Middlesex Regiment.
King's Royal Rifles. Highland Light Infantry.
Royal Irish Rifles. Connaught Rangers.
Rifle Brigade.

It will be seen from a glance at the appended casualty returns that a great many other regiments were present during the operations connected with the siege and capture of this fortress from the French, notably the Coldstream and Scots Guards. The losses of the two Battalions of Guards and of the Northamptons were far heavier than those of some of the regiments to whom the distinction of this battle honour has been granted.

CASUALTIES AT THE SIEGE AND CAPTURE OF CIUDAD RODRIGO.

Regiments.	Officers.		Men.		Regiments.	Officers.		Men.	
	K.	W.	K.	W.		K.	W.	K.	W.
Royal Artillery	—	2	1	19	45th Sherwood				
Roy. Engineers	1	5	—	2	Foresters ..	3	4	15	29
Coldstream Gds.	—	—	1	10	48th N'amptons	—	4	15	43
Scots Guards	—	—	4	17	52nd Oxford				
Northumber-					L.I. ..	1	5	7	52
land Fusiliers	1	8	35	58	King's Roy. R.	—	1	1	5
Roy. Fusiliers	—	—	2	8	74th Highland				
Royal Welsh					L.I. ..	—	4	5	17
Fusiliers ..	—	—	2	18	77th Middlesex	—	5	14	31
South Wales					83rd Roy. Irish				
Borderers ..	—	—	3	19	Rifles ..	—	2	10	31
40th S. Lancs	—	—	3	19	88th Connaught				
42nd Royal					Rangers ..	—	6	10	47
Highlanders	—	—	1	14	94th Connaught				
43rd Oxford					Rangers ..	2	7	11	51
L.I. ..	—	3	9	45	95th Rifle Brig.	—	6	9	47

NOTE.—The Coldstream and Scots Guards figure in the casualty returns for Ciudad Rodrigo, but do not bear the honour.

BADAJOZ, MARCH AND APRIL, 1812.

The losses incurred by the army under Wellington during the siege and at the assault of this fortress were most severe. The battle honour is borne by the

King's Own (Lancaster).
Royal Fusiliers.
Inniskilling Fusiliers.
South Staffords.
Oxford Light Infantry
Sherwood Foresters.
Middlesex.
Highland Light Infantry.
Connaught Rangers.

Northumberland Fusiliers.
Royal Welsh Fusiliers.
East Lancashire.
South Lancashire.
Essex.
Northamptons.
King's Royal Rifles.
Royal Irish Rifles.
Rifle Brigade.

In the year 1811 Wellington had made an unsuccessful attempt to seize Badajos, in which we suffered heavy loss. Now, with this fortress and Ciudad Rodrigo in his hands, the French were deprived of any rallying-point on the road to Madrid, and the English Commander-in-Chief at once opened a determined offensive campaign.

The gallantry displayed by our men at the assault are graphically described by Napier and by many contemporary historians, French and English ; it only remains for me to record the part played by each unit in the memorable siege.

CASUALTIES AT THE SIEGE AND ASSAULT OF BADAJOZ.

Regiments.	Officers.		Men.		Regiments.	Officers.		Men.	
	K.	W.	K.	W.		K.	W.	K.	W.
Royal Artillery	2	4	27	48	51st K. O. Yorks L.I.[1]	1	3	26	75
Roy. Engineers	3	7	5	21	52nd Oxford L.I. ..	5	16	66	295
Royal Scots ..	—	—	—	2					
K. O. Lancs. ..	2	15	40	173	King's Royal Rifles ..	1	4	6	37
Northumberland Fusiliers	1	4	20	55	74th Highland L.I. ..	2	11	20	104
Roy. Fusiliers	5	12	50	147	77th Middlesex	—	4	3	26
Royal Welsh Fusiliers ..	3	15	31	123	83rd Royal Irish Rifles	3	7	31	76
27th Roy. Inniskilling Fus.[1]	5	20	51	303	88th Connaught Rangers ..	5	10	55	180
30th E. Lancs	—	6	38	88	92nd Gordon Highlanders	—	1	—	—
38th S. Staffs	1	4	12	25	94th Connaught Rangers ..	1	3	14	77
40th S. Lancs[1]	2	24	83	387	97th W. Kent[1]	—	5	16	80
43rd Oxford L.I. ..	3	15	74	255	95th Rifle Brig.	8	16	61	297
44th Essex ..	2	7	37	88					
45th Sherwood Foresters ..	4	11	46	132					

SALAMANCA, JULY 22, 1812.

This was the first battle on a large scale ever fought by Wellington, and its name is borne on the colours and appointments of the

5th Dragoon Guards.	3rd Hussars.
4th Hussars.	11th Hussars.
14th Hussars.	16th Lancers.
Royal Scots.	Queen's.
King's Own.	Northumberland Fusiliers.
Royal Fusiliers.	Norfolks.

[1] These figures include the losses during the operations at Badajoz in 1811. The 51st and 97th were not present in 1812, so these regiments do not bear the battle honour " Badajoz."

Devons.	Royal Welsh Fusiliers.
South Wales Borderers.	Inniskilling Fusiliers.
Gloucesters.	Worcester.
East Lancashires.	Cornwall Light Infantry.
South Staffords.	South Lancashire.
Oxford Light Infantry.	Essex.
Sherwood Foresters.	Northamptons.
King's Own (Yorkshire Light Infantry).	Shropshire Light Infantry.
	King's Royal Rifles.
Durham Light Infantry.	Highland Light Infantry.
Cameron Highlanders.	Royal Irish Rifles.
Connaught Rangers.	Rifle Brigade.

CASUALTIES AT THE BATTLE OF SALAMANCA, JULY 22, 1812.

Regiments.	Officers.		Men.		Regiments.	Officers.		Men.	
	K.	W.	K.	W.		K.	W.	K.	W.
General Staff	2	5	—	—	43rd Oxford L.I. ..	—	1	1	15
5th Drag. Gds.	—	2	9	42	44th Essex ..	2	—	4	23
3rd Hussars ..	1	—	6	11	45th Sherwood				
4th Hussars ..	—	1	7	21	Foresters ..	—	5	5	45
12th Lancers	1	—	2	2	48th N'ampton	—	10	9	60
14th Hussars	—	—	1	7	51st K. O.				
16th Lancers	—	—	—	—	Yorks L.I.	—	—	—	2
Royal Artillery	—	—	2	6	52nd Oxford				
Coldstream Gds.	—	1	7	22	L.I. ..	—	—	—	2
Scots Guards	—	1	1	20	53rd Shropshire				
Royal Scots ..	—	8	23	131	L.I. ..	—	11	26	105
Queen's ..	1	6	13	77	58th N'ampton	—	—	—	3
K.O. Lancs. ..	—	1	2	40	60th K.R.R.	—	3	6	24
N'umberland F.	—	8	11	131	61st Gloucester	5	19	38	303
Royal Fusiliers	1	10	19	168	68th Durham				
Norfolk ..	—	1	3	42	L.I. ..	1	2	3	14
Devon	1	15	44	281	74th Highland				
Royal Welsh					L.I. ..	—	2	3	41
Fusiliers ..	1	6	9	90	79th Cameron				
27th Inniskil-					Highlanders	—	—	—	1
ling Fusiliers	—	1	1	7	83rd Roy. Irish				
30th E. Lancs	—	1	3	22	Rifles ..	—	2	13	30
32nd Cornwall					88th Connaught				
L.I. ..	2	9	15	111	Rangers ..	2	4	11	110
36th Worcester	4	4	16	74	94th Connaught				
38th S. Staffs	2	14	23	155	Rangers ..	1	3	3	21
40th S. Lancs	—	5	12	115	95th Rifle Brig.	—	—	3	24
42nd Bk. Watch	—	—	—	3					

NOTE.—It will be remarked that both the Coldstream and the Scots Guards figure in the casualty returns, but they have not been authorized to bear the honour.

In actual numbers the two armies were evenly matched, Wellington having some 42,000 men against an equal number of the French. There were, however, nearly 15,000 Portuguese in the allied army, and no one could assert that they were the equal of 15,000 British. The victory was complete. Our casualties, though severe, were little more than half of those sustained by the French, who lost upwards of 8,000 killed and wounded, whilst twelve cannon and two eagles remained in our hands. The road was now open to Madrid, and on August 12 Wellington entered that capital in triumph.

In the month of October came a damper in the shape of a decided reverse at Burgos, and the winter was spent by Wellington in reorganizing his forces for the final struggle in the coming summer. The French were heavily engaged in Eastern Europe, and Napoleon was unable to spare large bodies of men for the war in Spain. The stars in their courses were fighting for Wellington.

VITTORIA, JUNE 21, 1813.

This victory, which gave Wellington his baton of Field-Marshal, is borne on the colours of the

3rd Dragoon Guards.	5th Dragoon Guards.
3rd Hussars.	4th Hussars.
13th Hussars.	14th Hussars.
15th Hussars.	16th Lancers.
Royal Scots.	Queen's.
Buffs.	King's Own.
Northumberland Fusiliers.	Royal Warwicks.
Norfolk.	Royal Fusiliers.
Lancashire Fusiliers.	South Wales Borderers.
Royal Welsh Fusiliers.	Inniskilling Fusiliers.
Gloucesters.	East Lancashire.
East Surrey.	Border.
South Staffords.	Dorsets.
South Lancashire.	Oxford Light Infantry.
Sherwood Foresters.	Northamptons.
North Lancashire.	Royal Berkshires.
Royal West Kent.	King's Own (Yorkshire
Shropshire Light Infantry.	Light Infantry).
Middlesex.	King's Royal Rifles.
Durham Light Infantry.	Highland Light Infantry.
Gordon Highlanders.	Royal Irish Rifles.
Royal Irish Fusiliers.	Connaught Rangers.

Rifle Brigade.

CASUALTIES AT VITTORIA, JUNE 21, 1813.

Regiments.	Officers.		Men.		Regiments.	Officers.		Men.	
	K.	W.	K.	W.		K.	W.	K.	W.
General Staff	—	8	—	—	45th Sherwood Foresters ..	—	4	4	66
3rd Dragoon Guards ..	—	1	3	3	47th N. Lancs	2	4	18	88
5th Dragoon Guards ..	—	—	—	1	48th N'ampton	—	—	1	18
3rd Hussars ..	—	—	—	1	50th Roy. West Kent ..	—	7	27	70
10th Hussars	—	—	6	10	51st K. O. Yorks. L.I.	1	1	10	20
11th Hussars	—	1	—	—	52nd Oxford L.I.	1	1	3	18
12th Lancers	1	—	3	8	53rd Shropshire L.I. ..	—	—	4	6
13th Hussars	—	—	1	1	57th Middlesex	—	2	5	21
15th Hussars	—	2	10	47	59th E. Lancs	—	8	11	125
16th Hussars	—	2	7	12	60th K.R.R.	—	2	2	47
18th Hussars	1	2	10	21	66th Berkshire	—	1	2	22
Royal Artillery	—	1	9	53	68th Durham L.I. ..	2	10	23	91
Roy. Engineers	—	1	—	—	71st Highland L.I. ..	3	12	41	260
Royal Scots ..	—	7	8	96	74th Highland L.I. ..	—	5	13	64
King's Own Lancaster ..	2	6	11	72	82nd S. Lancs	1	3	5	22
Northumberland Fusiliers	2	6	22	132	83rd Royal Irish Rifles ..	3	4	32	74
Royal Fusiliers	—	—	2	2	87th Royal Irish Fusiliers	1	7	84	177
Lancs Fusiliers	—	—	3	1	88th Connaught Rangers ..	—	5	23	187
Royal Welsh Fusiliers ..	—	—	1	3	92nd Gordon Highlanders	—	—	4	16
27th Inniskilling Fusiliers	—	3	7	32	94th Connaught Rangers ..	—	7	5	59
28th Gloucester	—	17	12	171	95th Rifle Brig.	1	6	11	61
31st E. Surrey	—	1	1	13					
34th Border	—	3	10	63					
38th S. Staffs	—	2	—	6					
39th Dorset ..	—	8	28	181					
40th S. Lancs	—	3	5	34					
43rd Oxford L.I. ..	—	2	2	25					

In this battle Wellington, for the first time, had a decided superiority in numbers, having close on 80,000 men opposed to but 62,000 of the French ; but it must be conceded that the 20,000 Portuguese were by no means of the same value as 20,000 British infantry. The victory was undisputed. Practically the whole of the

French artillery—no less than 143 guns, with 1,000 prisoners—fell into our hands, and upwards of a million in treasure was the booty. The personal effects of King Joseph and an immense quantity of material was also taken. Our casualties amounted to more than 4,000 killed and wounded ; those of the French to upwards of 6,000.

Amongst the cavalry regiments which suffered losses at Vittoria, but which have not yet been authorized to assume the battle honour, are the 12th Lancers and 15th and 18th Hussars.[1]

PYRENEES, JULY 28 TO AUGUST 2, 1813.

This battle honour was granted as a distinction commemorative of the three days' hard fighting in the Pyrenees between July 28 and August 1, 1813. It is borne by the following regiments :

14th Hussars.	Queen's.
Buffs.	Royal Fusiliers.
Royal Warwicks.	Lancashire Fusiliers.
Devons.	South Wales Borderers.
Royal Welsh Fusiliers.	Gloucesters.
Royal Inniskilling Fusiliers.	East Surrey.
Worcesters.	Border.
Cornwall Light Infantry.	South Lancashire.
Dorsets.	Oxford Light Infantry.
Royal Highlanders.	Sherwood Foresters.
Northamptons.	Royal Berkshire.
Royal West Kent.	King's Own (Yorkshire
Middlesex.	Light Infantry).
Shropshire Light Infantry.	King's Royal Rifles.
Durham Light Infantry.	Highland Light Infantry.
Gordon Highlanders.	Cameron Highlanders.
Argyll Highlanders.	Rifle Brigade.

There were many reasons which compelled Wellington to refrain from prosecuting a vigorous pursuit after the decisive victory of Vittoria. The French were in possession of the two fortresses of Pampeluna and San Sebastian in the north, and they were far superior in numbers to the Allies in the south of the Peninsula. He pushed the

---

[1] The Household Cavalry do not bear the honour " Vittoria," nor do they figure in the casualty returns, but Lord Wellington, in submitting the medal rolls, included Major Camac of the 1st Life Guards, Captain Jackson of the 2nd Life Guards, and Major Packe of the Royal Horse Guards, as entitled to gold medals for having commanded their regiments in this battle.

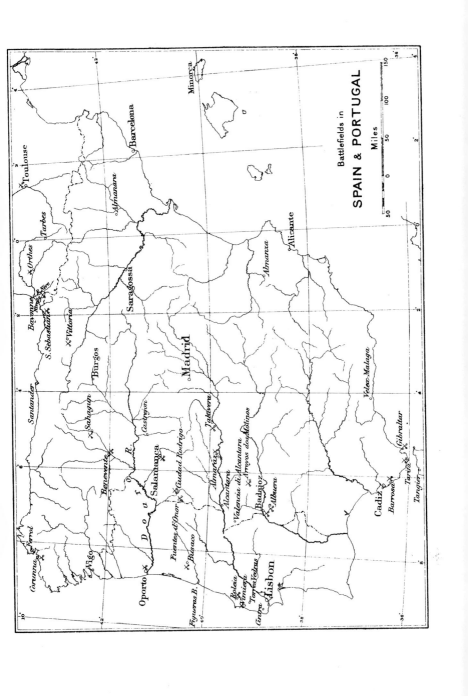

Battlefields in

SPAIN & PORTUGAL

Miles

Toulouse
Tarbes
Orthes
Bayonne
S.Sebastian
Vittoria
Santander
Sahagun
Burgos
Benevente
Corunna
Ferrol
Vigo
Oporto
Figueras B.
Busaco
Fuentes d'Onor
Ciudad Rodrigo
Salamanca
Castrejon
Madrid
Talavera
Almaraz
Alcantara
Valencia de Alcantara
Arroyos dos Molinos
Badajoz
Albuera
Roleia
Vimiero
Torres Vedras
Cintra
Lisbon
Saragossa
Almanara
Barcelona
Minorca
Almanza
Alicante
Velez Malaga
Gibraltar
Tarifa
Tangier
Cadiz
Barrosa
D o u r o   R.

enemy back slowly to the frontier, and at the same time he detached two of his own divisions, under Sir Thomas Graham, to reduce San Sebastian, whilst he entrusted the task of besieging Pampeluna to the Spaniards, resolving that, as soon as these two fortresses were in his possession, he would continue the work of expelling the French from the Peninsula. Emboldened by Lord Wellington's tactics, Soult turned and attacked the English at Roncesvalles and in the Maya Pass. At the latter engagement we were compelled to fall back, leaving some prisoners in the hands of the French ; but reinforcements coming up, Wellington resumed the offensive, and by August 1 had once more driven the French to the north of the Pyrenees. The fighting during these few days was excessively severe, our casualties amounting to upwards of 4,000 of all ranks killed and wounded.

CASUALTIES IN THE ACTIONS IN THE PYRENEES, JULY 25 TO AUGUST 2, 1813.

Regiments.	Officers.		Men.		Regiments.	Officers.		Men.	
	K.	W.	K.	W.		K.	W.	K.	W.
Royal Artillery	—	I	I	19	42nd Royal Highlanders	—	—	4	26
2nd Queen's ..	—	I	I	9	45th Derbysh.	—	I	—	7
3rd Buffs ..	I	I	3	27	48th N'amptons	2	10	12	109
6th Royal Warwicks ..	I	7	14	140	50th West Kent	3	12	30	198
7th Royal Fus.	I	10	52	187	51st K.O.L.I.	—	—	7	62
11th Devons ..	—	4	7	62	53rd Shrops.L.I.	—	I	I	20
20th Lancs Fusiliers ..	3	17	38	189	57th Middlesex	—	3	4	68
23rd Royal Welsh Fus.	3	8	23	85	58th N'ampton	—	6	10	61
					60th Royal R.	2	6	8	72
24th S. Wales Borderers ..	—	—	—	I	61st Gloucesters	—	4	3	38
27th Royal Inniskillings ..	3	11	58	228	68th Durham L.I. ..	I	3	8	41
28th Gloucester	I	6	9	121	71st Highland L.I. ..	2	7	28	181
31st E. Surrey	—	3	2	37	74th Highland L.I. ..	I	4	6	38
32nd Cornwall L.I. ..	—	4	4	51	79th Cameron H.	—	I	5	47
34th Border R.	I	5	48	122	82nd S. Lancs	4	6	17	146
36th Worcesters	—	3	8	35	91st H'landers	—	7	13	100
39th Dorsets ..	2	7	11	118	92nd Gordon Highlanders	—	26	55	363
40th S. Lancs	2	10	22	197	95th Rifle Brig.	—	2	7	28

San Sebastian, August, 1813.

On July 18, 1817, the following regiments were permitted to assume the battle honour for their services at the siege and capture of this fortress :

Royal Scots.
Norfolks.
South Staffords.

King's Own (Lancaster).
East Lancashire.
North Lancashire.

Immediately after the Battle of Vittoria, Lord Wellington detached two divisions to besiege this fortress, the possession of which was a necessary prelude to his further pursuit of the French. Unfortunately, our army was ill-provided with material for a siege, and two months were spent before the place was taken. Our losses during the siege and in the two assaults were very severe, as the accompanying casualty returns prove :

CASUALTIES AT THE SIEGE AND ASSAULT OF SAN SEBASTIAN, JULY AND AUGUST, 1813.

Regiments.	Officers.		Men.		Regiments.	Officers.		Men.	
	K.	W.	K.	W.		K.	W.	K.	W.
Royal Artillery	4	7	4	20	38th South Staffords	5	12	33	174
Roy. Engineers	3	3	14	111					
Coldstream Gds.	—	1	3	20	40th South Lancashires	—	1	3	8
Scots Guards ..	—	—	1	24					
Royal Scots ..	8	15	118	310	43rd Oxford L.I.	1	—	2	10
2nd Queen's ..	—	—	1	1					
4th K.O. Lancs.	5	6	117	170	47th Loy. North Lancs	7	6	106	130
7th Royal Fus.	—	—	—	6					
9th Norfolks ..	6	12	62	177	48th N. Staffs	—	1	4	1
20th Lancashire Fusiliers ..	1	1	2	9	52nd Oxford L.I.	1	2	1	7
23rd Roy. Welsh Fusiliers ..	—	1	4	4	53rd Shropshire L.I.	—	—	2	1
27th Roy. Inniskilling Fusiliers	1	—	5	2	59th E. Lancs	8	12	109	208
					95th Rifle Brig.	—	2	7	16

Nivelle, November 10, 1813.

The battle honour for this hard-fought action is borne by the

Queen's.
Northumberland Fusiliers.

Buffs.
Royal Warwicks.

Devons.	Royal Welsh Fusiliers.
South Wales Borderers.	Inniskilling Fusiliers.
Gloucesters.	Worcesters.
East Surrey.	Cornwall Light Infantry.
Border.	Dorsets.
South Lancashire.	Royal Highlanders.
Oxford Light Infantry.	Sherwood Foresters.
Northamptons.	Royal Berkshires.
King's Own (Yorkshire Light Infantry).	Shropshire Light Infantry.
	Middlesex.
King's Royal Rifles.	Durham Light Infantry.
Highland L. I.	Royal Irish Rifles.
Royal Irish Fusiliers.	Cameron Highlanders.
Argyll Highlanders.	Connaught Rangers.

Rifle Brigade.

CASUALTIES AT THE BATTLE OF THE NIVELLE, NOVEMBER 13, 1813.

Regiments.	Officers.		Men.		Regiments.	Officers.		Men.	
	K.	W.	K.	W.		K.	W.	K.	W.
General Staff	5	—	—	—	52nd Oxford L.I. ..	—	6	34	202
Royal Artillery	1	—	—	—	53rd Shropshire L.I. ..	—	1	3	20
12th Lancers	—	—	—	1	57th Middlesex	2	7	5	50
Coldstream Guards ..	—	1	—	9	58th N'ampton	—	—	—	3
2nd Queen's ..	—	—	2	26	59th E. Lancs	—	—	1	2
Buffs	—	1	3	8	King's Roy. R.	1	3	7	58
K.O. Lancs. ..	—	1	1	4	61st Gloucester	2	5	5	37
5th Northumberland Fus.	—	2	15	109	66th Berkshire	—	2	5	32
Roy. Warwicks	—	—	1	6	68th Durham L.I. ..	2	6	7	32
Devons ..	—	5	3	38	76th W. Riding	—	—	—	1
S. Wales Bord.	—	2	—	5	79th Cameron Highlanders	—	1	6	44
27th Inniskilling Fusiliers	1	3	9	51	82nd S. Lancs.	—	6	9	58
28th Gloucester	—	—	—	2	83rd Royal Irish Rifles ..	—	4	7	36
31st E. Surrey	—	1	1	13	84th York and Lancaster ..	—	—	2	5
34th Border R.	—	—	1	2	85th Shropshire L.I. ..	1	—	—	13
38th S. Staffs	—	2	—	2	87th Roy. Irish Fusiliers ..	1	5	74	133
39th Dorsets ..	—	—	1	5	91st Argyll Highlanders	1	6	13	105
40th S. Lancs	1	6	15	80	94th Connaught Rangers ..	1	2	10	60
42nd B. Watch	—	2	—	25	95th Rifle Brig.	—	8	11	76
43rd Oxford L.I. ..	2	9	6	60					
45th Sherwood Foresters ..	—	—	—	1					
48th N'amptons	—	4	7	57					
51st K. O. Yorks L.I. ..	2	2	22	73					

Wellington had made all his preparations for a general advance so soon as he should be in possession of the two fortresses of San Sebastian and Pampeluna. The former fell into our hands on August 31, but Pampeluna held out until the last days of October. Directly he was apprised of its fall, Wellington commenced his advance. Soult had profited by the delay, and had constructed three strongly entrenched positions, each of which was held with determination. The first has not been inscribed on our colours ; the second was on the banks of the River Nivelle, and before the French were driven from it Wellington had lost upwards of 1,200 men. It is worthy of note that, though the Coldstream Guards figure in the casualty return, they have not been awarded the battle honour of Nivelle.

NIVE, DECEMBER 9 TO 13, 1813.

This distinction is borne on the colours of the

16th Lancers.	Grenadier Guards.
Coldstream Guards.	Scots Guards.
Buffs.	Royal Scots.
Norfolk.	King's Own (Lancaster).
Gloucesters.	Devons.
East Lancashire.	Worcesters.
Cornwall Light Infantry.	East Surrey.
Border.	West Riding.
Dorset.	Royal Highlanders.
South Staffords.	Loyal North Lancashires.
Oxford Light Infantry.	Royal Berkshire.
West Kent.	Shropshire Light Infantry.
Middlesex.	King's Royal Rifles.
Wiltshires.	York and Lancaster.
Highland Light Infantry.	Gordon Highlanders.
Cameron Highlanders.	Argyll Highlanders.

Rifle Brigade.

This was Soult's last stand before he was driven across the frontier, and, as the casualty lists show, a very gallant stand did he make on those four December days. The heavy losses incurred by the Grenadier and Scots Guards failed to obtain for the Household Brigade this well-merited battle honour until the month of August, 1910, but full justice has not yet been done to the Brigade of Guards for its gallant services at Ciudad Rodrigo, Salamanca, and Sebastian.

CASUALTIES DURING THE CROSSING OF THE NIVE,
DECEMBER 9 TO 13, 1813.

Regiments.	Officers.		Men.		Regiments.	Officers.		Men.	
	K.	W.	K.	W.		K.	W.	K.	W.
General Staff	7	6	—	—	47th N. Lancs	—	2	12	53
Royal Artillery	—	—	2	15	50th West Kent	—	11	20	92
13th Hussars	—	—	—	3	52nd Oxford L.I. ..	—	3	2	15
14th Hussars	—	—	2	3	57th Middlesex	3	4	7	113
16th Lancers	—	—	2	5	59th E. Lancs	—	11	18	136
Grenadier Gds.	2	2	21	126	60th K.R.R. ..	—	2	9	76
Coldstream Gds.	—	1	—	13	61st Gloucesters	—	2	—	4
Scots Guards	1	3	7	54	66th Berkshire	—	1	9	68
Royal Scots ..	—	13	7	111	71st Highland L.I. ..	3	9	27	100
K.O. Lancs ..	—	15	13	154	76th W. Riding	—	—	1	15
Norfolk ..	2	6	26	160	79th Cameron Highlanders	—	1	5	26
Devons ..	—	1	1	16	84th York and Lancaster ..	2	6	24	100
28th Gloucester	—	5	13	129	85th K.O. Shrop. L.I.	—	1	1	11
31st E. Surrey	—	2	2	32	91st Argyll Highlanders	—	—	7	47
32nd Cornwall L.I. ..	—	—	2	5	92nd Gordon Highlanders	4	10	27	140
34th Border R.	—	—	1	12	95th Rifle Brig.	1	1	9	71
36th Worcesters	—	—	—	3					
38th S. Staffs	—	4	12	90					
39th Dorsets ..	—	1	3	26					
42nd B. Watch	2	1	—	11					
43rd Oxford L.I. ..	—	—	12	22					

ORTHES, FEBRUARY 27, 1814.

This, the first battle fought by Wellington on French soil, is borne on the colours of the

7th Hussars.
14th Hussars.
Northumberland Fusiliers.
Royal Fusiliers.
Lancashire Fusiliers.
South Wales Borderers.
Gloucesters.
East Surrey.
Cornwall Light Infantry.
South Lancashire.
Oxford Light Infantry.
Royal Highlanders.
Royal Berkshires.
King's Own (Yorkshire Light Infantry).
Royal Irish Fusiliers.

13th Hussars.
Buffs.
Royal Warwicks.
Devons.
Royal Welsh Fusiliers.
Inniskilling Fusiliers.
Worcesters.
Border.
Dorsets.
Royal Highlanders.
Sherwood Foresters.
Northamptons.
West Kent.
King's Royal Rifles.
Durham Light Infantry.
Highland Light Infantry.

Gordon Highlanders.

Royal Irish Rifles.   Royal Irish Fusiliers.
Connaught Rangers.   Argyll Highlanders.
Rifle Brigade.

The casualties fell heavily on the Sherwood Foresters and on the two Irish regiments which then bore the numbers 87th and 88th.

CASUALTIES AT THE BATTLE OF ORTHES, FEBRUARY 27, 1814.

Regiments.	Officers.		Men.		Regiments.	Officers.		Men.	
	K.	W.	K.	W.		K.	W.	K.	W.
General Staff	—	6	—	—	52nd Oxford L.I. ..	—	6	7	76
7th Hussars ..	—	3	4	6	58th N'ampton	—	3	3	25
10th Hussars	—	—	—	1	King's Roy. R.	—	2	3	31
13th Hussars	—	1	2	15	61st Gloucesters	—	—	1	6
14th Hussars	—	—	—	2	68th Durham				
15th Hussars	—	—	—	9	L.I. ..	—	1	3	27
Royal Artillery	1	1	3	23	74th Highland				
Roy. Engineers	1	—	—	—	L.I. ..	—	5	8	21
N'umberland F.	1	—	5	31	82nd S. Lancs	—	2	2	24
Roy. Warwick	2	8	24	111	83rd Roy. Irish				
Royal Fusiliers	—	4	6	56	Rifles ..	—	6	11	47
Lancs Fusiliers	2	6	16	97	87th Roy. Irish				
Roy. Welsh F.	—	3	16	75	Fusiliers ..	1	5	92	166
27th Royal In-					88th Connaught				
niskilling F.	—	1	1	4	Rangers ..	2	11	41	214
40th S. Lancs	—	—	1	4	91st Argyll				
42nd B. Watch	1	4	4	90	Highlanders	—	7	3	27
45th Sherwood					94th Connaught				
Foresters ..	1	9	14	106	Rangers ..	—	1	1	12
48th N'ampton	—	—	1	13					

NOTE.—In following up the retreating French the army had been sharply engaged on February 14, 17, 23, and 26, and subsequently to Orthes. A general action was fought at Tarbes on March 20, 1814, the brunt of the work falling on the Rifle Brigade.

TOULOUSE, APRIL 10, 1814.

This, the closing action of the Peninsular War, was fought after the abdication of Napoleon, and was the final act of the campaign which Sir Arthur Wellesley opened at the combat of Roleia on August 17, 1808. There are ten regiments which bear on their colours the names of the earliest and the last engagements, Roleia and Toulouse. Of these, only five suffered any loss in both engagements. The King's Royal Rifles, Highland

Light Infantry, and Rifle Brigade take pride of place, each having fifteen Peninsular battle honours on their appointments. Those to whom the battle honour " Toulouse " has been awarded are the

5th Dragoon Guards.	3rd Hussars.
4th Hussars.	13th Hussars.
Queen's.	Buffs.
Northumberland Fusiliers.	Royal Fusiliers.
Devons.	Lancashire Fusiliers.
Royal Welsh Fusiliers.	Inniskilling Fusiliers.
Gloucesters.	Worcesters.
South Lancashire.	Royal Highlanders.
Oxford Light Infantry.	Sherwood Foresters.
Northamptons.	Shropshire Light Infantry.
King's Royal Rifles.	Highland Light Infantry.
Cameron Highlanders.	Royal Irish Rifles.
Connaught Rangers.	Argyll Highlanders.

Rifle Brigade.

CASUALTIES AT THE BATTLE OF TOULOUSE, APRIL 10, 1814.

Regiments.	Officers.		Men.		Regiments.	Officers.		Men.	
	K.	W.	K.	W.		K.	W.	K.	W.
General Staff	—	3	—	—	48th N'ampton	—	4	5	39
5th Drag. Gds.	—	1	1	2	50th W. Kent	—	2	2	8
3rd Hussars ..	—	1	—	5	52nd Oxford L.I.				
4th Hussars ..	—	1	2	5	L.I.	—	—	—	5
10th Hussars	1	1	4	6	53rd Shropshire				
15th Hussars	—	—	—	4	L.I. (two cos.)	—	5	2	14
Royal Artillery	—	—	7	31	60th K.R.R. ..	—	3	11	48
Queen's (four					61st Gloucesters	1	18	16	140
companies)	—	—	—	12	71st Highland				
N'umberland F.	—	—	—	3	L.I. ..	—	—	3	13
Royal Fusiliers	—	—	1	3	74th Highland				
Devon ..	1	4	14	121	L.I. ..	—	7	32	72
Lancs Fusiliers	—	—	2	9	79th Cameron H.	3	15	26	179
Roy. Welsh F.	—	—	1	7	83rd Roy. Irish				
27th Inniskilling Fusiliers	2	5	23	76	Rifles ..	—	—	—	1
28th Gloucesters	—	3	3	25	87th Roy. Irish				
34th Border R.	—	1	2	11	Fusiliers ..	1	2	7	17
36th Worcester	1	9	38	104	88th Connaught				
39th Dorsets ..	—	1	—	4	Rangers ..		2	7	76
40th S. Lancs	—	8	7	71	91st Argyll				
42nd B. Watch	4	22	50	337	Highlanders	—	6	18	98
45th Sherwood					94th Connaught				
Foresters ..	1	8	7	72	Rangers ..	—	—	1	5
					95th Rifle Brig.	—	1	10	75

In this fight the 42nd (Royal Highlanders) was wellnigh annihilated.

PENINSULA, 1808-1814.

The following regiments bear this battle honour :

1st Life Guards.
Royal Horse Guards.
4th Dragoon Guards.
1st Royal Dragoons.
4th Hussars.
9th Lancers.
11th Hussars.
13th Hussars.
15th Hussars.
18th Hussars.
Grenadier Guards.
Scots Guards.
Queen's (Royal West Surrey).
K.O. (Royal Lancaster).
Royal Warwicks.
Norfolk.
Devons.
Royal Welsh Fusiliers.
Royal Inniskilling Fusiliers.
Worcester.
East Surrey.
West Riding.
South Staffordshire.
Dorset.
Black Watch.
Essex.
Loyal North Lancashire.
Royal Berkshire.
K.O. (Yorkshire L.I.).
Middlesex.
Wiltshire.
York and Lancaster.
Highland L.I.
Cameron Highlanders.
Royal Irish Fusiliers.
Argyll Highlanders.

2nd Life Guards.
3rd Dragoon Guards.
5th Dragoon Guards.
3rd Hussars.
7th Hussars.
10th Hussars.
12th Lancers.
14th Hussars.
16th Lancers.
20th Hussars.
Coldstream Guards.
Royal Scots.
Buffs.
Northumberland Fusiliers.
Royal Fusiliers.
Lincoln.
Lancashire Fusiliers.
South Wales Borderers.
Gloucester.
East Lancashire.
Cornwall Light Infantry.
Border.
Hampshire.
South Lancashire.
Oxford Light Infantry.
Sherwood Foresters.
Northampton.
Royal West Kent.
King's (Shropshire L.I.).
King's Royal Rifles.
Manchester.
Durham L.I.
Gordon Highlanders.
Royal Irish Rifles.
Connaught Rangers.
Rifle Brigade.

ROLL OF THE PRINCIPAL ACTIONS DURING THE PENINSULAR WAR.

Action.	Date.	Officers. K.	Officers. W.	Men. K.	Men. W.	Honours.
Roleia	1808. August 17	4	20	65	315	Medal, clasp, and battle honour.
Vimiera	,, August 21	4	37	185	497	,, ,, and battle honour.
Sahagun	,, December 21	—	—	2	18	,, ,, No battle honour.
Benevente	,, December 29	?	3	5	23	,, ,, battle honour.
Corunna	1809. January 16	?	?	?	?	Medal, clasp, and battle honour.
Douro	,, May 24	—	10	23	86	No medal or clasp. Battle honour.
Talavera	,, July 27	27	171	643	3,295	Medal, clasp, and battle honour.
Busaco	1810. September 27	5	35	102	408	,, ,, ,,
Barrosa	1811. March 4	7	45	182	881	,, ,, ,,
Fuentes d'Onor	,, May 5	11	62	157	576	,, ,, ,,
Albuera	,, May 16	39	165	850	2,567	,, ,, ,,
Arroyos dos Molinos	,, October 28	—	7	7	51	No medal or clasp. Battle honour.
Tarifa	,, December	2	3	7	24	,, ,, ,,
Ciudad Rodrigo	1812. January	8	60	122	436	Medal, clasp, and battle honour.
Badajos	,, March, April	60	269	751	2,539	,, ,, ,,
Almaraz	,, May 19	2	12	32	131	No medal or clasp. Battle honour.
Salamanca	,, July 22	28	178	360	2,536	Medal, clasp, and battle honour.
Vittoria	1813. June 21	22	173	490	2,704	,, ,, ,,
Pyrenees	,, July, August	28	221	510	3,295	,, ,, ,,
San Sebastian	,, September	35	70	535	1,038	,, ,, ,,
Nivelle	,, November 10	21	121	237	1,031	,, ,, ,,
Nive	,, December 9-13	19	140	200	2,055	,, ,, ,,
Orthes	1814. February 27	15	105	192	1,291	,, ,, ,,
Toulouse	,, April 10	16	134	298	1,661	,, ,, ,,

CHAPTER XII

WATERLOO, AND THE ORDER OF THE BATH
FOR THE NAPOLEONIC WARS

WATERLOO, JUNE 18, 1815.

THIS victory, generally considered the most glorious ever gained by British troops, was commemorated in divers manner. The first regiments of Guards were allowed to assume the title of Grenadiers ; all who participated were granted a medal bearing the effigy of the Prince Regent— the first medal ever given to all ranks by the British Government—and were permitted to count two years' service towards pension ; and the word " Waterloo " was inscribed on the colours and appointments of the following regiments :

1st Life Guards.	2nd Life Guards.
Royal Horse Guards.	1st Dragoon Guards.
Royal Dragoons.	Royal Scots Greys.
Inniskilling Dragoons.	7th Hussars.
10th Hussars.	11th Hussars.
12th Lancers.	13th Hussars.
15th Hussars.	16th Lancers.
18th Hussars.	Grenadier Guards.
Coldstream Guards.	Scots Guards.
Royal Scots.	King's Own Royal Lancasters.
West Yorkshire.	Royal Welsh Fusiliers.
Royal Inniskilling Fusiliers.	Gloucesters.
East Lancashire.	Cornwall Light Infantry.
West Riding Regiment.	South Lancashire.
Welsh.	Royal Highlanders.
Oxford Light Infantry.	Essex.
King's Own (Yorkshire Light Infantry).	Highland Light Infantry.
	Gordon Highlanders.
Cameron Highlanders.	Rifle Brigade.

The story of the Battle of Waterloo has been described in the minutest detail by the most accomplished military

THE DUKE OF WELLINGTON.

To face page 192.

historians in Great Britain, Germany, and France, so that nothing remains to be told on this head. As is well known, Napoleon, worn down by the successive campaigns which had been waged against him in Europe and in Spain, had at last abdicated, and was relegated to honourable exile in the Island of Elba. In the early spring of 1815 he violated his engagements, and returned to France, where the majority of his soldiery flocked to his standard. The Allies once more mobilized their armies, and prepared for war. Whilst Austria and Russia were advancing from the east, the armies of Prussia and of Great Britain pushed forward from the north. Napoleon endeavoured to defeat these before the arrival of the Russians and Austrians on his frontier. On June 16 he simultaneously attacked the Prussians at Ligny and Wellington at Quatre-Bras. The Prussians were undoubtedly worsted, and we at the best fought a very doubtful action at Quatre-Bras. The Allies then fell back, and it was agreed that a further stand should be made at Waterloo. Circumstances arose which prevented Blücher from arriving on the field as soon as was anticipated, and for four long hours the small British army withstood the onset of the whole of Napoleon's forces ; then, early in the afternoon, the effect of the Prussian advance on our left began to be felt, and as the divisions of our allies came successively into action, the success of the day was no more in doubt. By sundown the battle was won, the French in full retreat, and Napoleon's sun had set for ever.

The vexed question of the relative part played by the Prussians and ourselves will never be settled to the satisfaction of all. One point in regard to this question has, in my humble opinion, never been sufficiently brought out. The Prussian army was virtually an army of mercenaries, kept in the field by the large subsidies so generously voted by the English Parliament. It is true that we might have held our own without the arrival of the Prussians, but it is quite certain that we should never have inflicted the crushing defeat had not Blücher

13

arrived—not so opportunely, as some writers assert, but according to his promise. Then, we know that the battle was a part of the prearranged plan between the Duke of Wellington and Prince Blücher. This, however, is beyond all doubt—that had it not been for the generous subsidies voted to Prussia by the English Parliament, amounting to 3,000,000 sterling, in the years 1814-15, there would have been no Prussian army to assist us. Throughout the wars with Napoleon, Austria, Prussia, and Russia received large sums to enable them to keep their armies in the field. It was not only the King's German Legion which was paid with English gold, but the Prussian army also ; and when the Germans taunt the British army with being an army of mercenaries, it would be well for them to study the financial conditions under which they fought in the wars with France in the eighteenth and nineteenth centuries. The following figures, showing the pecuniary assistance afforded by England to her allies, are of passing interest :

	AUSTRIA.	PRUSSIA.	RUSSIA.
1814	£545,612	£1,757,669	£1,758,436
1815	£1,475,632	£2,555,473	£1,330,171
1816	£1,796,229	£2,382,823	£3,241,919

CASUALTIES DURING THE WATERLOO CAMPAIGN.

Regiments.	QUATRE-BRAS (JUNE 16).				(JUNE 17).				WATERLOO (JUNE 18).			
	Officers.		Men.		Officers.		Men.		Officers.		Men.	
	K.	W.	K.	W.	K.	W.	K.	W.	K.	W.	K.	W.
1st Life Guards	—	—	—	—	—	1	8	9	2	3	16	39
2nd Life Guards	—	—	—	—	—	—	—	—	1	—	16	40
Royal Horse Gds.	—	—	—	—	—	—	3	5	1	4	16	56
King's Drag. Gds.	—	—	—	—	—	—	—	—	3	4	40	100
Royal Dragoons	—	—	1	—	—	—	—	—	4	9	85	88
Roy. Scots Greys	—	—	—	—	—	—	—	—	3	8	96	89
6th Inniskillings	—	—	—	—	—	—	—	—	1	5	72	111

CASUALTIES DURING THE WATERLOO CAMPAIGN—*Continued.*

Regiments.	QUATRE-BRAS (JUNE 16). Officers.		Men.		JUNE 17. Officers.		Men.		WATERLOO (JUNE 18). Officers.		Men.	
	K.	W.	K.	W.	K.	W.	K.	W.	K.	W.	K.	W.
7th Hussars	—	—	—	—	1	—	6	21	—	6	56	96
10th Hussars	—	—	—	—	—	—	—	—	2	5	20	40
11th Hussars	—	1	—	—	—	—	—	—	1	4	11	34
12th Lancers	—	—	—	—	—	—	—	—	2	4	45	61
13th Hussars	—	—	—	—	—	—	—	—	1	9	11	69
15th Hussars	—	—	—	—	—	—	—	—	2	3	21	48
16th Lancers	—	—	—	—	—	—	—	—	2	3	18	18
18th Hussars	—	1	1	—	—	—	—	—	—	2	12	71
Royal Artillery	—	2	9	17	—	—	—	—	5	24	53	211
Royal Engineers	—	—	—	—	—	—	—	—	—	—	—	—
Grenadier Guards (1st Batt.)	2	4	23	256	—	—	—	—	1	5	50	96
Grenadier Guards (3rd Batt.)	1	6	19	235	—	—	—	—	3	6	81	245
Coldstream Gds.	—	—	—	—	—	—	—	—	1	7	54	242
Scots Guards	—	—	—	7	—	—	—	—	3	9	39	288
Royal Scots	6	12	20	180	—	—	—	—	2	13	13	115
4th King's Own	—	—	—	—	—	—	—	—	—	8	12	113
14th West Yorks	—	—	—	—	—	—	—	—	—	1	7	21
23rd R. Welsh F.	—	—	—	—	—	—	—	—	4	6	11	78
27th Inniskill. F.	—	—	—	—	—	—	—	—	2	13	103	360
28th Gloucesters	—	4	11	60	—	—	—	—	1	15	18	143
30th East Lancs	—	2	5	28	—	—	1	2	6	12	47	157
32nd Cornw. L.I.	1	16	21	152	—	—	—	—	—	9	28	137
33rd W. Riding	3	7	16	67	—	—	—	3	2	9	33	92
40th S. Lancs	—	—	—	—	—	—	—	—	2	10	30	159
42nd Roy. Highl.	3	14	42	228	—	—	—	—	—	6	5	39
44th Essex	2	15	10	94	—	—	—	—	—	4	4	57
51st King's Own Yorkshire L.I.	—	—	—	—	—	—	—	—	—	2	9	20
52nd Oxford L.I.	—	—	—	—	—	—	—	—	1	8	16	174
69th Welsh	1	4	37	110	—	—	—	3	3	3	14	50
71st Highland L.I.	—	—	—	—	—	—	—	—	2	14	24	160
73rd Roy. Highl.	—	4	4	43	1	—	3	—	5	12	47	175
79th Camerons	1	16	28	248	—	—	—	—	2	11	39	132
92nd Gordons	4	20	35	226	—	—	—	—	—	6	14	96
95th Rifle Brigade (1st Batt.)	1	4	8	51	—	—	—	—	1	11	20	124
95th Rifle Brigade (2nd Batt.)	—	—	—	—	—	—	—	—	—	14	34	179
95th Rifle Brigade (3rd Batt.)	—	—	—	—	—	—	—	—	—	4	3	36

The Order of the Bath.

At the close of the Peninsular War, the Order of the
Bath, which up till then had consisted of but one class
(the K.B.), was enlarged, and henceforth comprised three
classes, as at present.   The First Class, or Knight's Grand
Cross, was reserved for General and Flag Officers ; the
Second Class was open to officers not below the rank of
Post-Captain in the navy or Lieutenant-Colonel in the
army.   In order to obtain the Third Class of the Bath,
better known as the C.B., an officer must have been
mentioned in despatches for service in presence of the
enemy.   This qualification does not apply to the two
higher classes, and it has happened more than once that
officers have received the Grand Cross of the Bath who,
under its statutes, are ineligible for the lowest class !
The number of K.C.B.'s was limited to 180, and of these,
80 were bestowed on the Royal Navy and Royal Marines,
and 100 on the army, in the following proportion as to
ranks : 19 Admirals and 9 Lieutenant-Generals were
granted the Order ; 23 Vice and 25 Rear Admirals ; and
37 Major-Generals, 19 Post-Captains, and 22 Colonels ;
whilst 32 Lieutenant-Colonels commanding regiments or
Staff Officers received the same Order.   Three officers of
Marines were likewise granted the Order of the K.C.B.
It is very rare now for a regimental commanding officer,
still rarer for a Post-Captain, to obtain admission to the
Second Class of the Bath.

I think I am right in stating that the late Sir William
Peel and Sir Harry Keppel were the last Post-Captains
who obtained this distinction.   Sir Robert Sale and Sir
Harry Smith were actually Lieutenant-Colonels of the
13th Light Infantry and of the Rifle Brigade respectively
when they were advanced to the dignity of Grand Crosses
of the Bath, but they held the local rank of Major-General
in the East Indies.   The latter was almost immediately
promoted to the rank of substantive General Officer ;
the former was killed before reaching the higher grade.

The Battle of Waterloo was the first engagement for which the C.B. was granted.   It is true that in the same *Gazette* a number of officers received the decoration for their services in the Peninsular War, and of these not a few also appeared in the Waterloo *Gazette* with a star against their names, intimating that they had received the decoration for previous services.   The list of officers granted the dignity of K.C.B. was published in the *Gazette* of January 2, 1815 ; but the C.B.'s, both for the Peninsula and for Waterloo, appeared in the *Gazette* of September 4, 1815.

The following list gives the number of decorations conferred regimentally.   It will be noticed that a number of regiments do not figure in the list at all.   On the other hand, a number of regiments which participated in these honours have long since ceased to exist, amongst them the well-known King's German Legion and the little-known Greek Light Infantry.   Of these I have not given the details.

THE FIRST REGIMENTAL RECIPIENTS OF THE BATH.

| Regiments. | Peninsula. | | Waterloo. |
	K.C.B.	C.B.	C.B.
2nd Life Guards	—	—	1
Royal Horse Guards	1	—	1
King's Dragoon Guards	—	—	1
5th Dragoon Guards	—	1	—
7th Dragoon Guards	—	1	—
1st Royal Dragoons	—	—	1
Royal Scots Greys	—	—	2
3rd Hussars	—	1	—
7th Hussars	—	1	—
9th Lancers	—	1	—
10th Hussars	—	1	—
11th Hussars	—	1	—
12th Lancers	—	1	—
Royal Artillery	9	8	8
Royal Engineers	—	10	2
Grenadier Guards	6	4	6
Coldstream Guards	5	5	4

Regiments.	Peninsula.		Waterloo.
	K.C.B.	C.B.	C.B.
Scots Guards	2	4	2
Royal Scots	2	2	3
4th King's Own	—	3	—
5th Northumberland Fusiliers	1	2	—
6th Royal Warwicks ..	—	2	—
7th Royal Fusiliers	1	2	1
8th King's Liverpool Regiment	—	2	—
9th Norfolks	1	—	—
10th Lincolns	—	1	—
11th Devons	—	2	—
12th Suffolks	—	2	—
13th Somerset Light Infantry	1	—	—
14th West Yorkshires	—	3	1
21st Royal Scots Fusiliers ..	—	1	—
23rd Royal Welsh Fusiliers ..	2	4	2
24th South Wales Borderers ..	—	1	—
27th Royal Inniskilling Fus.	1	3	1
28th Gloucesters	1	1	2
30th East Lancashires.. ..	—	1	3
31st East Surreys	1	1	—
32nd Cornwall Light Infantry	—	1	1
33rd Duke of Wellington's ..	—	—	1
34th Border Regiment ..	—	2	—
35th Royal Sussex	1	1	—
36th Worcesters	—	3	—
38th South Staffords	1	3	—
39th Dorsets	—	2	—
40th South Lancashires ..	—	2	1
42nd Royal Highlanders ..	2	3	2
43rd Oxford Light Infantry ..	—	2	—
44th Essex	—	1	3
45th Sherwood Foresters ..	—	3	—
48th Northamptons	—	3	—
49th Royal Berkshires ..	—	1	—
50th Royal West Kent ..	—	3	—
51st King's Own Yorkshire L.I.	—	1	3
52nd Oxford Light Infantry ..	1	5	1
53rd Shropshire Light Infantry	1	1	—.
54th Dorsetshire	—	1	—
56th Essex	—	1	—
57th Middlesex	—	1	—
58th Northamptons ..	—	1	—
59th South Lancashire ..	—	2	—
60th King's Royal Rifles ..	—	4	—
62nd Wiltshire	—	1	—

Regiments.	Peninsula.		Waterloo.
	K.C.B.	C.B.	C.B.
66th Royal Berkshire	—	2	—
68th Durham Light Infantry	—	2	—
69th Welsh	—	1	—
71st Highland Light Infantry	—	2	2
73rd Royal Highlanders ..	—	—	2
74th Highland Light Infantry	1	1	—
77th Middlesex	—	2	—
78th Ross-shire Buffs	—	2	—
79th Cameron Highlanders ..	—	1	2
83rd Royal Irish Rifles ..	1	1	—
85th King's Shropshire L.I. ..	—	1	—
86th Royal Irish Rifles ..	—	1	—
87th Royal Irish Fusiliers ..	—	2	—
88th Connaught Rangers ..	—	3	—
89th Royal Irish Fusiliers ..	—	2	—
90th Scottish Rifles	—	1	—
91st Argyll Highlanders ..	1	—	—
92nd Gordon Highlanders ..	—	—	2
94th Connaught Rangers ..	—	1	—
Rifle Brigade	2	6	8

No regimental officers were granted the dignity of a
K.C.B. for the Battle of Waterloo.

CHAPTER XIII

BATTLE HONOURS FOR SERVICES IN INDIA, 1818-1826

Kirkee — Seetabuldee — Nagpore — Maheidpore — Corygaum — Nowah—Bhurtpore—Hindoostan—India.

THE SECOND MAHRATTA WAR, 1817-18.

THE conclusion of the First Mahratta War of 1803-04 left us nominally at peace with all the ruling Sovereigns in Central and Southern India. At the same time, the result of that campaign had in no way impaired their power for evil. Their armies were, so far as numbers went, enormously powerful, and in a measure well organized and equipped. In most cases they had been drilled by European instructors, and certainly for irregular warfare they constituted a very formidable foe. Although they had accepted peace, it was well known that there was not a ruling Prince in India who would not willingly see our downfall ; and in the event of war with one, it was doubtful who we should not find arrayed against us. The Governor-General, then, had to prepare for an alliance of all the central and probably of one or more of the southern rulers. Our possible enemies were the Peishwa, the hereditary chief of the Mahratta Confederacy ; Scindia, the Maharajah of Gwalior ; Holkar, the Maharajah of Indore; the Maharajah of Nagpore; the Nizam of Hyderabad, in whose dominions there was considerable disaffection ; Ameer Khan, a Moslem freebooter, who, though possessing neither territory nor population, had nevertheless a powerful and well-disciplined force at his command ; and, lastly, the Pindarees.

It must be borne in mind that at this time we had Subsidiary Forces, composed of native troops, maintained by the different rulers, but officered by Englishmen, at Hyderabad, Nagpore, Poona, and Gwalior ; and through these officers, as well as through the Residents at the Courts of these Princes, we were well able to judge of the numbers and value of the forces that could be brought against us. These forces were estimated to be as follows :

	CAVALRY.	INFANTRY.	GUNS.
Scindia ..	14,250	16,250	140
Holkar ..	20,000	7,900	107
The Peishwa	28,000	13,800	37
Nagpore	15,700	17,000	85
Ameer Khan	12,000	10,000	80
The Nizam	25,000	20,000	240
Pindarees	15,000	1,500	20

With but few exceptions, the cavalry was undisciplined and unorganized, but well mounted, and the men as a rule admirable swordsmen. To combat this possible alliance, the Marquess of Hastings determined to utilize the troops of all three Presidencies, and to take the field in person, and so assume the direction of the operations. The Bengal army would deal with Scindia, and then push to the south and west to assist the troops of the other Presidencies. The Madras troops, with Secunderabad as their base, after assuring the neutrality of the Nizam, would operate from the south, whilst the Bombay army was left to deal with the Peishwa, whose disaffection was beyond doubt.

The Bengal army was composed of four divisions, under the personal command of the Marquess of Hastings. These were commanded respectively by Major-Generals Browne, Donkin, Marshal, and Sir David Ochterlony. Each division comprised one cavalry and two infantry brigades. Of the troops which composed that army, few

regiments are left. The 24th Light Dragoons were disbanded shortly after the campaign, and the majority of
the native regiments fell away from their allegiance in
the unfortunate rebellion of 1857. Of the regiments
which went to make up the First Division, the 87th
(Royal Irish Fusiliers) still survive ; of the Second
Division, the 8th (Royal Irish) Hussars, the 14th (West
Yorkshires), and Gardner's Horse are yet on the rolls of
the army. The 67th (Hampshires) and the 2nd Gurkhas,
with Skinner's Horse, also survive.

The Madras army was under the command of Lieutenant-General Sir Thomas Hislop. Of its cavalry
brigade no representatives remain ; of its four infantry
brigades we have many survivors—first and foremost,
the Royal Scots and the Royal Dublin Fusiliers ; then the
1st Madras Europeans, which, with the 17th Madras
Infantry (now the 93rd Burmah Infantry), composed
the First Brigade. The Second Brigade was made up of
three light infantry regiments (native), of which the
63rd Palamcottah Light Infantry and the 74th Punjabis are with us. There were, all told, two regiments
of British and six of native infantry.

The Hyderabad Division, commanded by Major-General
Doveton, comprised a battalion of the Royal Scots and
ten regiments of Madras infantry ; whilst the Hyderabad
Subsidiary Brigade was made up of a wing of the 1st
Madras Europeans (now the Royal Dublins) and three
native regiments. Sir John Malcolm commanded the
Third Division of the Madras army. It comprised a
regiment of Madras cavalry, four battalions of Madras
infantry, 4,000 Mysorean horse, and three regiments of
what were so long known as the Hyderabad Contingent.

In the neighbourhood of Poonah was Sir Lionel Smith,
with the 65th (York and Lancasters), the 1st Bombay
Europeans (now the 2nd Royal Dublins), and four regiments of Bombay infantry.

Watching events in Guzerat was General Sir H. Grant
Keir, with the 17th Lancers, the 47th (Loyal North Lancashires), and four battalions of Bombay native infantry ;

whilst at Nagpore was Colonel Adams, with a regiment of Bengal and one of Madras cavalry, and seven battalions of Madras infantry.

Reserve Bombay Division (Brigadier Munro) : 22nd Light Dragoons, 7th Madras Cavalry, a battalion composed of the flank companies of the 34th, 53rd, 69th, and 84th Regiments, the 1st Bombay European Regiment, and three battalions of Bombay sepoys.

Prior to the army being put in motion, we had as garrisons at the various capitals, or in their immediate vicinity, the following troops :

At Secunderabad, watching the Nizam, a wing of the Madras European Regiment and three battalions of Madras sepoys.

At Poonah, watching the Peishwa, a detachment of the Bombay European Regiment and four battalions of Bombay sepoys, whilst another detachment of the 65th Foot (York and Lancaster) was on the march as a reinforcement.

At Nagpore were the 6th Bengal Cavalry, the Madras Bodyguard, and two battalions of sepoys.

KIRKEE, NOVEMBER 5, 1817.

This honour is borne on the colours of the

Royal Dublin Fusiliers.	102nd Grenadiers.
113th Infantry.	112th Infantry.
123rd Outram's Rifles.	

The attitude of the Peishwa's advisers left little room for doubt as to their intentions, and Colonel Burr, who was in command at Poona, took the necessary steps to secure the safety of the Resident and to maintain a hold on the capital of the Mahratta Confederacy. He concentrated his forces at Kirkee, where on November 5 he was attacked by the whole of the Peishwa's army. From a study of the casualties, it would appear that the British regiment was not engaged seriously, and there is no doubt that the brunt of the fighting fell on the Bombay sepoys, who behaved with exemplary steadiness. The result of the day was a serious check to the Peishwa's forces, our losses being inconsiderable. General Lionel Smith now pushed up reinforcements, and assumed command at Poona, where, on the 17th of the month, a second action was fought, known as the Battle of Poona; and though this is not borne on the colours of the regiments engaged, the troops present were awarded the India medal, with a clasp inscribed " Poona." Those who were at both engagements received one clasp, with the names of both actions engraved.

CASUALTIES AT THE ACTION AT KIRKEE, NOVEMBER 5, 1817.

Regiments.	Officers.		Men.		Regiments.	Officers.		Men.	
	K.	W.	K.	W.		K.	W.	K.	W.
Royal Artillery	—	—	—	2	112th Infantry	—	—	4	10
Dublin Fusiliers	—	—	1	1	113th Infantry	—	—	12	37
102nd Grena-					123rd Outram's				
diers	—	1	1	8	Rifles ..	—	—	1	7

CASUALTIES AT THE ACTION AT POONA, NOVEMBER 17, 1817.

Regiments.	Officers.		Men.		Regiments.	Officers.		Men.	
	K.	W.	K.	W.		K.	W.	K.	W.
Royal Artillery	—	—	—	4	105th Lt. Inf.	—	—	1	10
65th York and					107th Pioneers	—	—	2	4
Lancaster ..	—	—	—	2	112th Infantry	—	—	2	7
Dublin Fusiliers	—	1	5	13	113th Infantry	—	—	3	10

SEETABULDEE, NOVEMBER 26, 1817.

This distinction is borne on the colours and appointments of the Madras Bodyguard and the 61st Pioneers. Colonel Hopeton Scott, who was in command of the troops at Nagpore when hostilities broke out, withdrew his force to the fortified hill of Seetabuldee, in the immediate neighbourhood of Nagpore. He was more for-

tunately situated than Colonel Burr at Poona, inasmuch
as he had under his command a regiment of Bengal
cavalry, whose commanding officer was one of those
men not rarely met with in our Indian army—a born
leader of irregular troops, with no idea of shirking responsibility. On November 26 Colonel Scott found
himself attacked by the whole of the Nagpore army,
numbering some 18,000 men, with thirty-six guns. His
position was naturally a strong one, and the attacks were
never pressed home ; but his situation was critical, owing
to the immense numbers opposed to his small force. The
Bengal cavalry were by no means averse to testing the
metal of the Nagporeans, and, in spite of express orders
not to provoke a conflict, their commander, Captain
Fitzgerald, took every opportunity of charging into the
masses of the enemy whenever occasion offered, and
finally charged down on the flank of the Nagpore infantry
as they were recoiling from an attempt to carry the hill
by storm, and converted a momentary confusion into a
rout. In this he was supported by a small detail of the
Madras Bodyguard. Colonel Scott's men had sustained
a series of attacks extend'ng over eighteen hours, and a
glance at the list of casualties shows that the honour
" Seetabuldee " was well earned. More the pity that the
cavalry regiment which bore the major part in that
day's work no longer exists.

CASUALTIES AT SEETABULDEE.

Regiments.	Officers.		Men.		Regiments.	Officers.		Men.	
	K.	W.	K.	W.		K.	W.	K.	W.
Royal Artillery	—	1	2	15	1st Batt. 20th				
Madras Body-					Bengal Inf.	1	3	15	46
guard ..	—	—	—	—	Resident's Esc.	—	1	10	33
6th Bengal Cav.	—	3	23	24	Major Jenkin's				
61st Pioneers	2	3	55	99	Levies ..	—	3	8	13

NOTE.—It is worthy of remark that the total strength of the
force engaged at Seetabuldee amounted to 1,315 of all ranks, and
the casualties were 355 killed and wounded—a striking testimony
to the steadiness and devotion of the Sepoys of those days.

NAGPORE, DECEMBER 16, 1817.

On learning of the action at Seetabuldee, Brigadier Doveton pushed on to reinforce Scott, and on December 16 was fought this action, which is borne as an honorary distinction on the colours of the

Royal Scots.   6th Jat Light Infantry.
2nd Q.O. Sappers and Miners.   61st Pioneers.
62nd Punjabis.   81st Pioneers.
83rd Light Infantry.   86th Infantry.
88th Infantry.   97th Infantry.

The brunt of the fighting fell on the Royal Scots, who have ever shown themselves to the front in our Indian wars, and on the Berar Infantry, who were then fighting against their own ruler. The honour is borne by one of the representatives of Russell's brigade, yet, if contemporary returns are to be trusted, all the Hyderabad regiments did well at Nagpore.

With the repulse of the Nagporean army, Doveton's troubles were not at an end. A body of 300 Arabs withdrew into the fort, and before they surrendered the English commander was compelled to open a regular siege, in the course of which many casualties were incurred. On December 24 the Arabs came to terms, and we took possession of the city.

CASUALTIES AT THE ENGAGEMENTS IN THE NEIGHBOURHOOD
OF NAGPORE, NOVEMBER 16-24, 1817.

Regiments.	Officers.		Men.		Regiments.	Officers.		Men.	
	K.	W.	K.	W.		K.	W.	K.	W.
Royal Artillery	—	—	5	19	Royal Scots ..	1	—	29	97
Roy. Engineers	—	—	5	7	81st Pioneers	—	—	—	—
6th Jat Light Infantry ..	—	—	2	11	83rd Light Inf.	—	—	14	20
					86th Infantry	—	—	1	5
61st Pioneers	—	—	—	—	88th Infantry	—	—	—	—
62nd Punjabis	—	—	2	6	97th Deccan Inf.	—	—	12	45

MAHEIDPORE, DECEMBER 23, 1817.

This battle honour, which commemorates the only general action fought by the main army during the course of the Second Mahratta War, is borne on the colours and appointments of the

Royal Scots.
28th Light Cavalry.
63rd Light Infantry.
74th Punjabis.
88th Infantry.
94th Russell's Infantry.

Royal Dublin Fusiliers.
2nd Queen's Own Sappers and Miners.
87th Punjabis.
91st Light Infantry.
95th Russell's Infantry.

The distinction was granted in recognition of the services of the army under Sir Thomas Hislop, which resulted in the total defeat of the army belonging to the Maharajah Holkar, of Indore, at Maheidpore on December 22, 1817. Holkar's army far outnumbered the English in cavalry, as well as in guns. We captured no less than sixty-five of the latter. The Holkar force had the reputation of being well trained. For many years the Maharajah had availed himself of the services of English and French instructors, but on the outbreak of hostilities he had foully murdered all the English in his employ, and their absence, no doubt, shook the confidence of the men, who for so long had been accustomed to European leadership. From the returns it would appear that the 27th Light Cavalry (then the 3rd Madras Cavalry) suffered some casualties on this occasion.

CASUALTIES AT THE BATTLE OF MAHEIDPORE, DECEMBER 22, 1817.

Regiments.	Officers.		Men.		Regiments.	Officers.		Men.	
	K.	W.	K.	W.		K.	W.	K.	W.
Royal Scots ..	1	2	8	32	63rd Light Inf.	1	3	26	71
Royal Dublin					74th Punjabis	—	2	14	34
Fusiliers ..	1	1	7	51	87th Punjabis	—	1	1	11
Bombay Art.	—	3	5	12	88th Infantry	—	1	14	52
28th Light Cav.	—	—	4	8	91st Light Inf.	—	6	16	69
29th Deccan					94 and 95th				
Horse ..	—	—	19	47	Russell's Inf.	—	1	12	61

CORYGAUM, JANUARY 1, 1818.

This distinction is borne on the colours of the 34th Poona Horse and 102nd Grenadiers. It commemorates a very gallant stand made by a small body of Bombay Sepoys during the Second Mahratta War, in face of vastly superior forces. Colonel Burr, who was left in command of the troops at Poona after the defeat of the Peishwa in November, found that, owing to various circumstances, that army, though defeated, was by no means demoralized, and there was reason to fear a fresh attack. He therefore ordered Captain Staunton, who was at Seroor, some fifty miles distant, to fall back on Poona. Staunton had with him a couple of guns of the Madras Artillery, with twenty-six English gunners, 500 of the 2nd (now 102nd) Grenadiers, and 250 of what was then known as the Reformed Horse (now the 34th Prince Albert Victor's Own Poona Horse). Staunton moved off on receiving Colonel Burr's orders, but on nearing Corygaum found himself in the presence of the main body of the Peishwa's army, estimated at 18,000 men, with thirty-six guns. The village lent itself to defence, though the position was much cramped, especially for the large number of horses attached to his little force. Staunton knew that Sir Lionel Smith was within a couple of days' march, and that if he could hold out for that time he was sure of relief. He had taken the precaution to move with double the usual supply of ammunition, and he was seconded by eight British officers as gallant as himself.

On the evening of December 30 he occupied the village, which he proceeded to strengthen so far as was possible. The want of water was a great drawback, and, as I have said before, the large number of horses within such a confined space impeded the movements of the men. The fight was an exceedingly fierce one. The enemy on more than one occasion obtained an entrance into the village, and were able to seize the temporary hospital. The wounded were cruelly massacred, but a fine charge led by Dr. Wylie enabled Staunton to regain possession of this building.   On another occasion during an assault by an overwhelming number of the enemy one of the two guns was lost, but a counter-attack retrieved this loss.   For thirty-six hours the little force held its own.   Five out of the eight officers were *hors de combat*, only six men were left to work the guns, and the sepoy battalion had lost 150 out of 500 men.   On the evening of New Year's Day the fire of the assailants began to slacken, and ere nightfall it had died away. News had reached Sir Lionel Smith of the hard straits of Staunton's force, and he at once moved off to relieve him. The Peishwa's army was in no mood to face a well-organized British army, and it hurriedly withdrew from before Corygaum, leaving Staunton with the consciousness of having placed on record one of the finest feats of arms in the history of the Bombay army.   Both Staunton and Dr. Wylie ultimately received the Companionship of the Bath for their services, and a monument was erected at Corygaum to commemorate the fight.

CASUALTIES AT THE ACTION OF CORYGAUM, JANUARY I, 1818.

Regiments.	Officers.		Men.		Regiments.	Officers.		Men.	
	K.	W.	K.	W.		K.	W.	K.	W.
Bombay Art.	1	—	12	8	102nd Grenadiers	1	3	50	105
Poona Horse..	—	3	40	24					

NOWAH, JANUARY 21, 1819.

This name is inscribed on the colours of the 94th and 95th Russell's Infantry, and commemorates a little-known episode in the history of our dealings with the peoples of Southern India.   A mud fort held by a rebellious chief defied the power alike of the Hyderabad Nizam and the British Resident.   It became necessary to bring the

14

recalcitrant chief to reason, and the Resident despatched a portion of the Hyderabad contingent to reduce the fort. Fortunately, the operations were attended with no loss of English life, but a glance at the casualty list shows that the fighting was far more severe than in many actions which are recognized on the colours of better-known regiments than the direct representatives of Russell's brigade.

CASUALTIES AT THE SIEGE AND ASSAULT OF NOWAH,
JANUARY, 1819.

Regiments.	Officers.		Men.		Regiments.	Officers.		Men.	
	K.	W.	K.	W.		K.	W.	K.	W.
94th Russell's Infantry ..	—	1	12	58	95th Russell's I.	—	2	3	56
					96th Berar Inf.	—	1	6	44

MEDAL FOR THE SECOND MAHRATTA WAR.

For their services in this campaign the survivors were awarded the India General Service Medal, the issue of which was notified in the *London Gazette* of February 28, 1851. The following clasps were issued with the medal :

KIRKEE.—For the action on November 5, 1817.
POONA.—For the engagement on November 17, 1817.

Those who were present at both actions received one clasp, engraved " Kirkee—Poona."

SEETABULDEE.—For the action fought by Colonel Scott on November 26, 1817.
NAGPORE.—For General Doveton's action on December 16.

Those present at both engagements received but one clasp, inscribed " Seetabuldee—Nagpore."

MAHEIDPORE.—For the action fought by the army under the command of Sir Thomas Hislop on December 21.
CORYGAUM.—For the gallant defence of the village of Corygaum by Colonel Staunton on January 1, 1818.

BHURTPORE, JANUARY, 1826.

This battle honour has been conferred on the following corps :

11th Hussars.	16th Lancers.
West Yorkshire.	East Lancashire.
Royal Munster Fusiliers.	1st Skinner's Horse.
1st Prince of Wales's Own Sappers and Miners.	2nd Queen's Own Rajput Light Infantry.
1st Brahmins.	3rd Brahmins.
4th Rajputs.	1st Gurkhas.
2nd Gurkhas.	9th Gurkhas.

It commemorates the services rendered by the forces employed at the siege and capture of the famous fortress which twenty years before had successfully defied Lord Lake. In 1803 the Maharajah had thrown in his lot with the Mahratta Princes, and Bhurtpore was a depot of arms for the armies of Holkar. Lord Lake, after his successful actions at Deig, Delhi, and Laswarree, determined to effect its capture. On January 3, 1804, he appeared before the fortress with a force which included the 22nd (Cheshire), 65th (York and Lancaster), 71st (Highland Light Infantry), 76th (West Ridings), and the 1st Bengal European Regiment (Royal Munster Fusiliers). On January 9 the place was assaulted, and we were driven back, with a loss of 5 officers and 64 men killed, 23 officers and 364 men wounded. On the 21st of the same month a second assault was repulsed, our losses being 18 officers and 569 men killed and wounded. The siege was now carried on more systematically, but with a very inadequate train, and on February 20 and 21 two assaults were delivered, which cost us no less than 51 officers and 1,771 men *hors de combat.* Lake then raised the siege.

In 1826, when the British army once more appeared before its walls, the army of the Maharajah of Bhurtpore, remembering the successful defence in 1804, felt pretty confident of holding its own against the British. On our side, the Commander-in-Chief, Lord Combermere, a Peninsular veteran, determined to leave nothing to chance.

Two divisions were assembled—one at Agra, under Major-General Jasper Nicolls ; the second at Muttra, under Major-General Reynell, C.B. ; whilst Lord Combermere assumed the chief command in person.   The cavalry division was composed of two brigades, under Colonel Sleigh, of the 11th Hussars, who was given the rank of Brigadier-General.

First Cavalry Brigade—Brigadier Murray (16th Lancers) : 16th
    Lancers, 6th, 8th, and 9th Bengal Cavalry.
Second Cavalry Brigade—Brigadier Childers (11th Hussars) :
    11th Hussars, 3rd, 4th, and 10th Bengal Cavalry.

The infantry was composed as follows :

FIRST DIVISION : MAJOR-GENERAL T. REYNELL, C.B.

First Brigade—Brigadier M'Combe (14th Foot) : 14th Foot (West
    Yorkshire), 23rd and 63rd Bengal Infantry.
Fourth Brigade—Brigadier Whitehead (4th Bengal Infantry) :
    32nd, 41st, and 58th Bengal Infantry.
Fifth Brigade—Brigadier Paton, C.B. (18th Bengal Infantry) :
    6th, 18th, and 60th Bengal Infantry.

SECOND DIVISION : MAJOR-GENERAL JASPER NICOLLS, C.B.

Second Brigade—Brigadier Edwardes (14th Foot) : 59th Foot
    (East Lancashire), 11th and 31st Bengal Native Infantry.
Third Brigade—Brigadier Adams (14th Bengal Native Infantry) :
    33rd, 36th, and 37th Bengal Native Infantry.
Sixth Brigade—Brigadier Fagan (15th Bengal Native Infantry) :
    15th, 21st, and 25th Bengal Native Infantry.

The artillery of the force comprised eight horse and twelve field batteries, with a siege-train of 112 pieces, including twelve mortars of 10-inch and fifty-eight of 8-inch calibre.   The siege operations were under the directions of a very distinguished Company's officer, Brigadier Anbury, C.B.

On December 9, 1825, the two columns advanced from Muttra and Agra respectively, and on the 28th of the month the first battery opened fire.   On January 17 the breaches were reported practicable, and the Commander-in-Chief determined to assault, Major-General Reynell being placed in command of the three storming columns, which were detailed as follows :

Right Column—Colonel Delamain : 200 of the Munster Fusiliers, the 58th Bengal Infantry, and 2nd Sirmoor Gurkhas.

Centre Column—Brigadier M'Combe (14th Foot) : Four companies of the 14th (West Yorkshire), the 23rd and 63rd Bengal Infantry.

Left Column—Brigadier Whitehead : Two companies of the 14th Foot (West Yorkshire), the 18th and 60th Bengal Infantry.

Left Column—Brigadier Paton : Four companies of the 14th Foot (West Yorkshire), the 6th and 41st Bengal Infantry.

Reserve—Brigadier Whitehead : Two companies of the 14th Foot (West Yorkshire), the 21st and 32nd Bengal Infantry.

The remainder of the army was drawn up to the left of the fortress to afford general aid. The defence was most stubborn, all three commanders of the assaulting columns being badly wounded ; but the men of the 14th (the " Old Bucks " of those days, now the West Yorkshire) would not be denied, and ere sunset the fortress was in our possession. The individual losses of the existing regiments were :

British Troops.	Officers.		Men.		Native Troops.	Officers.		Men.	
	K.	W.	K..	W.		K.	W.	K.	W.
11th Hussars	—	1	2	7	2nd Q.O. Rajput Light Infantry ..	1	3	11	20
16th Lancers	—	1	1	5					
Bengal Artillery	—	2	8	11					
Bengal Enginrs.	2	7	13	30	3rd Brahmans	—	—	1	11
14th W. Yorks	2	7	31	99	1st Gurkhas ..	—	1	4	21
59th E. Lancs	2	8	16	97	2nd Gurkhas ..	—	—	3	15
101st Munster Fusiliers ..	—	3	10	42	1st Skinner's Horse ..	—	—	1	7

Note.—Of the many native infantry regiments above enumerated the 15th have become the 2nd Queen's Own Light Infantry, the 32nd the 3rd Brahmans, the 33rd is the 4th Rajputs, and the 63rd the 9th Gurkhas. The remainder, with the exception of the Gurkha regiments, were lost to us in 1857.

The prize-money distributed to the troops was considerable, but the enormous sums received by the Commander-in-Chief, compared with the pittance given to the private, provoked not a little indignation. At Seringapatam in 1792 Lord Cornwallis and General Meadows handed over their share for distribution amongst the non-commissioned officers and privates—an example which was not followed either by Lord Harris at Seringapatam in 1799 or by Lord Combermere at Bhurtpore. At the request of the officers of the force, a sum of £5,000 was retained for distribution amongst the widows of their comrades who had fallen in action.

DISTRIBUTION OF PRIZE-MONEY.

Commander-in-Chief	£59,500	Captains	.. ..	£476
General Officers	.. £5,900	Subalterns	.. ..	£238
Lieutenant-Colonels	£1,420	Sergeants	.. ..	£8
Majors	.. .. £950	Privates	.. ..	£4

Native Ranks.

Subadars	.. rupees 322	Havildars	.. rupees	53
Jemidars	.. ,, 282	Sepoys	.. ,,	26

HINDOOSTAN.

This honour has been conferred on the following regiments for their gallant services in the earlier campaigns which consolidated our power in our great Indian dependency :

8th Hussars.	Leicesters.
Worcesters.	Oxford Light Infantry.
Highland Light Infantry.	Seaforth Highlanders.
West Riding Regiment.	

8th Hussars.—In the month of March, 1825, the Royal Irish Hussars were authorized to add the harp as well as the battle honours " Laswarree " and " Hindoostan " to their colours and appointments. The 8th had been present with Lord Lake in his campaign against the Mahrattas ; they had served against the Rohillas in Bundulcund, and were with Rollo Gillespie in the gallant attack on the Gurkha fort of Kalunga, where a detachment of 100 dismounted men lost half its numbers. They had done right good work at the Siege of Hattrass, and assisted in many long-forgotten but arduous campaigns, in which our troops were so constantly engaged during the earlier years of the foundation of the Indian Empire.

17th (Leicestershire Regiment).—The honour was bestowed on the old 17th Foot on June 25, 1825, in recognition of the services of the regiment between the years 1804 and 1823. The 17th had been with Wolfe at Louisburg, but had missed the hard fighting in the Peninsula. In the course of its twenty years' Indian service it did right good work in several of those little-known campaigns in which there was hard work and little glory. At the storming of the fort at Chumar, in Bundulcund, it lost 2 officers and 56 men killed and wounded. In the following year (October, 1807), at the operations in connection with the reduction of the fort of Kamounah, near Allyghur, it lost no less than 4 officers and 47 men killed, 5 officers and 95 men wounded. In the Gurkha War of 1814 its casualties amounted to 74 men killed and wounded, and in the year 1817 it again suffered heavily at the capture of Jubbulpore.

36th (Worcestershire Regiment). — This distinguished corps, which already had the battle honour " Mysore " emblazoned on its colours, was authorized in October, 1835, to add the battle honour " Hindoostan " in recognition of its services from 1790 to 1793. In those three years it had lost 4 officers and 65 men in the action of Sattimungulum ; it had been present at the storming of Bangalore, Nundy Droog, Pondicherry, and Seringapatam (1792) ; and in the course of the latter operations it had lost 5 officers and 60 men killed and wounded.

52nd (Oxford Light Infantry).—In February, 1821, the 52nd was authorized to add this distinction to its long list of battle honours as a recognition of its gallant services in India between the years 1790 and 1793. The honour " Mysore," already granted, commemorated its connection with the army which Lord Cornwallis led against Tippoo Sultan in 1792. In the operations of that army the 52nd had borne a very distinguished part, having furnished details for the storming-party at the assault of Bangalore and Nundy Droog, and had lost heavily at the first capture at Seringapatam. There had been several occasions in which the 52nd had shown an earnest of their future greatness during those three years, and for which as yet they had received no recognition. At Cannanore their casualties amounted to 67 killed and wounded, including 4 officers. At Dindigul they had lost 23 men, and they had borne their fair share of the hardships and loss at the Siege of Pondicherry, as well as at the capture of the Island of Ceylon.

71st (Highland Light Infantry).—On January 20, 1837, the 71st and 72nd Regiments were authorized to add this battle honour to those already emblazoned on their colours. No regiment had better earned it than the old Highland Light Infantry. From the date of its landing in India in 1780, until its departure for home twenty years later, the regiment had been continually on active service. The flank companies had been present at Baillie's unfortunate defeat at the hands of the Mysoreans, when their casualties amounted to 6 officers and 181 men killed and wounded, the two companies being practically annihilated. They had shared in Eyre Coote's defeat of the same Mysorean army at the Battle of Porto Novo. At Cuddalore, on June 13, 1783, they lost 10 officers and 196 non-commissioned officers and men. The Commander-in-Chief, General Stuart, thus wrote of their services on this day : " I am also most grateful to Captain Lamont and the officers under his command, who so gallantly led the precious remnants of the 73rd Highlanders "—at that time the regimental number was 73— " through the most perilous road to glory, until exactly one - half the officers and men were either killed or wounded." The 71st furnished a detachment of stormers at the capture of Bangalore ; at the fortress of Nundy Droog in 1791 ; and at Seringapatam, in the following year, they enabled their commander, David Baird, to take a striking revenge for the indignities and cruelties inflicted on their comrades who had fallen into Tippoo Sultan's hands when Baillie met with his defeat. At the storming of Pondicherry the 71st were, as usual, well to the fore, and they formed a portion of the force which added Ceylon to the British Empire. No regiment has a better claim to the battle honour " Hindoostan " than the Highland Light Infantry.

72nd (Seaforth Highlanders).—It was not until the year 1837 that the 72nd were authorized to add the battle honour " Hindoostan " to their other distinctions, and the honour was then granted to commemorate the gallant services of the regiment during its tour of Indian service between the years 1782 and 1793. It had already been granted the distinctions " Mysore " and " Carnatic "— scanty recognition of fifteen years' continuous war. At Cuddalore, in 1783, its losses amounted to 60 killed and wounded, including 3 officers ; at Seringapatam (1792) they were rather more severe. At the Siege of Nundy Droog and of Pondicherry the Seaforths did not escape scathless, and, with the 52nd, they aided in the capture of Ceylon from the Dutch.

76th (West Riding Regiment).—This regiment from its earliest days was known as the " Hindoostan Regiment," and was the first regiment to bear the word " Hindoostan " on its colours—a distinction granted to it on the petition of Lord Lake in the year 1807. Few regiments have suffered more severely in action than did the 76th at Allyghur, Delhi, Laswarree, and Deig ; whilst in Lord Lake's attempt on Bhurtpore the regiment was again cut to pieces. Throughout the earlier phase of Lord Lake's campaign it was the only British infantry in his army, and, in recognition of its valour, the Commander-in-Chief bestowed upon the 76th a third colour—a distinction which has been disallowed by the War Office.

INDIA.

This distinction is borne by the

Suffolks.	West Yorkshire.
Hampshire.	Welsh.
York and Lancaster.	Gordon Highlanders.
Royal Irish Rifles.	

12th (Suffolk Regiment).—On p. 154 I have alluded to the services of the 12th Regiment at the defence of the Residency at Cochin. It was for this and other hard work performed in the early days of the last century that the 12th earned this well-merited distinction " India." During the rising in Travancore they lost heavily. A boat containing the sergeant-major and thirty-three men was wrecked on the coast below Quilon, and every man was massacred. At Quilon itself they lost 53 officers and men in an engagement with the Travancorean troops. Prior to this the 12th had served with General Harris in the war with Tippoo Sultan, and had earned the battle honour " Seringapatam."

West Yorkshire.—The old 14th Foot were actively employed on several campaigns between 1810 and 1825. They furnished the stormers at Bhurtpore when that fortress was captured by Lord Combermere, and they had previously borne a prominent part in the operations which led to the capture of Fort Hattrass in 1817.

65th (York and Lancaster).—This regiment was unfortunate enough to be deprived of the privilege of sharing in the victories gained by the army under Sir Arthur Wellesley in 1803. With the 86th they were selected to maintain order on the line of communications. A detachment was present at the engagements outside Poonah —engagements which are borne on the colours of the Royal Dublin Fusiliers under the name " Kirkee." They were present in many hard-fought actions in Guzerat, and were employed more than once in suppressing refractory Rajahs in the Bombay Presidency. Their conduct in expeditions against the Arab pirates on the Persian Gulf earned the distinction of " Arabia." These are described on p. 224.

67th (Hampshire Regiment).—The old 67th certainly lost more men in putting this battle honour on their colours than they did in the better-known but less arduous campaign in China in 1860. At the capture of the fort of Ryghur in 1817, and, two years later, at the storming of Asseerghur, they lost some 60 officers and men killed and wounded. Indeed, throughout their first tour of Indian service—from 1805 to 1826—they were almost continuously in the field.

69th (The Welsh Regiment).—In the early part of the nineteenth century the 69th was constantly employed on active service. It lost heavily in the suppression of the mutiny of the Madras troops at Vellore, and in the operations in Travancore in the year 1808 it defeated the rebels on more than one occasion, sharing with the 12th (Suffolks) the principal honours of that little-remembered campaign.

75th (Gordon Highlanders).—" Mysore " and " Seringapatam " on the colours of the old 75th testify to the work this fine regiment went through in Southern India ; but those honours by no means exhaust its claims on the honour list of the army. In the year 1802 it was engaged in a series of hard fights in Western India, in the province of Cambay, where its casualties amounted to 4 officers and 161 men killed and wounded. At the capture of the fort of Jemlanabad the losses were 67 of all ranks. These were some of the affairs which led King George III. to accord the 75th permission to add the honour " India " to the colours of the old Stirlingshire Regiment, now the Gordon Highlanders.

84th (York and Lancaster Regiment).—The 84th was one of those regiments whose duty it was to do garrison duty in the disaffected districts during the campaign which put " Assaye " on the colours of more fortunate corps. Between the years 1796 and 1819 it was constantly employed in little-heard-of expeditions, which entailed many hardships and not a little hard fighting. On one occasion, in Guzerat in 1801, it lost an officer and 19 men killed, and its total losses in those twenty-two years amounted to close on 200 killed and wounded. It is a strange coincidence that in Guzerat they should have been fighting side by side with the regiment which eighty years later became their 1st Battalion.

86th (The Royal Irish Rifles).—During the operations of the main army, under Sir Arthur Wellesley, the 86th were employed in keeping in check the turbulent tribes in Guzerat, and so they, like the 65th and 84th, missed sharing in the glories of Assaye. Their services in Guzerat, in Cambay, were sufficiently severe. At the capture of Kariah their casualties were no less than 67 of all ranks ; at Baroda they lost 37 killed and wounded ; at Baroach 4 officers and 39 men ; and at Lord Lake's attack on Bhurtpore the losses of the 86th were 112 of all ranks.

CHAPTER XIV

BATTLE HONOURS FOR MINOR CAMPAIGNS IN THE EAST, 1796-1857

Amboyna — Ternate — Banda — Cochin — Arabia — Bourbon —Java — Persian Gulf—Beni Boo Ali — Aden — Persia— Bushire—Reshire—Koosh-ab.

AMBOYNA, 1796 AND 1810.

THIS distinction is borne only by the Royal Dublin Fusiliers, as the lineal descendants of that most distinguished corps the 1st Madras European Regiment, which certainly has the right to bear with the Dorsets the title of " Primus in Indus."

From the earliest days of our association with the East Indies there had been mutual jealousies between the English and the Dutch merchants with regard to commerce in the Moluccas. So far back as the year 1623 the summary execution by the Dutch Governor of Amboyna of the commander of an East Indiaman nearly led to war between the two nations, and would have done so had not the States General disavowed the action of their colonial official. When Holland threw in her lot with France at the outbreak of the revolutionary wars, and granted the French fleets the hospitality of her Eastern harbours, it was determined to relieve the Dutch of these possessions.

In February, 1796, Admiral Rainier, commanding the fleet in the East Indies, sailed to Amboyna with a squadron consisting of the *Suffolk* (74), *Centurion* (50), *Resistance* (44), *Orpheus* (32), and *Swift* (16). The Dutch, recognizing the futility of resistance, surrendered, and

Amboyna passed into our possession. The small body of troops employed on this occasion, as well as the navy, reaped a rich harvest in the shape of prize-money, the share of the Commander-in-Chief amounting to £90,000, and that of the Captains of the Royal Navy to £13,000 each. A detachment of the Madras European Regiment, under Major Vigors, was embarked on Admiral Rainier's squadron, and participated beneficially in the booty, the shares that fell to the lot of the soldiers being :

	£	s.	d.		£	s.	d.
Major in command	13,583	0	0	Subalterns ..	636	0	0
Captains ..	1,314	0	0	Sergeants ..	229	0	0
				Privates ..	44	0	0

At the Peace of Amiens, Amboyna and the neighbouring islands were restored to the Dutch. In the year 1810 it was found necessary to reoccupy them, and Captain Edward Tucker, R.N., with the *Doris*, *Cornwallis*, and *Samarang*, embarked a detachment of 130 men of the 1st Madras European Regiment (Royal Dublin Fusiliers), with 50 men of the Royal Artillery, as well as some sepoys. Slight opposition was encountered, our losses being 3 men killed, 1 officer and 9 non-commissioned officers and men wounded. We maintained a garrison in the island until the year 1814, when by the Treaty of Paris it was once more restored to the Dutch, and the British Empire deprived of one of the richest islands in Eastern waters.

DETAILS OF FORCE LANDED.			CASUALTIES.			
			Officers.		Men.	
Force Engaged.	Officers.	Men.	K.	W.	K.	W.
Naval Brigade	8	235	—	1	1	4
Royal Artillery	1	46	—	1	—	1
Royal Dublin Fusiliers	5	130	—	—	2	4

TERNATE, 1801 AND 1810.

This honour is borne only by the Royal Dublin Fusiliers. It commemorates one of the many little oversea expeditions which we were compelled to undertake in the course of our wars with France between the years 1793 and 1815. Ternate is one of the Molucca Islands, and then, as now, belonged to the Dutch. Its harbours, however, were open to the French fleets, and gave refuge to vessels of war and to privateers, which preyed upon our China commerce. It became necessary, therefore, to reduce the island, and in the year 1801 a combined naval and military expedition was despatched for its subjugation. The Madras troops were under the command of Colonel Burr, and they encountered a stubborn resistance. It was not until after a siege of fifty-two days that the Dutch Governor surrendered. As was our custom, on the conclusion of peace in the following year Ternate was restored to its original owners.

In the year 1810 it again became necessary to take possession of the island, and, after the capture of Amboyna, Captain Tucker, with a small detachment of artillery and of the 1st Madras European Regiment, the latter under Captain Forbes, set sail for the island. There was but slight opposition, and on August 31 Ternate once more passed into our hands, only to be restored to the Dutch under the terms of the Treaty of Paris in 1814.

DETAILS OF TROOPS LANDED.			CASUALTIES.			
			Officers.		Men.	
Force Engaged.	Officers.	Men.	K.	W.	K.	W.
Naval Brigade	8	200	—	—	1	7
Royal Artillery	1	36	—	—	—	—
Royal Dublin Fusiliers	3	74	—	1	1	9

The troops received a small solatium in the shape of prize-money, the share of a Captain being £270, a Subaltern £120, a sergeant £32, and a private £13.

BANDA, 1796 AND 1810.

This distinction was granted by the Governor of Madras to the 1st Madras European Regiment, and is now borne only by the Royal Dublin Fusiliers. It commemorates the two occupations of the Island of Banda, in the Eastern Archipelago, by a detachment of the old Madras European Regiment, the first taking place in 1796, the second in 1810. No medal was issued to the land forces engaged, but on the institution of the Naval General Service Medal in 1847 the naval commanders of the *Caroline*, *Piedmontaise*, and *Barracouta* were awarded the naval gold medal for the capture of the island in 1810, and distinctive bronze arm-badges, in lieu of medals, were bestowed by the Governor of Madras on the sepoys. The detachment of the 1st Madras European Regiment (now the 1st Royal Dublin Fusiliers) was under the command of Captain Nixon. Their services were cordially acknowledged by Captain Coles, of H.M.S. *Caroline*, but the regiment does not appear to have suffered any casualties.

ARABIA, 1809.

This distinction was granted to the York and Lancaster Regiment by a notification in the *London Gazette* in the month of March, 1823, in recognition of the gallant services of the regiment during the operations on the coast of Arabia in the years 1809 and 1821. The old 65th Regiment, as it then was, had not been fortunate enough to have been present at any of the well-known campaigns during its tour of Indian service. Nevertheless, it had been engaged in several arduous and by no means bloodless minor expeditions, in which the soldierlike qualities of a regiment are as severely tested as in campaigns which bring in their train greater honours and rewards.   Such were the two expeditions for the punishment of piratical tribes on the Arabian coast.

The expedition in 1809 was under the command of Lieutenant-Colonel Lionel Smith, of the 65th Regiment. It was accompanied by the frigates *Chiffon* (Captain Wainwright) and *Caroline*.   The military force comprised the 65th (York and Lancaster), the flank companies of the 47th (North Lancashire), and the 2nd Bombay Native Infantry, now the 103rd Mahratta Light Infantry, with a company of artillery.   Nominally the pirates owned allegiance to the Sultan of Turkey, but his sovereignty was very shadowy, and as they had embraced Wahabiism they were looked upon more in the light of rebels than subjects.   For years they had interfered with our commerce in the Persian Gulf, and had treated their prisoners with the refinement of cruelty.   It therefore became necessary to root them out of their lair.

The little force left Bombay in the month of September, 1809, and proceeded to the pirate stronghold of Ras el Khima, on the Arabian coast.   The Arabs fought bravely, but our superior armament and discipline soon told, and the fort, which had originally been built by the Portuguese more than two centuries previously, was dismantled. On December 27 the flotilla arrived at Linga, another piratical haunt, and this, too, after making a show of resistance, was destroyed.   Hostages were brought to Bombay as security for the good behaviour of the tribes, and the force then returned to India, its total casualties having been :

CASUALTIES AT BENI BOO ALLI, 1809.

	Officers.		Men.		Regiments.	Officers.		Men.	
	K.	W.	K.	W.		K.	W.	K.	W.
Royal Navy ..	—	—	2	16	47th N. Lancs	1	—	3	10
65th York and Lancs Regt.	—	1	2	7	103rd Mahratta Light Inf. ..	—	—	2	31

NOTE.—For this expedition the 2nd Bombay Native Infantry was granted the battle honour " Beni Boo Alli."

BOURBON, JULY 8, 1810.[1]

This distinction has been granted to the

Welsh Regiment.	Royal Irish Rifles.
66th Punjabis.	84th Punjabis.

104th Wellesley's Rifles.

A medal was struck, by order of the Governor-General of India, for distribution to the officers and men of the Company's forces present during the expedition.

In the *London Gazette* of July 17, 1826, the 69th Foot (now the 2nd Welsh Regiment) was authorized to bear on its colours and appointments the word " Bourbon," in commemoration of the distinguished conduct of the regiment at the attack and capture of that island. Subsequently the same privilege was conferred on the 86th (2nd Battalion Irish Rifles).

Bourbon, now better known as Reunion, was a thorn in the side of the East India Company during our many wars with France. With Mauritius, then known as the Isle of France, it was a harbour of refuge for the many privateers which preyed upon our commerce, and a base of operations for the French fleet in Eastern waters. Its reduction became a necessity, but was from time to time deferred, until at last, in the month of September, 1809, the Governor-General, Lord Minto, despatched a force, under Colonel Keatinge, of the 56th Regiment (now the Essex), to report on the feasibility of the capture of both islands. With Keatinge was associated Commodore Josias Rowley, at the head of a squadron comprising the *Raisonnable, Sirius, Boadicea, Nereide,* and *Otter,* with the Honourable Company's cruiser *Wasp.* Keatinge's force consisted of his own regiment, the 56th (Essex), and the 2nd Bombay Native Infantry (now the ·104th Wellesley's Rifles). A descent was made on the island, the forts at the principal port destroyed, and some French men-of-war and armed Indiamen brought away ; but the

---

[1] Two companies of the Madras Sappers accompanied the expedition to Bourbon, but the battle honour has not yet been awarded to the 2nd Queen's Own Sappers and Miners.

force was altogether too small for Keatinge to retain possession.

In the following July, having received reinforcements, Keatinge and Rowley made a second descent. In the meantime they had occupied the Island of Rodriguez, which served as a valuable base of operations. In addition to the Essex and the Bombay Regiment, Keatinge now had the 69th (2nd Welsh), the 86th (2nd Irish Rifles), and the 6th and 12th Regiments of Madras Infantry (now the 66th and 84th Punjabis) ; and this force was strengthened by a naval brigade of seamen and Marines from the ships, the total numbering about 3,600 men. The French garrison made some show of resistance, but after a sharp engagement the Governor, seeing himself cut off from all hope of aid, surrendered, and until the conclusion of peace in 1814 Bourbon remained in our possession, Colonel Keatinge being installed as Governor, and a regiment being raised from the Creole inhabitants, which was borne on the rolls of our army as the Bourbon Regiment.

CASUALTIES AT THE CAPTURE OF THE ISLAND OF BOURBON, 1810.

Regiments.	Officers.		Men.		Regiments.	Officers.		Men.	
	K.	W.	K.	W.		K.	W.	K.	W.
12th Suffolk ..	—	2	2	5	69th Welsh ..	—	—	2	—
56th Essex ..	—	—	1	3	86th R. Irish R.	1	6	10	51

CASUALTIES AT THE ATTACK ON THE ISLAND IN 1809.

Regiments.	Officers.		Men.		Regiments.	Officers.		Men.	
	K.	W.	K.	W.		K.	W.	K.	W.
Royal Marines	—	2	7	17	104th Welles-ley's Rifles	—	1	2	11
56th Essex ..	—	—	6	27					

The Essex Regiment, by its participation in both descents on the island, seem to have some claim to this distinction.

JAVA, 1811.

This battle honour is borne on the colours of the

West Yorkshire.	East Lancashire.
Welsh.	Seaforth Highlanders.
Royal Irish Fusiliers.	Governor-General's Bodyguard.

2nd Queen's Own Sappers and Miners.

The expedition was under the command of General Sir Samuel Auchmuty, but the Governor-General of India, Lord Minto, himself accompanied the troops, in order to arrange for the civil administration of the Dutch islands, several of which, as I have shown, had already fallen into our hands.

The troops selected comprised two Madras and one Bengal division, and were brigaded as follows :

First Madras Division—Major-General R. R. Gillespie : 25th Light Dragoons (260), Horse Artillery (152), the 14th (West Yorkshire), a wing of the 59th (East Lancashire), the 89th (Royal Irish Fusiliers), and four companies of European Sappers.

Second Madras Division—Colonel Gibbs, of the 59th (East Lancashire) : 22nd Light Dragoons (154), Royal Artillery (98), a wing of the 59th (East Lancashire), the 69th (Welsh), and the 78th (Seaforth Highlanders).

The Bengal division was under the command of Major-General J. S. Wood, and consisted of the Governor-General's Bodyguard, the 1st Battalion of the Bengal Native Infantry, and five battalions of sepoys, who had volunteered from the whole of the regiments of the Bengal army, and who were designated as the 1st, 2nd, 3rd, 4th, and 5th Regiments of Bengal Volunteers. On the force being broken up, these men returned to their own regiments, receiving the medal which the Governor-General caused to be struck for the expedition, and so it comes about that, with the exception of the Bodyguard and the Madras Sappers, no native corps bears the distinction " Java " on its colours.

A powerful fleet, under the command of Admiral the
Hon. R. Stopford, convoyed the transports.   It comprised the following vessels :

Commander-in-Chief : Rear-Admiral the Hon. R. Stopford.
Commodore : W. R. Broughton.

	GUNS		GUNS		GUNS
Scipio ..	.. 74	Illustrious ..	74	Minden	.. 74
Lion ..	.. 64	Akbar	.. 44	Nisus	.. 38
Présidente	.. 38	Hussar	.. 38	Shœton	.. 38
Leda ..	.. 38	Caroline	.. 36	Modeste	.. 36
Phœbe	.. 36	Bucephalus ..	36	Doris	.. 36
Cornelia	.. 32	Psyche	.. 32	Drake	.. 32
Procris	.. 18	Barracouta ..	18	Hesper	.. 18
Harpy	.. 18	Hecate	.. 18	Dasher	.. 18
Samarang	.. 12				

HONOURABLE EAST INDIA COMPANY'S CRUISERS.

Malabar.	Aurora.	Mornington.
Nautilus.	Vestal.	Ariel.
Thetis.	Psyche.	

and fifty-seven transports carrying troops.

The total strength of the expeditionary force amounted
to 5,344 British and 5,770 native troops.   On August 4
the troops disembarked at a place called Chillingcherry,
some ten miles east of the capital, meeting with no opposition ; but on the 10th the advanced brigade, under
Gillespie, a most dashing officer, who had distinguished
himself greatly in the West Indies, had a sharp encounter
with the French, who were driven back, our casualties
amounting to 90 killed and wounded.   On the 20th the
siege of Fort Cornelis was commenced, the Admiral
landing a naval brigade and some heavy guns to aid in
the operations.   On the 26th the fort was carried by
assault, Gillespie again distinguishing himself, pursuing
the beaten enemy with the 22nd Light Dragoons for a
distance of thirty-five miles, capturing 2 general, 30 field,
and 214 other officers ; 280 guns and 6,000 prisoners fell
into our hands as a consequence of this bold attack, and
the operations were brought to a conclusion by the unconditional surrender of the island.   Gillespie, who was
left in command on the departure of the Governor-General,

experienced some difficulty in inducing the natives to learn submission, and a number of expeditions were necessary ere peace was fully restored. On the institution of the Land General Service Medal in 1847, the survivors of the expedition received that medal with a clasp inscribed " Java." The Governor-General, on his own initiative, at the conclusion of the operations, bestowed gold medals on field officers and silver medals on all other ranks ; but the privilege of wearing these was confined to officers and men in the service of the East India Company.

CASUALTIES IN THE EXPEDITION TO JAVA, 1811.

Regiments.	Officers.		N.C.O.'s and Men.	
	K.	W.	K.	W.
Royal Navy	—	5	15	55
Royal Artillery ..	I	2	I	9
Bengal Artillery	I	I	3	12
Madras Artillery	—	I	2	6
Bengal Engineers	—	I	—	—
Madras Engineers	—	I	—	—
22nd Light Dragoons ..	I	I	I	19
14th West York	I	5	11	90
59th East Lancastrian ..	5	10	18	128
69th Welsh	3	8	14	60
78th Seaforth Highlanders	I	7	33	137
89th R.I. Fusiliers	—	8	11	65
Governor-General's Bodyguard	—	I	I	5
Madras Pioneers	I	I	I	4
3rd Bengal Native Vols.	—	—	—	3
4th Bengal Native Vols.	—	2	11	28
5th Bengal Native Vols.	—	I	2	22
6th Bengal Native Vols.	—	3	4	22

PERSIAN GULF, 1819.

This distinction is borne only by the 121st Pioneers, formerly the Bombay Marine Battalion, and was awarded to that regiment by the order of the Governor of Bombay in Council as a recognition of its services when employed under Sir W. Grant Keir in the destruction of the piratical strongholds in the Persian Gulf in the year 1819. A previous expedition had been undertaken against the same tribes in the year 1809, when Sir Lionel Smith, with the 65th (York and Lancasters), the 47th (North Lancashire), and the 2nd Bombay Infantry had taught the pirates that they could not attack vessels flying the English flag with impunity. For some years the hot bloods of the Arabian coast abstained from exercising their predatory habits, but in the year 1817 they plundered several vessels, massacring their crews. The vessels of the East India Squadron had more than one sharp tussle with the pirates, but these were always able to escape to their lairs, where the seamen were unable to follow them. It was determined in 1819 to despatch a second expedition against the Joassma, the offending tribe. The command was entrusted to Major-General Sir W. Grant Keir, an officer who had conducted more than one successful campaign in Cutch and against other recalcitrant petty potentates. The troops selected were the 65th (York and Lancaster Regiment), and the flank companies of the 47th (Loyal North Lancashires). These two corps had been associated in the previous expedition in the year 1809. In addition to the British contingent, the 1st Battalion of the 2nd Bombay Native Infantry (now the 103rd Mahratta Light Infantry), the 11th Marine Battalion (now the 121st Pioneers), and the flank companies of the 1st Battalion of the 3rd Bombay Infantry (now the 105th Mahratta Light Infantry), also accompanied the force, which was convoyed by H.M.S. *Liverpool* and several of the Honourable East India Company's cruisers.

The whole force assembled at the Island of Larrack, in the Persian Gulf, on November 24, and the General at once proceeded in the *Liverpool* to Ras-el-Khima, the pirates' stronghold, where he made a careful reconnaissance. Attempts were made through the Imaum of

Muscat to open negotiations with the chief of the Joassma tribe, but to these he returned a defiant reply. The General thereupon sent for the transports, and on December 3 the whole force disembarked unopposed. It was evident that the fort had been considerably strengthened since 1809, and the General borrowed some 24-pounders from the *Liverpool* in order to construct and arm his shore batteries. Whilst the siege operations were in progress, the Arabs made more than one determined sortie ; but when the bombardment commenced in earnest, they made but a feeble reply. This is scarcely to be wondered at. Their guns were all of small calibre, and the *Liverpool* claimed that she had thrown upwards of 1,200 32 and 24 pound shot into the place in twenty-four hours.

On the evening of December 9 the breach was declared practicable, but when the storming-parties approached the place at dawn on the 10th it was found deserted. Information was received through the Imaum of Muscat that the Arabs had retreated to another stronghold farther inland. The General then re-embarked a portion of his force, and proceeded up the coast to Rhams, which also was found to be abandoned ; but here it was ascertained that the tribes were still defiant, and were massed in a hill fort of Zaya, some miles inland. The two British corps, with the artillery, were at once despatched to destroy this work, and on the 18th of the month Sir Grant Keir was able to report to Government the destruction of all the piratical strongholds and the submission of their chiefs.

The expedition had been attended with some loss, but the official report of the casualties in the *Bombay Gazette* tends to show that these fell on the British, and not on the native, corps engaged. The York and Lancaster Regiment have been accorded the distinction " Arabia " as a recognition of their services ; but the 47th (Loyal North Lancashires), although they were twice employed with the 56th on the by no means pleasing duty of chastising Arab pirates, have not as yet been permitted to add the word " Arabia " to the other battle honours which are embroidered on their colours.

CASUALTIES DURING THE EXPEDITION TO THE PERSIAN GULF IN 1819.

Regiments.	Officers.		Men.		Regiments.	Officers.		Men.	
	K.	W.	K.	W.		K.	W.	K.	W.
Royal Artillery	—	—	1	3	103rd Mahratta L.I. ..	—	—	—	5
47th North Lancashires ..	1	—	2	17	105th Mahratta L.I. ..	—	—	—	—
65th York and Lancasters	1	2	4	24	121st Pioneers	—	—	—	—

Considerable booty was found, and the sum of £38,958 was remitted to England by the prize agents for distribution amongst the men of the 47th (North Lancashire) and 65th (York and Lancaster) Regiments.[1]

BENI BOO ALLI, MARCH, 1821.

This distinction is borne by the

Royal Dublin Fusiliers.   103rd Mahratta Light Infantry.
104th Wellesley's Rifles.   105th Mahratta Light Infantry.
107th Pioneers.   113th Infantry.
121st Pioneers.

It was awarded to these regiments by the Governor of Bombay for their gallant services in destroying the strongholds of Arab pirates in the Persian Gulf. The 65th Regiment (York and Lancasters) was also employed in the same service, but it does not bear the honour.

The expedition was under the command of Major-General Lionel Smith, who, as a Lieutenant-Colonel, had carried through successfully a previous expedition in the year 1809.

On this occasion his force comprised the 65th (York

[1] Field Officers of the regiments employed received £527; Captains, £82; Subalterns, £40; sergeants, £12; and privates, £2 10s.

and Lancasters), the 1st Bombay European Battalion (now the 2nd Royal Dublin Fusiliers), the 1st Battalion of the 7th Regiment of Bombay Native Infantry, and the flank companies of the 1st Battalion of the 2nd, 2nd Battalion of the 2nd, 1st Battalion of the 3rd, and 1st Battalion of the 4th Regiments of Bombay Native Infantry, with the Bombay Marine Battalion (121st Pioneers), together with 200 Bombay artillerymen. H.M.S. *Topaze, Liverpool, Eden,* and *Curlew* also accompanied the force.

The Arabs were in a most defiant mood. They had inflicted a severe defeat on a native force which had been sent against them a short time previously. This force had been driven back, with a loss of nearly 400 sepoys killed, whilst five British officers were amongst the slain. Sir Lionel Smith's force landed without opposition under cover of the guns of the fleet, and on March 2 the stronghold of the Joassma tribe was carried, after a sharp fight. The Imaum of Muscat now endeavoured to induce the tribes to come to terms, but on the 10th they made a most determined attack on our camp. In this they were worsted, but our losses were considerable, the 1st Bombay Fusiliers and the 7th Regiment of Bombay Sepoys (now the 113th) suffering severely. The destruction of their forts and vessels by the fleet soon reduced the Arabs to reason, and they agreed to send hostages to Bombay for their future good behaviour. Our casualties during this expedition were as follows:

CASUALTIES AT BENI BOO ALLI.

Regiments.	Officers.		Men.		Regiments.	Officers.		Men.	
	K.	W.	K.	W.		K.	W.	K.	W.
Royal Navy ..	3	3	5	20	113th Pioneers (British) ..	1	2	—	—
65th York and Lancaster ..	—	2	4	35	113th Pioneers (Native) ..	—	2	21	122
2nd Dublin Fus.	1	3	17	34					

Aden, 1839.

This distinction is borne by the

Royal Dublin Fusiliers.   121st Pioneers.
124th Baluchistan Infantry.

It commemorates the expedition which transferred the sovereignty of the well-known coaling-station to the East India Company. So far back as the year 1799 an expedition from Bombay had occupied the Island of Perim, at the entrance of the Red Sea, and during the expedition to Egypt in the year 1801 we had a garrison on that inhospitable little islet. At the close of the war with France the garrison was withdrawn. With the advent of steam it became evident that the real route to India would be by the Red Sea, and the value of Aden as a coaling-station was borne on the minds of the Government of our great dependency. Commodore Haines, of the Indian Marine, an officer of exceptional attainments, was entrusted with the task of carrying on the necessary negotiations with the Arab ruler of Aden, and in the year 1835, in return for a cash subsidy and a promise of British protection, we became virtual rulers of the place. Disputes soon arose. The neighbouring chiefs disapproved of the action of the chief with whom we had negotiated, and in the year 1838 it became evident that it would be necessary for us to maintain a garrison there in order to assert our supremacy. No resistance was anticipated, and the force sent was small. It consisted of a wing of the 1st Bombay Fusiliers (now the Royal Dublin Fusiliers) and the 24th Bombay Native Infantry, the whole under Major T. M. Bailie, of the latter regiment. Two ships of the Royal Navy, the *Volage* and *Cruiser*, and a squadron of the Indian Marine also participated in the affair. On these were embarked the present 121st Pioneers, then known as the Bombay Marine Battalion.

On the arrival of the expedition at Aden, the Arabs declined to allow the troops to land or to supply them with either food or water. The works were then shelled, and under cover of this fire the troops disembarked and occupied the town, which had been abandoned, the Arabs having taken refuge in one of the forts, from which a white flag was displayed. After a little parleying, these men surrendered ; but in the act of disarming them a regrettable incident occurred, in which we lost some sixteen men killed and wounded ; otherwise, with the exception of one midshipman, who was hurt in the landing, Aden was acquired without bloodshed.

In the month of November following a half-hearted attempt was made to recapture the place. This was repulsed without loss, and in May, 1840, a second attempt was also repulsed. Since then our hold on Aden has been unchallenged, though on more than one occasion we have been compelled to undertake expeditions against the tribes in the hinterland, none of which, however, have been deemed of sufficient importance for special mention. Indeed, with so many hard-fought actions unrecorded, one is tempted to ask how comes it that the name " Aden " has been selected for a battle honour.

PERSIA, 1856-57.

This distinction is borne by the

14th Hussars.
Durham Light Infantry.
33rd Queen's Own Light Cavalry.
2nd Queen's Own Sappers and Miners.
120th Rajputana Infantry.
126th Baluchistan Infantry.
North Staffords.
Seaforth Highlanders.
34th Poona Horse.
35th Scinda Horse.
3rd Sappers and Miners.
104th Wellesley's Rifles.
123rd Outram's Rifles.
129th Duke of Connaught's Own Baluchis.

It recognizes the services of a force which was employed in Persia during the winter 1856-57, in a campaign for which no less than four battle honours were granted. The army was commanded by Lieutenant-General Sir James Outram, K.C.B., an officer of the

Bombay army, who was affectionately termed the Bayard of India. His force was organized as follows :

First Division : Major-General Stalker.
First Brigade — Brigadier N. Wilson, K.H : 64th (North Staffords), 120th Rajputana Infantry.
Second Brigade—Brigadier R. H. Honnor : 106th (Durham Light Infantry), and 104th Bombay Rifles.
Second Division : Major-General H. Havelock, C.B.
Third Brigade—Brigadier H. Hamilton : 78th (Ross-shire Buffs), 126th Baluchistan Infantry.
Fourth Brigade—Brigadier J. Hale : 123rd Outram's Rifles and 129th Baluchis.
Cavalry Brigade—Brigadier J. Jacob : 14th Hussars, 33rd Queen's Own Light Cavalry, 34th Poona Horse, and 35th Scinde Horse.

The *casus belli* may be summed up in one word— Herat. That city had long been considered the key of India, and when, early in 1856, the Persians captured it from the Afghans, we insisted on its restoration. On this being refused, it was determined to compel acceptance of our demands. Sir James Outram, who had been nominated to the chief command, was on his way from England, and, in order to lose no time, the First Division of the expeditionary force, under General Stalker, accompanied by a powerful squadron of vessels belonging to the Indian Marine, left Bombay on November 9 for the Persian Gulf. On December 5 the fleet bombarded the fortifications of Bushire, and the following day the troops disembarked unopposed.

No casualties were incurred either at the bombardment of Bushire or at the landing of the troops. It was a very cheaply won battle honour.

BUSHIRE, DECEMBER 5, 1856.

The following regiments have been authorized to bear this battle honour for the bombardment of Bushire :

North Stafford.	Durham Light Infantry.
33rd Queen's Own Light Cavalry.	34th P.A.V.O. Poona Horse.
3rd Sappers and Miners.	104th Wellesley's Rifles.
120th Rajputana Infantry.	129th P.W.O. Baluchis.

RESHIRE, DECEMBER 7, 1856.

This battle honour is borne on the colours of the

North Staffords.
33rd Queen's Own Light Cavalry.
104th Wellesley's Rifles.
Durham Light Infantry.

34th Poona Horse.
3rd Sappers and Miners.
120th Rajputana Infantry.
129th Baluchis.

On December 5 the first division of the Persian Expeditionary Force had disembarked in the near neighbourhood of the fortified city of Bushire. The Persians were holding an old redoubt which dated from the days of the Dutch occupation. Unfortunately, General Stalker made no attempt to shell the work, and when, in the early morning of December 7, the brigade carried it by assault, the 64th (North Staffords) and 104th Bombay Rifles were met by a well-sustained fire, which, however, died away as they neared the parapet. The Colonel of the 64th—Stopford—who was in command of the brigade, was shot dead as he led the men over the breastwork, and the 104th lost two officers mortally wounded. With this insignificant loss, the formidable work was carried, and on the following day the Governor of Bushire, thinking he had done enough for honour, surrendered the fortifications of the city to the General. The whole brigade now took up its position close to Bushire, to await the arrival of the Commander-in-Chief with the remainder of the army.

CASUALTIES AT THE ACTION OF RESHIRE, DECEMBER 7, 1856.

Regiments.	Officers.		Men.		Regiments.	Officers.		Men.	
	K.	W.	K.	W.		K.	W.	K.	W.
Royal Artillery	—	—	—	3	120th Rajputana Infantry	2	1	—	7
64th N. Stafford	—	—	2	5	106th Durham L.I.	—	—	2	7
33rd Q.O. Light Cavalry	1	—	—	3	34th Poona H.	—	—	—	—
104th Wellesley's Rifles	—	—	—	5	129th Baluchis	—	—	2	—

Koosh-ab, February 8, 1857.

This battle honour is borne on the colours and appointments of the

North Staffords.

Seaforth Highlanders.

34th Poona Horse.

3rd Sappers and Miners.

120th Rajputana Infantry.

Durham Light Infantry.

33rd Queen's Own Light Cavalry.

104th Wellesley's Rifles.

126th Baluchis.

129th Baluchis.

It recognizes the services of these regiments at the action of Koosh-ab, during the Persian campaign under Sir James Outram. The Persian infantry, which had been trained by British officers, were well handled, and actually threw themselves into square when threatened by our cavalry. These squares were broken by the 3rd Bombay Cavalry (now the 33rd Queen's Own Light Cavalry), and two officers obtained the Victoria Cross for their conduct on this occasion. Sir James Outram, who had a keen eye for personal gallantry, recommended no less than ten members of the regiment for this much-prized decoration, including some of the native ranks. The casualties which I append below show that the Persians evinced little determination, or else their shooting did not reflect much credit on their training :

Regiments.	Officers.		Men.		Regiments.	Officers.		Men.	
	K.	W.	K.	W.		K.	W.	K.	W.
Royal Artillery	—	—	1	7	33rd Q.O. Light Cavalry ..	—	1	1	14
64th N. Stafford	—	2	2	10					
106th Durham L.I. ..	—	1	2	9	34th Poona H.	—	—	3	8
					126th Baluchis	—	—	1	5

The other regiments present suffered no loss.

CHAPTER XV

BATTLE HONOURS FOR SERVICES IN BURMAH,
1824-1887

Ava—Kemmendine—Arracan—Pegu—Burmah.[1]

AVA, 1824-1826.

THIS distinction is borne by the following regiments :

Royal Scots.	90th Punjabis.
South Staffords.	Somerset Light Infantry.
Essex.	Welsh.
North Lancashire.	Sherwood Foresters.
Royal Irish Fusiliers.	Dorsets.
Governor-General's Body-guard.	Royal Dublin Fusiliers.
	26th Light Cavalry.
2nd Queen's Own Sappers and Miners.	61st Pioneers.
	67th Punjabis.
63rd Light Infantry.	72nd Punjabis.
69th Punjabis.	82nd Punjabis.
76th Punjabis.	88th Carnatic Infantry.
86th Carnatic Infantry.	92nd Punjabis.

It recognizes the services of these regiments in the long and harassing campaign in Lower Burmah, between the years 1824 and 1826.

Our relations with our Burmese neighbours had never been marked with cordiality. They had been in the habit of committing unprovoked raids across the Assam or Cachar borders, and had misconstrued our verbal remonstrances into a sign of weakness. So far back as the year 1784 they had annexed Arracan in the most unprovoked manner, and since that date on more than one occasion considerable bodies of Burmese troops had actually violated British territory in pursuit of what they

---

[1] The battle honour "Burmah" was awarded to the 121st Pioneers for services in the squadron operating on the Burmese coast in the campaign of 1824-1826.

were pleased to call fugitives from justice. In the year 1823 they committed a series of aggressions in Sylhet and Cachar, and finally occupied an island in the vicinity of Chittagong, which was undoubtedly British. To our remonstrances they retaliated with a threat to invade Bengal and drive us back to our island home. War was reluctantly decided upon, and it was resolved to invade Burmah with four separate columns :

I. A column composed entirely of Bengal troops under the command of Brigadier Richards, was to operate from the north, and, after capturing the old capital of Assam, was to threaten the kingdom from that direction.

II. A second Bengal column under Brigadier Shuldham, was to penetrate by way of Sylhet.

III. A mixed column of Bengal and Madras troops, under Brigadier-General W. Morrison, was to advance from Chittagong into Arracan, with the support of a flotilla of the Indian Marine.

IV. The main attack was entrusted to a joint Bengal and Madras army, under Major-General Archibald Campbell, of the 38th (South Stafford Regiment), an officer who had done good service in the Peninsula. The troops composing the main army comprised a Bengal brigade, which consisted of the 13th (Somerset Light Infantry), 38th (South Stafford), and the 20th Bengal Infantry. The 1st Madras Brigade comprised the 41st (Welsh Regiment), the Madras European Regiment (now the 1st Royal Dublin Fusiliers), and five battalions of Madras sepoys, with two companies of artillery.

The 2nd Madras Brigade consisted of the 89th (Royal Irish Fusiliers), five battalions of Madras sepoys, and two companies of artillery.

The Bengal and Madras troops assembled in Cornwallis Bay, in the Andaman Islands ; thence the main army proceeded to Rangoon, whilst Colonel McCreagh, of the 13th (Somersets), was detached to seize the island of Cheduba. Rangoon was occupied after very feeble resistance, but in the month of December the Burmese,

16

finding we were not disposed to advance farther into their country, made desperate attempts to retake the city. They found, however, that we were as good behind stockades as they were, and from that date the war resolved itself into a number of desultory expeditions, in which stockade after stockade was carried at the point of the bayonet, often with heavy loss. There was little glory to be gained in such a war, nor was there scope for any display of military talent ; but the gallantry of the officers and the ready valour of our men was never better exemplified.

The determined attack on Rangoon by the Burmese in the month of December, 1824, gave the 26th Madras, now the 86th Carnatic, Infantry an opportunity of putting an additional battle honour on their colours.

KEMMENDINE, NOVEMBER 30 to DECEMBER 9, 1824.

This battle honour is borne only by the 86th Carnatic Infantry, and was granted to that corps, then the 26th Madras Infantry, by the Governor of Madras, in recognition of the gallant defence of the Kemmendine stockade during the repeated attacks by the Burmese in the month of December, 1824. Kemmendine was the name given by the Burmese to one of the principal defences of Rangoon. We had captured it with some loss on the first occupation of the city. It was rightly looked upon as one of the most important works in the vicinity of Rangoon. In December, when the Burmese made their desperate attempts to retake Rangoon, the Kemmendine stockade was the object of their fiercest attacks. It was held by the 26th Madras Infantry, now the 86th Carnatics, a company of the Madras Europeans, and some gunners, the Honourable Company's cruiser *Sophie* being moored off its river face. The conduct of the Madras sepoys was beyond all praise, and even Havelock, ever chary of encomiums, except to his beloved 13th, wrote in the most eulogistic manner of the 26th. " The sepoys of the 26th acquired a lasting reputation for their firm-

ness at Kemmendine," wrote that distinguished General in his "History of the War in Ava." "Major Yates, who commanded them, sent for, and received, frequent supplies of ammunition, but never talked or dreamt of reinforcements, surrender, or retreat. Hungry and watching, pent in, outnumbered, and wearied by night and day, they repelled their assailants with slaughter." Another contemporary writer says : " Worn out with fatigue, they successfully repulsed the successive attacks of the enemy, contenting themselves with dry rice, not even laying aside their arms for cooking food." The safety of the stockade was entirely due to the ceaseless watchfulness of the little garrison. The Burmese had no stomach for an assault on a foe who was ready for them, and so it was that the garrison of Kemmendine escaped with few casualties.

Regiments.	Officers.		Men.	
	K.	W.	K.	W.
Dublin Fusiliers	—	1	4	13
86th Carnatic Infantry (British)	—	2	—	—
86th Carnatic Infantry (Natives)	—	2	6	21

The battle honour was only conferred on the 26th Madras Native Infantry, which also was allowed to assume the honour "Ava." The 1st Madras European Regiment, a detachment of which was so closely associated with them in the defence, has been obliged to content itself with the one distinction " Ava."

On December 7 the Commander-in-Chief determined to teach the Burmese a fresh lesson, and, attacking the besieging force (for Rangoon at this time was virtually besieged) in four columns, he inflicted on them a most crushing defeat, capturing over 200 pieces of ordnance.

In the course of the next few months our troops suffered terribly from climate and the criminal neglect of the most elementary precautions as regards shelter and

food. The British soldier fought in coatee, shako, and leather stock. Hundreds perished from sunstroke, more from scurvy and cholera. The 13th (Somersets), 38th (South Staffords), 41st (Welsh), 45th (Sherwood Foresters), 49th (Royal Berkshires), and 87th (Royal Irish Fusiliers) buried 3,586 men in eight months; whilst the two regiments sent to Arracan, the 44th (Essex) and 54th (Dorsets), lost 595 out of a strength of 1,004.

Not only were our troops suffering from the climate, but the resistance of the enemy was found to be far more formidable than was anticipated. It was found necessary to call for more reinforcements, and early in 1825 the Royal Scots, the 44th (Essex), the 45th Sherwood Foresters, and the 87th (Royal Irish Fusiliers) joined Sir Archibald's army. The want of cavalry had been apparent, so the Governor-General's Bodyguard and a regiment of Madras cavalry were also despatched to Rangoon. In the course of the cold weather expeditionary columns had been sent to Tenasserim and Martaban, both of which provinces had been occupied with but little loss. A force despatched to Kykloo, however, met with a serious repulse, and the Commander-in-Chief felt that it would be necessary to carry the war still farther into Burmese territory. In February the main army advanced towards Prome, Brigadier Sale, of the 13th (Somersets), being detached to Bassein, which he occupied after a sharp fight. Sir Archibald Campbell met with a check at Donabew in the month of March, but towards the end of April Prome was occupied, and the summer was passed by the army with that city as its headquarters. Advances on our part, with a view to opening negotiations, were construed by the Burmese into an acknowledgment of our weakness, and as soon as the season permitted, fresh hostilities commenced. It was not until the month of February, 1826, that we were enabled to meet the enemy in the open. So little did they dread our attacks, and so little had they taken to heart the numerous defeats we had inflicted on them, that they actually withstood our attack in the open

at Pagahm, not far from Prome.   This was the lesson they needed.   Hitherto the want of cavalry and the density of jungle had prevented our following up our successes, but at Pagahm the Governor-General's Bodyguard was able to reach the flying Burmese, cutting up a large number.   The result of this was a renewal of peace negotiations ; this time the advance was on their part.

The result of the war was a considerable extension of our territory to the east of Bengal.   Tenasserim, Martaban, and Rangoon, all fell into our hands, and the King of Burmah renounced all sovereignty over Arracan and Assam.

ARRACAN, 1825.

This distinction was conferred by the Governor-General in Council on the Bengal native regiments which took part in the invasion of the ancient kingdom of Arracan during the operations in Burmah in the year 1825.   The British and Madras regiments employed bear the same honour as that bestowed on the regiments which accompanied the main army under Sir Archibald Campbell. The only regiments now left with the distinction " Arracan " are the 2nd Gardner's Horse and the 5th Light Infantry.

The force destined for the invasion of Arracan was placed under the command of Brigadier-General W. Morrison, of the 54th (Dorsets), and acted in co-operation with a strong flotilla of the Indian Marine.   It was composed of three brigades—two of Bengal, the third of Madras troops :

First Brigade—Lieutenant-Colonel W. Richards : 26th Bengal Infantry, 44th (Essex Regiment), 49th and 62nd Bengal Infantry.

Second Brigade — Lieutenant-Colonel Grant, C.B. (54th Foot) : 54th (Dorsets), 42nd (now the 5th Light Infantry), and 61st Bengal Infantry.

Third Brigade—Lieutenant-Colonel Fair (10th Madras Infantry) : 10th and 16th Madras Infantry (the latter now the 76th Punjabis).

A couple of companies of Bengal and one of Madras Artillery, as well as two squadrons of Gardner's Horse, accompanied the force.

CASUALTIES OF THE ARRACAN FIELD FORCE.

Regiments.	Officers.		Men.		Regiments.	Officers.		Men.	
	K.	W.	K.	W.		K.	W.	K.	W.
44th Essex	—	—	—	11	5th Light Infantry	—	1	1	18
54th Dorsets	—	2	3	25	76th Punjabis	1	3	10	30
2nd Gardner's Horse	—	—	—	8					

CASUALTIES IN ACTION DURING THE OPERATIONS IN BURMAH, 1824.

Regiments.	Officers.		Men.		Regiments.	Officers.		Men.	
	K.	W.	K.	W.		K.	W.	K.	W.
Royal Scots	—	1	2	5	Governor-General's Bodygd.	—	1	3	3
Somerset L.I.	5	18	21	138	26th Light Cav.	—	—	—	—
South Staffords	2	6	25	130	61st Pioneers	—	3	6	24
41st Welsh	2	2	12	98	63rd Light Infantry	1	3	10	58
44th Essex	1	5	3	14	67th Punjabis	—	—	—	—
45th Sherwood Foresters	—	—	—	—	69th Punjabis	—	2	5	16
47th N. Lancs	1	5	10	80	72nd Punjabis	—	1	1	11
54th Dorsets	—	3	3	27	76th Punjabis	1	3	10	30
87th Roy. Irish Fusiliers	—	—	—	—	82nd Punjabis	—	—	—	—
89th Roy. Irish Fusiliers	3	8	21	147	86th Carnatic I.	—	2	4	57
1st Roy. Dublin Fusiliers	1	3	22	120	88th Carnatic I.	—	3	2	22
					90th Punjabis	—	1	1	12
					92nd Punjabis	—	—	—	—

The force suffered much from sickness, owing to the unhealthy nature of the country traversed, and experienced many hardships. The resistance was not very serious, but on one or two occasions the Burmese fought well. The total casualties amounted to about 130 killed and wounded, the Dorsets and 76th Punjabis being the principal sufferers.

The casualties in action barely reached 3 per cent., those by disease exceeded 56 per cent., of the troops present !

PEGU.

This distinction was granted to the following regiments, in recognition of their services during the campaign in Burmah in the years 1852-53 :

Royal Irish.
King's Own Yorkshire Light Infantry.
2nd Queen's Own Sappers and Miners.
69th Punjabis.

South Staffords.
Royal Munster Fusiliers.
Royal Dublin Fusiliers.
54th Sikhs.
61st Pioneers.
79th Carnatic Infantry.

86th Carnatic Infantry.

The continual infractions of the Treaty of 1826 by the King of Burmah, his arbitrary seizure of the persons and property of British merchants, and his insolent reply to communications addressed to him by the Governor-General of India, rendered it necessary for us to take steps to uphold the dignity of our flag. Early in 1852 a force, furnished by the armies of Madras and Bengal, was placed under the command of General Godwin, an officer who had served in the war of 1834, and who prior to that had taken part in almost every engagement of note in the Peninsular War, under Wellington. At the outset of the operations it was thought that a brigade from each presidency would prove sufficient, but before the end of 1852 the army under General Godwin's command was organized into no less than five brigades, as under :

Madras Brigade—Brigadier-General W. H. Elliott: 51st King's Own Light Infantry, 1st, 9th, and 35th Regiments of Madras Infantry (now the 61st Pioneers, 69th and 72nd Punjabis).
First Bengal Brigade—Brigadier-General T. S. Reignolds : 18th (Royal Irish), the 40th and 67th Regiments of Bengal Infantry.
Second Bengal Brigade—Brigadier-General T. Dickenson : 80th (North Staffords), 10th Bengal Infantry, and the 54th Sikhs.
Third Bengal Brigade—Brigadier-General H. Huishe : 1st Battalion Munster Fusiliers, and the 37th Bengal Infantry.

Of these five Bengal regiments, the 54th Sikhs alone remains to bear the honour.

The campaign calls for little remark. The General, whilst waiting for the Madras Brigade, seized Martaban, and on April 19 Rangoon was captured, with a loss to us of 149 officers and men killed and wounded, our trophies amounting to no less than ninety-two guns, mostly of large calibre. In the month of August the 1st Madras Fusiliers (now the 1st Battalion of the Dublin Fusiliers) arrived from Madras, and in October Pegu was captured. The war now resolved itself into a succession of attacks on dacoits, or petty chieftains, and is noticeable for the fact that in one of these, when matters were looking very serious for us, a young officer—Ensign Garnet Wolseley, of the 80th—showed himself possessed of determined gallantry and ready resource. He was badly wounded on this occasion, but it is not every Ensign that is fortunate enough to be mentioned in despatches in his first action.

The result of the campaign was a considerable addition to our Indian Empire—or, rather, to the dominions then administered by the East India Company—and the annexation of the maritime provinces of the Burmese kingdom. The casualties show the serious nature of the fighting which took place :

Regiments.	Officers.		Men.		Regiments.	Officers.		Men.	
	K.	W.	K.	W.		K.	W.	K.	W.
Royal Artillery	4	3	—	—	1st Madras Fus. (Dublins) ..	—	2	2	27
18th Royal Irish ..	2	5	12	71	2nd Q.O. Sappers and Min.	—	3	3	13
51st K.O. Yorkshire L.I. ..	2	4	5	31	54th Sikhs ..	1	3	6	20
80th North Staffords ..	5	4	4	40	61st Pioneers..	—	1	4	17
1st Bengal Fus. (Munsters) ..	2	1	3	11	69th Punjabis	—	2	3	18
					79th Carnatic I.	—	—	—	—
					86th Carnatic I.	—	—	—	—

BURMAH, 1885-1887.

This distinction was awarded to the regiments named below, who shared in the long and arduous operations in Burmah which led to the annexation of that province in the years 1885-1887 :

The Queen's (R.W. Surrey).	King's Liverpool.
Somerset Light Infantry.	Royal Scots Fusiliers.
Royal Welsh Fusiliers.	South Wales Borderers.
Hampshire.	King's Own Yorkshire L.I.
Royal Munster Fusiliers.	Rifle Brigade.
7th Hurriana Lancers.	26th P.W.O. Light Cavalry.
27th Light Cavalry.	31s Lancers.
2nd Q.O. Rajput Light Infantry.	1st P.W.O. Sappers and Miners.
3rd Sappers and Miners.	2nd Q.O. Sappers and Miners.
1st Brahmins.	4th Rajputs.
10th Jats.	5th Light Infantry.
12th Pioneers.	11th Jats.
18th Infantry.	16th Rajputs.
27th Punjabis.	26th Punjabis.
61st Pioneers.	33rd Punjabis.
72nd Punjabis.	63rd Light Infantry.
74th Punjabis.	73rd Carnatic Infantry.
76th Punjabis.	75th Carnatic Infantry.
83rd Light Infantry.	81st Pioneers.
87th Punjabis.	86th Carnatic Infantry.
95th Russell's Infantry.	90th Punjabis.
101st Grenadiers.	96th Berar Infantry.
107th Pioneers.	105th Mahratta Light Infantry.
123rd Outram's Rifles.	125th Napier's Rifles.
127th Baluch Light Infantry. 3rd Gurkhas.	
8th Gurkhas.	

The absurd pretensions of the Court of Burmah had led to a cessation of all diplomatic intercourse between the British and Burmese Governments since the year 1879. In 1884 King Thebaw gave cause for further remonstrances by the high-handed treatment accorded to an English company trading in his kingdom, and on October 22, 1885, a contemptuous reply to an ultimatum led to a war which placed the battle honour " Burmah, 1885-1887 " on the colours of so many of our regiments. Our Intelligence Department was by no means well informed as to the nature of the interior of the kingdom, beyond the main facts that roads were non-existent, and that it consisted for the most part of thick jungle. In the operations of 1824-1826, and again during the campaign of 1882, no efforts had been made to reach the capital, but it was now determined that no durable peace was possible until the King himself had felt the power of our arms. Fortunately, the officials of the Bombay-Burmah Trading Company possessed a number of steamers, the officers of which were excellent pilots, knowing the upper reaches of the river well, and their knowledge enabled the naval authorities to carry the operations to a rapid and successful conclusion. The officer selected to command the expeditionary force was Sir Harry Prendergast, of the Madras Engineers. He had well won a Victoria Cross for an act of exceptional gallantry in the Mutiny, and he had the reputation, besides personal gallantry, of possessing high powers of organization. The force at his command numbered upwards of 9,000 men, with 67 guns, and it was accompanied by a flotilla of no less than 55 river steamers. with a naval brigade of 600 men and 26 guns. The land force was divided into three brigades, each composed of one British and two native regiments, commanded by Brigadiers Foord, F. B. Norman, and G. S. White respectively. There were, as divisional troops, a battalion of native pioneers and six batteries of artillery. On November 14, 1885, no answer having been received to the ultimatum of the Viceroy, the force advanced ; on the following day the forts at Minhla, on the Irawadi River, were carried by General Norman's brigade, and on the following day we silenced the various forts between our frontier and the capital. On the 26th, as we neared the capital, envoys arrived announcing the unconditional surrender of King Thebaw, and on the 28th we entered Mandalay, and the official war was over, our losses having been comparatively very trifling. Unfortunately, although a certain number of the Burmese troops laid down their arms at Mandalay, a very large number escaped into the jungle, to commence a harassing campaign of dacoitry. A force of three brigades and 9,000 men had been considered sufficient for the subjugation of the country ; now five brigades and 30,000 men were mobilized to restore order.

On January 1 the Viceroy published a proclamation, by the terms of which the sovereignty of Burmah passed into our hands : " By command of the Queen-Empress, it is hereby notified that the territories formerly governed by King Thebaw will no longer be under his rule, but have become part of Her Majesty's dominions, and will, during Her Majesty's pleasure, be administered by such officers as the Viceroy and Governor-General of India may from time to time appoint." With this simple announcement 88,000 square miles of territory passed into our possession.

CASUALTIES AT MANDALAY.

Regiments.	Officers.		Men.		Regiments.	Officers.		Men.	
	K.	W.	K.	W.		K.	W.	K.	W.
King's Liverpool Regt. ..	—	—	—	4	83rd W.L.I. ..	1	—	1	3
					Roy. Welsh Fus.	—	1	2	14
Hampshires ..	—	—	—	—	2nd Q.O.L.I. ..	1	—	6	15
11th Rajputs	1	—	3	15	72nd Punjabis	—	5	1	6

CHAPTER XVI

BATTLE HONOURS FOR THE FIRST AFGHAN WAR, 1839-1842

Afghanistan, 1839-1842—Ghuznee, 1839—Khelat, 1839—Kahun, 1840 — Jelalabad — Khelat-i-Ghilzai — Candahar, 1842 — Ghuznee, 1842—Cabool, 1842—Cutchee.

AFGHANISTAN.

THIS distinction is borne by the

4th Hussars.	Somerset Light Infantry.
The Queen's.	Royal Munster Fusiliers.
Leicesters.	31st D.C.O. Lancers.
3rd Skinner's Horse.	3rd Sappers and Miners.
34th Poona Horse.	2nd Q.O. Light Infantry.
5th Light Infantry.	6th Light Infantry.
16th Lancers.	119th Multan Regiment.

It commemorates their share in the ill-judged campaign which had for its object the forcible imposition of an unpopular Sovereign on an unwilling people. Many of the oldest and most experienced of our Indian statesmen foretold disaster from the outset. The Duke of Wellington expressed himself in no measured terms on the folly of endeavouring to overthrow the *de facto* ruler of Afghanistan, and to put on his throne a monarch who did not own an acre of land nor a rupee which he did not owe to our bounty. Unsuccessful negotiations were entered into with Runjeet Singh, the ruler of the Punjab, with a view to permitting our army to march through the Punjab. This favour was refused, and the Bengal troops, which mobilized at Ferozepore, were compelled to march down the left bank of the Sutlej, through Bhawulpore, and then, crossing the Indus by a bridge of boats thrown across that river at Bukkur, to traverse the desert of Scinde, and, ascending the Bolan Pass, to enter Afghanistan by way of Kandahar. The chief command it was intended should have been held by Sir Harry Fane, the Commander-in-Chief in India, but at the last moment—indeed, after the army had assembled at Ferozepore—its composition was considerably reduced, and Sir John Keane, the Commander-in-Chief in Bombay, assumed the command. The troops destined for the expedition consisted of some 27,000 men, including the reserve divisions at Ferozepore and in Scinde, and were brigaded as under :

Cavalry Division—Major-General E. Thackwell : Wing of the 4th Hussars, 16th Lancers, the 2nd and 3rd Bengal Light Cavalry, a wing of the 1st Bombay Cavalry (now the 31st Duke of Connaught's Own Lancers), the 34th Poona Horse, the 1st and 4th Local Horse (now the 1st Duke of York's Own Lancers), and the 3rd Skinner's Horse.

This fine force of cavalry was formed in three brigades :

First Infantry Division—Major-General Sir W. Cotton.
First Brigade—Brigadier-General J. R. Sale, C.B. : 13th (Somerset Light Infantry), the 16th and 48th Regiments of Bengal Infantry.
Second Brigade—Major-General W. Nott, C.B. : 31st, 42nd, and 43rd Regiments of Bengal Infantry.
Third Brigade—Brigadier-General A. Roberts : 2nd Bengal European Regiment, 30th, 35th, and 37th Regiments of Bengal Infantry.

The 35th Bengal Infantry was left at Bukkur to hold the bridge over the Indus, and preparations were made to punish the Scinde Sirdars, who evinced a determination to oppose the passage of our troops through their country. Wiser counsels prevailed, possibly due to the fact that H.M.S. *Wellesley* had with a couple of broadsides knocked the forts at Kurrachee into pieces, and that the Bombay troops were advancing from the south. On reaching Quettah, the Bombay column, which was under Sir John Keane, the Commander-in-Chief, joined hands with the Bengal army. This force consisted of the 4th Hussars, the two Bombay cavalry regiments named above, the 2nd (Queen's), 17th (Leicesters), and the 19th (now the 119th) Bombay Infantry. Leaving the 43rd Bengal Infantry at Quettah, the army pushed on to Kandahar, losing an immense number of its baggage animals *en route*, and suffering much from marauding Baluchis, and still more from the terrible heat in the passes. It must be remembered that the men marched in leather stocks, in leather shakos, and red coatees ! In June the army reached Kandahar, and thence a force was detached, under Brigadier Sale, to the Helmund River, meeting with a certain amount of opposition. Leaving a strong garrison under Colonel Herring in Kandahar, and entrusting the chief command in Southern Afghanistan to General Nott, the Commander-in-Chief advanced to the north towards the end of June, reaching the neighbourhood of Ghuznee on July 21, where the first serious opposition was encountered, the Afghans being signally worsted by our cavalry, who were well handled by General Thackwell, a Peninsular veteran, who had lost an arm at Waterloo.

Ghuznee, 1839.

This battle honour was the first granted during the reign of Queen Victoria, and was awarded to the following regiments, who were present at the storming of the Afghan fortress by Sir John Keane on July 23, 1839 :

4th Hussars.	16th Lancers.
The Queen's (R.W. Surrey)	13th Somerset L.I.
17th Leicesters.	1st Bengal Fus. (Munsters).
3rd Skinner's Horse.	31st Duke of Connaught's
34th Poona Horse.	Lancers.
3rd Sappers and Miners.	119th Multan Regiment.

All the regiments of the old Bengal army which participated in this feat of arms, or in the subsequent operations in Afghanistan, were swept away in the Mutiny of 1857.

Sir John Keane, against the advice of his artillery officers, had left his siege-train behind, owing to difficulties of carriage, and there was nothing to be done but to carry Ghuznee by storm. There were men present who had assisted at the storming of Bhurtpore in 1826, and all remembered the terrible losses incurred by Lord Lake's army at the unsuccessful assaults of that fortress in 1805. The prospect was not a pleasing one, but with the Oriental *l'audace, l'audace, toujours l'audace* is the best policy in the long-run.   On July 23 Keane carried the place by assault with but trifling loss, and so earned a peerage.

CASUALTIES AT THE STORMING OF GHUZNEE, JULY 28, 1839.

Regiments.	Officers.		Men.		Regiments.	Officers.		Men.	
	K.	W.	K.	W.		K.	W.	K.	W.
4th Hussars ..	—	—	—	—	Bengal Artillery	—	—	—	—
16th Lancers..	—	—	—	—	Bombay Artlly.	—	—	—	—
2nd Queen's ..	—	6	4	27	Bombay Engrs.	—	1	—	—
17th Leicester	—	—	—	—	3rd Skinner's H.	?	?	?	?
13th Somerset					31st Lancers ..	?	?	?	?
L.I. ..	—	1	1	30	34th Poona H.	—	—	—	—
Munster Fus.	—	9	1	51	119th Mult. R.	—	—	—	—

On August 8 the army reached Kabul, and the puppet Shah Sujah was installed on the throne, the brave Dost Mohammed flying before our arms, only to rally for a fresh desperate venture for the kingdom.   The Bombay column was now ordered back by way of Ghuznee and Kandahar, and the Commander-in-Chief, with the 16th Lancers and some details of the 13th Light Infantry and of the Bengal regiments, returned to India by the Khyber.

KHELAT, NOVEMBER 13, 1839.

This battle honour is borne by the

Queen's (Royal West Surrey).
3rd Sappers and Miners.

Leicesters.
3rd Skinner's Horse.
2nd Q.O. Rajput L.I.

It commemorates a scarcely remembered, but very successful, affair carried out by a column of the invading army of Afghanistan.   On the capture of Ghuznee (p. 254) and the flight of Dost Mohammed, it was erroneously anticipated that the people of the country were willing to accept Shah Sujah as their Sovereign. Sir John Keane, misled by the political officers, determined to send back a large portion of his army to India, and whilst one column was to return by the Khyber Pass, in the north, another was told off to return by the Bolan, in the south. This column was placed under the command of Major-General Willshire, and comprised the regiments above named, with a company of Bombay Artillery and one of Sappers. All were much under their proper strength, and this I touch upon in passing, as it brings out into stronger relief the nature of the task achieved by General Willshire's force.

STRENGTH OF BRITISH TROOPS.

The Queen's	..	13 officers,	331 other ranks.
Leicesters ..	.. 24	,,	374 ,, ,,
Artillery ..	.. 2	,,	38 ,, ,,

STRENGTH OF NATIVE TROOPS.

| 2nd Q.O. Light Inf. | 11 officers, | 373 other ranks. |
| Sappers .. | .. 3 ,, | 127 ,, ,, |

The Baluch tribes had shown themselves uniformly hostile towards us during the whole course of the expedition to Afghanistan. They had attacked our convoys, murdered officers, and cut up camp followers with impunity, and apparently with the full approval of their chiefs. General Willshire, on the return march of the Bombay column, was instructed to inflict condign punishment on the Khans of Khelat. These, on the other hand, determined to make a sturdy resistance. On approaching Khelat the General found the Baluchis massed on the heights surrounding the city, and he at once took measures to attack them. Whilst the Bombay artillery shelled the heights, three columns of infantry, each consisting of but four weak companies, pushed up the three principal spurs, the remainder of the force, under the General's own personal command, being held in reserve. The Bombay artillery always held the reputation of being second to

none, and the accuracy of their fire not only silenced the
few Baluch guns which were posted on the heights, but
compelled the enemy to seek shelter behind the walls of
the fortress before the advancing columns had come to
close quarters.　The General, seeing the enemy streaming
towards the walls, endeavoured to forestall them, and it
became a race as to who should reach the open gateway
first.　Although in this we were beaten by a short head,
yet we were so close in rear of the Baluchis that they were
unable to make any very well-organized stand : our men
were close at their heels.　The gates were blown in, and
British private, well supported by the Bengal sepoy,
pressed into the place.　If we compare the numbers
present at Khelat with those which assisted at the storming of Ghuznee, and then study the two casualty lists, it
will at once be seen that, although the name of Khelat may
not be so familiar as that of Ghuznee, the feat of General
Willshire's army is in no way inferior to that which gained
for Sir John Keane the title of Baron Keane of Ghuznee.

CASUALTIES AT THE STORMING OF KHELAT.

Regiments.	Officers.		Men.		Regiments.	Officers.		Men.	
	K.	W.	K.	W.		K.	W.	K.	W.
Royal Artillery	—	1	1	3	2nd Q.O. L.I.	—	2	2	17
The Queen's ..	1	5	2	42	Bombay Saps.				
Leicesters ..	—	1	6	32	and Miners	—	—	2	6

KAHUN, 1840.

105th Mahratta Light Infantry.

In the month of March, 1841, the Governor of Bombay
issued the following Order in Council :

" In order to testify his admiration of the gallantry,
prudence, and perseverance which distinguished Captain
Brown in the defence of Kahun, and the fidelity and

bravery of the officers and men under his command, the 5th Regiment of Native Infantry shall be permitted to have ' Kahun ' inscribed on their colours and borne on their appointments."

Outside the ranks of the 105th Mahratta Light Infantry there are few who know of the gallant deed which this one word commemorates. On his return to India after the successful capture of Ghuznee, Sir John Keane deemed it advisable to occupy the forts of Quetta and Kahun, commanding as they did two passes between Afghanistan and the Lower Indus. Quetta is well known to the present generation of soldiers, but Kahun is still in the territory of the Murri tribe. It is situated in a valley some ten miles long by five broad, at the western extremity of an exceedingly difficult pass. The town in 1840 was surrounded by a lofty wall, 25 feet in height, with six bastions, but unprovided with a ditch. The force told off to hold the fort consisted of 300 men of the 105th Mahratta Light Infantry (then the 5th Bombay Infantry), under a Captain Lewis Brown, of that corps. He was instructed to move in with six months' supplies, as it was considered quite possible that the Baluchis would refuse to supply him with provisions. The 500 camels, with provisions, were to be escorted back to Sukkur, on the Indus, by a company of the 5th and a squadron of the Scinde Irregular Horse, under Lieutenant Clarke of the 5th, who were to march up to Kahun under Brown's orders. Two guns were at first told off for this force, but this order was afterwards countermanded. However, Brown, contrary to orders, did succeed in taking one gun with him. Leaving Sukkur late in April, Brown reached Kahun on May 12, his march having been vigorously opposed by the Baluchis. On the 15th he sent back the camels, adding a second company to the infantry escort, as he considered the attitude of the tribes very threatening. He thus reduced his force to 140 bayonets, 12 gunners, and 1 gun. On the return march Clarke's little force was attacked by a large body of Baluchis and totally annihilated. Brown now saw that he would have to fight for life. He at once commenced to strengthen the walls, levelled all houses in the immediate neighbourhood, cut down all trees within musketry range, and dug a ditch round the place. On August 31 an effort was made to relieve him. Major Clibborn, of the 101st Grenadiers, with 300 bayonets of his own regiment, 200 sabres of the Scinde Horse, with three guns, reached the foot of the pass, within sound of gunshot of the beleaguered garrison. There Clibborn was attacked by an overwhelming force of Baluchis, and after a stubborn fight was driven back, with the loss of all his guns, 5 officers and 190 men killed. The garrison had long since been deprived of all meat rations, and on September 5 Brown found that he had but six bags of flour left. On this day he received an official letter from the Brigade-Major at Sukkur, informing him of the defeat of the relieving force, and further adding that it would be impossible to make another attempt, as there were no more troops available. Brown was therefore told that he must act on his own resources, and either cut his way out or make arrangements with the Baluch chiefs for a safe conduct to Sukkur. On more than one occasion Dodah Khan, the head of the Murri tribe, had offered to allow Brown to march through his country if he would hand over the fort, but without superior orders Brown felt he was not entitled to treat. Now he had full power to act on his own responsibility, and on September 12, after a close siege of four months, the gallant Brown entered into an arrangement with the Baluch chief, and evacuated the fort which he had held so nobly. The Baluchis, unlike the Afghans at Kabul, held to their word. Brown's return march was unmolested, and early in October the remains of his own wornout, half-starved garrison reached Quetta. Few battle honours have been more worthily earned than Kahun.

The forebodings of the prophets of evil came to pass. We had placed Shah Sujah on the throne of his fathers, but it was not in our power to enthrone him in the hearts of his people. Expedition after expedition was undertaken to punish tribes which refused to accept his rule, and who in doing so showed active hostility to ourselves. In 1841 it was determined to evacuate the country, but a rising of the tribes in the Khyber Pass effectually cut off all communication between Kabul and India. Sir Robert Sale was despatched with a brigade to open the pass, but he found that he was compelled to fight his way at every step, and finally threw himself into Jelalabad, a semi-fortified town midway between Kabul and Peshawur. Shortly after his arrival he learnt of the murder of the Envoy, Sir William Macnaghten, and of the attempt of the Kabul garrison to reach the shelter of Jelalabad. Of the army which left Kabul, but one man reached the shelter of Sale's defences, the 44th Foot being abso-lutely annihilated. Lady Butler's picture, " The Rem-nant of an Army," depicts Dr. Bryden riding, sorely wounded, into the snowed-in fortress.[1]

JELALABAD.

This battle honour, with a mural crown, is borne by the Somerset Light Infantry, and commemorates their gallant defence of Jelalabad in the winter of 1841-42. As a feat of arms the defence was not of any striking value. The garrison suffered from want of food, and they were exposed to attack on the part of the Afghan tribes ; but as a matter of fact they were left pretty much undisturbed, their casualties during the six months' siege being but 4 men killed, 2 officers and 14 men wounded. On April 5 Sale made a sortie, driving off the besiegers, and so reliev-ing himself before the arrival of the avenging army under Pollock. In this action the 13th lost their gallant Colonel Dennie, a soldier whose loss would have dimmed a far more glorious victory than that won under the walls of Jelalabad ; the losses on this day were, in addition to the Colonel, 8 men killed, 2 officers and 31 men wounded. As the native infantry regiment which shared with the 13th the glories of the defence of Jelalabad no longer exists, I have not given the casualties incurred by any corps but the

[1] The 44th (Essex) lost 22 officers and 645 N.C.O.'s and men in this disastrous retreat.

Somerset Light Infantry. The total casualties of the 13th throughout the campaign amounted to 4 officers and 62 men killed, 19 officers and 238 non-commissioned officers and men wounded.

KHELAT-I-GHILZAI.

This honour, with the word " Invicta," is borne by the 12th Pioneers (the Khelat-i-Ghilzai Regiment). During our occupation of Afghanistan certain strategic points had necessarily been held in order to maintain our communications with India. Amongst these were the forts of Ghuznee and Khelat-i-Ghilzai, between the capital and Kandahar. The former was entrusted to a Colonel Palmer, of the 27th Bengal Infantry ; the latter to Captain Craigie, with a regiment of infantry raised in Hindustan for the army of the Shah Sujah. Unfortunately, the Ghuznee garrison was compelled to surrender, but Craigie and his men weathered the storm, and though besieged for four long months, and reduced to sore straits for food, they repelled more than one assault. For its gallant defence of Khelat-i-Ghilzai the Shah's regiment was brought on the establishment of the Bengal army, and now remains with us as the 12th Pioneers (the Khelat-i-Ghilzai Regiment). In addition to the name " Khelat-i-Ghilzai," the regiment is allowed to carry an honorary standard, and bears on its colours the proud motto " Invicta."

CANDAHAR, 1842.

This battle honour was conferred on the troops which, advancing from Kandahar under General Nott, aided in the release of the captives in Kabul, and in the punishment of the Afghans for the murder of our Envoy in 1841. The regiments still entitled to bear this honour are the

South Lancashire.	Welsh.
1st Skinner's Horse.	34th Poona Horse.
5th Light Infantry.	6th Light Infantry.
12th Pioneers (Khelat-i-Ghilzai Regiment).	

Throughout the winter of 1841-42 General Nott had been subject to considerable annoyance from the tribes of Southern Afghanistan. On two occasions he had been attacked at Kandahar, and he had experienced some difficulty in keeping open his communications with India by the Bolan Pass. It was not until he had heard that General Pollock was at Jelalabad that he was able to commence his advance towards Kabul. His force was divided into two brigades of infantry, with a small, but very efficient, force of cavalry, consisting of the 3rd Bombay Cavalry (now the 33rd Queen's Own Light Cavalry), and two regiments of irregular cavalry, one of which is still with us as Skinner's Horse. His artillery comprised two batteries of horse and two of field artillery. The First Infantry Brigade was under Brigadier Wymer, and consisted of the 40th (South Lancashire Regiment), the 16th and 38th Regiments of Bengal Infantry, and the 12th Khelat-i-Ghilzai Regiment, this last alone being with us.

The Second Brigade comprised the 41st (Welsh Regiment), the 42nd and 43rd Regiments of Bengal Infantry (now the 5th and 6th Regiments of Light Infantry).

On passing Khelat-i-Ghilzai, which all through the winter had been most gallantly defended by the 3rd Regiment of the Shah's infantry, under Captain Craigie, Nott, in obedience to instructions, destroyed the fortifications. At Ghuznee he met with his first opposition, and was able, with but little loss, to inflict a sharp defeat on the Afghans.

GHUZNEE, 1842.

This distinction was conferred on the regiments which marched up from Kandahar, under General Nott, and were present at the successful little skirmish outside the fortress of Ghuznee in August, 1842. The regiments authorized to bear this honour are the

South Lancashire.	The Welsh.
33rd Q.O. Light Cavalry.	5th Light Infantry.
6th Jat Light Infantry.	12th Khelat-i-Ghilzais.

The losses were slight ; indeed, when we examine the casualty returns of nearly all the engagements that have been inscribed on the colours of the British army for services in Afghanistan, it is impossible to avoid the conclusion that the honours have been very liberally bestowed.

CASUALTIES AT GHUZNEE, 1842.

Regiments.	Officers.		Men.		Regiments.	Officers.		Men.	
	K.	W.	K.	W.		K.	W.	K.	W.
Royal Artillery	—	—	—	3	Christie's Horse	—	1	7	14
40th S. Lancs.	—	1	—	12	5th Light Inf.	—	—	—	—
41st Welsh ..	—	—	—	4	6th Jat. Lt. Inf.	—	—	—	—
33rd Q.O. Light				7	12th Khelat-i-				
Cavalry ..	2	2	15		Ghilzais ..	—	—	—	

CABOOL, 1842.

This distinction was granted to all the regiments which participated in the operations in Afghanistan, having for their object the release of the captives in the hands of Akbar Khan, or of the relief of the garrisons at Jelalabad and Khelat-i-Ghilzai. The command of the army operating from Peshawur was entrusted to General George Pollock, of the Bengal Artillery, whilst the Southern army, which advanced from Kandahar, was, as we have seen, commanded by General Nott, a distinguished officer of the Indian army. The regiments authorized to bear this distinction are the

3rd Hussars.
Somerset Light Infantry.
South Lancashire.
33rd Q.O. Light Cavalry.
5th Light Infantry.

Norfolk.
East Surrey.
Welsh.
4th Rajputs.
6th Light Infantry.

12th Khelat-i-Ghilzai.

Pollock's army was mobilized at Peshawur, in virtue of an arrangement with Runjeet Singh, the Sovereign of the Punjab, who had consented to send an army to act in conjunction with our own. It was not until the commencement of April that General Pollock had collected sufficient carriage for his advance. We were now under no delusions as to the feeling of the people of Afghanistan, and we also knew that the tribes in the Khyber Pass would oppose every step of our way. Sir Robert Sale had relieved himself before General Pollock started, and it was intended that his troops should join in the advance, and take their share in carrying out the punishment to be inflicted on the city of Kabul. Sale's brigade was numbered the First of Pollock's army, which was thus constituted :

Commanding the Forces : General George Pollock.
Second in Command : Major-General John McCaskill.
First Brigade—Major-General Sir Robert Sale : 13th (Somerset Light Infantry), 35th Light Infantry, and tribal levies.
Second Brigade—Brigadier-General Tulloch : 9th (Norfolk Regiment), 26th and 60th Regiments of Bengal Infantry.
Third Brigade—Brigadier-General Wilde : 30th, 53rd, and 64th Regiments of Bengal Infantry.
Fourth Brigade—Brigadier-General Monteath : 31st (East Surrey), 6th and 33rd Regiments of Bengal Infantry.

The cavalry brigade was under Brigadier-General White, and consisted of the 3rd Hussars, the 1st and 10th Regiments of Bengal Light Cavalry, and two corps of Irregular Horse.

The artillery comprised two batteries of horse artillery, three of field, and one mountain battery, under Brigadier-General H. Delafosse.

Pollock determined to advance before the arrival of his Third Brigade, leaving that to join him at Jelalabad. He left Peshawur on April 5, and, after one or two sharp skirmishes, arrived at Jelalabad on the 16th of the same month. Here the army was reorganized, Sir Robert Sale being made a Divisional General, and placed in command of the second division, which was to consist of the 9th (Norfolks), the 13th (Somerset Light Infantry), the 16th and 26th Regiments of Bengal Infantry.

General McCaskill, in command of the first division, had under him the 31st (East Surrey), the 33rd and 60th Regiments of Bengal Infantry, and the Sikh army.

In the month of August the army continued its advance on Kabul. Some opposition was experienced in forcing the passes in which our troops in the preceding winter had met their doom, but by the end of September retribution had been exacted ; the captives, amongst whom were Sir Robert Sale's wife and daughter, had been released ; the Bala Hissar, or citadel, in Kabul had been destroyed, and Nott's army had joined hands with the Commander-in-Chief. The retirement to Peshawur was effected with comparatively little loss, and in the beginning of November the army was once more on the left bank of the Sutlej, in British territory.

Pollock's force met with opposition in the Khyber, both in going up to relieve the garrison of Jelalabad as well as in the return march from Kabul to Peshawur, the casualties of his and Nott's force being—

Regiments.	Officers.		Men.		Regiments.	Officers.		Men.	
	K.	W.	K.	W.		K.	W.	K.	W.
3rd Hussars ..	—	—	—	8	40th South				
9th Norfolk ..	1	5	26	90	Lancs ..	1	4	15	33
13th Somerset					41st Welsh ..	2	3	11	48
L.I... ..	—	1	2	19	5th Light Inf.	—	2	8	17
31st E. Surrey	1	2	5	40	6th Light Inf.	—	3	12	76

CUTCHEE, 1839-1842.[1]

This distinction, which is borne on the appointments of the 35th Scinde Horse and the 36th Jacob's Horse, was awarded to those regiments for their services in the province of Cutchee during the operations in Afghanistan in 1839-1842. Cutchee is a province of Southern Baluchistan, and the inhabitants had been enriching themselves at the cost of the East India Company by a very comprehensive system of attacks on our convoys. No general action was fought, and the actual losses incurred by the two regiments were trifling ; but the work was none the less arduous for the absence of fighting, and Sir Charles Napier felt it would be an encouragement to the two newly-raised regiments if they received some outward token that the Sirkar appreciated their good and gallant conduct. On several occasions the regiments had shown considerable dash, and had never hesitated to follow their British officers against any number of Baluchis.

[1] Skinner's Horse, the 101st Grenadiers, and the 105th Mahratta Light Infantry were actively employed in Cutchee in 1839 under Colonel Billamore, but they have not been awarded the battle honour.

CHAPTER XVII

BATTLE HONOURS FOR SERVICES IN INDIA, 1843

Scinde—Meeanee—Hyderabad—Maharajpore—Punniar.

SCINDE, 1843.

THIS distinction was accorded to the Cheshire Regiment for its services in Scinde—services which brought to the regiment the two battle honours " Meeanee " and " Hyderabad." The distinction has not been conferred on the Bombay native regiments which fought side by side with the Cheshires in the brilliant and hardly-contested campaign on the banks of the Indus.

MEEANEE, FEBRUARY 17, 1843.

This battle honour, which commemorates the victory gained by the army commanded by General Sir Charles Napier over the Amirs of Scinde, is borne by the following regiments :

Cheshires.	34th Poona Horse.
35th Scinde Horse.	36th Jacob's Horse.
2nd Queen's Own Sappers and Miners.	112th Infantry.
	125th Outram's Rifles.

The hostilities with the Amirs of Scinde were the direct but inevitable result of the first Afghan War. With some difficulty we had succeeded in obtaining the consent of some of the Amirs to the passage of the Bombay column of the army of Afghanistan through their country ; but the people themselves were very averse to this concession. It was laying them open to future annexation, as they wisely conjectured. The passage of our convoys through their territories was an irresistible attraction to Baluch marauders, and, not content with robbery, they cut up stragglers with impunity. Then we demanded satisfaction, and finally the Amirs undertook to enter into a treaty, by which they were compelled to pay the cost of a force which we maintained in Scinde for the purpose of safeguarding our lines of communication. Our reverses in Afghanistan, as well as the defeat they themselves inflicted on our troops in the neighbourhood of Kahun, and one or two other regrettable incidents, led the Amirs to underrate our strength. They not only neglected to keep up the payments for the army of occupation, but they consistently violated the treaty in every possible way. Frequent attacks were made on parties of troops, and it was evident either that the Amirs would not, or could not keep their people in order.

Sir Charles Napier was despatched to Hyderabad to compel respect to the treaty. The Amirs retaliated by attacking the Residency. Fortunately, a small vessel belonging to the Indian Marine was lying in the Indus, some few miles from the Residency, and Major (afterwards General) Sir James Outram was enabled to beat off his assailants, and to reach the steamer in safety. Napier was a man of action. Knowing that the Amirs were within a few miles of the city, he at once marched to attack them. He calculated their numbers at between 30,000 and 40,000 men, well armed with matchlock and sabres. His own force was just 2,600 men, with twelve guns. This included but one British battalion—the 22nd (Cheshires)—barely 600 men, all armed with the old flint-lock Brown Bess—a weapon which, though a more rapid loader than the matchlock, was its inferior in range. The Amirs had taken up a strong position in a large wooded game-preserve, surrounded with a low mud wall. The one entrance Napier closed with a company of the 22nd, and then he assaulted the place, after he had thoroughly shaken the defenders with a searching fire from his twelve guns. The Baluchis fought well, but this happened to be one of the sepoys' fighting days, and, after three hours' hard firing, the Baluchis were driven off in confusion. Estimates vary as to their losses. Napier himself put it at 5,000 killed ; others put it as low as 500.

If the General's estimate was a correct one, then we must put aside the old saying that it took a ton of lead to kill a man with Brown Bess. When we consider the strength of the position held by the Baluchis and their enormous superiority in numbers, the losses incurred in gaining such a decisive victory were by no means excessive.

CASUALTIES AT MEEANEE.

Regiments.	Officers.		Men.		Regiments.	Officers.		Men.	
	K.	W.	K.	W.		K.	W.	K.	W.
22nd Cheshires	1	5	23	52	9th Bengal Cavalry ..	1	5	3	29
Royal Artillery	—	—	1	4	101st Grena-				
34th Poona H.	—	—	—	—	diers ..	—	—	1	4
35th Scinde H.	—	—	—	—	112th Infantry	3	2	12	45
36th Jacob's H.	—	—	—	—	125th Outram's				
3rd Q.O. Sap-					Rifles ..	1	2	16	27
pers.. ..	—	—	—	3					

NOTE.—The 101st Grenadiers were present at Meeanee, were mentioned in Sir C. Napier's despatch and captured a Baluch standard, but they have not as yet been awarded the battle honour.

The 9th Bengal Cavalry, which behaved with the greatest gallantry at Meeanee, is, unfortunately, no longer represented in the Army List. The regiment was swept away in the Mutiny of 1857, and the present 9th Regiment of cavalry was raised by the immortal Hodson in 1857, whose name it bears.

HYDERABAD, MARCH 24, 1843.

This battle honour is borne by the

Cheshires.	34th Poona Horse.
35th Scinde Horse.	36th Jacob's Horse.
2nd Queen's Own Sappers	101st Grenadiers.
and Miners.	108th Infantry.
112th Infantry.	121st Pioneers.

125th Outram's Rifles.

It commemorates a second victory gained by Sir Charles Napier over the Amirs of Scinde, and was fought, as the name suggests, in the immediate neighbourhood of Hyderabad, on the Indus, just one month after Meeanee. That month had been spent in fruitless negotiations. Outram, the Political Officer, thought he could induce the Amirs to accept our terms without further bloodshed. The hot weather was drawing on apace, and Napier felt there was no time for further delay. He had been reinforced by a couple of sepoy battalions from Bombay and by two field batteries from Bengal, and already some regiments were on the march from the Sutlej to support him. On March 24 he attacked the Amirs, and, though the action was a severe one, it was never for one moment in doubt. The losses in the 22nd Cheshires were sensibly higher than at Meeanee, and the 34th Poona Horse, for the second time in their history, had a fair opportunity of showing of what material they were made. They emerged from the ordeal with a reputation they have maintained to this day.

CASUALTIES AT HYDERABAD.

Regiments.	Officers.		Men.		Regiments.	Officers.		Men.	
	K.	W.	K.	W.		K.	W.	K.	W.
22nd Cheshires	—	5	23	119	101st Grena-				
Royal Artillery	1	—	—	5	diers	—	—	2	1
34th Poona H.	—	1	3	17	108th Infantry	—	—	1	1
35th Scinde H.	—	—	—	—	112th Infantry	—	—	2	1
36th Jacob's H.	—	—	—	—	121st Pioneers	—	2	4	22
2nd Q.O. Sap-					125th Outram's				
pers.. ..	—	—	—	2	Rifles ..	—	—	3	23

The result of the campaign was the annexation of Scinde, and the perpetration of the canard that in announcing his second victory Napier telegraphed to the Governor of Bombay the one word " Peccavi."

The troops were well rewarded for their short campaign. Considerable booty was found in the Amirs' palaces, and Sir Charles at last, after nearly forty years of arduous service, found himself the richer by £68,000, which was his share of the prize-money.

THE GWALIOR CAMPAIGN.

MAHARAJPORE AND PUNNIAR, DECEMBER 29, 1843.

These two general actions, fought on the same day, recall one of the shortest campaigns on record—a campaign forced unwillingly on the Government of India by the truculent conduct of the military oligarchy in the Mahratta State of Gwalior. This spirit was no doubt intensified by the feeling—or, rather, by the hope—that, owing to our recent disasters in Afghanistan, the British would be unwilling to trust to the arbitrament of the sword.

" Maharajpore " is borne on the colours of the

16th Lancers.	Dorsetshire.
East Lancashires.	Governor-General's Body-
3rd Skinner's Horse.	guard.
2nd Q.O. Rajput Light	6th Jat Light Infantry.
Infantry.	12th Khelat-i-Ghilzai.

" Punniar " on the colours of the

9th Lancers.	Buffs.
Royal West Kent.	6th P.W.O. Cavalry.

On the refusal of the Gwalior Council of Regency to disband their army, which was a standing menace to the peace of our North-West Frontier, the Governor-General determined to undertake the task of that disbandment himself. A large camp of exercise was therefore formed at Agra, under the direct superintendence of Sir Hugh Gough, the Commander-in-Chief ; and a second force was assembled at Jhansi, under General Sir George Grey. The former force is responsible for the victory of Maharajpore, the latter for that of Punniar.

Sir Hugh Gough's army was composed of one cavalry and three infantry divisions :

Cavalry Brigade—Major-General Sir Joseph Thackwell : 16th
 Lancers, the Bodyguard, and four native cavalry regiments.
First Infantry Brigade—Major-General Sir John Littler : 39th
 Regiment (Dorsets) and 56th Bengal Infantry.
Second Infantry Brigade—Major-General Valliant : 40th Regi-
 ment (South Lancashires), 2nd and 16th Bengal Infantry.
Third Infantry Brigade—Brigadier-General Stacey : 14th, 31st,
 and 45th Bengal Infantry.

The plan of attack was simple, and one which has been
invariably successful against an Oriental foe. The Mahrattas were found holding a strong position around the
village of Maharajpore. The Commander-in-Chief ordered
Sir John Littler, with his own and the Second Cavalry
Brigade, to make a direct attack on the enemy's position,
covered by a heavy artillery fire, Stacey's brigade being
held in reserve. At the same time Sir Joseph Thackwell,
with the First Cavalry Brigade and Valliant's infantry,
turned the enemy's left. The Gwalior troops made a
very determined resistance, but if they thought that the
disasters in Afghanistan were in any way due to deterioration on the part of the British army, they were woefully
disillusioned. Littler found the Gwalior troops holding
a series of entrenched positions, from which they were
successively driven at the point of the bayonet, not without heavy loss, our total casualties being 36 officers and
750 men killed and wounded.

CASUALTIES AT THE BATTLE OF MAHARAJPORE,
DECEMBER 29, 1843.

Regiments.	Officers.		Men.		Regiments.	Officers.		Men.	
	K.	W.	K.	W.		K.	W.	K.	W.
16th Lancers ..	—	—	2	7	Bengal Artillery	1	—	6	36
39th Dorset ..	1	10	29	174	Bengal Engrs.	—	—	—	—
40th S. Lancs	—	8	23	151	6th Jat Light Infantry ..	—	—	1	4
Governor-Gene-ral's Body-guard ..	—	—	—	—	12th Pioneers (Khelat - i - Ghilzai Regt.)	—	—	2	7
2nd Q.O.L.I.	—	1	3	16					

On the same day General Grey found another division of the Gwalior army entrenched at Punniar. On this occasion our losses amounted to 35 killed and 182 wounded, our trophies to twenty-four guns. The result of the two engagements was the destruction of the military power of Gwalior.

CASUALTIES AT THE BATTLE OF PUNNIAR.

Regiments.	Officers.		Men.		Regiments.	Officers.		Men.	
	K.	W.	K.	W.		K.	W.	K.	W.
9th Lancers ..	—	—	—	—	Roy. W. Kent	1	1	8	32
The Buffs ..	1	3	10	56	6th K.E. Cav.	—	—	1	3

CHAPTER XVIII

BATTLE HONOURS FOR THE CONQUEST OF THE PUNJAB

Moodkee — Ferozeshah — Aliwal — Sobraon — Chillianwallah — Multan—Goojerat—Punjab.

THE British conquest of the Punjab embraces two distinct phases—the one represented by the Sutlej Campaign of 1845-46, the other better known as the Punjab War of 1849. The extension of our dominions to the North-West, the gradual break-up and absorption of the hitherto independent principalities in Southern and Central India, had brought our frontiers conterminous with those of the powerful Sikh monarchy of Runjit Singh. That monarch was a well-wisher—outwardly, at any rate—of his neighbours, and during the Afghan War he proved his loyalty to us. On his death the sovereignty of the Sikhs fell into the hands of a group bitterly hostile to the English, and it was evident that there were members of the Sikh Regency who believed that the overthrow of the British was a matter of comparative ease. Into the merits of the quarrel it is not my province to enter. Suffice it to say that on December 11 the Sikh army crossed the Sutlej, the boundary river between the two kingdoms, and that the crossing constituted an act of war.

In those far-off days our frontier stations were Ferozepore and Ludhiana, with Umballa in support. Ferozepore was the headquarters of a division, commanded by a sterling soldier, who had done good service in the Gwalior Campaign—Sir John Littler. It consisted of the

62nd (Wiltshire) Regiment, two batteries of horse, and two of field artillery, two regiments of native cavalry, and seven battalions of native infantry.

At Ludhiana, some eighty miles to the east, lay another division, under Brigadier Wheler, comprising the 50th (Royal West Kent), two batteries of horse artillery, three regiments of native cavalry, and five battalions of native infantry.

At Umballa, under Sir Walter Gilbert, a well-known soldier and equally well-known sportsman, were the 9th (Norfolks), 31st (East Surrey), and 80th (South Staffords), the 3rd Light Dragoons (now 3rd Hussars), two regiments of native cavalry, with the Governor-General's Body-guard and five battalions of native infantry. At Kussowlie was the 29th (Worcesters), and at Subathoo the 1st Bengal Europeans (now the 1st Royal Munster Fusiliers), both these battalions being at the disposal of Sir Walter Gilbert.

Thus, at the three frontier stations there was a total force of some 22,000 men ready to face the Sikh advance. At Meerut, which was the headquarters of the Bengal Artillery, there were three horse and three field batteries, the 9th and 16th Lancers, the 10th Foot (the Lincolns), and a considerable force of native infantry, with one regiment of native cavalry.

The Sikh army was known to be superior in every way to any army we had yet met in India, both in training and in material. There were a considerable number of foreign officers in the employ of the Sikhs, and the men had a high reputation, which they maintain to this day, of being equal to the best material of which any army, whether European or Asiatic, can boast. Of its numbers at that time we had no accurate estimate. The Chief Political Officer, Major Broadfoot, who fell gloriously at Ferozeshah, reported that it consisted of upwards of 100,000 men, and that the Sikh plan of campaign was to invade British India with two powerful armies of 50,000 each—with the one to overwhelm Littler at Ferozepore, with the other to attack Wheler at Ludhiana. Fortunately for us, at the moment when their services and their friendly co-operation were most needed, both the Governor-General and the Commander-in-Chief were on the spot. The Governor-General, Sir Henry Hardinge, was a soldier of renown. He had served with Moore at Corunna, had rallied the men at Albuera with the now historic saying, " Die hard, my men—die hard !" and had lost an arm at Ligny, when attached to Blücher's army, the day before Waterloo. The Commander-in-Chief was a well-known fighter, and the forerunner of a family of equally heroic men. Sir Hugh Gough was an old comrade of the Governor-General's. He, too, had fought throughout the Peninsular War, but he had won his spurs at the capture of the Cape of Good Hope in 1805. At Barrosa under Graham, at Tarifa under Skerret, and in many a hard tussle under Wellington, Gough and the 87th (Royal Irish Fusiliers) had won imperishable renown. He had in more recent days shown himself as good a leader of an army as he had been commander of a regiment. In the China War of 1842 he had paved the way for the victory at Maharajpore. With two such soldiers in the field, the Khalsa army, despite its numbers, its organization, and the bravery of its men, was likely to meet its match.

Hard though the campaign was—and for some days the fate of our Indian Empire hung in the balance—no blame can be attached to the military authorities for any shortcomings that were disclosed during this campaign. On December 11 the Sikhs, crossing the Sutlej, cut in between Ferozepore and Umballa. On the following day the Commander-in-Chief moved out of Umballa to meet them. The din of battle was music in the ears of the war-worn Governor-General, and he blithely accompanied the army. On the 17th the Ludhiana division joined that of Umballa, and on the 18th the Sikhs and British met at Moodkee. Our troops had covered 150 miles in seven days, and, as Sir Charles Gough puts it in terse and soldier-like language, " wearied with long and incessant marching, the troops were enjoying a well-earned rest, when reports came in from the cavalry patrols that a large force of Sikhs was advancing upon them." Orders were at once given to fall in, and in a very few moments the force was formed in order of battle. The cavalry, with the horse artillery, immediately advanced, under Sir Hugh Gough's personal direction, and formed line in front of the Sikh position, the guns occupying the centre, with the cavalry on either flank. The infantry formed up in second line and moved forward. On the extreme right was Wheler's brigade, the next stood Bolton's, and then in succession a brigade of native regiments belonging to Gilbert's division, which had not yet been joined by the British battalions from Kussowlie ; whilst to the left stretched Sir John McCaskill's division, which comprised the 9th (Norfolks) and the 80th (South Staffords), with three native battalions ; and so commenced the opening scene in the drama which culminated at Goojerat two years later.

MOODKEE, DECEMBER 18, 1845.

This battle honour was conferred on the regiments present under Lord Gough at the stubbornly contested fight at Moodkee. It is now borne by the following regiments :

3rd Hussars.	Norfolk.
East Surrey.	Royal West Kent.
South Staffords.	Gov.-General's Bodyguard.
3rd Skinner's Horse.	6th K.E.O. Cavalry.
5th Light Infantry.	7th Rajputs.

Moving forward with his cavalry and horse artillery, Sir Hugh Gough opened a heavy fire on the Sikh line, in order to give time for his infantry to deploy and his field batteries to come up into line. Then the cavalry opened out and threatened both flanks of the enemy. The infantry pushed resolutely forward. They were received with equal resolution on the part of our gallant foes. Night put an end to the conflict, but the success was ours.

Seventeen guns remained in our hands. Our losses had
been most severe, numbering 872 of all ranks killed and
wounded.

CASUALTIES AT THE BATTLE OF MOODKEE.

Regiments.	Officers.		Men.		Regiments.	Officers.		Men.	
	K.	W.	K.	W.		K.	W.	K.	W.
General and Divnl. Staff	5	11	—	—	80th S. Staffs	—	1	4	19
3rd Hussars ..	2	3	58	32	Gov.- General's Bodyguard	1	2	6	17
Royal Artillery	2	4	18	23	3rd Skinner's H.	—	—	2	4
9th Norfolk ..	—	1	2	49	6th K.E.O. Cav.	—	—	4	8
31st E. Surrey	2	6	24	125	5th Light Inf.	1	1	26	61
50th W. Kent	1	5	11	92	7th Rajputs ..	—	1	6	8

The casualties in the native regiments which have
disappeared from the Army List are not given.

FEROZESHAH, DECEMBER 21, 1845.

This battle honour is inscribed on the colours of the

3rd Hussars.
Worcesters.
Royal West Kent.
South Staffords.
Governor-General's Body-
    guard.
1st P.W.O. Sappers and
    Miners.

Norfolk.
East Surrey.
Wiltshire.
Royal Munster Fusiliers.
3rd (Skinner's Horse).
6th K.E.O. Cavalry.
4th Rajputs.
5th Rajputs.

7th Rajputs.

On the 20th, the day after Moodkee, the two battalions
of British troops—the 29th (Worcesters) and 1st Europeans (Munster Fusiliers)—joined the army, and Gough
at once advanced again to meet the Sikhs, and at the
same time Sir John Littler moved out of Ferozepore to
effect a junction with headquarters, leaving two native
battalions to hold the cantonment. The force now at
Sir Hugh Gough's disposal was as follows :

First Division : Sir Harry Smith.
First Brigade—Brigadier Hicks : 31st (East Surrey), 24th and 47th Bengal Infantry.
Second Brigade—Brigadier Ryan : 50th (Royal West Kent), 42nd and 48th Bengal Infantry.
Second Division : Major-General Sir Walter Gilbert.
Third Brigade—Brigadier Taylor (29th Foot) : 29th (Worcesters), 80th (South Staffords), and 41st Bengal Infantry.
Fourth Brigade—Brigadier McClaren : 1st Europeans (1st Royal Munsters), 16th and 45th Bengal Infantry.
Third Division—Brigadier-General Wallace : 9th (Norfolks), 2nd and 73rd Bengal Infantry.
Fourth Division—Major-General Sir John Littler.
Seventh Brigade—Brigadier Reid : 62nd (Wiltshires), 12th and 14th Bengal Infantry.
Eighth Brigade—Brigadier-General the Hon. T. Ashburnham : 33rd, 44th, and 54th Bengal Infantry.

At 3 a.m. the force, under the Commander-in-Chief, struck its camp, and four hours later Littler also left his cantonments. It was the intention of the Commander-in-Chief to attack the enemy without waiting for the junction of Littler's force, but the Governor-General vetoed the plan, so that it was nearly dusk before the Sikh entrenchments were attacked. The Sikhs fought even more stubbornly than at Moodkee. Littler's attack on the left was checked, the 62nd (Wiltshires) losing 20 officers and 281 non-commissioned officers and men in twenty minutes. The fault was not theirs ; they were not properly supported by the Bengal regiments. As one eyewitness put it : " Jack Sepoy fights well enough on occasions, but this was not one of his fighting-days." The 12th and 14th Bengal Infantry, however, did show much courage and determination. It was the purely native brigade, under Ashburnham, which hung back, and this was attributed to the fact that it contained no British battalion to stiffen the sepoy corps. Littler's check took place before the Commander-in-Chief had delivered his attack. The Sikhs, triumphant in having driven back one British column, fought with more than usual determination. The main assault took place by echelon from the right, Sir Hugh Gough leading that column in person, whilst the Governor-General cheered on the centre, he having placed his services at the disposal of the Commander-in-Chief.

Night fell on a scene of great confusion. On the extreme right Gilbert's division had carried the Sikh entrenchments, on the left Littler had been repulsed, and in the centre Sir Harry Smith's division had borne away to the left, and was cut off from the main army. Men and officers were worn out with fatigue and chilled with the bitter cold of a Punjab night. It was impossible to light fires without drawing down the fire of the enemy, who were much elated at the result of the engagement, and who throughout the night kept up an incessant artillery fire on our bivouac. One heavy gun in particular caused especial annoyance, and Sir Henry Hardinge called upon the 80th to silence it. The men nobly responded to the call. In perfect silence they advanced to the edge of the Sikh entrenchments, and then, headed by their Colonel, Bunbury, and supported by the " Dirty Shirts " (Royal Munsters), they dashed over the parapet with a cheer, bayoneting the gunners, spiking the gun, and driving off all the Sikhs in the vicinity. This little episode showed the Sikhs that the fight was not yet won. The Commander-in-Chief determined to renew it on the morrow, and the Governor-General, who felt that the fate of India hung in the balance, was equally firm in his resolve to support the Chief. " Better that our bones should bleach honourably on the field of battle than retire," was the response to a suggestion to fall back.

When dawn broke on the 22nd it was found that Sir Harry Smith, who had clung to the village of Ferozeshah during the night, had effected a junction with the division under Littler, and that both divisions were now in front of the extreme right of the Sikh position. They were too distant to join in the final attack on the entrenchments, which was delivered in the early dawn, the Commander-in-Chief leading the division on the right, the Governor-General that on the left. The attack was preceded by a heavy artillery fire, and under its cover the infantry, forgetting fatigue, cold, and hunger, swept forward with unhesitating devotion, and carried the entrenchments at the point of the bayonet. Our losses in this battle were terribly severe—not merely in numbers. Whole regiments were decimated, but amongst the dead were men who had helped to build up our Indian Empire, and whose names are imperishably engraved on the military history of our country. The total casualties amounted to 2,415 killed and wounded, including 115 British officers.

No means existed of ascertaining the enemy's losses, but that they were most severe was undoubted. They abandoned their entrenched position, and recrossed the frontier, leaving seventy-three guns in our hands. But the campaign was not over. Reinforcements were called up from Meerut, Delhi, and Cawnpore, and on January 6 Sir John Grey arrived at headquarters with the 9th and 16th Lancers, the 10th Foot (Lincolns), two regiments of native cavalry and three of native infantry, whilst the 53rd (Shropshire Light Infantry) was within a few days' march.

CASUALTIES AT THE BATTLE OF FEROZESHAH.

Regiments.	Officers.		Men.		Regiments.	Officers.		Men.	
	K.	W.	K.	W.		K.	W.	K.	W.
3rd Hussars ..	2	7	53	86	Gov.-General's				
Royal Artillery	2	4	39	84	Bodyguard	—	—	—	2
9th Norfolk ..	3	7	67	197	3rd Skinner's				
29th Worcesters	3	3	52	192	Horse ..	—	—	9	8
31st E. Surrey	2	6	59	96	6th K.E.O. Cav.	—	—	4	9
50th Roy. West					4th Rajputs				
Kent ..	2	6	24	89	(Natives) ..	1	3	7	37
62nd Wiltshire	7	11	97	184	5th Rajputs				
80th S. Stafford	4	4	39	73	(British) ..	1	2	—	—
Royal Munster					Do. (Natives)	2	—	12	40
Fusiliers ..	4	4	51	164	7th Rajputs				
Staff	6	12	—	—	(Natives) ..	—	—	9	26

The Sikhs, too, were by no means disheartened, and towards the middle of January a strong force crossed the

Sutlej and threatened our line of communication at Ludhiana. Sir Harry Smith was detached to attack them, which he did at Aliwal, having fought a successful little action on January 20 at Buddiwal.

ALIWAL, JANUARY 28, 1868.

The following regiments have been awarded this battle honour :

16th Lancers.	East Surrey.
West Kent.	Shropshire Light Infantry.
Gov.-General's Bodyguard.	3rd Skinner's Horse.
7th Rajputs.	13th Shekhawati Regiment.
1st Gurkhas.	2nd Gurkhas.

Sir Harry Smith, the hero of Aliwal, was an officer who had seen considerable service in the Rifle Brigade, having been present at practically every engagement during the Peninsular War, either as Adjutant of the Rifle Brigade or on the staff of the Light Division. He at this time wore only the Waterloo medal, for a grateful country had not as yet recognized the services of the Peninsular veterans. His division constituted a very efficient fighting force. There were four batteries of horse and one of field artillery. His cavalry was in two brigades—

First Cavalry Brigade—Brigadier MacDowell : 16th Lancers, 3rd Light Cavalry, and 4th Irregulars.
Second Cavalry Brigade—Brigadier Stedman : Governor-General's Bodyguard, 1st and 5th Light Cavalry.

—the two brigades being under a distinguished officer, Brigadier-General Cureton, who was to fall two years later at the head of the cavalry brigade at Ramnuggur.

First Infantry Brigade—Brigadier Hicks : 31st (East Surrey), 24th and 36th Bengal Infantry.
Second Infantry Brigade—Brigadier Wheler : 50th (West Kent), 48th Bengal Infantry, and the 2nd Gurkhas.
Third Infantry Brigade—Brigadier Wilson : 53rd (Shropshire Light Infantry), 30th Bengal Infantry, and the Shekhawati Battalion (now the 13th Bengal Infantry).
Fourth Infantry Brigade—Brigadier Godby : 47th Bengal Infantry and the 1st Gurkhas.

The total strength was 3,000 cavalry and 7,100 infantry, with twenty-eight field-guns and two 8-inch howitzers.

Covering his front with his cavalry and horse artillery,
Sir Harry Smith, who was a consummate drill, advanced
in true light division order against the Sikhs, who held a
position with their rear resting on the River Sutlej, close
by the village of Aliwal. On the extreme right was Stedman's cavalry brigade, then in succession Godby's and
Hick's infantry, with three batteries and the howitzers in
the centre ; then came Wheler's and Wilson's brigades,
with two batteries between them, and on the left the 16th
Lancers, with the 3rd Bengal Light Cavalry.

CASUALTIES AT THE BATTLE OF ALIWAL.

Regiments.	Officers.		Men.		Regiments.	Officers.		Men.	
	K.	W.	K.	W.		K.	W.	K.	W.
16th Lancers ..	2	6	56	77	3rd Skinner's				
31st E. Surrey	—	1	1	14	Horse ..	1	—	—	2
50th West Kent	1	10	9	59	7th Rajputs ..	—	—	1	9
53rd Shropshire					13th Shekha-				
L.I.	—	—	3	8	wati ..	—	—	2	13
Gov.-General's					1st Gurkhas ..	—	—	6	16
Bodyguard	—	—	—	—	2nd Gurkhas ..	—	1	9	39

The village of Aliwal was carried at the point of the
bayonet by the brigades of Godby and Hicks, whilst those
of Wheler and Wilson attacked the Sikh entrenchment.
Cureton, a born cavalry leader, was watching his opportunity, and as the infantry swarmed over the entrenchments, the 16th swept down on the Sikh infantry through
an opening on the extreme right. The Sikhs hurriedly
threw themselves into squares. The Red Lancers charged
ere they had time to complete their formation, and, reforming on the far side, charged again in splendid style.
The infantry brigade gave effective support to Cureton's
cavalry, never allowing the Sikhs a moment to rally, but
pressing them back step by step to the river, into which
at last they were driven in utter rout, with the loss
of sixty-seven guns and all their camp equipage. Our

total losses in this engagement were 580 men killed and wounded, but the results were far-reaching, for the whole of the Cis-Sutlej provinces of the Sikh Raj made their submission to the British, and passed away for ever from the domination of the Khalsa.

SOBRAON, FEBRUARY 10, 1846.

This, the final defeat of the Sikhs on the banks of the Sutlej, is commemorated on the colours and appointments of the

3rd Hussars.	9th Lancers.
16th Lancers.	Norfolks.
Lincoln.	Worcesters.
East Surrey.	Royal West Kent.
Shropshire Light Infantry.	Wiltshires.
South Staffords.	Royal Munster Fusiliers.
Gov.-General's Bodyguard.	2nd (Gardner's Horse).
6th K.E.O. Cavalry.	4th Rajputs.
5th Light Infantry.	6th Jat Light Infantry.
1st P.W.O. Sappers and	7th Rajputs.
Miners.	8th Rajputs.
1st Gurkhas.	2nd Gurkhas.

9th Gurkhas.

The undoubted success gained by Sir Harry Smith at Aliwal infused fresh spirit into our troops, and now every preparation was made for the final bout with the Sikhs. On February 7 the siege-train arrived in the Commander-in-Chief's camp, and on the following day Sir Harry Smith rejoined headquarters. The Sikhs had not been idle. They had thrown up most formidable entrenchments at Sobraon, on the banks of the Sutlej, covering the ford on the direct road to Lahore. To attack this was no easy task, for the Commander-in-Chief had to provide against a counter-attack on the part of our gallant foes, who in point of numbers, as in mobility, were far our superiors. To avoid this contingency, Sir John Littler, with his division, watched the fords in front of Ferozepore; Sir John Grey, with three battalions of sepoys and a regiment of native cavalry, watched those midway between that place and Sobraon; whilst Brigadier-General Wheler fronted the Sutlej near Ludhiana.

The cavalry was now under the command of Sir Joseph Thackwell, an officer of the highest distinction, who had served throughout the Peninsular War, lost an arm at Waterloo, and finally added to his reputation in Kabul and at Maharajpore. He, with the 16th Lancers and three regiments of native cavalry, was to threaten the Sikh left above Sobraon. Next to him came the division led by Sir Harry Smith, consisting of the 31st (East Surrey), the 50th (West Kent), and four sepoy battalions. Our centre was composed of Sir Walter Gilbert's division, which contained the 29th (Worcesters), 1st Bengal Europeans (1st Munsters), and four sepoy battalions. On our left was a division commanded by another Peninsular and Waterloo veteran—Sir Robert Dick. This, which was to lead the attack, comprised the 10th (Lincolns), 53rd (Shropshire Light Infantry), 80th (South Stafford), with three battalions of sepoys ; and in Dick's second line were the 9th (Norfolks), 62nd (Wiltshire), with one sepoy battalion. The artillery, which numbered sixty guns, was distributed throughout the whole front.

The troops got under arms at 2 a.m., it being the intention of the Commander-in-Chief to attack at dawn ; but such a dense fog hung over the river that the actual advance was delayed until nine o'clock, when the three horse batteries attached to Sir Robert Dick's division galloped to the front, and opened a very heavy fire on the Sikh entrenchments. Under cover of this, Stacey's brigade, which included the Lincolns and Shropshires, moved steadily forward. When within 300 yards of the entrenchments, they were threatened by a body of cavalry, and also came under the enfilading fire of a battery, which inflicted heavy loss on the 53rd. Then, cheering on his men, Dick carried the first line of trenches with a charge, the brave old General meeting his death-wound in the *mêlée*. On the extreme right Sir Harry Smith's attack had been no less successful, but in the centre Gilbert's advance had been checked, owing to the nature of the breastworks in the front, which were from

8 to 10 feet in height, the men having to mount on each other's shoulders before they could force their way in. On Dick's left the 3rd Hussars had also found an entrance to the entrenchments, and were charging down on the enemy, driving them in confusion towards the one bridge which was their one and only chance of safety.

CASUALTIES AT THE BATTLE OF SOBRAON.

Regiments.	Officers.		Men.		Regiments.	Officers.		Men.	
	K.	W.	K.	W.		K.	W.	K.	W.
Genl. and Divl. Staff ..	4	8	—	—	4th Rajputs (British) ..	1	1	—	—
3rd Hussars ..	—	4	5	22	Do. (Natives)	1	4	4	55
9th Lancers ..	—	—	1	1	5th Light Inf. (British) ..	—	2	—	—
16th Lancers ..	—	—	—	—	Do. (Natives)	—	3	8	53
Royal Artillery	1	1	6	46	6th Jat L.I. (British) ..	—	2	—	—
9th Norfolks ..	—	1	5	28	Do. (Natives)	—	4	7	90
Lincoln ..	1	2	30	100	7th Rajputs (British) ..	—	4	—	—
29th Worcesters	—	12	32	129	Do. (Natives)	1	4	8	64
31st E. Surrey	—	7	35	112	8th Rajputs (British) ..	—	1	—	—
50th West Kent	1	11	41	186	Do. (Natives)	—	1	4	59
53rd Shropshire L.I. ..	1	8	7	105	1st Gurkhas (British) ..	—	1	—	—
62nd Wilt-shire ..	1	1	3	43	Do. (Natives)	—	2	6	74
80th S. Staffs	—	4	13	74	2nd Gurkhas (British) ..	1	—	—	—
Royal Munster Fusiliers ..	3	9	33	152	Do. (Natives)	—	4	13	126
Gov.-General's Bodyguard	—	4	6	38	9th Gurkhas (British) ..	—	3	—	—
2nd Gardner's Horse ..	—	—	1	5	Do. (Natives)	—	1	3	30
6th K.E.O. Cavalry ..	—	—	—	—					

By noon the day was ours, but our loss had been enormous. It is true that the Sikh army was in full retreat, and that sixty-seven guns, chiefly of large calibre, were in our hands, but our casualties amounted to close on 2,400 killed and wounded. The little graveyard at Ferozepore bears testimony to the severity of the fighting in the Sutlej Campaign. In no war in which Great Britain has been engaged have the Staff suffered so severely, and in none has the proportion of General Officers been so high, Generals Sir Robert Sale, Sir Robert Dick, and Sir John McCaskill, with Brigadier-Generals Taylor, Bolton, and Wallace, being killed, and no less than eight Brigadiers wounded, in the short campaign. The casualties amongst the British regiments were appalling. The Governor-General had spared neither himself nor his Staff, every single member of which was either killed or wounded.

PUNJAUB.

All regiments employed in the operations in the Punjab against the Sikhs in the year 1848-49 were awarded this distinction. Some bear it in addition to one of the three battle honours " Chillianwalla," " Mooltan," and " Goojerat," granted for this campaign. Others, which were not present at any of these general actions, but which were actually under fire, bear only the word " Punjaub." The following regiments carry this word on their colours and appointments :

3rd Hussars.	9th Lancers.
14th Hussars.	Lincolns.
South Wales Borderers.	Gloucester.
Worcester.	Cornwall Light Infantry.
Shropshire Light Infantry.	King's Royal Rifles.
North Staffords.	Royal Munster Fusiliers.
Royal Dublin Fusiliers.	2nd Gardner's Horse.
5th Cavalry.	31st Lancers.
35th Scinde Horse.	36th Jacob's Horse.
Q.O. Corps of Guides.	1st P.W.O. Sap and Min.
2nd Sappers and Miners.	2nd Q.O. Light Infantry.
11th Rajputs.	51st Sikhs.
52nd Sikhs.	103rd Light Infantry.
104th Wellesley's Rifles.	109th Infantry.
119th Multan Regiment.	121st Pioneers.

The victory over the Sikhs at Sobraon had been complete. That battle had been fought on February 10 ; on the 20th of the month our troops entered Lahore, the capital of the Sikh kingdom. The conditions of peace were galling enough to a high-spirited and warlike race like the Sikhs, but they were indispensable for our security in India. Their army was reduced to reasonable dimensions, all the artillery was handed over to us, the whole of the territories on the left bank of the Sutlej were annexed by Great Britain, and a war indemnity of £1,500,000 was exacted. The conduct of the administration was placed in the hands of a Council of Regency, which was supposed to be favourable to our cause, and a British Resident was appointed at the Court of Lahore, in which city a strong British garrison was retained until all the terms had been complied with.

It was soon evident that the Council of Regency was unable to govern the country. Spasmodic outbursts of anti-British fanaticism culminated in the murder of two English officers at Multan, and in the early summer of 1848 it was clear that we must be prepared to conquer and to administer the Punjab. Multan was in the hands of men opposed, not only to the British, but also to the nominal rulers of the kingdom (the Council of Regency), and a British force, under General Whish, was despatched to retake the fortress. This was composed of two troops of horse artillery and a siege-train manned by four companies of English gunners. Five companies of sappers, under Major Robert Napier, later known as Field-Marshal Lord Napier of Magdala, the 10th (Lincoln) and 32nd (Cornwall Light Infantry), with four sepoy battalions, made up the regular forces. To these must be added some 15,000 native levies, who had flocked to the call of a subaltern—Lieutenant Herbert Edwardes—and some loyal Sikhs. A column was under orders from Bombay to assist Whish. This comprised the King's Royal Rifles, the 1st Bombay European Regiment (now the 2nd Royal Dublin Fusiliers), and four sepoy battalions. The task before Whish was more than his force, without the aid of the Bombay troops, could encompass, and the check to his operations had a disastrous effect throughout the Punjab. All the malcontents threw in their lot against us, and on December 16 Lord Gough crossed the Ravi

River, and commenced the final conquest of the Land of the Five Rivers. His army was composed as under :

DISTRIBUTION OF THE ARMY OF THE PUNJAB, 1849.

Commander-in-Chief : General Lord Gough, G.C.B.

Cavalry Division : Lieutenant-General Sir Joseph Thackwell, K.C.B.

First Cavalry Brigade—Brigadier M. White : 3rd Hussars, 5th and 8th Light Cavalry.

Second Cavalry Brigade—Brigadier Pope : 9th Lancers, 14th Hussars, 1st and 6th Light Cavalry.

First Infantry Division : Major-General Whish, at Multan.

First Brigade—Brigadier Markham : 32nd Foot (Cornwall Regiment), 49th and 51st Bengal Infantry.

Second Brigade—Brigadier Hervey : 10th Foot (Lincolns), 8th and 72nd Bengal Infantry.

Second Infantry Division—Major-General Sir Walter Gilbert, K.C.B.

First Brigade—Brigadier Mountain : 29th Foot (Worcesters), 30th and 56th Bengal Infantry.

Second Brigade—Brigadier Godby : 2nd Bengal Europeans (2nd Munsters), 31st (now the 2nd Q.O. Light Infantry), and the 70th Bengal Infantry (now the 11th Rajputs).

Third Division : Brigadier-General Colin Campbell, C.B.

First Brigade—Brigadier Pennycuick : 24th Foot (South Wales Borderers), 25th and 45th Bengal Infantry.

Second Brigade—Brigadier Hoggan : 61st Foot (2nd Gloucesters), 15th, 36th, and 46th Bengal Infantry.

Third Brigade—Brigadier Penny : 15th, 20th, and 69th Regiments Bengal Infantry.

Artillery Division—Brigadier-General Tennant : Six batteries of horse artillery, three field and two heavy batteries.

Ever since the advance from Sobraon we had retained a strong force at Lahore, as well as at Ferozepore, but no success had attended our efforts to keep down the numbers of the Sikh army ; in fact, at that time the Sikhs were a race of warriors, every man carrying arms, and every second man had undergone military training. Lahore, it is true, was no longer the headquarters of their army, but Lord Gough soon found that the Sikh forces drawn up on the far side of the Chenab were no whit inferior to those he had met and with difficulty overthrown on the banks of the Sutlej. On November 23 the opening action of the campaign took place at Ramnuggur,[1] where the

---

[1] Ramnuggur : 4 officers and 34 men killed ; 13 officers and 72 men wounded.

14th Hussars showed themselves worthy of the high reputation they had made in the Peninsula ; and on the 30th of the month Sir Joseph Thackwell, in command of the cavalry, fought the successful action of Sadoolapore.[1]

CHILLIANWALLAH, JANUARY 13, 1849.

This battle honour, which commemorates one of the hardest fights ever waged in India, is borne by the following regiments :

3rd Hussars.	9th Lancers.
14th Hussars.	South Wales Borderers.
Gloucesters.	Worcesters.
Royal Munster Fusiliers.	2nd Q.O. Light Infantry.
	11th Rajputs.

On January 10 Lord Gough received orders from the Governor-General to attack the Sikhs. Up to this date it had been the intention of the Commander-in-Chief to await the arrival of General Whish's division from Multan, the fall of which was daily expected. On January 13 Gough found the enemy in a strongly entrenched position at Chillianwallah, and attacked them in his usual formation, with his cavalry on the flanks, the advance being preceded by a heavy artillery fire. The Sikhs far outnumbered our forces, and their front, it is said, extended to a distance of no less than six miles, so that a turning movement with the small numbers at his disposal would have exposed Lord Gough to the piercing of his line by a counter-attack. The ground was much broken and covered with thick jungle, which rendered it exceedingly difficult for any General to exercise efficient control over even one brigade. Some confusion was the inevitable result, for it must be borne in mind that the only means of communication then known was by mounted orderlies, and I am afraid it must be admitted that this was not one of the Bengal sepoys' fighting-days. The Sikhs had abandoned their stereotyped plan, and had advanced

---

[1] Sadoolapore : 2 officers and 14 men killed ; 4 officers and 45 men wounded.

from their entrenched position, and literally forced the hand of the Commander-in-Chief. They relied on the nature of the ground to hide their dispositions, and in this they were to a certain extent successful. The result of the day was by no means satisfactory. Our losses were abnormally heavy, amounting to 2,338 officers and men killed and wounded. The Sikhs, it is true, were driven from their position and fell back during the night, but they retired unmolested and carried off all their artillery.

The Commander-in-Chief was subjected to a great amount of harsh criticism for his conduct of the operations—criticism based on but a very partial knowledge of the real facts—and in deference to public opinion, too often the offspring of the fertile brains of armchair critics, Sir Charles Napier, the conqueror of Scinde, was sent out to India to relieve the brave Gough. It is but fair to state that the Commander-in-Chief had never lost the love or confidence of the officers and men under him, and the stars fought for the genial Irishman. Multan fell ; Whish, with his own and the Bombay division, joined headquarters, and before the new Chief arrived Gough had inflicted a crushing defeat on the Sikhs at Goojerat, and the Punjab had passed into our hands for ever.

CASUALTIES AT THE BATTLE OF CHILLIANWALLAH,
JANUARY 13, 1849.

Regiments.	Officers.		Men.		Regiments.	Officers.		Men.	
	K.	W.	K.	W.		K.	W.	K.	W.
3rd Hussars ..	—	2	24	14	29th Worcester	—	4	34	203
9th Lancers ..	—	—	4	8	61st Gloucester	—	3	11	100
14th Hussars ..	1	1	3	14	2nd Bengal				
Bengal Artillery	1	3	18	39	Europeans				
24th S. Wales					(Munster				
Borderers ..	11	10	237	266	Fusiliers) ..	—	2	6	59
2nd Q.O. L.I.	—	1	3	14	11th Rajputs	2	—	3	20

NOTE.—I have not given the casualties in the native regiments which no longer exist.

MOOLTAN, JANUARY, 1849.

This distinction was conferred on the troops engaged in the siege of Multan, under General Whish, during the Second Punjab Campaign. It is borne on the colours and appointments of the following regiments :

Lincolns.	Cornwall Light Infantry.
King's Royal Rifles.	Royal Dublin Fusiliers.
5th Cavalry.	31st Lancers.
35th Scinde Horse.	36th Jacob's Horse.
Q.O. Corps of Guides.	1st P.W.O. Sappers and
3rd Sappers and Miners.	Miners.
103rd Mahratta L.I.	104th Wellesley's Rifles.
109th Infantry.	119th Multan Regiment.

The siege of Multan was of necessity begun in the very height of the hottest season of the year—the month of July. In order to spare the men, the British troops dropped down the rivers by boat, whilst the native troops marched. I have already, on p. 288, given the composition of the force with which General Whish undertook the siege. Herbert Edwardes, a subaltern of that distinguished corps the 1st Bengal Fusiliers, was already on the spot with a large force of irregulars, who, owing to his personal magnetism, had flocked to our standard ; but the Sikhs, aware of the approach of the British force, busied themselves steadily in strengthening the works at Multan. It was not until the commencement of September that the whole of the siege-train was present, and then Whish summoned the Sikhs to surrender. This was an empty form. It was well known that the Sikhs had no intention of submitting to our rule, and that ere our flag should be hoisted over the walls of Multan many a gallant soldier would have met his death.

On September 7 the siege commenced, with, it must be confessed, very inadequate means. The Pathan and Baluch levies, who had been won over by Edwardes, fought gallantly enough in the field, but they resolutely declined to undergo the fatigue of siege-work, all of which fell on the British and sepoy battalions. The siege dragged slowly on until December 12, when General Dundas arrived with two strong brigades, consisting of the

2nd Battalion King's Royal Rifles, the 1st Battalion Royal Dublin Fusiliers, three regiments of native cavalry, and five of native infantry. Now the siege was pushed on with vigour, and on January 21 all preparations were made for an assault. The Sikhs, however, never waited for this, and on January 22 Mulraj, the Sikh commander, surrendered at discretion. Whish was now free to push on to the north, and afford much-needed aid to the Commander-in-Chief.

CASUALTIES AT THE SIEGE AND CAPTURE OF MULTAN, JANUARY 22, 1849.

Regiments.	Officers.		Men.		Regiments.	Officers.		Men.	
	K.	W.	K.	W.		K.	W.	K.	W.
10th Lincoln ..	1	4	13	113	35th Scinde H.	—	—	—	—
32nd Cornwall L.I. ..	2	11	17	104	36th Jacob's H.	—	—	—	—
60th K.R.R. ..	1	2	10	28	Q.O. Corps of Guides ..	—	—	—	—
Artillery ..	1	6	21	94	103rd Mahratta				
Bengal Engrs.	—	9	30	96	L.I. ..	—	2	1	20
Roy. Dublin F.	1	6	16	86	104th Welles-				
Indian Navy ..	1	2	1	3	ley's Rifles..	—	2	29	72
5th Cavalry ..	—	—	2	6	109th Infantry	1	2	1	10
31st Lancers ..	—	—	—	—	119th Multan	—	2	6	42

NOTE.—The four regiments of Bengal infantry which took part in the siege of Multan have ceased to exist. Their casualties, therefore, are not given.

GOOJERAT, FEBRUARY 21, 1849.

This distinction is borne on the colours and appointments of the

3rd Hussars.
14th Hussars.
South Wales Borderers.
Worcesters.
Shropshire Light Infantry.
Royal Munster Fusiliers.
35th Scinde Horse.
Q.O. Corps of Guides.
3rd Sappers and Miners.
2nd Q.O. Light Infantry.
103rd Light Infantry.

9th Lancers.
Lincolns.
Gloucesters.
Cornwall Light Infantry.
King's Royal Rifles.
Royal Dublin Fusiliers.
36th Jacob's Horse.
1st P.W.O. Sappers and Miners.
11th Rajputs.
119th Multan Regiment.

THE COLOURS OF THE ROYAL DUBLIN FUSILIERS.

(Formerly the Bombay Europeans.)

On February 21 General Whish, with the First Division strengthened by the Bombay troops, joined the Commander-in-Chief, so that, in addition to the force enumerated on p. 288, Lord Gough had with him for the final attack on the Sikh position two additional battalions of British soldiers (the 2nd Battalions of the King's Royal Rifles and Royal Dublin Fusiliers), two regiments of native cavalry, and two of native infantry. His artillery was brought up to the respectable total of ninety-six field-guns, which included three heavy batteries. The Sikhs occupied a strong position, their flanks resting on two villages, which they had fortified, and their whole front was covered by a series of entrenchments. Whish, with the Bombay troops, as I have said, joined the Commander-in-Chief on February 21 at dawn ; on the morrow Lord Gough launched his attack. As the British army approached the broad sandy nullah which ran along the front of the Sikh line, the guns opened on us, disclosing their whole front. To this fire the ninety-six pieces at once replied, and for two hours a storm of shell was poured on the entrenchments ; then, shortly before noon, Gough moved forward the whole line. The Sikhs fought, as is their wont, with consummate gallantry, and the Afghan Horse on our right made a gallant effort to retrieve the fortunes of the day. They were met in an equally gallant manner by the Scinde Horse, supported by the 9th Lancers, and on this flank being uncovered the horse artillery galloped up and enfiladed the Sikh entrenchments. " By half-past twelve," writes Sir Charles Gough, who, as a subaltern, took part in the campaign, " the whole Sikh army was in full flight. By one o'clock Goojerat itself, the Sikh camp, their baggage, and most of the guns, were in possession of the victors." Sir Walter Gilbert, at the head of 12,000 men, pressed the retreating Sikhs hard, never slackening his pursuit until he had driven their Afghan allies through the Khyber Pass and received the unconditional surrender of their leaders.

At Goojerat the victory was complete, and the Sikhs,

recognizing the inevitable, acknowledged British rule. Heavy was the price we paid for the conquest of the Punjab, but the blood shed on the banks of the Sutlej was not shed in vain, for England has no more faithful subjects, no braver soldiers in her armies, than the Sikhs who stood so bravely before us in the campaigns of 1846-1849.

CASUALTIES AT THE BATTLE OF GOOJERAT.

Regiments.	Officers.		Men.		Regiments.	Officers.		Men.	
	K.	W.	K.	W.		K.	W.	K.	W.
3rd Hussars ..	—	—	—	1	61st Gloucesters	—	—	—	9
9th Lancers ..	—	—	—	—	Roy. Munster F.	1	5	9	135
14th Hussars	1	2	—	4	Roy. Dublin F.	—	—	—	—
10th Lincolns	—	1	7	53	35th Scinde H.	—	1	2	11
24th S. Wales					36th Jacob's H.	—	—	—	—
Borderers ..	—	—	—	—	Q.O. Corps of				
29th Worcesters	—	—	2	6	Guides ..	—	—	—	—
32nd Cornwall					2nd Q.O. Light				
L.I. ..	—	1	1	4	Infantry ..	—	5	11	127
53rd Shropshire					11th Rajputs	—	6	10	38
L.I. ..	—	—	—	—	103rd Light Inf.	—	—	—	—
King's Royal R.	—	—	—	1	119th Multan	—	—	—	—

CHAPTER XIX

Alma—Balaclava—Inkerman—Sevastopol.

THE perennial quarrel between Russia and Turkey entered on a new phase in the year 1854, when England and France, espousing the Ottoman cause, despatched their fleets into the Baltic and a combined naval and military expedition to the Crimea. The command of the British army was entrusted to General Lord Raglan—a veteran officer, who had served on the Duke of Wellington's Staff in the Peninsula and at Waterloo, where he lost an arm, and who for many years had held the important post of Military Secretary at the Horse Guards. He had never exercised the command of an independent body of troops, and his experience of war was not of recent date. The whole campaign was grievously mismanaged, but the chief blame rested with the authorities at the War Office, who neglected to provide the army with the thousand and one requisites for troops waging war in such a climate as a Crimean winter. It was retrieved by the bravery of our troops and their cheerful endurance of sufferings—sufferings that might have been avoided by the exercise of common forethought.

The army that landed in the Crimea on September 14, 1854, numbered some 27,000 men, with fifty-four guns, and was distributed as under :

Commander-in-Chief : Field-Marshal Lord Raglan.

Cavalry Division : General the Earl of Lucan.

Heavy Brigade—Brigadier-General J. Yorke Scarlett : The 4th and 5th Dragoon Guards, the Scots Greys, and the Inniskilling Dragoons.

Light Cavalry Brigade—Major-General the Earl of Cardigan :
4th, 8th, 11th, and 13th Hussars, and the 17th Lancers.

First Division : H.R.H. the Duke of Cambridge.

Brigade of Guards : A battalion of the Grenadier, Coldstream,
and Scots Guards.

Highland Brigade—Major-General Sir Colin Campbell : The
42nd (Royal), 79th (Cameron), and 93rd (Sutherland Highlanders).

Second Division : Lieutenant-General Sir de Lacy Evans.

Third Brigade—Brigadier-General Adams : 41st (Welsh), 47th
(North Lancashire), and 49th (Royal Berkshires).

Fourth Brigade—Brigadier-General Pennefather : The 30th (East
Lancashire), 55th (Border Regiment), and the 95th (Derbyshire).

Third Division : Lieutenant-General Sir Richard England.

Fifth Brigade—Brigadier-General Sir John Campbell : 4th (King's
Own), 38th (South Staffords), and the 50th (Royal West
Kent).

Sixth Brigade—Brigadier-General Eyre : The Royal Scots, 28th
(Gloucesters), and 44th (Essex).

Fourth Division : Major-General Sir George Cathcart.

Seventh Brigade—Brigadier-General Torrens : 20th (Lancashire
Fusiliers), 21st (Royal Scots Fusiliers), and the 68th (Durham
Light Infantry).

Eighth Brigade : 46th (Cornwall Light Infantry), and the 57th
Middlesex (arrived after the landing of the troops on
September 14, not in time to take part in the Battle of the
Alma).

Light Division : Lieutenant-General Sir George Brown.

First Brigade—Major-General W. Codrington : 7th (Royal
Fusiliers), 23rd (Royal Welsh Fusiliers), and the 33rd (West
Riding Regiment).

Second Brigade—Major-General G. Buller : The 19th (Yorkshires),
77th (Middlesex), and the 88th (Connaught Rangers).

In addition to the above, the 2nd Battalion of the Rifle
Brigade was also present, but in the earlier stages of the
campaign it acted as a divisional battalion.

Acting in co-operation with us was a strong French
army, under Marshal St. Arnaud, a division of which was
commanded by one of the Napoleon Princes, and a
Turkish force of 8,000 men, under Omar Pasha.

In the spring of 1855 a division of the Sardinian army
also arrived, and was sharply engaged with the Russians
at the Battle of the Tchernaya.

The army was reinforced from time to time by regiments from home and from India, and when peace was

declared in 1856 it was composed of close on 50,000 well-equipped men, capable of carrying on the Siege of Sevastopol to a satisfactory conclusion.   The casualties during the campaign, apart from those incurred at the Battles of Alma, Balaclava, Inkerman, and the two assaults on the Redan, were not heavy, the losses in some regiments being remarkably small ; but the losses from disease were regrettably severe—the more regrettable as, with proper forethought, many hundreds—nay, thousands—of valuable lives might have been saved.   The campaign is memorable as the first in which the whole of our infantry were armed with a *percussion* arm, and also the first in which a body of lady nurses was organized for service in military hospitals.   The honoured name of Florence Nightingale must for ever be associated with the war in the Crimea.   It was also the first in which officers and men were authorized to accept and to wear foreign medals and decorations ; and, lastly, it was to recognize the bravery of subordinate officers and men in the campaign that the decoration of the Victoria Cross was instituted.

ALMA, SEPTEMBER 20, 1854.

This battle honour is borne by the following regiments :

4th Hussars:
11th Hussars.
17th Lancers.
Coldstream Guards.
Royal Scots.
Royal Fusiliers.
Lancashire Fusiliers.
Royal Welsh Fusiliers.
East Lancashires.
Border.
Welsh.
Sherwood Foresters.
Royal Berkshire.
Middlesex.
Durham Light Infantry.
Connaught Rangers.
Rifle Brigade.

8th Hussars.
13th Hussars.
Grenadier Guards.
Scots Guards.
King's Own (Lancasters).
Yorkshire.
Royal Scots Fusiliers.
Gloucesters.
West Riding.
South Staffords.
Royal Highlanders.
North Lancashire.
West Kent.
Manchester.
Cameron Highlanders.
Argyll and Sutherland Highlanders.

At the Alma the Russians occupied a strong natural position, following the crest of a range of hills dominating the valley of the Alma River. Their front was covered by one or two redoubts, but no serious effort had been made to strengthen it. Had this been done, the disparity in numbers would have been compensated for. The actual strength of the combatants and casualties are as follows :

Troops Engaged.	Men.	Guns.	Officers.		Men.	
			K.	W.	K.	W.
British	27,000	54	26	73	327	1,557
French	23,000	72	3	54	253	1,033
Turks	6,500	?	?	?	?	?
Russians	37,500	96	45	100	1,762	2,720

A good-sized library might be filled with the literature on the Crimean War. Most of the more valuable books, such as Hamley's, Kinglake's, Clarke's, and Sir William Russell's " Letters to the *Times*," are in every library, so that it is quite unnecessary to deal in any detail with the events of this campaign. At the Alma the French took the right, their right flank resting on the sea. We advanced, covered by the Rifle Brigade, with the Cavalry Division on our outer or left flank. The Second Division, on our right, kept touch with the French, and had in support the Third Division, under Sir Richard England. On our left the Light Division, under Sir George Brown, led, supported by the division under the Duke of Cambridge, who in this, his first engagement, showed the hereditary courage of our Royal Family. In the course of the advance through the vineyards at the foot of the hill, and before the final advance took place, the troops suffered much from the artillery fire of the Russians, and were thrown into some confusion. Few amongst the senior officers had seen any service since the Peninsular War, and the number of regimental officers who had heard the whistle of a bullet was infinitesimal ; yet the behaviour of all was excellent, and after three and a half hours of hard fighting the Russians were in full retreat, leaving a couple of guns in our hands. Unfortunately, we were in no condition to follow up our advantage. The Russians were able to retire unmolested into Sevastopol, and we were compelled to embark on a siege of indefinite length, with totally inadequate means.

It was necessary to secure a harbour as a base of operations, and the allied armies carried out a flank march within striking distance of the Russians. No advantage was taken of this movement, and by the commencement of October our troops were in possession of the little land-locked harbour of Balaclava, and the labours of the long-drawn-out siege commenced.

CASUALTIES AT THE BATTLE OF THE ALMA.

Regiments.	Officers.		Men.		Regiments.	Officers.		Men.	
	K.	W.	K.	W.		K.	W.	K.	W.
11th Hussars	—	—	—	—	44th Essex ..	—	—	1	7
13th Hussars	—	—	—	—	47th N. Lancs	—	4	4	61
17th Lancers	—	—	—	—	49th R. Berks	—	—	2	13
Royal Artillery	3	—	9	21	50th West Kent	—	—	—	—
Grenadier Gds.	—	3	11	116	55th Border ..	2	6	11	96
Coldstream Gds.	—	2	—	27	63rd Man-				
Scots Guards	—	11	26	123	chester ..	—	—	—	—
Royal Scots ..	—	—	—	—	68th Durham				
K.O. Lancaster	—	2	3	8	L.I. ..	—	—	—	—
Royal Fusiliers	1	11	42	168	77th Middlesex	—	—	3	17
Yorkshire ..	2	6	45	174	79th Cameron				
Lancashire Fus.	—	—	—	1	Highlanders	—	—	2	7
R. Welsh Fus.	8	5	45	152	88th Connaught				
Gloucester ..	—	—	—	—	Rangers ..	—	1	5	16
30th E. Lancs	1	4	11	63	93rd Suther-				
33rd W. Riding	1	6	55	177	land Highl.	1	—	7	44
38th S. Stafford	—	—	—	—	95th Sherwood				
41st Welsh ..	—	—	4	23	Foresters ..	6	11	48	128
42nd R. High.	—	—	7	32	Rifle Brigade	—	1	11	39

BALACLAVA, OCTOBER 25, 1854.

This battle honour is borne by the

4th Dragoon Guards.	5th Dragoon Guards.
Royal Dragoons.	Royal Scots Greys.
Inniskilling Dragoons.	4th Hussars.
8th Hussars.	11th Hussars.
13th Hussars.	17th Lancers.

Sutherland Highlanders.

The defence of the country surrounding Balaclava had been entrusted to the Turks, who in a series of actions on the banks of the Danube had shown that they could fight well behind stone walls. Some redoubts had been thrown up on the neighbouring heights, and these were armed with ships' guns, lent by us to the Turks. In Balaclava itself was one battalion—the 93rd (Sutherland Highlanders)—and the command of the place had been entrusted to one of the few veterans of the army who had seen modern war. Sir Colin Campbell had served under Wellington in the Peninsula, and had earned mention in more than one despatch when still a subaltern. For his conduct at Barrosa and at San Sebastian, at both of which actions he was wounded, he was promoted to a company in the 60th Rifles. In the China War he had commanded the 98th, and was made an Aide-de-Camp to the Queen. In the Punjab Campaign he had added to his reputation by his masterly handling of a brigade in the hard-fought battles of Chillianwallah and Goojerat, and he had earned still higher laurels when in command of the troops at Peshawur in the early days of our occupation of the Punjab frontier.

On the early morning of October 25 the Russians, who had no very great opinion of the Turkish troops, made a determined attack on Balaclava. The valley leading down to the sea is cut in two by a low range of hills, and down these two valleys they advanced. The Turks, after one or two rounds, incontinently abandoned the redoubts, and fled in haste to the refuge of the town. Sir Colin moved up the 93rd Highlanders, and awaited the advance of the Russian cavalry division. He had a firm faith in the new weapon with which his troops were armed, and a still firmer belief in his Highlanders. On swept the Russians, and, as they came within range, a volley from the 93rd at 600 yards emptied many saddles, but did not stop the advance ; then, as the dense Russian columns neared the " thin red streak, tipped with steel," a second volley, at 150 yards, rang out, and as the smoke cleared away the Russians were seen moving to the rear. Now was the opportunity for our cavalry, and the Heavies were not slow in taking advantage of it. Scarlett moved forward his brigade in two lines, the Greys and Inniskillings leading, with the 5th and 4th Dragoon Guards on the right and left flanks respectively, and the Royal Dragoons in support, the total strength being some 750 men. As Russell graphically wrote, while the Russians fell back, Scarlett charged into them. " By sheer steel and courage the Inniskillings and Scots were winning their desperate way right through the enemy's squadrons, and already grey horse and red coat had disappeared right at the rear of the mass, when the Royals, 4th Dragoon Guards, and 5th Dragoon Guards rushed at the remnants of the first line of the enemy, and went through it like pasteboard. In less than five minutes after they met our Dragoons the Russians were flying at full speed from a foe not half their strength."

Lord Raglan had in the meantime moved down the First and Fourth Divisions to reinforce Balaclava, and, recognizing the military genius of the Brigade Commander, ordered the Duke of Cambridge to take his instructions from Sir Colin Campbell. The services of the infantry were not called into requisition, but, owing to some inconceivable blunder, never yet properly explained, the Light Brigade of cavalry, without any supports, were ordered to attack the Russian troops in the westernmost valley. Here there was a whole division of Russian cavalry, with a force of six battalions of infantry supporting thirty-six guns, and at this force the little cavalry brigade, just 636 strong, was let loose. " C'est magni-

fique, mais ce n'est pas la guerre !" was the comment of
a French General who witnessed the spectacle. The Earl
of Cardigan was not wanting in personal courage, but he
was totally inexperienced in war. He led his men
straight at the guns, and escaped scathless himself, but
he acted in defiance of all the canons of the art of war.
The charge of the Light Brigade has been immortalized
by Tennyson, but, alas ! the men who participated in it
were rewarded with the same decoration as the infantry
soldiers who marched down from the camp to act as
spectators of that gallant charge. The clasp " Balaclava "
means nothing ; the name on the colours is the battle
honour.

CASUALTIES AT THE BATTLE OF BALACLAVA.

Regiments.	Officers.		Men.		Regiments.	Officers.		Men.	
	K.	W.	K.	W.		K.	W.	K.	W.
Staff	2	4	—	—	4th Hussars ..	2	2	32	22
4th Drag. Gds.	—	—	1	4	8th Hussars ..	2	2	30	23
5th Drag. Gds.	—	2	2	11	11th Hussars	—	3	32	23
Roy. Dragoons	—	4	2	7	13th Hussars	3	—	24	14
R. Scots Greys	—	4	2	53	17th Lancers	3	4	33	34
Inniskilling Dragoons ..	—	—	2	13	Sutherland Highlanders	—	—	—	—

INKERMAN, NOVEMBER 5, 1854.

This battle honour is borne by the

4th Hussars.　　　　　8th Hussars.
11th Hussars.　　　　13th Hussars.
17th Lancers.　　　　Grenadier Guards.
Coldstream Guards.　Scots Guards.
Royal Scots.　　　　King's Own.
Royal Fusiliers.　　Yorkshire.
Lancashire Fusiliers.　Royal Scots Fusiliers.
Royal Welsh Fusiliers.　Gloucesters.
East Lancashire.　　West Riding.
Border.　　　　　　South Staffords.
Welsh.　　　　　　Essex.
Sherwood Foresters.　North Lancashire.

Royal Berkshires.   West Kent.
Middlesex.   Manchesters.
Durham Light Infantry.   Connaught Rangers.
Rifle Brigade.

This was indeed a soldiers' battle. In the early dawn of November 5 a large Russian force, taking advantage of a dense fog, issued from Sevastopol and surprised our troops in the trenches. Reinforcements were hurried up from the camp, and the men—the few men on duty in the trenches and in the advanced siege-works—behaved with unexampled heroism. As each fresh regiment came up it was hurried into action, without any regard to brigades or divisions, and, indeed, in many cases men were found fighting in groups under officers of different regiments. The Allies were not merely surprised : they were outnumbered, as the following table shows :

Troops Engaged.	Men.	Guns.	Officers.		Men.	
			K.	W.	K.	W.
British ..	8,500	38	44	102	616	1,878
French ..	7,500	18	14	34	118	1,299
Russians	42,000	106	2	47	4,976	10,162

After an heroic struggle, in which the Russians displayed the greatest gallantry, they were driven back, with terrible slaughter, the fire of those of our regiments which were armed with the Minié rifle doing fearful execution in the dense columns of the enemy. It will hardly be believed that many regiments were still armed with the Brown Bess with which we fought in the Peninsula, although the Minié rifle had in the Kaffir War three years before proved itself a most formidable weapon.

The losses of the army during the winter of 1854-55 were appalling, but the men bore them without a murmur. With the spring active operations were renewed, and on June 18, the anniversary of Waterloo, an attempt was made to carry the fortress by storm. In this disastrous attack our losses were 22 officers and 247 men killed, 78 officers and 1,207 men wounded. Ten days later the Commander-in-Chief, Lord Raglan, died, and the command was given to his Chief of the Staff, another Peninsular veteran, Sir James Simpson, an officer who did not enjoy the confidence of the army, and who practically owned that he felt himself unfitted to exerc'se its command.

On September 8 a second attack was made on the Redan, the outwork which had defied our attempt on June 18. Again we were driven back, after our men had made good their footing in the place. This defeat was entirely due to the neglect to support the stormers, who had shown the habitual gallantry of the British soldier.

CASUALTIES AT THE BATTLE OF INKERMAN.

Regiments.	Officers. K.	Officers. W.	Men. K.	Men. W.	Regiments.	Officers. K.	Officers. W.	Men. K.	Men. W.
Staff	5	12	—	—	33rd W. Riding	1	2	6	55
8th Hussars ..	—	—	—	—	38th S. Stafford	—	—		
11th Hussars	—	—	—	—	41st Welsh ..	5	6	55	101
13th Hussars	—	—	—	—	44th Essex ..	—	—		
17th Lancers	1	—	—	1	47th N. Lancs	—	2	19	45
Royal Artillery	2	4	13	76	49th R. Berks	—	—		
Grenadier Gds.	3	6	101	124	50th West Kent	1	1	8	21
Coldstream Gds.	8	5	65	116	55th Border ..	—	5	18	58
Scots Guards	1	8	49	119	57th Middlesex	2	3	13	75
1st Royal Scots	—	—	1	—	63rd M'chester	3	7	12	93
4th K.O. Lancs	—	—	—	—	68th Durham L.I. ..	2	2	16	33
7th Royal Fus.	—	5	13	49	77th Middlesex	1	—	20	37
19th Yorkshire	1	—	1	3	88th Connaught Rangers ..	—	2	22	80
20th Lancs Fus.	1	8	40	122	95th Sherwood Foresters ..	—	4	27	104
21st R. Scots F.	1	6	24	90	Rifle Brigade	2	4	35	109
25th R.Welsh F.	1	1	18	20					
28th Gloucester	—	—	—	—					
30th E. Lancs	2	5	29	101					

On the following day the Redan was found to be evacuated, and our men entered unopposed. This was the last general action of the war. The Russians now abandoned the city, and retired to the far side of the harbour, and, though actual fighting was at an end, the winter was passed as if on active service. In the spring overtures of peace were made, and in the summer of 1856 the army returned to England, Sevastopol being restored to the Russians.

In writing of battle honours, I must not omit to mention that our allies, the French, Turks, and Sardinians, bestowed a certain number of decorations on our officers and men. The French distributed crosses of the Legion of Honour, which were, as a rule, given to officers. In some exceptional cases a cross was given to a non-commissioned officer, and in some very few cases to privates. The French war medal was bestowed on a certain number of men in each battalion, and one was given to H.R.H. the Duke of Cambridge. The Turks showered the Order of the Medjidieh with no niggardly hand, and the Sardinians gave a few crosses of the Order of St. Maurice and St. Lazarus to senior officers, and a few medals to each regiment. The distribution of these foreign decorations gave rise to considerable dissatisfaction. There were certain regiments which had fought throughout the campaign ; there were others which had landed at the very close of the operations, and had not lost a man in action. All shared equally, like the labourers in the vineyard.

There were few officers on the Staff or in the Brigade of Guards who did not receive four decorations for this campaign, and, in truth, the Guards deserved all they received. They not only took their fair share of trench duty, but at the Alma and at Inkerman they suffered most severely. A party of Guardsmen who happened to be on fatigue duty at Balaclava the morning of the battle were collected by a young officer, and fell in on the left of the 93rd. That young officer afterwards acted as Brigade-Major to the heroic Nicholson at the Siege of Delhi, and as I write is, I believe, the only living officer who saw Sevastopol and Delhi fall. I allude to Lieu-

20

tenant-General Sir Seymour Blane, who served as a subaltern of the Scots Guards in the Crimea. Afterwards exchanging into the 52nd, he marched down with Nicholson to Delhi, and was by his side when the hero of the siege was shot down inside the Cashmere Gate.

SEVASTOPOL.

This distinction was awarded to all regiments which landed in the Crimea prior to September 8, 1855, the date of the last storming of the Redan :

King's Dragoon Guards.
5th Dragoon Guards.
Royal Dragoons.
4th Hussars.
8th Hussars.
11th Hussars.
13th Hussars.
Grenadier Guards.
Scots Guards.
Buffs.
Royal Fusiliers.
Somerset Light Infantry.
Leicester.
Yorkshire.
Royal Scots Fusiliers.
Scottish Rifles.
East Lancashire.
Cornwall Light Infantry.
Border.
Dorsets.
Welsh.
Essex.
North Lancashire.
Royal Berkshires.
Middlesex.
Manchester.
Highland Light Infantry.
Cameron Highlanders.
Connaught Rangers.
Rifle Brigade.

4th Dragoon Guards.
Carabiniers.
Royal Scots Greys.
Inniskilling Dragoons.
10th Hussars.
12th Lancers.
17th Lancers.
Coldstream Guards.
Royal Scots.
King's Own (Lancaster).
Norfolks.
West Yorkshire.
Royal Irish.
Lancashire Fusiliers.
Royal Welsh Fusiliers.
Gloucesters.
East Surrey.
West Riding.
South Staffords.
South Lancashire.
Royal Highlanders.
Sherwood Foresters.
Northamptons.
West Kent.
Wiltshire.
Durham Light Infantry.
Seaforth Highlanders.
Royal Irish Fusiliers.
Argyll and Sutherland Highlanders.

In addition to the following casualties in action, between the landing of the army in the Crimea on September 14, 1854, and the storming of the Redan on September 8, 1855, 11,375 non-commissioned officers and men were invalided and 16,037 died of disease !

CASUALTIES DURING THE CAMPAIGN IN THE CRIMEA (INCLUDING THE BATTLES OF ALMA, BALACLAVA, AND INKERMAN).

Regiments.	Officers. K.	Officers. W.	Men. K.	Men. W.	Regiments.	Officers. K.	Officers. W.	Men. K.	Men. W.
K. Drag. Gds.	—	—	—	—	38th S. Staffs.	3	7	43	210
4th Drag. Gds.	—	—	2	12	39th Dorsets ..	1	1	9	46
5th Drag. Gds.	1	3	2	4	41st Welsh ..	9	13	145	426
Carabiniers ..	—	—	—	—	42nd R. Highlanders ..	1	2	39	119
Roy. Dragoons	—	4	3	7					
Scots Greys ..	—	4	8	57	44th Essex ..	4	8	64	156
4th Hussars ..	2	2	19	24	46th Cornwall				
Inniskillings ..	—	—	3	14	L.I. ..	1	2	32	71
8th Hussars ..	2	3	26	23	47th N. Lancs	2	9	120	216
10th Hussars	—	—	—	4	48th N'ampton	—	2	12	60
11th Hussars	1	2	29	29	49th Berkshire	7	10	204	325
12th Lancers..	—	—	—	—	50th West Kent	2	4	56	67
13th Hussars	3	—	14	31	55th Border ..	6	18	145	412
17th Lancers	4	5	39	34	56th Essex ..	—	1	8	13
Royal Artillery	12	30	173	632	57th Middlesex	8	11	81	237
Roy. Engineers	15	13	55	86	62nd Wiltshire	7	7	37	121
Grenadier Gds.	6	12	144	410	63rd Manchester	6	8	65	127
Coldstream					68th Durham				
Guards ..	10	6	128	197	L.I. ..	6	4	51	71
Scots Guards	4	23	109	336	71st Highland				
Royal Scots ..	3	10	58	225	L.I. ..	—	—	—	1
Buffs	3	13	78	259	72nd Seaforth				
King's Own ..	2	5	38	142	Highlanders	1	—	12	48
Royal Fusiliers	8	23	174	381	77th Middlesex	5	11	411	606
Norfolks ..	1	2	20	83	79th Cameron				
Somerset L.I.	—	—	—	11	Highlanders	—	2	12	55
14th W. Yorks	—	—	16	46	82nd S. Lancs	—	—	—	—
Leicesters ..	1	5	34	134	88th Connaught				
Royal Irish ..	3	10	87	267	Rangers ..	7	16	159	400
Yorkshire ..	4	20	138	502	89th R. Irish F.	—	1	13	73
20th Lancs F.	3	10	83	81	90th ScottishR.	4	15	92	221
R. Welsh Fus.	16	15	193	495	93rd Sutherland				
28th Gloucesters	—	9	42	89	Highlanders	2	2	19	95
30th E. Lancs	10	19	144	364	95th Derbysh.	7	21	184	360
31st E. Surrey	2	1	25	84	97th West Kent	8	9	108	198
33rd W. Riding	8	21	116	293	Rifle Brigade				
34th Border ..	7	18	118	375	(two batts.)	9	20	245	781

The Sultan of Turkey, in addition to the Order of the Medjidieh, bestowed a silver medal on every officer and man present in the Crimea, and Queen Victoria in like manner granted the Crimean Medal to every French, Sardinian, and Turkish soldier or sailor present in the campaign.

DECORATIONS BESTOWED BY OUR ALLIES DURING THE CRIMEAN WAR.

Regiments.	Legion of Honour.	Medjidieh.	Sardinian Medal.	French War Medal.	Regiments.	Legion of Honour.	Medjidieh.	Sardinian Medal.	French War Medal.
General officers	22	16	8	1	28th Gloucester	5	13	8	9
Staff officers ..	47	35	8	—	30th E. Lancs	6	17	6	9
Med. officers	31	85	—	—	31st E. Surrey	2	7	1	5
1st Drag. Gds.	—	3	—	—	33rd W. Riding	6	14	7	9
4th Drag. Gds.	2	7	6	4	34th Border ..	4	13	6	8
5th Drag. Gds.	3	6	—	4	38th S. Staffs	5	12	6	9
6th Drag. Gds.	—	2	2	—	39th Dorsets ..	4	10	3	6
Roy. Dragoons	2	5	3	3	41st Welsh ..	7	12	6	9
R. Scots Greys	2	5	3	4	42nd R. Highl.	6	13	6	8
4th Hussars ..	3	6	4	4	44th Essex ..	6	13	8	8
8th Hussars ..	3	5	4	3	46th Corn. L.I.	5	16	6	7
10th Hussars	—	7	1	1	47th N. Lancs	6	17	9	7
11th Hussars	2	7	2	5	48th N'amptons	2	9	2	4
12th Lancers	—	4	2	1	49th R. Berks	6	12	7	9
13th Hussars	2	5	4	2	50th R. W. Kent	5	12	8	7
17th Lancers	2	6	4	3	55th Border ..	3	13	6	9
Royal Artillery	74	124	50	60	56th Essex ..	1	—	—	4
Roy. Engineers	26	22	15	7	57th Middlesex	6	13	6	8
3rd Batt. Grenadier Guards	6	31	7	9	62nd Wiltshire	5	13	6	8
1st Batt. Coldstream Gds.	6	32	7	9	63rd Manchester	2	8	4	8
1st Batt. Scots Guards ..	7	32	9	7	68th Durham L.I. ..	7	11	6	9
Royal Scots (two batts.)	7	25	7	7	71st Highland L.I. ..	2	10	4	6
Buffs	4	10	3	5	72nd Seaforth Highlanders	2	8	1	4
4th King's Own	4	13	6	9	77th Middlesex	5	12	6	7
7th Roy. Fus.	8	14	6	9	79th Cameron Highlanders	5	12	7	8
9th Norfolk ..	4	10	3	7	88th Connaught Rangers ..	6	14	9	10
13th Somer. L.I.	2	10	5	—	89th R. Irish F.	4	10	4	5
14th W. Yorks	2	10	5	6	90th Scottish R.	5	11	5	8
17th Leicesters	3	12	2	6	93rd Sutherland Highlanders	4	14	6	9
18th Roy. Scots	3	11	4	7	95th Derbyshire	6	11	6	8
19th Yorkshire	7	11	6	9	97th West Kent	5	11	5	8
20th Lancs F.	5	13	6	9	Rifle Brigade (two batts.)	11	33	13	18
21st R. Scots F.	6	11	7	9					
23rd R. Welsh Fusiliers ..	7	10	6	10					

THE VICTORIA CROSS.

This decoration dates from the Crimean War, and was instituted, as is well known, as a reward open to all ranks for conspicuous bravery in presence of the enemy.   During the campaign the following regiments were able to add to their other honours the Victoria Cross :

Royal Scots Greys ..	..	2	19th (Yorkshire)	2
4th Hussars	..	1	23rd (Royal Welsh Fus.) ..	4
Inniskilling Dragoons	..	1	30th (East Lancashire) ..	1
11th Hussars ..	..	1	34th (Border Regiment) ..	2
13th Hussars ..	..	1	41st (Welsh)	2
17th Lancers ..	..	3	44th (Essex)	1
Royal Artillery ..	..	9	47th (North Lancashire) ..	1
Royal Engineers ..	..	7	49th (Royal Berkshire) ..	3
Grenadier Guards ..	..	4	55th (Border)	2
Coldstream Guards	..	3	57th (Middlesex)	2
Scots Guards ..	..	5	68th (Durham Light Inf.)	1
Royal Scots ..	..	1	77th (Middlesex)	2
The Buffs	..	2	90th (Scottish Rifles) ..	2
4th (King's Own) ..	..	1	97th (West Kent)	2
7th (Royal Fusiliers)	..	5	1st Batt. Rifle Brigade ..	4
17th (Leicestershire)	..	1	2nd Batt. Rifle Brigade ..	3
18th (Royal Irish) ..	..	1		

The following table is of interest, as showing the total losses incurred by the army in the Crimea in the different arms :

	CAVALRY.		ARTILLERY.		ENGINEERS.		INFANTRY.	
	Officers.	Men.	Officers.	Men.	Officers.	Men.	Officers.	Men.
Killed in action	9	114	11	121	9	32	125	2,331
Died of wounds	4	26	1	52	6	23	73	1,832
Died of disease	23	1,007	10	1,298	5	175	105	13,414
Total	36	1,147	22	1,471	20	230	303	17,577
Wounded in action	26	237	30	632	13	86	435	10,406

From the above it will be seen that, whilst 2,769 officers and men were killed in action or died of their wounds, the losses by disease amounted to no less than 16,037 ! For every ten officers killed in action, six died from disease, whereas in the proportion of the men who fell the figures were reversed. For every ten who fell in action or as a result of their wounds no less than sixty died of disease.

CHAPTER XX

BATTLE HONOURS FOR THE INDIAN MUTINY, 1857-1859

India — Delhi — Lucknow — Central India — Defence of Arrah
—Behar.

INDIA, 1857-1859.

FOR some inscrutable reason, the colours of those regiments which were employed in the suppression of the Indian Mutiny bear no record of their services unless they happened to have been employed at the Siege of Delhi or in the operations at Lucknow or in Central India. There is, indeed, one notable exception. A group of Sikhs, but fifty in number, aided Mr. Wake in his determined defence of Arrah, and subsequently the regiment was engaged in maintaining peace in the province of Behar. For these services the 45th Rattray's Sikhs are authorized to bear the words " Defence of Arrah " and " Behar " on their colours and appointments. Yet British and native troops —aye, civilians and delicately-nurtured women—were engaged for many weary months in a daily contest with battle and with wounds, with plague, pestilence, and famine. Throughout the length and breadth of the northern portion of Hindustan we were waging a life-and-death struggle for the maintenance of British supremacy in India. The details of many incidents in that struggle we never shall know. Our Indian graveyards are filled with tombs recording the losses of those days, from Generals who, like Nicholson, fell in the hour of victory, to wee bairnies who perished from want of the bare necessaries of life, and, alas ! also from the sword and bullet of our foes. The whole peninsula is hallowed with the unknown graves of our gallant dead.

The history of the Siege of Delhi, where a force of less than 10,000 men besieged a city defended by four times their number of disciplined troops for a period of twelve long weeks in the hottest season of the year, is only equalled by the dauntless bravery with which Lucknow was defended against incalculable odds. Loyal native vied with his British comrade in upholding the honour of our flag, whilst the cheerful heroism and self-abnegation of the women who bore such a noble part in the struggle is deserving of more than a passing tribute of homage. The romantic interest that centred round Havelock's relief of Lucknow has dwarfed the marvellous achievements of the Delhi force—an achievement never surpassed in the military annals of our own or any other country.

The losses suffered by the troops at the siege of that fortress exceeded in number the total casualties incurred by the rest of the army in the suppression of the rebellion. The " morning states " of September 13—the day before the storm of the city—showed a total strength of 9,366 effectives ; on the evening of the 20th, when the entire city was in our hands, there were but 5,520. No less than 3,846 officers and men had been killed and wounded ; yet four days afterwards General Wilson was enabled to despatch a little column to aid in the relief of Lucknow. It consisted of three batteries of Bengal Artillery, 300 men of the 9th Lancers, the headquarters of the 8th and 75th Regiments, totalling only 450 men, so grievously had these battalions suffered in the siege. Four squadrons of native cavalry and two battalions of Punjab troops brought the total strength of the brigade to just under 2,000 men.

DELHI, MAY TO SEPTEMBER, 1857.

The regiments authorized to bear the battle honour " Delhi " on their colours and appointments are the

Carabiniers.	9th Lancers.
King's (Liverpool).	Gloucesters.
Oxford Light Infantry.	King's Royal Rifles.

Gordon Highlanders.	Royal Munster Fusiliers.
9th Hodson's Horse.	10th Lancers.
21st Daly's Horse.	22nd Sam Browne's Horse.
25th Cavalry.	Q.O. Corps of Guides.
1st P.W.O. Sappers and Miners.	54th Sikhs.
	55th Coke's Rifles.
56th Punjab Rifles.	57th Wilde's Rifles.
127th Baluch Light Infantry.	2nd Gurkhas.
	3rd Gurkhas.

It will be noted that the Carabiniers is the only corps which bears the two honours " Delhi " and " Sevastopol."

On the first news of the mutiny at Meerut reaching the Commander-in-Chief at Simla on May 12, he at once moved down with the Headquarters Staff to Umballa, where the regiments at Kussowlie, Dugshai, and Subathoo, had been ordered to assemble. The 9th Lancers and two troops of Bengal Artillery were quartered at that station, and at Meerut were the Carabiniers, the 60th Rifles, and the headquarters of the Bengal Artillery.

Much unavoidable delay occurred in procuring carriage for the troops, and, of course, it was necessary to provide for the safety of the Punjab. It was not until May 24 that the Commander-in-Chief was able to move. Two days afterwards he died of cholera at Kurnal, and the command devolved upon General Barnard—a gallant officer who had been Chief of the Staff during the latter part of the Crimean War, but who was new to India. The force moving down from Umballa consisted of two brigades, and was to be joined before reaching Delhi by the Meerut garrison. This junction took place on June 7. The Meerut force had fought a successful action with the mutineers a week previously, capturing five guns.

On the 7th General Barnard found the mutineers drawn up in a strong position at Budli-ka-Serai to dispute his advance. They had thrown up some works, in which heavy guns were placed. After a sharp fight, in which we lost 51 killed and 131 wounded, the rebels were driven out of their vantage-ground, with the loss of thirteen guns, and from this day the siege may be said to have commenced. Just one month later General Barnard died of cholera, which was daily claiming victims from all ranks. Indeed, until the close of the siege, this scourge was never absent. From time to time, as circumstances permitted, reinforcements of both British and native troops were pushed down from the Punjab, and the loyal Sikh chiefs also sent contingents, which, though not of great fighting value, served to keep open our communications with Lahore, and to a certain extent, no doubt, did aid in the work of the siege.

Between June 7 and September 14—the day of the assault—the besieging force fought no fewer than thirty-two engagements, and so heavy were the duties thrown on officers and men that it was impossible to relieve the guards, men remaining for days at a time on duty, whilst staff officers took their turn in the batteries and trenches. On the morning of September 13 the decision was taken to carry the city by storm. Two breaches were declared practicable on the northern side of the walls at the Water and Kashmir bastions. Practically the whole available force was detailed for the assault. The first, second, and third columns, under the command of General John Nicholson, were to act on the left ; the fourth, under Major Reid, of the 2nd Gurkhas, on the right. It consisted of Major Reid's own gallant regiment (now well known to all soldiers as the 2nd Gurkhas), the infantry of the Guides, and such men as could be spared from the picquets of the British regiments on the ridge. No. 1 column of the force, under Nicholson, was composed of the 75th (now the Gordon Highlanders), the 1st Bengal Fusiliers (now the 1st Munsters), and the 2nd Punjab Infantry (now the 56th Rifles). This stormed the breach at the Kashmir bastion. No. 2 column, under Colonel Jones, of the 61st, consisted of the 8th (Liverpool) Regiment, the 2nd Bengal Fusiliers (now the 2nd Munsters), and the 4th (now the 54th Sikhs). The third column, under Colonel Campbell, of the 52nd, was composed of the 52nd (Oxford Light Infantry), the 3rd Gurkhas, and Coke's Rifles. The total strength of the three columns amounted to 2,800 men, whilst the fourth, under Major Reid, was 680 strong, but it had in support 1,200 men of the Kashmir contingent. The reserve was under Colonel Longfield, of the 8th, and comprised the 61st Foot (2nd Gloucesters), the 4th Punjab Infantry (now the 57th), Wilde's Rifles, and the Baluch battalion (now the 127th Baluch Light Infantry).

CASUALTIES AT THE SIEGE AND ASSAULT OF DELHI,
MAY TO SEPTEMBER, 1857.

Regiments.	BRITISH TROOPS.				NATIVE TROOPS.			
	Officers.		Men.		Officers.		Men.	
	K.	W.	K.	W.	K.	W.	K.	W.
General Staff	4	9	—	—	—	—	—	—
Royal Artillery ..	4	24	43	216	1	1	26	49
Royal Engineers ..	3	19	6	3	2	1	34	60
6th Carabiniers ..	1	2	18	9	—	—	—	—
9th Lancers	1	2	26	64	—	—	—	—
8th (King's Liverpool)	3	7	41	129	—	—	—	—
52nd (Oxford L.I.) ..	1	4	28	75	—	—	—	—
60th (King's Roy. Rifles)	4	10	109	266	—	—	—	—
61st (Gloucestershire)	2	7	30	112	—	—	—	—
75th (Gordon Highl.) ..	5	14	79	184	—	—	—	—
1st Roy. Munster Fus.	3	11	95	210	—	—	—	—
2nd Roy. Munster Fus.	4	6	79	156	—	—	—	—
Hodson's Horse ..	—	—	—	—	—	—	—	—
21st Daly's Horse ..	—	—	—	—	—	—	—	3
22nd Sam Browne's H.	—	—	—	—	—	—	—	—
25th Cavalry	—	—	—	—	—	—	—	—
Q.O. Corps of Guides	2	6	—	—	5	10	65	215
54th Sikhs	1	3	—	—	2	7	43	116
55th Coke's Rifles ..	3	5	—	—	3	5	71	141
56th Rifles	1	2	—	—	2	4	41	103
57th Wilde's Rifles ..	1	1	—	—	—	2	9	59
127th Baluchis ..	1	—	—	—	—	1	7	48
2nd Gurkhas (Sirmoor Rifles)	1	6	—	—	2	8	80	219
3rd Gurkhas	1	2	—	—	—	3	20	33

NOTE.—I regret that I have been unable to trace the losses in those three fine regiments, now the 21st, 22nd, and 25th Cavalry.

The story of the siege and the assault is an epic which will remain a monument of the heroism of our troops, British and native, to all time. Those who stand on that famous ridge and gaze at the stupendous walls before them, must wonder, as I have wondered, at the audacity which conceived and the gallantry which achieved such a feat of arms. As I have said, by September 20 the city, with its arsenal, was in our hands, and on the following day a small brigade of all arms was at once despatched to open up communications with the North-West Provinces, and to aid in the tranquillization of the country. Our losses during the siege were grievously heavy. Out of a total strength of 640, the 60th Rifles lost 389 of all ranks ; the 2nd Gurkhas lost 310 out of 540 ; the Guides 303 out of 550. Coke's Rifles had all its officers killed or wounded, and more than half the men. The 52nd had arrived from Sialkot just a month prior to the assault. It marched into camp 640 strong ; on the morning of September 14 it paraded 240 rank and file, having lost 74 men from cholera and sunstroke in one short month ! The table on p. 315 tells its own tale.

LUCKNOW.

The following regiments are authorized to bear this battle honour on their colours and appointments :

Queen's Bays.	7th Hussars.
9th Lancers.	Northumberland Fusiliers.
King's Liverpools.	Royal Welsh Fusiliers.
Lincolns.	Lancashire Fusiliers.
Border.	Scottish Rifles.
Cornwall Light Infantry.	South Staffords.
South Lancashire.	Black Watch.
Royal West Kent.	Shropshire Light Infantry.
North Staffords.	York and Lancaster.
Seaforth Highlanders.	Gordon Highlanders.
Cameron Highlanders.	Sutherland Highlanders.
Royal Munster Fusiliers.	Royal Dublin Fusiliers.
Rifle Brigade.	9th Hodson's Horse.
10th Hodson's Horse.	11th Probyn's Lancers.
21st Daly's Horse.	22nd Sam Browne's Horse.
25th Cavalry.	1st P.W.O. Sappers and
2nd Q.O. Sappers and Miners.	Miners.
14th Sikhs.	16th Lucknow.
32nd Pioneers.	56th Punjabi Rifles.

57th Wilde's Rifles.

This one battle honour, " Lucknow," covers four distinct military operations—the memorable defence of the Residency under Sir Henry Lawrence ; the first relief, or rather reinforcement, of the beleaguered garrison by Sir Henry Havelock ; the final relief and withdrawal of the women and children by Sir Colin Campbell ; and, lastly, the siege and capture of the city in March, 1858. With the medal granted for the Indian Mutiny clasps were issued for the Relief, the Defence, and one simply superscribed " Lucknow," which covered the final operations only. Wearers of the medal are enabled to show the distinctive part they played in the grand struggle in and around Lucknow, but survivors are now few and far between. In a very few short years there will be no wearers of the Mutiny Medal left. Whilst the men by their clasps showed the share they took in the operations, the regiments bear no distinctive mark showing the part they played. The Somerset Light Infantry and the 12th Khelat-i-Ghilzai Regiment are authorized to bear a mural crown as a distinctive honour for their defence of Jelalabad and Khelat-i-Ghilzai ; the 16th Lucknow Regiment wears a battlemented gateway, to connect it with the memorable defence of the Residency ; the 45th Sikhs bear the words " Defence of Arrah "; and the regiments which formed the garrison, under Sir George White, were granted the honour " Defence of Ladysmith," to differentiate them from their comrades who, under Sir Redvers Buller, effected their relief. It is true that the 32nd were made light infantry as a recognition of their conduct at Lucknow, but so little is this fact remembered that in the month of January, 1910, a leading service paper gravely asserted that the Cornwalls were given their bugles in the year 1832 ! *Sic transit gloria mundi*.

Defence of Lucknow.

Lucknow, the capital of the newly-annexed kingdom of Oude, was in 1857 a city of some 150,000 inhabitants, known to be fanatically hostile to our rule. Only the

year before the Mutiny the King had been deposed, and
with good cause. Misgovernment and tyranny were
rampant throughout his kingdom, and we were performing a mere act of justice towards his people in
removing him from power. We have not yet learnt the
lesson that a nation prefers bad government under its
own rulers to the best form of government under an alien
administration. The unpopularity of the annexation was
felt beyond the confines of Oude. A very large proportion of the sepoys of the Bengal army were recruited from
this very country, and their sympathies were naturally
with their fallen King.

Fortunately, Lord Dalhousie, the Governor-General
responsible for the annexation, had selected one of the
very best soldier-statesmen in India for the post of Chief
Commissioner—Sir James Outram, a tried soldier of the
Bombay army. At this moment he was absent from his
post, having been selected to command the troops in the
Persian Expeditionary Force. His successor, Sir Henry
Lawrence, was, like Outram, a soldier—one of that
gallant band of brothers whose names will last so long
as does our Indian Empire. He commenced his career
in the Bengal Artillery, had seen a great deal of service
as a gunner, and had earned a still higher reputation in
the early days of the administration of the Punjab.
Fortunate it was for England that she had such a man
in Lucknow. The Mutiny caused no surprise to Henry
Lawrence. Fifteen years previously, in the pages of the
Calcutta Review, he had predicted an attempt on the part
of the pampered sepoy to gain the upper hand, but his
warnings had fallen on deaf ears. Now he was ready for
the emergency—ready so far as his means permitted.
The garrison of Lucknow consisted of one British battalion—the 32nd (Cornwall Regiment), numbering 19
officers and 517 other ranks—one weak company of the
84th—one officer and 48 men. There were, in addition,
six regiments of native infantry, two of native cavalry,
and two batteries of native artillery.

The news of the mutiny at Meerut and of the capture
of Delhi by the adherents of the old Mogul Emperor was
known in Lucknow on May 12, and then Lawrence commenced to take steps to meet the coming storm. Measures
were adopted to render the Residency defensible—no
easy task. It was in the heart of the city, surrounded
by a few buildings erected for the convenience of the
staff of the Resident. These were in plots of ground,
separated by low mud walls. Within easy range were
several masonry palaces, which afforded good shelter to
an enemy. It was impossible to include all of the staff
houses in the scheme of defence, owing to the smallness
of the garrison. All that could be done was to connect
the various buildings by a breastwork, and to excavate
a ditch all round. Provisions and ammunition were
brought in, and all the civilians, as well as the British
troops, were concentrated as near the Residency as
possible.

On May 29 the native garrison threw off all semblance
of loyalty, murdered their officers, including the Brigadier
(Handscomb), and moved out of their lines, which they
fired. They were from time to time joined by other
mutineers, who had committed grievous outrages in other
stations in Oude. No attack, however, was made on the
Residency.

On June 29 Lawrence determined to undertake the
offensive, and he moved out to Chinhut, where the
mutineers were massed, to attack them. He met with
a sharp reverse, losing some of his guns, whilst the wing
of the 32nd, who were with him, lost 115 killed out of 300
men engaged. The following morning Lawrence blew up
the magazine, containing 249 barrels of powder and
594,000 rounds of ammunition, which it was found impossible to carry into the Residency, and made final preparations for the siege. His garrison consisted of under
2,000 men, of whom 100 were civilians and 765 loyal
natives—men of the mutinied regiments who had determined to throw in their lot with the Sirkar. With

them were nearly 200 pensioners—men mostly past work.

It is not within the scope of this work to deal with the details of that heroic defence, where civilian vied with soldier, native with Englishman, to uphold the honour of our name ; where delicately-nurtured women and the no less devoted wives of the privates shared all the dangers, all the privations, of the humblest sepoy. Many women and children died from want of the bare necessaries of life ; more than one babe was shot in its mother's arms, and more than one woman fell a victim to the bullets of our foes. For a long eighty-seven days did the siege last, and then the little band under Have-lock forced its way through the many thousands of the besieging force, and brought the welcome reinforcement of British bayonets to the beleaguered garrison. The figures below tell the sad tale of the severe losses which were endured by the heroic garrison of Lucknow :

CASUALTIES IN THE DEFENCE OF LUCKNOW.

Regiments.	Officers.		Men.		Regiments.	Officers.		Men.	
	K.	W.	K.	W.		K.	W.	K.	W.
32nd Corn. L.I.	7	8	192	171	84th York and Lancs (one company) ..	—	1	12	8
Royal Bengal Artillery ..	1	2	52	18					

No fewer than eighty-nine women and children also perished.

Relief of Lucknow by General Sir Henry Havelock.

The most serious problem that faced the Governor-General in India, as soon as the real gravity of the Mutiny was realized, was to effect the relief of the beleaguered garrisons of Lucknow and Cawnpore, where large numbers of women and children were hemmed in by the mutineers, and were in daily peril of their lives. It was well known that at both places the defences were utterly inadequate, and that the garrisons were all too small. By a fortunate coincidence, a strong force was on its way to China for the purpose of compelling a respect for treaty rights, and the regiments composing that force were stopped at Singapore and diverted to Calcutta. At the same time, the regiment at the Mauritius was despatched with all haste to India, and the return of the two battalions—the 64th (North Staffords) and the 78th (Ross-shire Buffs)—from the Persian Campaign enabled Lord Canning, the Governor-General, to send these up to Allahabad, and so to form the nucleus of a relieving army.

The officer selected for the command of the relieving force was Colonel Henry Havelock, an officer who had recently commanded a brigade in the Persian War. Havelock had seen an immensity of service in India, mostly on the Staff. He had been Adjutant of the 13th Light Infantry, and had served with that distinguished regiment throughout the Burmese War of 1824. In Afghanistan he had earned a Brevet and a C.B. for his exceptional services at the defence of Jelalabad. He had been present at Maharajpore, where he had earned a second Brevet. But he was a disappointed man. Success had come to him late in life, for he had been twenty-three years a subaltern, and had been purchased over times without number.

Immediately on his arrival in Calcutta Havelock learned of his new command, and he at once pushed up to Allahabad to take over charge from Colonel Neill, of the Madras Fusiliers, already at that station. The force was all too weak for the task imposed upon it. It barely numbered 1,350 bayonets, including 500 Sikhs. Its cavalry numbered just twenty sabres, composed of officers of regiments which had disappeared in the storm and a

few brave planters. The following are the details of the
brigade with which Havelock essayed the relief of Lucknow :

Royal Artillery ..	..	..	..	76	men.
64th (North Staffords) ..	..	..	435	,,
78th (Ross-shire Buffs) ..	..	..	284	,,
84th (York and Lancaster)	..	..	191	,,
Madras Fusiliers	..	..	..	376	,,
Ferozepore Sikhs	..	..	..	448	,,
Volunteer cavalry	..	..	..	20	sabres.

Arriving at Allahabad on June 30, Havelock immediately moved forward ; but the weather was terrific,
and his men suffered much—not only from heat, but also
from cholera. Not a day passed without some victim
being claimed by one or other of these deadly foes.
To-day it was a drummer of the Highlanders, to-morrow
the senior Staff Officer of the army. Still, no heart
quailed. The danger that faced their countrywomen
nerved all, but, alas ! their gallant efforts were doomed
to failure. When the Nana saw the net closing round
him, he gave the order for the murder of the women and
children who, trusting to his honour, had surrendered to
him at Cawnpore ; and when Havelock's force entered
the place, they were met with the most ghastly evidence
of cruelties which had been perpetrated by the man who
for many years professed himself a loyal ally of the
English.

Weakened by losses in action, as well as by disease,
Havelock was compelled to halt at Cawnpore for reinforcements. These reached him in the shape of the 5th
(Northumberland Fusiliers)—the Fighting Fifth—from
the Mauritius, and six companies of the 90th (Scottish
Rifles)—a regiment which, under its Colonel, Campbell,
had earned a great reputation for dash in the Crimea.
With the reinforcements came the unwelcome news that
he had been superseded by Sir James Outram, who was
reappointed to his old post of Chief Commissioner of
Oude, with the supreme command of all the troops in
that province. Sir James, however, with rare self-

denial, refused to deprive Havelock of the honour of carrying out the relief, and published an order announcing his intention to act in the ranks of the volunteer cavalry until Lucknow was entered.

It was not until the middle of September that Havelock was enabled to continue his onward march. He was opposed at every step, but the troops would not be denied; and on the 25th of that month a welcome reinforcement of nearly 2,000 fighting men was thrown into Lucknow, and the lives of the sorely-pressed garrison assured.

Havelock lived just long enough to know that his services had been appreciated at last, and that he had been gazetted a Major-General for distinguished service in the field, and raised to the dignity of a K.C.B. The baronetcy conferred upon him was not gazetted until after his death. The final relief I deal with on p. 326. A dark shadow was cast over that glorious achievement. Havelock was able to drag his sorely stricken frame across the breastwork to welcome Sir Colin Campbell and the relieving army, and then, worn out by toil and anxiety, he sank into his grave. In a shady grove of trees hard by the Alumbagh they made his humble tomb, and Campbell, Outram, Inglis, Peel, and many a stout soldier who had followed him in that stern march from Cawnpore, now followed his remains to their last resting-place. So long as gallant deeds and noble aspirations and spotless self-devotion are cherished in our midst, so long will Havelock's lonely tomb, hard by the scenes of his triumphs and of his death, be regarded as one of the most sacred spots where England's soldiers lie.

RELIEF OF LUCKNOW BY SIR COLIN CAMPBELL, NOVEMBER, 1857.

No sooner was Delhi in our hands than General Wilson, as I have shown on p. 312, despatched a small force towards Agra, where, unfortunately, the civil and military authorities had not shown themselves possessed of those qualities which have built up our Indian Empire. Few indeed were the men that Wilson could spare, but on the morning of September 21 Brigadier Greathed, Colonel of the 8th (King's), now the Liverpool Regiment, marched towards Agra at the head of the little movable column. His force consisted of two troops of horse and one battery of field artillery ; the 9th Lancers (300 strong) ; the 8th and 73rd Regiments, which, in consequence of their heavy losses, only numbered 450 men ; four squadrons of the 21st, 22nd, and 25th Cavalry and of Hodson's Horse, the four squadrons some 500 strong ; and the 2nd and 4th Punjab Infantry (now the 56th and 57th Rifles). All told, the brigade numbered 800 cavalry, 1,650 infantry, 200 sappers, and 18 guns.

On the 10th of the following month Greathed reached Agra, where he was attacked by the rebels. To their astonishment, these gentry found they had a totally different stamp of men to deal with than the Agra garrison, and Greathed, with the loss of but 13 killed and 54 wounded, drove them off, capturing thirteen guns. During the short halt at Agra, General Hope Grant, Colonel of the 9th Lancers, arrived in camp with some 300 British soldiers, convalescents of the regiments at Delhi, and took over command. Pushing on to Cawnpore, he found a wing of the 93rd (Sutherland Highlanders) and some men of the regiments which had gone into Lucknow with Havelock.

The relief of Lucknow was now the principal objective, and Hope Grant, in obedience to orders received from Calcutta, moved towards that city, halting at Bhantira until the arrival of Sir Colin Campbell, who, on the first news of the Mutiny reaching England, had been sent out to assume the post of Commander-in-Chief in India. The new Chief possessed the confidence not only of the Ministry in England, but of every man in the army. Probably he was the most deservedly popular General who had up till then ever commanded an army in the

FIELD-MARSHAL COLIN CAMPBELL : LORD CLYDE.

To face page 324.

field. He had a wide experience of war. As a subaltern he had served in the Peninsula, been repeatedly
mentioned in despatches for gallantry—a rare thing to
happen to a subaltern in Wellington's days. He commanded a regiment in China in the war of 1842, a brigade
in the Punjab Campaign of 1849, was in chief command
in many of the early expeditions on the Punjab frontier,
and was one of the very few General Officers who emerged
from the Crimean War with enhanced credit. The vast
majority of the reinforcements despatched from England
for the suppression of the Mutiny had served in the
Crimea, and to them the name of Colin Campbell was
that of a man who could lead and whom they were proud
to follow.

On November 9 Sir Colin arrived at Bhantira, and
assumed the command of the army. Sir Colin was fully
alive to the imperative necessity of withdrawing the
beleaguered garrison from its perilous position at Lucknow. Sir James Outram, who, as I have shown, assumed
command on reaching the Residency, was besieged by a
disciplined army numbering 60,000 men. He was en-
cumbered with 1,500 sick men, women, and children, and
the Residency, over which our flag had been kept flying
for thirteen weary weeks, was but an ordinary Indian
building, commanded on all sides by masonry palaces,
which had been converted into siege-batteries. To carry
through this formidable task Sir Colin had but 4,500
men, distributed as under :

Cavalry Brigade—Brigadier Little (9th Lancers) : Two squadrons
    9th Lancers, one squadron 21st Daly's Horse, one squadron
    22nd Sam Browne's Horse, one squadron 25th Cavalry, one
    squadron Hodson's Horse.

These native troops were under Lieutenants Watson,
Probyn, Younghusband, and Hugh Gough respectively,
and it is worthy of note that of these four subalterns one
(Younghusband) was killed ; the other three were all
wounded in action, and all three lived to wear the Victoria
Cross and the Grand Cross of the Bath.

Artillery Brigade—Brigadier Crawford, R.A. : Two troops of
    Bengal Horse Artillery, two batteries of Field Artillery, two
    companies of Royal Artillery, eight guns of the Naval Brigade
    under the gallant Sir William Peel, with 250 seamen and
    Marines.
First Brigade—Brigadier Adrian Hope : 93rd Highlanders, a
    wing of the 53rd (Shropshires), and the 57th Wilde's Rifles.
Second Brigade—Brigadier Greathed : 8th (King's Liverpool
    Regiment), a battalion made up of detachments of British
    regiments in Lucknow, and the 56th Punjab Rifles.
Third Brigade—Brigadier Russell : 84th Regiment, 23rd (Royal
    Welsh Fusiliers), and two companies of the 82nd (South
    Lancashires).

To keep open communication with Allahabad and Calcutta, Sir Colin had left General Wyndham at Cawnpore
with a force of British troops. Wyndham had earned a
great reputation for coolness under fire at the storming
of the Redan, but he had no experience of Indian warfare,
and had never exercised an independent command in his
life. At Cawnpore he did not show to advantage as a
commander.

During Sir Hope Grant's halt prior to Sir Colin's arrival
the most energetic measures had been adopted to obtain
the necessary carriage to enable the Commander-in-Chief
to carry out his design of withdrawing the garrison, so
that, on his assuming command, all was ready for an
immediate advance ; and on November 17, after some
hard fighting, which entailed a loss of 45 officers and 496
men killed and wounded, the relieving force entered the
Residency, and the garrison was saved. Ten days subsequently the evacuation of the Residency had been successfully accomplished, and the whole force was *en route*
for Cawnpore, where Wyndham had suffered a sharp
reverse at the hands of the mutinous Gwalior contingent.

Siege and Capture of Lucknow.

When Sir Colin Campbell withdrew the garrison from
the Residency, he felt that but half of his task was done.
His force was not strong enough to warrant his attacking
the mutineers, and so crushing the rebellion in Oude.

This must be left until the arrival of the reinforcements from England, and undertaken when he was not hampered with a large convoy of sick and wounded, women and children. In order to maintain a certain hold on the country around Lucknow, Sir Colin left Sir James Outram with a considerable force to occupy the Alumbagh—an old shooting-lodge of the Kings of Oude, situated in a park about three miles from the suburbs of Lucknow. Outram's force numbered over 4,000 men, and comprised the 5th (Northumberland Fusiliers), 75th (Gordon Highlanders), 78th (Seaforths), 90th (now the Scottish Rifles), and the 2nd Bengal Fusiliers (now the 2nd Munsters), with 450 gunners of the Bengal Artillery and 150 sabres. Opposed to Outram were, according to his report, no less than 96,000 armed men ; and from the end of November, when the Residency was evacuated, until March 21, when Sir Colin finally defeated the mutineers and retook Lucknow, Outram's force was practically besieged in the Alumbagh.

The months of December, 1857, January, February, and March, 1858, were occupied in preparing for the final advance on Lucknow and the break-up of the many bodies of mutineers scattered over Oude, Bundulcund, and the North-West Provinces. Reinforcements were daily arriving from England, but it was not until the beginning of March that Sir Colin was able to commence his advance on Lucknow. His army now numbered upwards of 20,000 men, with 180 guns. Never in the history of India had such a large number of British troops taken the field.

The Cavalry Division, under Sir Hope Grant, included the Queen's Bays, 7th Hussars, 9th Lancers, Hodson's Horse, Daly's Horse, Sam Browne's Horse, and the 25th Cavalry, in addition to the division under Outram.

The Second Division, under Sir Edward Lugard, was composed of the Third Brigade (Brigadier Guy)—34th, 38th, and 53rd Regiments ; Fourth Brigade (Adrian Hope) —42nd, 93rd, and 57th Wilde's Rifles.

The Third Division, under General Walpole, comprised the Fifth Brigade (Brigadier Douglas)—23rd, 79th, and 1st Munster Fusiliers ; Sixth Brigade (Horsford)—2nd and 3rd Battalions Rifle Brigade and 56th Rifles.

The artillery was under the command of Sir Archdale Wilson, who had been made a K.C.B. for the capture of Delhi.

CASUALTIES AT THE RELIEF OF LUCKNOW BY HAVELOCK.

Regiments.	Officers.		Men.		Regiments.	Officers.		Men.	
	K.	W.	K.	W.		K.	W.	K.	W.
5th Northumberland Fus.	1	2	23	29	90th Scottish Rifles ..	4	7	39	62
64th N. Staffs.	1	3	7	81	102nd R. Dublin Fusiliers	1	4	33	83
78th Ross. Buffs	2	6	47	85	14th Ferozepore Sikhs ..	—	1	7	37
84th York and Lancaster ..	2	4	25	55					

CASUALTIES AT THE RELIEF OF LUCKNOW BY SIR COLIN CAMPBELL, NOVEMBER, 1857.

Regiments.	Officers.		Men.		Regiments.	Officers.		Men.	
	K.	W.	K.	W.		K.	W.	K.	W.
Staff	2	6	—	—	82nd Regiment	1	1	1	13
Naval Brigade	1	3	4	17	84th Regiment	—	—	1	8
9th Lancers ..	—	—	—	—	90th Light Inf.	1	3	6	22
Royal Artillery	1	6	14	59	93rd H'landers	2	7	33	62
Roy. Engineers	—	1	3	17	102nd R. Dublin Fusiliers ..	1	—	3	12
5th Fusiliers ..	—	—	5	3	21st Cavalry ..	—	—	2	3
8th King's ..	—	—	—	1	22nd Sam Browne's H.	—	—	1	2
23rd R. Welsh Fusiliers ..	—	1	3	18	25th Cavalry	—	—	—	3
53rd Shropshire L.I. ..	—	3	10	63	56th Punjab R.	1	1	5	18
64th Regiment	—	—	4	7	57th Wilde's R.	1	2	13	50

CASUALTIES AT THE SIEGE AND CAPTURE OF LUCKNOW,
MARCH, 1858.

Force employed.	Officers.		Men.		Force employed.	Officers.		Men.	
	K.	W.	K.	W.		K.	W.	K.	W.
Naval Brigade	1	1	1	13	78th Seaforth				
The Bays ..	1	1	2	5	Highlanders	—	—	—	1
7th Hussars ..	—	3	—	3	79th Cameron				
9th Lancers ..	—	1	1	4	Highlanders	—	2	7	21
Royal Artillery	1	3	6	33	90th Scottish				
Roy. Engineers	3	3	19	34	Rifles ..	—	1	5	28
5th Fusiliers ..	—	1	—	3	93rd Sutherland				
10th Lincolns	—	1	4	23	Highlanders	2	2	12	59
20th Lancs F.	—	2	7	28	97th Royal W.				
23rd R. Welsh					Kent ..	1	—	2	21
Fusiliers ..	—	3	4	25	Rifle Brigade				
34th Border ..	—	—	—	4	(two batts.)	1	2	—	19
38th S. Staffs	—	3	1	22	22nd Sam				
42nd Royal					Browne's Cav.	—	1	1	9
Highlanders	—	1	5	39	25th Cavalry ..	—	1	—	6
53rd Shropshire					56th Punjab R.	1	1	8	32
L.I. ..	—	2	1	27	57th Wilde's R.	1	3	9	30

CENTRAL INDIA, 1857-58.

The regiments authorized to bear this distinction are the

8th Hussars.	12th Lancers.
14th Hussars.	17th Lancers.
Inniskilling Fusiliers.	South Staffords.
Sherwood Foresters.	Highland Light Infantry.
Seaforth Highlanders.	Royal Irish Rifles.
Connaught Rangers.	Leinster.
30th Gordon's Horse.	31st Duke of Connaught's
32nd Lancers.	Own Lancers.
33rd Q.O. Light Cavalry.	2nd Q.O. Sappers and Miners
3rd Sappers and Miners.	2nd Q.O. Light Infantry.
44th Merwara Infantry.	61st Pioneers.
79th Carnatic Infantry.	96th Berar Inafntry.
98th Infantry.	104th Wellesley's Rifles.
110th Mahratta L.I.	112th Infantry.
113th Infantry.	124th Baluchis.

125th Napier's Rifles.

Although as a whole the Princes of Central India remained loyal to our rule, their armies threw in their lot with the mutineers, and the honour " Central India " was conferred on the regiments which were employed in stamping out rebellion in those provinces during the winter of 1857-58 and in the ensuing hot weather. A number of independent columns were so engaged, but the brunt of the fighting fell on the troops under that dashing leader Sir Hugh Rose, afterwards Lord Strathnairn. The capture of Kotah, Jhansi, Calpee, and Gwalior all bear witness to the heroism of our troops and to the sufferings they endured during that terrible hot-weather campaign of 1858, when men died of cholera and of sunstroke by hundreds, and when the survivors struggled on manfully to retain our hold on Hindustan.

The rapidity of the movements of Sir Hugh Rose has often been held up as a contrast to the slowness of those of Sir Colin Campbell, but it must be borne in mind that when Sir Hugh took the field the back of the Mutiny had been broken. His duty was to hunt down and to destroy all bodies of armed rebels in the field, and right nobly did he perform his task. Sir Colin had to organize a force for the relief of Lucknow (where close on 300 women and children were besieged), to break the power of the rebel army in Oude, and to maintain peace in Bengal. His one line of communications was a narrow strip of railway open to destruction at many points, and he had in the field against him over 100,000 trained troops, possessed of large stores of arms and munitions. The tasks before the two Generals were entirely different. Whether, had Sir Colin been in command in Central India, he would have acted with the rapidity that Sir Hugh showed is a mere matter of opinion. This much is certain—that Sir Hugh never could have achieved success had not Northern India been in our hands, and that it was in our hands was due first to the gallantry of the Delhi Field Force, and secondly to the well-organized, if slowly carried out, campaign by which Sir Colin swept the rebels out of Oude.

The Central India Campaign divides itself into a

number of well-executed operations in different parts of the country. First we may take the Malwa Field Force, under Brigadier C. S. Stuart, which consisted of the 14th Hussars, 86th (Royal Irish Rifles), 3rd Hyderabad Cavalry, and 125th Napier's Rifles, which was in the field from July to December, 1857.

CASUALTIES IN CENTRAL INDIA.

Regiments.	Officers.		Men.		Regiments.	Officers.		Men.	
	K.	W.	K.	W.		K.	W.	K.	W.
8th Hussars ..	—	9	18	34	32nd Lancers	1	3	3	12
12th Lancers ..	—	1	2	16	33rd Q.O. Light				
14th Hussars ..	1	4	15	73	Cavalry ..	—	2	4	15
17th Lancers ..	—	1	2	11	2nd Q.O. Sap.				
Royal Artillery	2	6	11	37	and Miners	1	4	6	29
Roy. Engineers	—	—	—	—	3rd Sappers and				
71st High. L.I.	1	1	9	15	Miners ..	—	1	2	11
72nd Seaforth					44th Merwara				
Highlanders	—	1	3	14	Infantry ..	—	—	—	
83rd R. Irish					61st Pioneers	—	—	2	5
Rifles ..	2	1	7	28	79th Carnatic				
86th R. Irish					Infantry ..	—	4	3	27
Rifles ..	1	10	26	109	96th Berar Inf.	2	1	14	22
88th Connaught					98th Infantry	—	1	7	32
Rangers ..	—	2	7	54	104th Welles-				
95th Derbys ..	2	7	4	37	ley's Rifles	—	1	5	13
3rd Madras Eur.					110th Mahratta				
(2nd Innis.F.)	—	—	3	12	L.I. ..	—	1	2	22
3rd Bomb. Eur.					112th Infantry	1	1	3	6
(2nd Leinst.)	—	6	17	92	113th Infantry	—	—	2	14
30th Gordon's					124th Baluchis	—	1	12	20
Horse ..	—	1	7	18	125th Napier's				
31st Lancers ..	1	4	6	19	Rifles ..	2	6	11	37

Then we have Sir Hugh Rose commanding two brigades, the one under the same Brigadier C. S. Stuart, the other under Colonel Stewart, of the 14th Hussars. His first act was to relieve Saugor, then defended by the 2nd Queen's Own Rajput Light Infantry. A Madras column had been toiling up to effect this, but General Whitlock was impeded by many obstacles. In April Sir Hugh carried Jhansi by storm ; in May Calpee was taken ; and then the General was reinforced by a column from the north, commanded by Brigadier-General Sir Robert Napier (afterwards Lord Napier of Magdala). In June Gwalior was recaptured, and with this the real operations of the Central India Field Force came to an end, though the appearance in the field of a rebel General, Tantia Topee, and the assumption of the title of Peishwa by the notorious Nana Sahib compelled the Commander-in-Chief once more to organize a number of flying columns, whose work procured for the regiments which composed them the battle honour " Central India."

I have found it an impossible task to ascertain the losses suffered by some of the regiments. The casualties given in the table on p. 331 show, however, that the distinction " Central India " was not earned without hard fighting.

Defence of Arrah—Behar, 1857.

These two distinctions are the peculiar property of the 45th Rattray's Sikhs, and demand a passing notice.

When the Mutiny broke out, there was but one British regiment in the long stretch of nearly a thousand miles between Calcutta and Lucknow—the 10th Foot, at Dinapore. Here, too, was a large native garrison—the 7th, 8th, and 40th Regiments of Bengal Infantry. Dinapore is the military cantonment of the city of Patna, the hotbed then of Wahabiism, with a population of 150,000, of whom some 38,000 were Mussulmen. It is the capital, too, of the province of Behar, the centre then of the indigo trade, and the home of a number of English planters—gentlemen and sportsmen, whose sporting instincts stood England in good stead in that hour of trial.

The General at Dinapore had plenty of warning as to the temper of his troops and of the neighbouring population, but no measures were taken to deal with the crisis ; and when the sepoy garrison mutinied, the men were allowed to leave the station unmolested. A few hours later a feeble attempt was made to follow them up, but the detachment of the 10th (Lincolns) returned to Dinapore, having failed to overtake the mutineers. These marched at once on Arrah, a civil station, the head of the railway engineers, some twenty-five miles distant. There, fortunately, were a handful of Englishmen unfettered by red tape. Herewald Wake, the Commissioner, and Vicars Boyle, the railway engineer, had foreseen the coming storm, and, to meet it, had converted the billiard-room in Boyle's garden into a little fort, in which ammunition and provisions had been stored. Its garrison consisted of sixteen Englishmen, one Moslem gentleman, and fifty men of Rattray's newly-raised regiment of Sikhs.

On the 27th the Dinapore garrison—three regiments of sepoys, reinforced by a disaffected Rajput, Rajah Kunwar Singh, who possessed two pieces of artillery—appeared on the scene, and demanded the surrender of the treasure. On that day the siege commenced in earnest.

Two days afterwards the Brigadier at Dinapore sent out a force, consisting of some men of the 10th (Lincolns) and 37th (Hampshires), to relieve Arrah. The affair was mismanaged from the outset, and the column was driven back with heavy loss. Fortunately, there was a man at hand capable of dealing with the situation. Major Vincent Eyre, of the Bengal Artillery, was bringing up his battery to the aid of Havelock, and, hearing of the distress of the little garrison in Arrah, he undertook its relief. With but 150 men of the Northumberland Fusiliers, 40 of his own battery, and 18 gallant planters, who for the nonce converted themselves into a corps of cavalry, he attacked the besieging force, and after a sharp fight was enabled to bring off the garrison without loss. The siege lasted but five days, but the devotion of the 45th Sikhs and the gallantry of Vicars Boyle and Herewald Wake stand out in striking contrast to the supineness of the military authorities at Dinapore.

For many months subsequently the 45th were employed

in hunting down rebels in the province of Behar, unsupported by any British troops, and for these services, in which the men were exposed to many attempts on their fidelity, the 45th bear the word " Behar " on their colours and appointments. Their losses during these operations were unusually severe, 2 British officers and 43 of all ranks having been killed or died of wounds, and 1 native officer and 75 other ranks having been wounded.

It is impossible to close this chapter without adverting to the injustice meted out in the distribution of the battle honours for the Indian Mutiny. Every regiment that served on the line of communications in Afghanistan or in South Africa has been granted a battle honour. The regiments which maintained peace in the Punjab, which disarmed mutinous soldiery, which hunted down rebels in Lower India, have been denied all share in the distinctions granted for the Mutiny. The Inniskilling Fusiliers at Peshawar, the 24th (South Wales Borderers) at Jhelum, the 81st (Loyal North Lancashire) at Lahore, the 13th (Somerset Light Infantry) at Azimghur, all contributed to the maintenance of our hold on India, and many of these regiments suffered severely in action.[1] It is not too much to say that, had it not been for the 81st at Lahore, we should never have held the Punjab. The conduct of this regiment at the disarming of the native garrison at Meean Meer was one of the finest feats in those dark days. Again, what are we to think of the failure to recognize the conduct of the 31st (now the 2nd Queen's Own Rajput Light Infantry) at Saugor, where they defended a large number of Englishwomen and children ? There was no stiffening of British bayonets, as at Lucknow or at Cawnpore, but there were a number of British officers who had earned the confidence of their men ; and when the mutinous 42nd Bengal Infantry endeavoured to seduce the then 31st Bengal Infantry from their duty, the answer

---

[1] At Jhelum the 24th lost 4 officers and 70 men killed and wounded ; the losses of the 13th at Azimghur were but little inferior.

was not merely a refusal, but the regiment, under its own native officers, sallied out from the fort at Saugor, attacked their mutinous *bhaibunds*, drove them off in confusion, and captured a couple of guns. For the defence of Arrah by one weak company, the 45th Sikhs bear on their colours the honour " Defence of Arrah." Was the defence of Saugor one whit less deserving of reward ?

Victoria Crosses for the Mutiny.

Queen's Bays	2	60th (King's Royal Rifles)	8
7th Hussars	2	61st (Gloucesters)..	1
8th Hussars	5	64th (North Staffords)	1
9th Lancers	12	71st (Highland L.I.)	1
14th Hussars	1	72nd (Seaforth H'landers)	1
17th Lancers	1	75th (Gordons)	3
Royal Artillery	19	78th (Ross-shire Buffs)	8
Royal Engineers	8	84th (York and Lancaster)	6
Northumberland Fusiliers	3	86th (Royal Irish Rifles)	4
10th (Lincolns)	3	90th Light Infantry	6
13th (Somerset L.I.)	2	93rd (Highlanders)	7
23rd (Royal Welsh Fus.)	2	95th (Derbyshires)	1
32nd (Cornwall L.I.)	4	101st (Royal Munsters)	4
34th (Border Regiment)	1	102nd (Royal Dublin Fus.)	4
42nd (Royal Highlanders)	8	103rd (Royal Munster Fus.)	1
43rd Light Infantry	1	109th (Royal Leinster)	1
52nd (Oxford L.I.)	2	Rifle Brigade	3
53rd (Shropshires)	5		

CHAPTER XXI

BATTLE HONOURS FOR SERVICES IN CHINA, 1842-1900

Chinese War of 1840-1842—Canton—China, 1857-1860—Taku Forts—Pekin—China, 1900—Pekin, 1900.

CHINA, 1840 (WITH THE DRAGON).

THIS distinction was conferred on the regiments which participated in the first China War, under Sir Hugh (afterwards Lord) Gough, and is borne by the

Royal Irish.	Cameronians.
Border Regiment.	Royal Berkshires.
North Staffords.	2nd Queen's Own Sappers
62nd Punjabis.	and Miners.
66th Punjabis.	74th Punjabis.

The first China War, generally known as the " Opium War," while not entailing any very severe fighting, cost us many hundred lives, owing to the neglect of the most elementary precautions on the part of the officials who were responsible for the fitting out of the expedition. The actual *casus belli* was the refusal of the Chinese Government to permit the importation of opium into the Empire. British merchants had been in the habit of importing the drug from India, and large fortunes had been amassed in this trade. When the edict was issued, there were large stocks of the drug in the warehouses of our fellow-countrymen, and its seizure entailed, it is said, a loss of £3,000,000. The British Commissioner on the spot insisted on the right of disposing of the opium, but the Chinese authorities put this beyond a doubt by destroying the forbidden article. We then demanded compensation, which was refused, and a force was despatched from India to enforce satisfaction and pecuniary compensation. This consisted of the 18th (Royal Irish), the 26th (Cameronians), and the 49th (Royal Berkshires), with a battalion of Bengal infantry, composed of volunteers from the whole of the Bengal army. Chusan was occupied with but little loss, and the Viceroy of the province sued for peace. Terms were arranged, the Chinese ceding Hong-Kong and paying an indemnity of 6,000,000 dollars. Grave doubts were felt as to the permanence of this arrangement, and our troops occupied certain points in the country. No efforts were made to provide them with suitable clothing or food, and the mortality was appalling, the Cameronians losing no less than 286 men between July 1, 1840, and January 1, 1841.

Early in 1841, weary of the vacillation of the Chinese, the British Government sent out considerable reinforcements, and Lieutenant-General Sir Hugh Gough was placed in supreme command. His little army was thus composed :

First Brigade—Major-General Lord Saltoun : 26th (Cameronians), 98th (North Staffords), and Bengal Volunteers.
Second Brigade—Major-General Schoedde : 55th (Border Regiment), 2nd (now the 62nd), 6th (now the 66th), and 37th Regiments of Madras Native Infantry.
Third Brigade—Major-General Bartley : 18th (Royal Irish), 49th (Royal Berkshires), and 14th (now the 74th) Madras Infantry.

Early in May, 1841, the forts at the entrance of the Canton River were bombarded and captured. The fleet then passed up the river, and on May 24 Canton itself was taken, after slight resistance, our losses being 14 killed and 91 of all ranks wounded. In the month of August Amoy was occupied, and in October Chusan was reoccupied, our losses being an officer and 19 men killed and wounded.

The winter of 1841-42 was spent in fruitless negotiation, and with the opening of the spring Sir Hugh Gough recommenced operations. In March, 1842, Ningpo was taken, and in the month of May Chapoo was captured,

22

after a sharp fight, in which our losses were 6 officers and
51 of all ranks killed and wounded. In the month of July
the fleet pushed up the Yangtse Kiang River, with a view
of showing the Chinese that we could and we would
reach the very heart of their country. A more determined
resistance was met with at Ching-Kiang-Foo, which was
carried with a loss of 13 officers and 111 of all ranks.
This broke the back of the war-party. Emissaries came
in suing for peace. The fresh terms included a war indemnity of 21,000,000 dollars and the opening of a
number of ports to free and unrestricted trade.

LIST OF CASUALTIES.

Regiments.	Officers.		Men.		Regiments.	Officers.		Men.	
	K.	W.	K.	W.		K.	W.	K.	W.
18th Roy. Irish	2	6	8	73	98th N. Staffs	—	—	13	1
26th Camer'ians	2	2	6	24	62nd Punjabis	—	3	1	8
49th R. Berks	1	8	7	49	66th Punjabis	—	1	1	11
55th Borders	1	3	5	40	74th Punjabis	—	1	1	13

The little army was well rewarded for its arduous
services, and the following list of honours conferred for
the China War of 1840-1842 effectually dispels the legend
that the lavish distribution of rewards for military services
is a product of the later Victorian era. Sir Hugh Gough
was created a Baronet, the three Brigadiers received the
Knighthood of the Bath, three officers were made Aides-
de-Camp to Queen Victoria, twenty-nine received the
Companionship of the Bath, eight were made Brevet
Lieutenant-Colonels, and thirteen received the Brevet of
Major. The young Queen was graciously pleased to allow
the East India Company to strike a medal commemorative of the campaign, and officers and men of her regiments
were authorized to wear this decoration. At the same
time Her Majesty expressed her opinion that in future

medals should only be granted by the Sovereign, and that it should not be left to a company of "merchant venturers" trading to the East Indies to issue decorations to her soldiers.

CANTON (1858).

This distinction was conferred on the 59th Foot (now the East Lancashire Regiment) for its services when holding the city of Canton during the second Chinese War of 1857-1860.

The terms of the treaty entered into after the war of 1842 had never been faithfully observed by the Chinese. At last the seizure of a vessel called the *Arrow*, flying the British flag, compelled us to demand reparation. This was contemptuously refused, and in the early spring of 1857 a force was despatched from England to enforce respect to our flag. The outbreak of the Indian Mutiny necessitated the diversion of the regiments from China to India, so the punishment was delayed. General Straubenzee was then in command of the troops in China, which consisted of the 59th (East Lancashires), four battalions of sepoys, and a couple of battalions of Royal Marine Light Infantry.

Sir Michael Seymour, the naval Commander-in-Chief, who was in supreme command of the naval and military forces, was acting in conjunction with a French brigade, and it was deemed advisable to seize Canton with the available forces, rather than allow the Chinese to strengthen its defences, and so increase the difficulties of capture.

In the month of January, 1858, the Admiral, after consultation with General Straubenzee, determined to attempt the capture of Canton. The force at his disposal consisted of the 59th (East Lancashires), two strong battalions of Royal Marines, and a brigade of bluejackets numbering 1,800 men. This force was placed under the command of Major-General Straubenzee. The Chinese showed considerable determination, but the energy and gallantry of our bluejackets carried all before them, and Canton was occupied, with a total loss of 2 officers and 14 men killed, 4 officers and 112 men wounded, the 59th (East Lancashires) contributing to the casualty list 2 officers and 2 men killed, 1 officer and 17 men wounded.

CHINA (1857-1860).

This distinction was conferred on the regiments which took part in the operations in China during the years 1857-1860, and is now borne by the following corps of the Indian Army :

7th Rajputs.	10th Jats.
11th Rajputs.	15th Sikhs.
22nd Punjabis.	27th Punjabis.
105th Mahratta L.I.	

The necessity for putting forth our whole strength in the suppression of the rebellion in India led, as I have said on p. 321, to a temporary cessation of the military operations in China. Lord Elgin, who had been deputed by the Home Government to carry through the negotiations, was naturally anxious to do so without the effusion of blood. He had a considerable naval force at his disposal, and a number of native troops had been sent from India, more with a view of removing them from the sphere of temptation than with the intention of their carrying out serious military operations.

In 1858 the Chinese Commissioners agreed to our demands that the treaty of peace between the two nations should be concluded at Pekin ; but on realizing that Lord Elgin was determined to carry out this clause, every obstacle was thrown in his way. Finally, when Sir Frederick Bruce attempted to pass up the Peiho River, he was fired on, and three of our gunboats sunk. The Indian Mutiny was now at an end, and Sir Hope Grant, who as a cavalry leader had gained great distinction in its suppression, was nominated to the chief command of the China Expeditionary Force. Sir Hope had a double claim to this distinction, for he had acted as Brigade Major to Lord Saltoun in the war of 1840-42. It was very evident from the tone of the correspondence of the Chinese Commissioners that all memory of the defeats they had experienced in the war of 1840-1842 had been effaced. Our Envoys were treated with supercilious disdain, and we were gravely warned of the dangers we were incurring in thus treating the Celestial Empire. In reply to our ultimatum they wrote :

" The contents of the letter of the English Envoy fills us with the greatest astonishment, and the demand for an indemnity is against all decorum. The language in which the English letter is couched is too insubordinate and extravagant even to be discussed. In future the British Ambassador must not be so wanting in decorum, or he will give cause for serious trouble."

In face of such language as this, it was evident that nothing short of a sharp lesson inflicted at the capital itself would teach this irrepressible people the power of our arms, and preparations were at once made for the final advance of the troops, under Sir Hope Grant.

CASUALTIES DURING THE OPERATIONS IN CHINA, 1858-1861.

Regiments.	Officers.		Men.		Regiments.	Officers.		Men.	
	K.	W.	K.	W.		K.	W.	K.	W.
7th Rajputs ..	—	—	—	—	22nd Punjabis	—	—	—	—
10th Jats ..	—	—	—	—	27th Punjabis	—	—	—	—
15th Sikhs ..	—	—	—	—	105th Mahr. L.I.	—	—	—	—

NOTE.—I have been unable to ascertain the losses of the Sepoy battalions during the occupation of the Chinese Ports, 1857-62.

CHINESE EXPEDITIONARY FORCE OF 1860.

The army, under the command of Lieutenant-General Sir Hope Grant, which was to act in conjunction with a French force, numbered some 16,000 all told, and was brigaded as under :

Cavalry Brigade—Brigadier-General Pattle (King's Dragoon Guards) : King's Dragoon Guards, 11th Probyn's Lancers, 19th Fane's Horse.

First Infantry Division—Major-General Sir John Mitchell, K.C.B.

First Brigade—Brigadier-General Staveley, C.B. : The Royal Scots, 31st (East Surrey Regiment), and 15th Ludhiana Sikhs.

Second Brigade—Brigadier-General Sutton : 2nd (Queen's), 60th (King's Royal Rifles), and 23rd Sikh Pioneers.

Second Division—Major-General Sir Robert Napier, K.C.B.

Third Brigade—Brigadier-General Jephson : The Buffs, 44th (Essex Regiment), and 20th Brownlow's Punjabis.

Fourth Brigade—Brigadier-General Reeves : 67th (Hampshires), 99th (Wiltshires), and 19th Punjabis.

To each infantry division a field battery was attached, and a troop of horse artillery acted with General Pattles' cavalry brigade. At the immediate disposal of the Commander-in-Chief were three field and two mountain batteries, a battalion of Sikhs, a company of Royal Engineers, under that fine soldier the late Sir Gerald Graham, who had recently gained the Victoria Cross for a series of acts of gallantry in the Crimea, and with him were two companies of the Madras Sappers and Miners.

The 87th (Royal Irish Fusiliers) were left to garrison Hong-Kong, whilst other points on the coast were occupied by native troops from Bengal and Madras.

TAKU FORTS (AUGUST 12, 1860).

This battle honour was awarded to the regiments which assaulted the Taku Forts at the commencement of the second phase of the Chinese War of 1860 :

King's Own Dragoon Guards.	Royal Scots.
Queen's.	Buffs.
East Surrey.	Essex.
King's Royal Rifles.	Hampshire.
11th Probyn's Horse.	19th Fane's Horse.
2nd Queen's Own Sappers and Miners.	20th Brownlow's Punjabis.
	23rd Pioneers.

Early in June, 1860, the force, under Sir Hope Grant, disembarked in Talien-Wan Bay, where the 99th (Wiltshire) and the 19th Punjabis were left to hold the base, whilst preparations were made for the advance on Pekin. The first objective was the capture of the Taku Forts, at the entrance of the Peiho River—the forts which had inflicted such a serious blow to our prestige in the previous year. On August 20 these were carried by storm by Napier's division, the colours of the 44th and the 67th being almost simultaneously placed on the ramparts by Lieutenants Rogers and Chaplin of those regiments. Both of these officers received the Victoria Cross for their heroism, both having been badly wounded in their gallant dash for the prize of honour.

CASUALTIES AT THE STORMING OF THE TAKU FORTS.

Regiments.	Officers.		Men.		Regiments.	Officers.		Men.	
	K.	W.	K.	W.		K.	W.	K.	W.
Royal Artillery	—	2	—	15	44th Essex ..	—	2	10	50
2nd Queen's ..	—	—	—	—	Royal Marine L.I.	—	5	1	24
3rd Buffs ..	—	—	—	2					
31st E. Surrey	—	—	—	—	67th Hampshire	—	8	6	63

PEKIN (OCTOBER 12, 1860).

This battle honour is borne by the regiments which accompanied General Sir Hope Grant to Pekin during the second Chinese War of 1860 :

King's Dragoon Guards.
Queen's R.W. Surrey.
Hampshire.
11th K.E.O. Lancers (Probyn's Horse).
20th Brownlow's Punjabis.

Royal Scots.
King's Royal Rifles.
Wiltshire.
19th Lancers (Fane's Horse).
2nd Q.O. Sappers and Miners.
23rd Pioneers.

After the fall of the Taku Forts, the Chinese Envoys made every effort to induce Sir Hope Grant to forgo his march on the capital, but both the English and the French commanders felt this was a point that could not be waived. In the course of the negotiations some members of the Staff were seized by the Chinese, and, after undergoing the most brutal torture, were foully murdered. Such conduct merely emphasized the necessity for the occupation of the capital, and on October 5 the allied armies entered Pekin, having experienced but slight opposition during the advance, the survivors of the little band who had been so treacherously captured having been previously released.

OTHER CASUALTIES IN ACTION DURING THE MARCH TO PEKIN.

Regiments.	Officers.		Men.		Regiments.	Officers.		Men.	
	K.	W.	K.	W.		K.	W.	K.	W.
K. Drag. Gds.	—	1	1	10	19th Fane's H.	—	2	3	24
2nd Queen's ..	—	—	1	2	20th Brown-			2	6
3rd Buffs	—	—	—	3	low's Punjs.	—	—	2	6
11th Probyn L.	—	2	4	16	23rd Pioneers	—	1	1	8

CHINA, 1900.

This distinction is borne by the regiments which took part in the expedition to China in the year 1900, under the command of General Sir Alfred Gaselee, in conjunction with the allied army, which was entrusted to the supreme command of Field-Marshal the Count Waldersee, a German officer of distinction.

15th Cavalry.
2nd Q.O. Light Infantry.
2nd Q.O. Sappers and Min.
6th Jat. Light Infantry.
20th Brownlow's Punjabis.
57th Wilde's Riffes.
63rd Light Infantry.
91st Punjabis.
122nd Rajputana Infantry.

33rd Q.O. Light Cavalry.
1st K.E.O. Sappers and Min.
3rd Sappers and Miners.
14th Sikhs.
34th Pioneers.
61st Pioneers.
88th Carnatic Infantry.
98th Infantry.
130th Baluchis.

4th Gurkhas.

Anti-dynastic and anti-Christian troubles had been rife in China for some time previous to the Boxer Rising of 1900. Little is really known of the Boxers, except that they formed a secret society, having as their object the extermination of all Christians and the overthrow of the existing dynasty. The murder of some English missionaries in the neighbourhood of the capital and a general sense of insecurity led the various foreign Ministers in Pekin to call up a mixed force of Marines and blue-jackets from the allied fleets in Chinese waters for the defence of the Embassies. This step was replied to by the Chinese by the murder of the German Minister and a general attack on the Embassies, which for a period of eight weeks were exposed to one of the closest sieges of modern times. Thanks to the gallantry of the British Minister, Major Sir Claude Macdonald—a soldier who had served his apprenticeship in that excellent regiment the Highland Light Infantry, and who was unanimously nominated to the supreme command of the little garrison, numbering only 400 officers and men—the Legations, though hard pressed, were enabled to hold out until assistance arrived.

In June, 1900, on learning of the precarious situation of the Legations, Admiral Seymour, commanding our fleet in Chinese waters, and the senior of the foreign Admirals, essayed to march to their relief with a mixed force of 2,000 seamen and Marines from the various fleets. His little force included Americans, Austrians, French, German, Italian, and Russians, as well as our own men, our contingent numbering close on half the total. The Admiral found his force too small to cope with the hordes of Boxers, and he was compelled to make a stand at Tientsin. In the meantime the European Powers, together with Japan, were hastily despatching troops for the double relief of the Legations and of the Admiral. On June 16 the allied fleets bombarded and seized the Taku Forts, as well as the Chinese flotilla, the torpedo-boats built by the Germans for the Chinese fleet being gallantly cut out from under the guns of the forts by a young English Lieutenant, Roger Keyes. By the beginning of August the Indian brigades, under Sir Alfred Gaselee, reached the mouth of the Peiho, and after a series of small engagements pushed its way up to Pekin, and on August 14 the relief of the beleaguered Legations was accomplished.

PEKIN, 1900.

This honour was awarded to the regiments which accompanied General Sir Alfred Gaselee to the relief of the beleaguered Embassies in Pekin, when besieged by Chinese during the Boxer Rising of 1900 :

Royal Welsh Fusiliers.	1st Duke of York's Own Lancers.
7th Rajputs.	51st Sikhs.
	24th Punjabis.

I have given on p. 344 the names of the regiments which are entitled to bear the distinction " China, 1900," on their colours and appointments. It is difficult to fathom the reasoning which has denied this distinction to the regiments which accompanied General Gaselee to Pekin. As well deny a regiment the honour " Sevastopol " because it had been already granted one for the Alma. Sir Alfred Gaselee's task was no easy one. The relieving force was composed of many nationalities, and international jealousies were not unknown. Some of the allied commanders were desirous of delaying the advance until the arrival of the whole of their contingents. Gaselee and General Chaffee, the chief of the American contingents, set their faces against this. The lives of women and children were at stake, and the English General let it be distinctly understood that he was going to march on a certain day, whatever the others might decide. The Americans and the Japanese were one with him. On August 14 the relieving force started.

International Force.	*Men.*	*Guns.*	*British Force.*	*Men.*
Japanese ..	10,000	24	Royal Welsh Fusiliers	300
Russians ..	4,000	16	1st Bengal Lancers	400
British	3,000	12	7th Rajputs ..	500
U.S.A.	2,000	6	24th Punjabis ..	300
French	800	12	51st Sikhs	500
Germans ..	20	—	Chinese Regiment ..	100
Austrians ..	100	—	Hong-Kong Regiment	100
			Naval Brigade ..	300

Little resistance was met with, and on August 20 General Gaselee had the satisfaction of learning that, thanks to his decision, the lives of the beleaguered garrison of the Legations had been saved. The force he took with him was dangerously small, but he had been compelled to leave a strong detachment, under Generals O'Moore Creagh and Lorne Campbell, to guard his long line of communications, as well as to leave garrisons at Hong-Kong and Shanghai, where there was a considerable amount of anti-Christian feeling. Originally his brigades had been organized as under :

First Brigade—Brigadier-General Sir Norman Stewart : 7th Rajputs, 24th Punjabis, 51st Sikhs, and 126th Baluchis.

Second Brigade—Brigadier-General O'Moore Creagh, V.C. : 2nd Queen's Own Light Infantry, 14th Sikhs, 1st Battalion 4th Gurkhas, and 130th (Prince of Wales's Own) Baluchis.

Lines of Communications—Brigadier-General Lorne Campbell : 63rd Palamcottah Light Infantry and 122nd Rajputana Infantry.

Divisional Troops : 1st Bengal Lancers, 61st Pioneers, and two batteries of artillery.

Sir Norman Stewart, as the second senior officer, and as the one who had the widest experience of war, was selected by General Gaselee to command the brigade which was to have the honour of relieving the garrisons.

CHAPTER XXII

BATTLE HONOURS FOR SERVICES IN SOUTH AFRICA, 1806–1879.

Cape of Good Hope, 1806—South Africa, 1835—South Africa, 1846-47—South Africa, 1851-1853—South Africa, 1877-1879.

CAPE OF GOOD HOPE, 1806.

THIS distinction has been conferred on the following regiments :

South Wales Borderers.	East Lancashire.
Highland Light Infantry.	Seaforth Highlanders.
Royal Irish Rifles.	Sutherland Highlanders.

Before touching on the capture of the Cape in 1804, it will be advisable briefly to allude to the previous capture in 1795.

When Holland threw in her lot with revolutionary France, the Cape became a subsidiary base for the French fleets, which put in there for provisions and water, as well as for refit. As the islands of Rodriguez, Bourbon, and Mauritius, belonged to France, it became necessary for the safety of our Indian possessions that we should seize all those points which were detrimental to the preservation of the trade route to India. The reduction of the French islands necessitated the employment of a force larger than we at that time could dispose of, but the Dutch settlements presented no such difficulties. It was therefore determined to despatch a joint naval and military expedition from England, which should be reinforced by troops from India.

Admiral Sir Keith Elphinstone was selected for the naval command, his force consisting of the *Monarch* (74 guns),

Tremendous (74), *America* (64), *Stately* (64), *Ruby* (64), *Sceptre* (64), *Trident* (64), *Jupiter* (50), *Crescent* (50), *Sphinx* (24), and *Moselle* (16). Major-General Craig embarked on the fleet with the 78th Highlanders, having instructions to pick up the St. Helena Regiment at that island. Detachments of the 25th and 27th Light Dragoons also embarked, the idea being to horse them on arrival at the Cape.

Commodore Blanket, then commanding the fleet in the East Indies, had instructions to proceed south to cooperate with the Admiral, and he was to convoy a force under the command of Sir Alured Clarke, composed of the 84th, 95th, and 98th Regiments. Leaving Spithead in the *Monarch* on April 5, Elphinstone arrived at the Cape on July 11, and Craig at once disembarked his troops. Desultory skirmishing took place with the Boers until September 3, when the Indian contingent arrived. The Dutch, seeing the futility of further resistance, surrendered. In the meantime Elphinstone had taken possession of the Dutch fleet of eight fine ships—the *Dordrecht* (66 guns), *Revolution* (66), *Admiral Tromp* (54), *Castor* (44), *Brave* (40), *Bellona* (28), *Sirene* (28), and *Havik* (18). The total casualties amounted to 9 men killed, 3 officers and 53 men wounded, and fell, as will be seen, chiefly on the force commanded by General Craig.

CASUALTIES AT THE CAPTURE OF THE CAPE OF GOOD HOPE
IN 1795.

Regiments.	Officers.		Men.		Regiments.	Officers.		Men.	
	K.	W.	K.	W.		K.	W.	K.	W.
78th Seaforth Highlanders	—	2	6	24	Royal Navy ..	—	1	3	15
84th York and Lancaster ..	—	—	—	1	98th (now Argyll Highlrs.)	—	—	—	3
					95th	—	—	—	6

CAPE OF GOOD HOPE, 1806.

In accordance with our time-honoured Parliamentary custom, the Cape, which had been captured in 1795, was restored, by the terms of the Treaty of Amiens, to the Dutch, thus necessitating its recapture on the renewal of the war in 1803. It was known that efforts had been made to render this more difficult, and therefore it was determined to employ a larger force. The command of the troops was entrusted to Sir David Baird, a soldier who had shown conspicuous gallantry on several occasions in India, and who had displayed considerable resource when in command of the Indian division of the Egyptian Expeditionary Army in 1801. With him was associated Admiral Sir Home Popham, whose squadron, comprised the *Diadem, Raisonnable, Belliqueux, Diomed, Leda, Narcissus, Espoir,* and *Encounter.*

The troops forming the expedition were the 20th Hussars ; a Highland brigade, under Brigadier Ronald Fergusson, an officer who had distinguished himself as Lieutenant-Colonel of the 84th at the capture of the Cape in 1795, and had added to that reputation by his conduct in Flanders under Abercromby. This brigade consisted of the 71st (Highland Light Infantry), 72nd (Seaforths), and 93rd (Sutherland Highlanders). The Second Brigade, under General Beresford, afterwards the well-known commander of the Portuguese army in the Peninsular War, under Wellington, consisted of the 24th (South Wales Borderers), the 38th (South Staffords), 59th (East Lancashires), and the 83rd (Royal Irish Rifles).

On January 7 the troops were landed, General Beresford, with the 20th Hussars and the South Staffords, being sent round to Saldanha Bay to effect a diversion, his brigade being handed over to Colonel Baird, of the 83rd. In landing, the 93rd unfortunately lost thirty-six men by the upsetting of a boat. On the following day— January 8—the Dutch were driven from their entrenched position on the Blue Mountain by the Highland Brigade, and on the 9th the General capitulated.

When the order was issued conferring this distinction on certain of the regiments which had taken part in this expedition, the two corps which were detached under Beresford were for some reason omitted from the list. There would seem no reason why the 20th Hussars and South Staffords should not now be allowed to assume the honour. The casualties amounted to 15 killed and 189 wounded, and fell chiefly on the Highland Brigade.

CASUALTIES AT THE CAPTURE OF THE CAPE OF GOOD HOPE IN 1806.

Regiments.	Officers.		Men.		Regiments.	Officers.		Men.	
	K.	W.	K.	W.		K.	W.	K.	W.
24th S. Wales Borderers ..	1	—	3	16	72nd Seaforth Highlanders	—	2	2	36
59th E. Lancs	—	1	2	5	83rd R. Irish R.	—	—	—	6
71st Highland L.I... ..	—	2	6	7	93rd Sutherland Highlanders	—	5	2	57

SOUTH AFRICA, 1835.

This distinction is borne by the

Royal Inniskilling Fusiliers.   Seaforth Highlanders.
Gordon Highlanders.

Our difficulties at the Cape may be said to have commenced with its first capture in 1795, and to have lasted until the conclusion of peace with the Boers more than a century later. In the year 1819 we had to embark on a campaign with the Kaffirs, and now, in the early part of 1835, there was a general rising of the Kaffirs against the European settlers in South Africa. Delagoa Bay was attacked, the Portuguese Governor killed, and the fort captured. Our own Colony was overrun, and it became necessary to use force against force. The garrison of the

Colony had been reduced to a dangerous level. There were but three weak battalions of the line, one company of artillery, and that fine old regiment the Cape Mounted Rifles. Fortunately, we had as Governor a man well qualified to deal with the crisis. Sir B. D'Urban was an officer who had acted as Adjutant-General to Lord Beresford throughout the Peninsular War, and he now had as his Adjutant-General Colonel Harry Smith, subsequently known as the victor of Aliwal, and whose name will be associated with a later war in South Africa.

Leaving the 98th (North Staffords) to garrison Cape Town, General Sir B. D'Urban moved up the 72nd (Seaforths) to Grahamstown, then held by a wing of the 75th (now the 1st Gordons). A laager was constructed round Port Elizabeth, and the inhabitants formed into battalions of irregulars, and placed under the command of regular officers. A similar proceeding was adopted at Grahamstown, and in April Colonel Harry Smith was ready to take the field. His force did not number more than 3,000 men. It was composed of the 72nd (Seaforths), Cape Mounted Rifles, some 1,500 mounted Boers, and two weak battalions of armed Hottentots. Desultory fighting continued for some weeks—indeed, it was not until the month of December that a permanent peace was concluded, our frontiers being pushed still farther to the north.

SOUTH AFRICA, 1846-47.

This distinction commemorates a long-forgotten campaign, and is borne by the

7th Dragoon Guards.	Royal Warwicks.
Scottish Rifles.	Inniskilling Fusiliers.
Royal Highlanders.	Sherwood Foresters.
Argyll Highlanders.	Rifle Brigade.

For some considerable time prior to the outbreak of hostilities our relations with the Gaikas, a powerful tribe on the Natal frontier, had been on the verge of breaking-point ; and as no embargo was placed on the importation of arms, it was foretold that as soon as these gentry felt themselves strong enough a struggle for the mastery was inevitable.   In the early spring of 1846 the storm broke by the Gaikas attacking a convoy of prisoners and releasing some of their own tribesmen, and for a time Grahamstown was practically besieged.   There was but a small force in the Colony to make head against the insurrection, but as the Boers had as much, if not more, to lose at the hands of the Kaffirs, large numbers of them were enrolled for defence.   The Governor of the Colony was General Sir Peregrine Maitland, and he promptly moved up to the front with all the available troops.   Fortunately, a transport conveying the 90th (Scottish Rifles) from Ceylon to England had put into Port Elizabeth in distress, and the regiment was at once disembarked and sent up to the front.

In April, Colonel Somerset, of the Cape Mounted Rifles, took the field, with the 7th Dragoon Guards, the 91st (Argyll Highlanders), and his own regiment, strengthened by some Burghers and Hottentot levies, and on April 16 inflicted a sharp defeat on the enemy.   The 6th (Royal Warwicks), 27th (Inniskilling Fusiliers), 45th (Sherwood Foresters), and the Rifle Brigade were successively sent out to reinforce Sir Peregrine.   In the early part of 1847 an advance was made into the Amatole Bush, and after a few trifling skirmishes the Gaikas sued for peace, and our frontier was pushed up to the Kei River.

SOUTH AFRICA, 1851-52-53.

The following regiments are entitled to bear this distinction, for which a medal was granted by an Army Order of November 21, 1854

12th Lancers.	Queen's Royal West Surrey.
Royal Warwick.	Suffolks.
Royal Highlanders.	Oxford Light Infantry.
King's Royal Rifles.	Highland Light Infantry.
Argyll Highlanders.	Rifle Brigade.

Sandilli, the Gaika chief, had never reconciled himself to accepting loyally the terms of the treaty entered into after the war of 1847. In December, 1851, a party of the 45th (Sherwood Foresters) was surprised and cut up, although we were supposed to be at peace with the tribes. The Governor of the Colony, Sir Harry Smith, was a man of energy, and one who knew the country well, for he had been in actual command of the troops during the war of 1835. Since then he had added to his reputation in India, both in the Gwalior and Sikh Wars. He was not the man to sit down tamely under such an insult. He at once proceeded to Grahamstown to judge for himself the necessity of the case, and then wrote home for reinforcements. Without waiting for these, he commenced operations by an invasion of the Amatole Bush with two columns, the one commanded by Colonel Fordyce, of the 74th, the other by Colonel Mitchell; these operations were not unattended with loss, and further movements in the Waterkloof Mountains cost the 74th their Colonel and some thirty men.

In the autumn reinforcements commenced to arrive from England. These included the same battalion of the Rifle Brigade which had done so well in the previous campaign; but this time the Rifles were armed with the Minié, a weapon which ranged up to 1,000 yards. A few of the same weapons were served out to each company of the other regiments, and though perhaps in close Bush fighting the old Brown Bess was effective enough, yet, when it happened, which it often did, that the Kaffirs were holding a position with open country in its front, the long range of our weapons won the day before our men began to suffer any loss.

The policy of Sir Harry Smith did not commend itself to the Home Government, and in the early part of 1852 General Sir George Cathcart was sent out to the Cape to replace him. Sir George had earned a high reputation as a writer on military subjects, and was an officer of considerable experience. He had acted on the staff of his father, who was attached to the Russian army during the campaign of Leipsic, as well as in that of 1813-14 against

Napoleon, and he had been Aide-de-Camp to the Duke of Wellington at Waterloo. It was not until the commencement of 1853 that Sandilli sued for peace, when Sir George Cathcart returned home. He subsequently became Adjutant-General of the army, but resigned that position to take command of a division in the Crimean War, and he fell gallantly leading on his men at the Battle of Inkerman on November 5, 1855.

SOUTH AFRICA, 1879.

The regiments entitled to bear this distinction on their colours and appointments are the

King's Dragoon Guards.	17th Lancers.
Buffs.	King's Own Lancasters.
Somerset Light Infantry.	Royal Scots Fusiliers.
South Wales Borderers.	Scottish Rifles.
South Staffords.	Northamptons.
Middlesex.	King's Own Royal Rifles.
Wiltshires.	Connaught Rangers.
Argyll Highlanders.	

The campaign was undertaken with a view of punishing the Zulus, a powerful tribe bordering our Colony of Natal, for continual violations of our territory. The Zulus were undoubtedly the most powerful tribe in Southern Africa, and on more than one occasion they had defeated the Boers. We unfortunately entered on the campaign with our usual contempt for the forces opposed to us. The General in command was Major-General Lord Chelmsford, an officer who had considerable war experience, and who had held the highest staff appointments in India, both in war and in peace. He had served in the Crimea, first as a regimental officer in the Grenadier Guards, and subsequently on the staff. Exchanging into the 95th (Derbyshire Regiment), he served with that fine old corps in Central India, and in 1867 he was Adjutant-General to the Abyssinian Expeditionary Force.

The invasion of Zululand was to have been carried out by five columns, the Commander-in-Chief exercising a general supervision of the whole, but at the outset moving with the two centre columns.

No. 1 column was under the command of Colonel Pearson, of the Buffs, and consisted of the 2nd Battalion of the Buffs, the 99th (Wiltshires), a strong naval brigade, and some native levies. It numbered 4,750 men, with four guns.

No. 2 column was under the command of Colonel Durnford, of the Royal Engineers. It consisted entirely of native levies, commanded by British officers, and was 3,300 strong. Its commander had considerable colonial experience, and was generally looked upon as the best officer in South Africa for dealing with native questions.

No. 3 column was under the command of Colonel Glyn, of the 24th (South Wales Borderers). It consisted of both battalions of that unfortunate regiment, one of native levies, with six guns. Its strength was 4,700 men.

No. 4 column was under Colonel (better known as Field-Marshal Sir Evelyn) Wood, V.C., C.B., of the 90th (Scottish Rifles). He had with him the 13th (Somerset Light Infantry), his own corps, and native levies, including a regiment of Frontier Light Horse, under Colonel Redvers Buller, V.C., C.B. Its strength was 2,270 men, with six guns. In composition and leadership there is no doubt that this was the best organized of the five columns.

No. 5 column was under that exceptionally fine soldier Colonel Hugh Rowlands, V.C. It consisted of the 80th (South Staffords), with a number of native levies, bringing up its strength to 1,600 men, with three guns. The duty of this column was to watch the western frontiers of Zululand, and to keep a watch over another recalcitrant chieftain, Sekukuni, who had to be dealt with in the near future.

The army crossed the frontier in three columns—No. 1, under Pearson, following the easternmost road, near the sea, to Etshowe; Nos. 3 and 4, with the Commander-in-Chief, crossing the Tugela River at Rorke's Drift; whilst Sir Evelyn Wood took a more northerly course. On

January 22 Lord Chelmsford, leaving Colonel Durnford at Isandhlwana, within the Zulu border, with his own and the greater part of Colonel Glyn's column moved forward to reconnoitre. No means were taken to keep touch with Durnford's column, which was attacked by an overwhelming force of the enemy, and the whole force annihilated, the 24th losing no less than 21 officers and 591 non-commissioned officers and men. To the credit of the corps it must ever be remembered that not a man fell back; all died at their post. The colours were borne away at the distinct orders of the commanding officer by two young officers, Lieutenants Coghill and Melville, whose dead bodies were found some days after in the bed of the Tugela River, with the blood-stained standards lying safe beside them. A few hours later the Zulus followed up this success by a vigorous attack on the post at Rorke's Drift, on the Tugela River, held by one company of the 24th. Its commander, Lieutenant Bromhead, came of a famous fighting family, and he was associated with a sapper officer, Lieutenant Chard. The post was defended with unsurpassed heroism. After some hours the Zulus, unable to stand against the accurate shooting of the 24th, fell back, and so the communications with the Cape were maintained, and the Commander-in-Chief, who, although within hearing of the firing, was ignorant of the true state of affairs, was enabled to fall back and to reorganize his army.

Colonels Pearson and Wood held on to their positions. Wood was attacked on the 25th by the Zulus at Kambula, but beat them off after a sharp engagement with but slight loss, his two regiments showing themselves worthy of their high reputations as light infantry corps.

Pearson, on the other hand, was shut up in Etshowe, and was only relieved some days later by the Commander-in-Chief, who on his march to Etshowe inflicted a defeat on the Zulus at Ginghelovo.

The news of the disaster to the 24th caused a strong sensation in England. Reinforcements were hurried out to the Cape, and the command of the forces entrusted to Sir Garnet Wolseley. On his arrival in Natal he reorganized his army, which was now constituted as under :

First Division : Major-General Hope Crealock.

First Brigade—Brigadier C. Pearson : 2nd Battalion 3rd Buffs, 88th (Connaught Rangers), and 99th (Wiltshires).

Second Brigade—Brigadier-General J. Mansfield Clarke : 57th (Middlesex), 3rd Battalion King's Royal Rifles, and 91st (Argyll Highlanders).

Divisional Troops : Naval brigade (800 strong), ten mountain guns, one company of sappers, and two battalions of native troops.

Second Division : Major-General Newdigate.

First Brigade—Colonel Glyn : 2nd Battalion 21st (Royal Scots Fusiliers) and the 58th (Northamptons).

Second Brigade—Colonel Collingwood : 1st Battalion 24th (South Wales Borderers) and the 94th (Connaught Rangers).

Divisional Troops : Three battalions of native levies, one company of Royal Engineers, and three batteries of artillery.

Flying Column—Colonel Evelyn Wood, V.C., C.B. : 1st Battalion 13th (Somerset Light Infantry), 90th (Scottish Rifles), 80th (South Staffords), Buller's Frontier Horse, and two squadrons of mounted infantry.

Cavalry Brigade—Major-General Marshal : King's Dragoon Guards, 17th Lancers, and native mounted troops.

Lines of Communications—Major-General Hugh Clifford, V.C., C.B. : 88th (Connaught Rangers) and details.

Before Sir Garnet Wolseley had time to arrive at headquarters, Lord Chelmsford moved up from Ginghilovo, and defeated the Zulus in a serious engagement at Ulundi. Our losses were trifling, those of the enemy extremely heavy. With this defeat the active opposition of the Zulus ceased, and Sir Garnet Wolseley at once organized a number of flying columns to traverse the country and to effect the capture of the King. This brought the war to a close.

Early in the following year Sir Garnet turned his attention to King Sekukuni, whose stronghold was captured by a portion of the army which had been engaged at Ulundi.

The troops who took part in the campaigns against the Zulus and against Sekukuni were honoured by being awarded the South African War Medal, with a clasp bearing the date "1879" or "1880," as the case may be, and the regiments were authorized to add the words " South Africa " to the other distinctions on their colours. If we except the losses incurred by the 24th Regiment at Isandhlwana and the cutting up of a company of the 80th (South Staffords), the losses in the campaign were not of a very serious nature, as the appended casualty return shows :

CASUALTIES IN SOUTH AFRICA, 1877-1879.

Regiments.	Officers.		Men.		Regiments.	Officers.		Men	
	K.	W.	K.	W.		K.	W.	K.	W.
Royal Artillery	3	2	68	4	57th Middlesex	—	1	—	3
Roy. Engineers	1	—	4	—	58th N'amptons	—	2	1	10
K. Drag. Gds.	—	—	—	—	3rd Batt. 60th				
17th Lancers ..	1	3	1	4	Rifles ..	1	—	1	5
Buffs	—	—	3	3	80th S. Staffs.	1	—	60	1
4th King's Own	—	—	—	—	88th Connaught				
13th Somerset					Rangers ..	—	—	—	—
L.I. ..	1	2	8	28	90th Scottish R.	2	3	15	46
2nd Batt. 21st					91st Argyll				
Roy. Scots F.	—	4	3	24	Highlanders	—	—	1	8
1st Batt. S.					94th Connaught				
Wales Bdrs.	16	—	404	2	Rangers ..	—	2	2	22
2nd Batt. S.					99th Wilts ..	1	—	2	4
Wales Bdrs.	5	—	187	4	Naval Brigade	2	1	8	15

CHAPTER XXIII

BATTLE HONOURS FOR MISCELLANEOUS ACTIONS

Jersey, 1781—Rodney's Victory of April 12, 1782—The Glorious
First of June, 1794—St. Vincent—Fishguard—Copenhagen—
New Zealand—Abyssinia—Ashantee.

JERSEY, 1781.

THIS distinction is borne on the colours of the

1st Royal Jersey Light	2nd Royal Jersey Light
Infantry.	Infantry.

3rd Royal Jersey Light Infantry.

It commemorates the gallant conduct of these three
regiments in repelling the French attack on that island
in the year 1781. In the early dawn of January 6 a
French force, under the command of the Baron de Rullecourt, made a sudden descent on the island of Jersey,
landing a short distance to the east of St. Helier, the
capital. Entering the town, they occupied the central
square, and surrounded the house of the Lieutenant-
Governor, who was at once made a prisoner. He was
compelled to sign a capitulation of the island, although
he explained to the French commander that such an act
would, of course, be ignored by the next senior officer.
However, under cover of a flag of truce, the French commander, accompanied by the unfortunate Governor, approached Elizabeth Castle, which dominates the town of
St. Helier, and demanded the surrender of the garrison.

The troops at that time in the island, detachments of
which were in the castle, consisted of the 78th Highlanders, 83rd Glasgow Volunteers (now the 71st Highland

Light Infantry), and the 95th Regiment (the forerunners
of the Rifle Brigade), together with the three regiments
of Militia named above. The senior officer was Major
Pierson, of the 95th. So far from obeying the orders of
the Lieutenant-Governor, who, of course, being a prisoner,
was deprived of all vestige of authority, Major Pierson
replied to the French commander that unless the Governor
was released and the French troops laid down their arms
within ten minutes he would open fire on them. Rullecourt retorted that unless the castle accepted his terms he
would hang the Governor. It is said that Pierson's reply
was brief and to the point : " Hang, and be damned !"
said he. The French officer was allowed to rejoin his
troops, then Pierson, moving a couple of companies
of the 78th to a hill on the opposite side of St. Helier,
which had not been occupied by the French, descended
into the square. The French made a brave resistance,
but at the end of an hour Rullecourt, who had been shot
through the jaw, surrendered. Our losses were by no
means small, the most serious being the death of the
gallant Pierson, who fell at the head of his men, and whose
gallant conduct and heroic death are commemorated by a
monument in the square of St. Helier.

CASUALTIES IN JERSEY, JANUARY 6, 1781.

Regiments.	Officers.		Men.		Regiments.	Officers.		Men.	
	K.	W.	K.	W.		K.	W.	K.	W.
Royal Artillery	—	1	—	—	1st R. Jersey L.I.	—	—	—	4
78th Highlanders	—	—	1	3	2nd R. Jersey L.I.	—	3	—	6
83rd Glasgow Volunteers	—	—	6	8	3rd R. Jersey L.I.	—	—	4	24
95th Regiment	1	—	2	13					

A Naval Crown, superscribed April 12, 1782.

This distinction is borne by the Welsh Regiment in commemoration of the part played by a detachment of the old 69th Regiment, which were acting as Marines on the fleet in the action when Rodney defeated De Grasse off the island of Martinique, taking the French Admiral a prisoner, with his flagship, the *Ville de Paris*, of 120 guns.

The total losses in this engagement were 10 officers and 237 men killed, 22 officers and 766 men wounded, the 69th losing 5 officers and 29 men killed and wounded.

A Naval Crown, superscribed June 1, 1794.

This distinction was conferred on the Queen's (Royal West Surrey) and the Worcester Regiment for their services when acting as Marines on the ships composing Lord Howe's fleet in the memorable action on the Glorious First of June.   Our prizes included two line-of-battle ships of eighty and four of seventy-four guns, whilst the sinking of the *Vengeur* afforded our adversaries material for a pretty piece of fiction.   The total losses in this battle were 15 officers and 235 men killed, 39 officers and 669 men wounded.   To this total the regiments above mentioned contributed as under:

CASUALTIES ON JUNE 1, 1794.

Regiments.	Officers.		Men.		Regiments.	Officers.		Men.	
	K.	W.	K.	W.		K.	W.	K.	W.
The Queen's ..	1	1	—	—	Worcesters ..	1	1	11	24

St. Vincent, February 14, 1797.

This battle honour has been conferred on the Welsh Regiment in recognition of the services of a detachment of this regiment, under Lieutenant Pierson, when acting as Marines in Lord Nelson's ship, the *Captain*, at the battle which gave Sir John Jervis his peerage. The gallantry of a sergeant of the 69th, who smashed in the quarter gallery of the Spanish flag-ship, was specially mentioned by Nelson, who also begged to be allowed to retain the services of Lieutenant Pierson on board his ship.[1]

FISHGUARD, FEBRUARY 24, 1797.

This distinction is borne on the appointments of the Pembrokeshire Yeomanry, and, with the exception of " Jersey, 1781," borne on the colours of the three regiments of Jersey Militia, is the only battle honour granted for services in the United Kingdom. It recognizes the promptitude with which that regiment turned out to repel an incursion of French troops on the coast of Pembrokeshire on the date above mentioned. Strangely enough, in the despatches in which Lord Cawdor, the senior officer on the spot, and Lord Milford, the Lord-Lieutenant of the county, report the circumstance to the Duke of Portland, the Prime Minister, no mention whatever is made of the Yeomanry being present. Lord Cawdor wrote that, hearing that three French ships of war and a lugger had anchored in a small roadstead near Fishguard, he at once proceeded to the spot " with a detachment of the Cardigan Militia and all the provincial forces " he could collect. He found that 120 men had disembarked, and in the course of the evening the French commandant surrendered unconditionally. Lord Milford, the Lord-Lieutenant of the county, reported that " before the troops arrived many thousands of the peasantry turned out, armed with pikes and scythes, to attack the enemy." It does not appear that any shots were exchanged, or that Monsieur Tate, Chef-de-Brigade, made any effort to regain his ships or to oppose the armed peasantry who were ready to attack him. The name Tate has not a very Gallic flavour. One of the French ships, *La Résistance*, was captured on March 9 by H.M.S.

---

[1] The Detachment of the 69th lost 3 men killed and 4 wounded.

Nymphe, and brought into the navy under her new name *Fishguard,* thus connecting the navy with her battle honour.

1800.

This distinction is borne on the appointments of the King's Own Malta Regiment of Militia, and has been awarded to that corps for its services during the defence of the island against the French.

COPENHAGEN, APRIL 2, 1801.

This distinction has been conferred on the Berkshire Regiment and the Rifle Brigade for the services they rendered as Marines on the fleet under Sir Hyde Parker and Sir Horatio Nelson when the Danish fleet was destroyed at Copenhagen. The casualties suffered by the troops were slight. It is worthy of remark that the Queen's, Worcester, and Welsh Regiments have been granted permission to add a naval crown to the dates of the fleet actions which they bear on their colours. The Berkshires and Rifle Brigade have not been accorded this augmentation.

CASUALTIES AT COPENHAGEN, 1801.

Regiments.	Officers.		Men.		Regiments.	Officers.		Men.	
	K.	W.	K.	W.		K.	W.	K.	W.
Berkshire ..	—	2	13	40	Rifle Brigade..	—	—	3	4

COPENHAGEN, 1807.

The regiments that would be entitled to this battle honour are the

Coldstream Guards.
K.O. Royal Lancaster.
King's Liverpool.
Gloucester.
Oxford Light Infantry.
Royal West Kent.
Gordon Highlanders.

Scots Guards.
Royal Fusiliers.
Royal Welsh Fusiliers.
Cornwall Light Infantry.
South Lancashire.
Cameron Highlanders.
Rifle Brigade.

It is difficult to understand why the troops which took part in the expedition to Copenhagen in 1807 should be denied the battle honour conferred on the Berkshires and Rifle Brigade for their services as Marines in the expedition of 1801. In neither case were the losses severe, but the later expedition was in no way less successful than the former. The attitude of the Danes and the fear that their fine fleet would fall into the hands of the French led the Ministry of the day to assemble a powerful fleet and a by no means inconsiderable army in order to carry out their policy.

The former, which consisted of no less than twenty-six line-of-battle ships, was under the command of Sir James Gambier ; whilst General the Lord Cathcart was in command of the land forces. The troops employed were thus brigaded :

Right Division : Lieutenant-General Sir G. Ludlow.

Brigade of Guards—Major-General Finch : Coldstream, Scots Guards.

Second Brigade—Brigadier-General J. Walsh : 1st Battalion 28th (Gloucester) and 79th (Cameron Highlanders).

Left Division : Sir David Baird.

Third Brigade—Major-General Grosvenor : 1st Battalion 4th (King's Own Lancaster) and 1st Battalion Royal Welsh Fusiliers.

Fourth Brigade—Major-General Spencer : 32nd (Cornwall Light Infantry), 50th (Royal West Kent), and 82nd (South Lancashire).

Fifth Brigade—Brigadier-General Macfarlane : 1st Battalion 7th (Royal Fusiliers) and 1st Battalion 8th (King's Liverpool Regiment).

Reserve Division—Sir Arthur Wellesley : 1st Battalion 43rd (Oxford Light Infantry), 2nd Battalion 52nd (Oxford Light Infantry), 1st Battalion 92nd (Gordon Highlanders), and 1st Battalion 95th (Rifle Brigade).

There was, in addition, a strong division of the King's German Legion, under Lieutenant-General the Earl of Rosslyn, comprising three regiments of cavalry, ten battalions of infantry, two batteries of horse and four companies of field artillery. For siege purposes, ten companies of the Royal Artillery, under Major-General Bloomfield, and three of Royal Engineers, under Colonel D'Arcey, accompanied the force.

On July 18 the troops, numbering upwards of 27,000 men, embarked on 377 transports, and on the 15th of the following month disembarked without opposition at Wibeck, a few miles from Copenhagen. On the 28th of the month the Reserve Division, under Sir Arthur Wellesley, had a sharp brush with the Danes, capturing ten guns and 1,500 prisoners ; and on September 1, the siege-works being complete, the city was summoned to surrender. General Peiman, the Danish Commander-in-Chief, returned a bombastic reply, intimating that the Danes were ready to die to a man rather than surrender their capital or their fleet. On the following day the batteries opened fire, and on the 5th the General surrendered unconditionally. Our trophies included eighteen line-of-battle ships and fifteen frigates, the prize-money accruing to the two Commanders-in-Chief amounting to upwards of £300,000 ! On October 15 the troops re-embarked, and in the course of the following month troops and prizes arrived in England. It is worthy of note that of the huge convoy of 377 transports, few of which exceeded 500 tons burden, only six were wrecked. Five, unfortunately, were picked up by French frigates.

CASUALTIES DURING THE EXPEDITION TO COPENHAGEN, 1807.

Regiments.	Officers.		Men.		Regiments.	Officers.		Men.	
	K.	W.	K.	W.		K.	W.	K.	W.
Royal Artillery	1	—	2	4	43rd Oxf. L.I.	—	—	—	3
Scots Guards ..	—	—	—	3	50th Royal W.				
4th K.O. Royal					Kent ..	—	1	2	15
Lancasters ..	—	—	1	3	79th Cameron				
Royal Fusiliers	—	—	2	—	Highlanders	—	—	1	3
8 t h King's					82nd S. Lancs	1	2	4	17
Liverpool ..	—	—·	1	1	92nd Gordon H.	—	—	3	5
23rd R. W. Fus.	1	—	4	5	95th Rifle Bde.	—	—	1	4

The total casualties amongst the troops amounted to 4 officers and 39 men killed, and 6 officers and 139 men wounded. Amongst the latter was Sir David Baird, who had been badly wounded, as we have seen, in India, and who was destined to lose an arm at Corunna in the following year.

NEW ZEALAND.

This distinction has been conferred for three separate campaigns, but no attempt has been made by the addition of dates, as in the case of the wars in South Africa, to differentiate between the various operations.

NEW ZEALAND, 1846-47.

The first campaign took place in the years 1846-47, and the regiments which obtained the honour for these operations are the

> Northamptons.   Manchesters.   Wiltshires.

NEW ZEALAND, 1860-61.

The regiments which earned this distinction are the

> Suffolk.   West Yorkshire.
> South Lancashire.   Middlesex.
> York and Lancaster.

At the time of the dispute which led to these operations there was but one British battalion in the islands, and so critical was the situation that the city of Auckland was practically besieged by the natives. Urgent messages were sent to Australia and to Tasmania, where at that time we had garrisons, and the 12th (Suffolks) and 40th (North Lancashires) arrived very shortly from Sydney and Melbourne respectively. At the same time, on the news reaching England, the 68th (Durham Light Infantry) was ordered from Burmah, the 57th (Middlesex) and 70th (East Surrey) from India, and the 2nd Battalion of the 14th, a newly-raised corps, from the Curragh. General Pratt, who had arrived from Australia, took command of the operations, but some dissatisfaction was expressed at his strategy, and in March, 1863, he was superseded by Sir Duncan Cameron, an officer who had done good service in the Crimea.

The New Zealanders—or rather the Maori—showed themselves most gallant foes. Their *pahs*, or stockades, were constructed with much skill, and until these had been thoroughly searched out with artillery fire we found them almost impossible to carry.

It was generally conceded that the war was one which, with a little exercise of forbearance on the part of the Colonial Government, might have been avoided, and there was a good deal of friction between the civilian and military elements in consequence, many of the soldiers openly expressing an opinion that their foes had not been fairly dealt with. In the spring of 1861 a hollow truce was patched up. Our casualties during the operations, so far as the regular troops were concerned, had not been heavy, except in the case of the 40th (North Lancashires) and 65th (York and Lancasters).

Regiments.	Officers.		Men.		Regiments.	Officers.		Men.	
	K.	W.	K.	W.		K.	W.	K.	W.
Royal Artillery	1	—	2	12	40th N. Lancs	2	3	38	58
Roy. Engineers	—	1	1	4	57th Middlesex	—	—	—	6
12th Suffolks ..	—	1	1	7	65th York and				
14th West					Lancaster ..	1	1	5	38
Yorks ..	—	—	—	2	Naval Brigade	—	2	5	20

New Zealand, 1863-1866.

The regiments which were present during the operations, which lasted for nearly three years, are the

Suffolks.
Royal Irish.
Oxford Light Infantry.
Middlesex.
    Durham Light Infantry.
West Yorkshire.
North Lancashire.
Royal West Kent.
York and Lancaster.

The same causes which led to the war in 1860 were once more the origin of armed resistance to the Government. The natives considered that they were not being dealt fairly with in the matter of the sale of their lands, and, as I have said before, there was a very strong party in the Colony who sympathized with them. At the same time, it was felt that the Government must be supported until peace had been restored, and that then, but not till then, could the cause of the disturbance be removed. The troops, which included all the regiments named above, were under the command of Sir Duncan Cameron, and he had on his staff a number of exceptionally good men—men who came to the fore in our later wars—amongst them being Sir George Greaves and Sir Thomas Baker, both of whom became Adjutant-General in India. With them were Sir Henry Havelock and Sir John MacNeill, the latter of whom obtained the Victoria Cross in the campaign.

CASUALTIES IN NEW ZEALAND, 1864.

Regiments.	Officers.		Men.		Regiments.	Officers.		Men.	
	K.	W.	K.	W.		K.	W.	K.	W.
Naval Brigade	3	8	13	34	57th Middlesex	2	2	23	47
Royal Artillery	1	2	5	8	65th York and				
12th Suffolks	1	—	7	24	Lancaster ..	2	8	24	49
14th W. Yorks	2	8	13	29	68th Durham				
18th Roy. Irish	1	1	19	44	L.I. ..	—	4	9	41
40th N. Lancs	2	3	22	42	70th E. Surrey	1	2	8	16
43rd Oxford L.I.	7	2	13	19					
50th W. Kent	1	3	18	30	Colonial Troops	6	15	650	

Although the war dragged on for so long, it calls for no special remark. It resolved itself into the attack of the Maori stockades, which were constructed with great skill. On more than one occasion we certainly came off second best. One point, however, is worthy of note. It was found that the red coats and shakos of the soldiers were not the most suitable garments for Bush warfare, and, to the distress of the old soldiers of the leather stock and pipeclay school, the men fought in blue jumpers and forage-caps.

In the month of June we experienced rather a serious

reverse at what was known as the Gate Pah ; but the distinguished regiment which suffered heavily on that day showed a few weeks later that it had lost none of the dash for which it had been so famous in Wellington's days. In the early spring of 1866 peace was declared, and since then there have been no more loyal servants of the Crown than our Maori fellow-subjects.

ABYSSINIA, 1867-68.

The following regiments are authorized to bear this battle honour :

3rd Dragoon Guards.	King's Own Lancasters.
Cameronians.	West Riding.
Sherwood Foresters.	10th Hodson's Horse.
12th Cavalry.	33rd Q.O. Light Cavalry.
2nd Q.O. Sappers and Miners.	3rd Sappers and Miners.
	21st Punjabis.
23rd Pioneers.	102nd K.E.O. Grenadiers.
103rd Mahratta Light Infantry.	104th Wellesley's Rifles.
	121st Pioneers.
125th Napier's Rifles.	127th Baluch Light Infantry.

The above regiments formed the expeditionary force, under Sir Robert Napier, then Commander-in-Chief in Bombay, which had for its object the release of a number of English and German prisoners held in captivity by Theodore, King of Abyssinia. Until the year 1861 our relations with this half-savage, half-Christian potentate had been of the most cordial nature. He looked on Mr. Plowden, the British Consul, as his most trusted adviser, and amongst the members of his personal household was more than one Englishman. On Mr. Plowden's death a change occurred. The new Consul seems not to have been on the best terms either with the King or with the Foreign Office, and the neglect of the latter to take any notice of an autograph letter addressed to our Queen by King Theodore led to an open rupture. The King swept all Europeans into prison, including the Consul, and on remonstrances being made detained other emissaries. As Theodore had contracted a habit of doing away with his prisoners, it was considered necessary to back up verbal remonstrances with force, and the conduct of the negotiations was removed from the Foreign Office and placed in the hands of the Commander-in-Chief in Bombay.

Little was known of the country, and the most pessimistic forebodings were indulged in by the English Press. The result proved the falsity of the critics. Sir Robert Napier was a master of the art of organization, and from the date of the landing of the troops in Zoulla Bay until their final embarkation there was not a single mishap. There was practically no fighting. The army traversed close on 300 miles of country destitute of roads, crossed mountain-ranges 9,000 feet in height, stormed what Theodore fancied was an impregnable fortress, effected the release of the European prisoners, and freed the Abyssinians from the tyranny of a bloodthirsty King, without the loss of a single man killed in action, and of only thirty-seven who died by disease. The result was due to one man, and to one man alone, and it proved the wisdom of not interfering with the General in command when once he has been entrusted with the conduct of military operations. The House of Commons grumbled at the cost of the expedition, but Sir Robert Napier judged the value of a British soldier at a higher price than mere pounds, shillings, and pence, and preferred that the tax-payer should pay for the mistakes of the Foreign Office in hard cash rather than that the army should pay in the lives of its men.

Thirty years later the Italians tried their 'prentice hand in the same country. The annihilation of their army threw into stronger relief the wisdom of the tactics employed by Lord Napier, where, by utilizing native labour for the construction of the necessary military roads, he saved the health and the lives of his soldiers.

It is impossible to write of the Abyssinian Expedition without adding a word as to the marvellous manner in which the disembarkation and final embarkation of the army was conducted, without hitch or loss, by the Quarter-master-General at Zoulla Bay, then Major Fred Roberts,[1]

---

[1] Afterwards Field-Marshal the Earl Roberts, V.C., K.G.

The casualty rolls are instructive, and may be compared with advantage with those of the Italian army which was cut to pieces in Abyssinia thirty years later :

CASUALTIES IN ABYSSINIA, 1867-68.

Regiments.	Officers.		Men.		Regiments.	Officers.		Men.	
	K.	W.	K.	W.		K.	W.	K.	W.
Roy. Engineers	—	I	—	3	33rd Q. O. Light				
4th King's Own	—	I	—	6	Cavalry ..	—	—	—	I
33rd West					23rd Punjab				
Riding ..	—	—	—	5	Pioneers ..	—	—	—	12

ASHANTEE, 1873.

This distinction has been conferred on the

23rd (Royal Welsh Fusiliers). Black Watch.
Rifle Brigade. West India Regiment.

It commemorates the services of a force, under the command of Major-General Garnet Wolseley (now Field-Marshal Viscount Wolseley), which was organized for the purpose of putting a stop to the intolerable cruelties and depredations of the Ashantee monarch on the West Coast of Africa. In February, 1873, King Coffee Kalkali, not content with ravaging the territories of our allies, actually invaded our own territories in the neighbourhood of Cape Coast Castle. He was beaten off by Colonel Harley, then in command of the troops, and a second invasion was also repulsed by Colonel Festing, of the Royal Marine Artillery. Our relations with the Ashantees had been clouded by the memory of a severe defeat we suffered at their hands when Sir Charles Macartney, the Governor of the Colony, had been killed, and his head carried in triumph to Coomassie, the capital. It was now deemed imperative to teach the Ashantees that the English arm was longer than they imagined, and Sir Garnet Wolseley, who had only recently carried through a most successful little

expedition in the North-West Territory of Canada, was
selected for the command of the Ashantee Expeditionary
Force.   With him were associated a number of special-
service officers, whose duty it was to raise regiments from
the tribes which had suffered at the hands of King Coffee
Kalkali, and to act in co-operation with our own advancing troops.

The expedition was perfectly successful.   After pene-
trating to the capital, the force returned to the coast,
and re-embarked for England.   There were several sharp
skirmishes during the advance, in which the 42nd (Royal
Highlanders) particularly distinguished themselves, and
in which they suffered severely.   The expedition, however,
is more noticeable in that it produced a school of officers
for long known as " the Wolseley Gang," to whom the
army and the nation owe a deep debt of gratitude for the
institution of many of the most valuable military reforms.

At the conclusion of the war a medal was granted to
the officers and men who took part in the expedition,
with a special clasp—" Coomassie "—to those who were
fortunate enough to have been present at the final
advance on the capital.

CASUALTIES IN ASHANTEE WAR, 1873.

Regiments.	Officers.		Men.		Regiments.	Officers.		Men.	
	K.	W.	K.	W.		K.	W.	K.	W.
Staff	—	3	—	—	R. Welsh Fus.	—	1	—	4
Royal Artillery	1	1	1	6	42nd R. Highl.	—	11	6	120
Roy. Engineers	1	1	—	4	Rifle Brigade	—	3	3	30
Naval Brigade	—	7	—	32	Native Levies	2	11	5	122

SIERRA LEONE, 1898.

This distinction is borne by the West India Regiment
and West African Regiment, and commemorates their
conduct in the campaign undertaken for the purpose of

putting down the rebellion in the Colony of Sierra Leone
in that year.   The rising was a most serious one, and for
a time the lives of all the whites on the West Coast were
in danger.   Nominally the cause of offence was the imposition of a hut-tax ; in reality the grievance was a
stricter interpretation of the laws regarding slavery.
Little heed was paid to the warnings of disaffection.   A
number of towns in the hinterland were burnt and many
English were massacred before we were in a position to
cope with the rebels.   The command of the operations
was entrusted at first to Major-General Woodgate, who
afterwards met a soldier's death at the head of his brigade
at the Battle of Spionkop, in the Boer War.   On his
falling ill, the operations were brought to a successful
conclusion by Colonel Cunningham, of the Cornwall Light
Infantry.   The losses of the West India Regiment
amounted to 3 officers and 8 men killed, 8 officers and
39 men wounded.

WEST AFRICA.[1]

WEST AFRICA, 1887.

The above distinction is borne on the colours of the
West India Regiment, and has been conferred on that
hard-working corps for a series of arduous campaigns on
the West Coast of Africa.

The campaign of 1887 was under the command of
Major-General Sir Francis de Winton, the troops being
accompanied by a naval brigade furnished by H.M.S.
Icarus and *Royalist.*   It was undertaken for the subjugation of a powerful tribe called the Yonnies, who had
carried fire, sword, and rapine through the hinterland of
the Colony.

WEST AFRICA, 1892.

The campaign of 1892 was under the command of
Colonel Scott, an officer who had served in the 42nd

---

[1] In these operations—West Africa, 1887, 1892-3-4—the West
India Regiment lost 3 officers and 15 men killed, 4 officers and
72 men wounded.

Highlanders through the Crimea, the Mutiny, and the two Ashantee wars of 1874 and 1890. It was necessitated by the conduct of the Egbas and Jebus, two tribes who were blocking all the trade-routes from Lagos into the interior.

WEST AFRICA, 1893.

The campaign of 1893 was under the command of Colonel Ellis, of the West India Regiment, and was undertaken for the punishment of the Sofas, a tribe which had been giving much trouble on our own and on the French frontier. The expedition was marred by an unfortunate contretemps between our forces and the French Senegalese troops, in which we lost three officers killed, the subaltern in command of the French detachment falling a victim to the mistake of his men.

WEST AFRICA, 1894.

This year was marked by two expeditions—the one from Bathurst, under Captain Gamble, of the Royal Navy, accompanied by a detachment of the West India Regiment. In this the navy were roughly handled, losing 3 officers and 14 men killed, 6 officers and 32 men wounded. In the following month Major Fairtlough, of the Royal Artillery, took up the threads of the affair, and brought it to a successful conclusion. The recalcitrant chief, Foda Silah, took refuge in French territory, and was handed over to us for deportation.

In the month of September, 1904, the attitude of the ruler of Benin compelled us to destroy the armed towns on his frontier. Admiral Bedford, commanding the Cape of Good Hope Station, was entrusted with the chief command. The bulk of the forces were drawn from the ships on the Cape Station, but a detachment of the West India Regiment well and worthily upheld the fame of that corps. Our trophies included 106 guns of all calibres, a large number of small arms, 14 tons of gunpowder, and 8,300 dozens of gin !

BRITISH EAST AFRICA, 1896-1899, 1901.

This battle honour has been conferred on the

104th Wellesley's Rifles.
124th D.C.O. Baluchistan Infantry.

116th Mahrattas.
127th P.W.O. Baluch Light Infantry.

It commemorates arduous work, of which little is heard in England, in tropical regions of East Africa and the fever-haunted hinterland of Zanzibar. Split up into a number of small detachments, these regiments have showed themselves worthy successors to the old Bombay army, which more than a century ago broke the power of the Mahrattas and set the stamp of civilization on the coast of Malabar. The list of casualties shows that sickness was not the only foe these distinguished regiments had to face.

CASUALTIES DURING THE OPERATIONS IN EAST AFRICA.

Regiments.	Officers.		Men.		Regiments.	Officers.		Men.	
	K.	W.	K.	W.		K.	W.	K.	W.
104th Wellesley's Rifles ..	1	—	27	4	116th Mahrattas	—	1	2	6
124th D.C.O. Baluchis ..	—	—	—	—	127th P.W.O. Baluch L.I.	2	3	19	20

ASHANTI, 1900.

This distinction has been conferred on the West African Regiment, in commemoration of its services in the campaign undertaken for the relief of the Residency of Coomassie during the rebellion in Ashantee in the year 1900. The practical annexation of the kingdom of Ashantee after the campaign of 1890, for which no battle honour was granted, though a bronze decoration was awarded to the troops, had not been accepted with any degree of heartfelt loyalty by the people, and, though peace had been maintained, it was known that this was due to the personal ascendancy of successive Residents rather than to the acquiescence of the people in the new state of affairs. During the absence of the permanent Resident it was determined to obtain possession of the Golden Stool, the emblem of royalty. To effect this, a small expedition was despatched from Kumassi, the capital and seat of the Residency. This expedition was repulsed, and the repulse was followed by a general upheaval of the tribes. The Residency was closely besieged, and there were no troops on the coast to despatch to its relief.

Brigadier-General Willcocks, an officer who to youth added experience, was selected to command an expeditionary force ; but, in consequence of the war in South Africa, it was found inexpedient to employ British troops. The General set out on his mission with a mixed force, made up of detachments from the various corps in West Africa. The West India Regiment furnished its quota, as did the West African Frontier Force, the Central African Frontier Regiment, and the West African Regiment, of which the greater part was engaged. The country was an exceedingly difficult one, but its difficulties were known. Although the rising commenced in the month of April, it was not until July that Sir William James Willcocks was ready to move forward. His force numbered, all told, 152 whites and 2,800 natives, the former including a number of invaluable non-commissioned officers. It was fiercely opposed the whole way from the coast to Kumassi, and the severity of the fighting may be gauged from the fact that the total losses amounted to 9 Englishmen and 113 natives killed, and 53 English and 680 natives wounded.

CHAPTER XXIV

BATTLE HONOURS FOR THE SECOND AFGHAN WAR

Afghanistan, 1878-1880—Ali Masjid—Peiwar Kotal—Charasiah
—Kabul, 1879—Ahmad Khel—Kandahar, 1880.

AFGHANISTAN, 1878-1880.

THIS battle honour was granted to all regiments which took part in any of the operations during the course of the war in Afghanistan between the years 1878 and 1880. In the two campaigns there were no less than thirty-one regiments of cavalry and eighty battalions employed, and though few of these were actually under fire, yet all were accorded the distinction. It is borne on the colours of the following regiments :

Carabiniers.	8th Hussars.
9th Lancers.	10th Hussars.
11th Hussars.	15th Hussars.
Northumberland Fusiliers.	Royal Fusiliers.
King's Liverpool.	Norfolks.
Devons.	Suffolks.
West Yorkshire.	East Yorkshire.
Leicesters.	Royal Irish.
K.O. Scottish Borderers.	East Lancashire.
East Surrey.	Hampshire.
North Lancashire.	Berkshire.
K.O. Yorkshire L.I.	Shropshire L.I.
King's Royal Rifles.	Manchester.
Seaforth Highlanders.	Gordon Highlanders.
Rifle Brigade.	1st Skinner's Horse.
3rd Skinner's Horse.	4th Cavalry.
5th Cavalry.	8th Cavalry.
10th Hodson's Horse.	11th Probyn's Lancers.
12th Cavalry.	13th Watson's Horse.
14th Murray's Lancers.	15th Cureton's Lancers.
17th Cavalry.	18th Tiwana Lancers.
19th Fane's Lancers.	21st Daly's Horse.
22nd Sam Browne's Horse.	23rd Cavalry.
25th Cavalry.	26th Light Cavalry.

32nd Lancers.
34th Poona Horse.
36th Jacob's Horse.
39th Central India Horse.
1st P.W.O. Sappers and Miners.
2nd Q.O. Light Infantry.
4th Rajputs.
6th Light Infantry.
9th Bhopal Infantry.
12th Pioneers.
14th Sikhs.
16th Rajputs.
19th Punjabis.
21st Punjabis.
23rd Pioneers.
25th Punjabis.
27th Punjabis.
29th Punjabis.
31st Punjabis.
42nd Deoli Infantry.
45th Sikhs.
52nd Sikhs.
55th Coke's Rifles.
57th Wilde's Rifles.
61st Pioneers.
75th Carnatic Infantry.
90th Punjabis.
104th Wellesley's Rifles.
108th Infantry.
110th Mahratta L.I.
115th Mahrattas.
124th Baluchistan.
128th Pioneers.
1st Gurkhas.
3rd Gurkhas.

33rd Light Cavalry.
35th Scinde Horse.
38th Central India Horse.
Q.O. Corps of Guides.
2nd Q.O. Sappers and Miners.
3rd Sappers and Miners.
3rd Brahmins.
5th Light Infantry.
8th Rajputs.
11th Rajputs.
13th Rajputs.
15th Sikhs.
17th Loyal Regiment.
20th Brownlow's Punjabis.
22nd Punjabis.
24th Punjabis.
26th Punjabis.
28th Punjabis.
30th Punjabis.
32nd Pioneers.
44th Merwara Infantry.
51st Sikhs.
53rd Sikhs.
56th Punjab Rifles.
58th Vaughan's Rifles.
64th Pioneers.
81st Pioneers.
101st Grenadiers.
105th Mahratta L.I.
109th Infantry.
113th Infantry.
119th Multan.
127th Baluch L.I.
130th Baluchis.
2nd Sirmoor Rifles.
4th Gurkhas.

5th Gurkhas.

A very large number of these regiments were employed in keeping open the three lines of communication with Afghanistan—viz., by the Khyber, the Kuram, and the Bolan Passes. Though they did not participate in any of the actions which appear on the colours of certain more fortunate regiments, they were nevertheless exposed to continuous hardship, and some to constant attack by the fanatical tribes who inhabit the borderland between Hindustan and the territories of the Amir. Some, indeed, suffered more heavily in these long-forgotten skirmishes than did many of the regiments which added two or three names to their list of battle honours.

In consequence of the Russo-Turkish War of 1877, our relations with Russia became very strained, and owing to what the Sultan of Turkey considered our neglect to afford him material support against Russia, the long-standing friendship between England and Turkey was imperilled. Both nations turned towards the Amir of Afghanistan as the one potentate who could assist them to indulge in the policy of pinpricks towards England, and both nations despatched Missions to Kabul with this end in view. The Afghan Amir soon showed a change in his policy towards us. In accepting a Russian Mission at Kabul he defied treaty rights, and in refusing to accept an English Mission he inflicted on us a deliberate insult. The English Cabinet in the month of October, 1878, presented an ultimatum, and on November 21 our armies crossed the frontier.

The plan of campaign was simple. Afghanistan was to be invaded by three columns, operating respectively by the Khyber route from Peshawar, by the Kuram route from Kohat, and by the Bolan Pass on Kandahar. The detail of the northern force was as under :

PESHAWAR VALLEY FIELD FORCE.

Lieutenant-General Sir Samuel Browne, V.C., K.C.S.I., C.B., commanding.

Cavalry Brigade—Brigadier-General C. J. S. Gough, V.C., C.B. : Two squadrons 10th Hussars, 11th Probyn's Lancers, Guides Cavalry.

Commanding Royal Artillery—Colonel W. J. Williams : One horse, one field, three heavy, and three mountain batteries.

First Infantry Brigade—Brigadier-General H. T. Macpherson, V.C., C.B. : 4th Battalion Rifle Brigade, 20th Brownlow's Punjabis, 4th Gurkhas.

Second Infantry Brigade—Brigadier-General J. A. Tytler, V.C., C.B. : 1st Battalion Leicestershire, Guides Infantry, 51st Sikhs.

Third Brigade—Brigadier-General F. Appleyard, C.B. : 81st (North Lancashire), 14th Sikhs, 27th Punjabis.

Fourth Infantry Brigade—Brigadier-General W. Browne : 51st (King's Own Yorkshire Light Infantry), 6th Jat Light Infantry, 45th Sikhs.

Mobilizing at Peshawar in the early days of November, 1878, the column crossed the frontier at Jumrood on

November 21, and advanced on Ali Masjid, the hill fortress at the Afghan entrance of the Khyber Pass. Some show of fight was made, and Sir S. Browne deferred making the assault until the arrival of all his troops. In the course of the night the Afghans evacuated the fort, which was occupied by our men. Thus, with a casualty list of under sixty, the main road to Kabul had been opened.

ALI MASJID.

This battle honour is borne by the

10th Hussars.	Loyal North Lancashires.
Leicester.	K.O. Yorkshire L.I.
Rifle Brigade.	11th Probyn's Lancers.
Q.O. Corps of Guides.	6th Light Infantry.
1st P.W.O. Sappers and	14th Sikhs.
Miners.	20th Brownlow's Punjabis.
27th Punjabis.	45th Rattray's Sikhs.
51st Sikhs.	4th Gurkhas.

The casualties incurred were :

Regiments.	Officers.		Men.		Regiments.	Officers.		Men.	
	K.	W.	K.	W.		K.	W.	K.	W.
Royal Artillery	—	—	1	9	14th Sikhs ..	—	1	8	24
51st K.O. York-					20th Punjabis	—	—	—	1
shire L.I. ..	—	—	1	1	27th Punjabis	2	—	4	6

KURAM VALLEY FIELD FORCE.

Major-General F. S. Roberts, V.C., C.B., commanding.

Cavalry Brigade—Brigadier-General Hugh Gough, V.C., C.B. : One squadron 10th Hussars, 12th and 25th Cavalry.

Commanding Royal Artillery—Colonel A. H. Lindsay : One horse, one field, and two mountain batteries.

First Infantry Brigade—Brigadier-General A. H. Cobbe : 1st Battalion Liverpool Regiment, 23rd Pioneers, 29th Punjabis, and 58th Vaughan's Rifles.

Second Infantry Brigade—Brigadier-General J. B. Thelwall : 72nd (Seaforth Highlanders), 21st Punjabis, 56th Rifles, and 5th Gurkhas.

The Central, or Kuram Valley, Field Force assembled at Kohat, and advanced up the Thull Valley to be ready to cross the frontier on November 21. The Afghans were known to be holding the Peiwar Kotal in force, but the approaches to this position were well known, having been accurately surveyed many years before by Sir Frederick Roberts, predecessor in the post of Quartermaster-General Sir Peter Lumsden. A frontal attack was out of the question, and there were elements of weakness in Sir Frederick Roberts's army. One of his British regiments was dangerously weak, both in physique and in numbers, and one of his native regiments was disaffected. However, this did not deter the officer, who throughout his career had ever displayed, not only great personal gallantry, but quickness of decision and a long-acquired habit of accepting to the full all responsibility in cases of doubt. The frontier was crossed on the exact date, the Peiwar Kotal reconnoitred, its defences accurately estimated, and on December 2 the Kuram route was in our hands.

PEIWAR KOTAL, DECEMBER 2, 1879.

The regiments authorized to bear this distinction are the

King's Liverpool.	Seaforth Highlanders.
12th Cavalry.	23rd Pioneers.
29th Punjabis.	56th Punjab Rifles.
58th Vaughan's Rifles.	5th Gurkhas.

A medal and clasp, inscribed " Peiwar Kotal," were issued to the troops engaged.

The battle honour commemorates a sharp little fight between the Kuram column of the Afghan army, commanded by Major-General Frederick Roberts, of the Royal Artillery, and the Afghan army. The Afghans were drawn up behind a strongly entrenched position on the summit of the Peiwar Kotal, a pass at the entrance of the Kuram route to Kabul.   Their numbers were estimated at 10,000 men, and they had a well-equipped force of artillery. The position was capable of being turned by a well-known but exceedingly difficult path, known as

the Spin Gawi. Roberts determined to turn the position
with the bulk of his force, numbering only 2,263 men,
with eight guns, whilst a frontal attack was entrusted to
Brigadier Cobbe, with 1,000 men and five guns. Starting
at midnight, the turning column pushed up an almost
inaccessible path in the dead of night, and as dawn broke
appeared on the left flank of the astonished Afghans.
The resistance was for a time stubborn, but as the troops
were enabled to form across the ridges and bring a rifle-
fire to bear on the enemy, the issue soon was put beyond
doubt, and so the future Earl Roberts was able to secure
his first victory.

CASUALTIES AT THE ACTION OF THE PEIWAR KOTAL,
DECEMBER 2, 1879.

Regiments.	Officers.		Men.		Regiments.	Officers.		Men.	
	K.	W.	K.	W.		K.	W.	K.	W.
Royal Artillery	1	—	—	3	29th Punjabis	—	—	5	12
8th K. Liverpl.	—	1	1	7	56th Punjabi Rifles ..	—	—	7	11
72nd Seaforth Highlanders	—	1	2	9	58th Vaughan's Rifles ..	—	—	—	4
12th Cavalry ..	—	—	—	—	5th Gurkhas ..	—	—	2	16
23rd Pioneers	1	—	2	7					

The army destined for the invasion of Afghanistan
from the south was double the strength of the northern
columns. It was composed of two divisions, which were
under the command of Lieutenant-General Donald
Stewart, an officer of the Indian army who had held a
high staff appointment at the Siege of Delhi, had subsequently commanded the Bengal division in the expedition to Abyssinia, and who had seen a considerable amount
of service on the Peshawar frontier when Adjutant of a
native regiment. He had held responsible staff appointments in peace, and had earned a good reputation for
handling large bodies of troops at manœuvres. The

command of the Second Division was entrusted to Major-General Michael Biddulph, an artillery officer who had done good service in the Crimea, and had served in many situations in India, in all of which he had displayed high military qualifications. This army, the composition of which is given below, was intended to provide for the occupation of Southern Afghanistan, and also to despatch one division to join hands with the northern army at Kabul, should such a step be deemed advisable. From Multan and Quetta as bases, the Kandahar army advanced on the capital of Southern Afghanistan, which was occupied without resistance.

KANDAHAR FIELD FORCE.

First Division : Lieutenant-General Donald Stewart commanding.

Cavalry Brigade—Brigadier-General Walter Fane, C.B. : 15th Hussars, 8th Cavalry, 19th Fane's Lancers.

Commanding Royal Artillery—Brigadier-General C. G. Arbuthnot, C.B. : One horse, three field, two heavy, three siege, and one mountain battery.

First Infantry Brigade—Brigadier-General R. Barter, C.B. : 2nd Battalion King's Royal Rifles, 15th Sikhs, and 25th Punjabis.

Second Infantry Brigade—Brigadier-General W. Hughes : 59th (East Lancashire), 12th Kelat-i-Ghilzai Regiment, 1st and 3rd Gurkhas.

Second Division : Major-General M. A. S. Biddulph, C.B.

Artillery—Colonel Le Mesurier commanding : One field and two mountain batteries.

Cavalry Brigade : Brigadier-General C. H. Palliser, C.B. : 21st Daly's Horse, 22nd Sam Browne's Horse, and 35th Scinde Horse.

First Infantry Brigade—Brigadier-General R. Lacy : 70th (East Surrey), 19th Punjabis, and 127th Baluchis.

Second Infantry Brigade—Brigadier-General T. Nuttall : 26th Punjabis, 32nd Pioneers, 55th Coke's Rifles, and 129th Baluchis.

The three columns now proceeded to occupy strategic positions in the country until the Amir should accede to our demands. Sir S. Browne pushed up the Khyber Pass to Gundamak, General Roberts undertook the pacification of the tribes bordering on the Kuram route, and General Stewart despatched his Second Division to the Helmund. In the spring of 1879 the Amir Shere Ali died, and his successor at once opened negotiations with the Indian Government. A fresh treaty was concluded, under which the Amir assented to the nomination of a British Envoy at Kabul. Sir Louis Cavagnari was selected for this important post, and towards the end of July left for the Afghan capital, accompanied by a small escort of the Corps of Guides. Our troops were recalled within the new frontier, and all boded well, but on September 3 the Mission was attacked in the Residency at Kabul, and every member slain, the little escort of the Guides adding to the reputation of the regiment by refusing all overtures from their co-religionists, and dying by the side of their officers. Such an outrage demanded swift retribution, and Sir Frederick Roberts at once took up the command of the troops in the Kuram Valley, and prepared for an advance on Kabul. His army was composed as under :

DETAILS OF THE KABUL FIELD FORCE.

Major-General Sir Frederick Roberts, K.C.B., V.C., commanding.

Cavalry Brigade — Brigadier - General Dunham Massey : 9th Lancers, 12th Cavalry, 14th Lancers, and 25th Cavalry.

Royal Artillery—Brigadier-General B. L. Gordon : Two horse and two mountain batteries.

First Infantry Brigade—Brigadier-General Herbert Macpherson, V.C., C.B. : 67th (Hampshire Regiment), 92nd (Gordon Highlanders), and 28th Punjabis.

Second Infantry Brigade—Brigadier-General T. D. Baker, C.B. : 72nd (Seaforths), 53rd Sikhs, 23rd Pioneers, 58th Vaughan's Rifles, and 5th Gurkhas.

Third Brigade—Brigadier-General J. Tytler, V.C., C.B. : 85th (Shropshire Light Infantry), 11th and 13th Rajputs, and 20th Punjabis.

Fourth Brigade—Brigadier-General T. E. Gordon : 2nd Battalion King's Liverpool Regiment, 7th Rajputs, 21st and 29th Punjabis.

Leaving his Third and Fourth Brigades to maintain communications with India, Sir Frederick at once pushed on to Kabul, meeting with no opposition until in the immediate vicinity of the capital. On the way he had been joined by the new Amir, who wished to disclaim all participation in the attack on the Residency. His presence was not an unmixed blessing. It was more than suspected that he was in close communication with the malcontents, and that he was cognizant of the intention of his troops to hold the position at Charasiah, where, on October 6, Sir Frederick fought and dispersed the Afghan army, with but little loss on our side.

CHARASIAH, OCTOBER 6, 1879.

This battle honour is borne by the following regiments :

9th Lancers.
Seaforth Highlanders.
12th Cavalry.
25th Cavalry.
23rd Pioneers.
28th Punjabis.

Hampshires.
Gordon Highlanders.
14th Murray's Lancers.
1st P.W.O. Sappers and Miners.
58th Vaughan's Rifles.

5th Gurkhas.

The force at Sir Frederick Roberts's disposal only amounted to 4,000 men and eighteen guns. The enemy occupied a series of hills some three miles in extent, and dominating the plain to a height of over 3,000 feet. The brunt of the fighting fell on the two Highland regiments. Again the British General, who showed himself an adept in mountain warfare, essayed a turning movement with Baker's brigade, and, with a loss of but 88 killed and wounded, made his way into Kabul.

CASUALTIES AT THE ACTION OF CHARASIAH, OCTOBER 6, 1879.

Regiments.	Officers.		Men.		Regiments.	Officers.		Men.	
	K.	W.	K.	W.		K.	W.	K.	W.
9th Lancers ..	—	—	—	1	14th Murray's Lancers ..	—	—	—	—
Royal Artillery	—	—	—	—	25th Cavalry	—	—	1	2
67th Hampshire	—	—	—	—	23rd Pioneers	—	1	1	2
72nd Seaforth Highlanders	—	1	3	33	28th Punjabis	—	—	—	—
92nd Gordon Highlanders	—	—	3	6	58th Vaughan's Rifles ..	—	1	4	4
12th Cavalry	—	—	—	—	5th Gurkhas ..	—	—	4	7

On the issue of the medal for Afghanistan, a clasp inscribed " Charasiah " was issued to all the troops engaged.

KABUL, 1879.

This battle honour was granted to the regiments which took part in the operations in the neighbourhood of Kabul under Sir Frederick Roberts in the month of December, 1879. It is borne on the colours and appointments of the

9th Lancers.	Norfolk.
Hampshires.	Seaforth Highlanders.
Gordon Highlanders.	12th Cavalry.
14th Murray's Lancers.	25th Cavalry P.F.F.
Q.O. Corps of Guides.	1st P.W.O. Sappers and
23rd Pioneers.	Miners.
28th Punjabis.	53rd Sikhs.
58th Vaughan's Rifles.	2nd Gurkhas.
4th Gurkhas.	5th Gurkhas P.F.F.

With his entry into Kabul, which was effected without further opposition after the Battle of Charasiah, the difficulties of Sir Frederick Roberts's army were only at their commencement. The Amir was in our camp, but it was clear that he was heart and soul with his people, and that they were bitterly opposed to us was self-evident. They appeared forgetful of the ease with which they had been defeated at Ali Masjid, at the Peiwar Kotal, and again at Charasiah ; but they remembered the campaign of 1842, when they had annihilated a British army. Early in December the clouds broke, and after a few engagements, in which we were not uniformly successful, Sir Frederick Roberts withdrew his whole force into an entrenched position at Sherpur, just outside the city, and there awaited the attack. His dispositions were thoroughly sound. Reinforcements were ordered up from the line of communications, but these were delayed, owing to determined attacks by the tribes on our posts at different points between Kabul and Peshawar.

From December 14 to 24 Sir Frederick was practically besieged in Sherpur. On the 23rd the much-vaunted attack was delivered, but the troops vied with their commander in steadiness. None had lost confidence in him owing to the unfortunate failure of his combinations against the enemy at the commencement of the month— a failure for which the General-in-Chief was by no means responsible. If the Afghans thought that they were likely to catch a British army asleep at midnight, the attack on Sherpur must have woefully disappointed them. In spite of the fact that 100,000 men had assembled to sweep the British out of the land, the assault was repelled before the arrival of a single man of the reinforcing troops, and with a loss of but 57 officers and men killed and wounded during the siege of ten days.

A clasp was added to the Afghan medal for this brilliant feat of arms.

CASUALTIES IN THE ENGAGEMENTS NEAR KABUL,
DECEMBER 11 TO 23, 1879.

Regiments.	Officers.		Men.		Regiments.	Officers.		Men.	
	K.	W.	K.	W.		K.	W.	K.	W.
9th Lancers ..	3	4	20	28	25th Cavalry P.F.F. ..	2	2	8	6
Royal Artillery	2	—	3	8	Q.O. Corps of				
Roy. Engineers	2	1	—	—	Guides ..	1	3	15	37
67th Hampshire	—	—	1	11	23rd Pioneers	—	—	—	1
72nd Seaforth					28th Punjabis	—	—	—	1
Highlanders	2	2	12	39	53rd Sikhs ..	—	5	5	9
92nd Gordon					58th Vaughan's				
Highlanders	1	1	3	25	Rifles ..	—	—	4	17
12th Bengal C.	—	—	5	4	5th Gurkhas ..	1	1	4	10
14th Lancers	1	1	8	7					

The complicity of the Amir Yakub Khan in the attack on the Residency was never clearly proved, but it was very evident that he made no attempt to save the lives of the Envoy and his Staff. His desire, therefore, to abdicate was encouraged, and he was deported as a State prisoner to India. His successor, the Amir Abdur Rahman, had been a fugitive on Russian soil for many years, and his hold on the people was but slight. It was deemed advisable to show our strength in those parts of the country where no British army had been seen, and in the month of March, 1880, Sir Donald Stewart, who was in command at Kandahar, left the capital of Southern Afghanistan for Kabul. His force consisted of :

Cavalry Brigade—Brigadier-General C. H. Palliser, C.B. : 19th Fane's Lancers, 21st Daly's Horse, and 22nd Cavalry.
Royal Artillery : One horse, one heavy, and two mountain batteries.
First Infantry Brigade—Brigadier-General R. Barter : 2nd Battalion King's Royal Rifles, 19th and 25th Punjabis.
Second Infantry Brigade—Brigadier-General R. J. Hughes : 59th (East Lancashire), 15th and 52nd Sikhs, and 3rd Gurkhas.

In all, some 2,000 British and 5,000 native troops.

Leaving Kandahar on the last day of March, Sir Donald found himself attacked by a strong body of Afghans on nearing Ghuznee, and though for a moment things looked threatening, at the end of an hour the enemy were in full retreat, and the name " Ahmad Khel " had been added to the colours of the

East Lancashires.	King's Royal Rifles.
19th Fane's Horse.	21st Daly's Horse.
22nd Sam Browne's Horse.	1st P.W.O. Sappers and
15th Sikhs.	Miners.
19th Punjabis.	25th Punjabis.
52nd Sikhs.	3rd Gurkhas.

Our casualties being—

Regiments.	Officers.		Men.		Regiments.	Officers.		Men.	
	K.	W.	K.	W.		K.	W.	K.	W.
Royal Artillery	—	1	—	2	21st Daly's H.	—	—	—	19
East Lancashire	—	2	1	10	22nd Sam				
2nd Batt. K.					Browne's H.	—	2	3	20
Royal Rifles	—	—	4	1	25th Punjabis	—	—	—	3
19th Punjabis	—	—	—	3	52nd Sikhs ..	—	—	1	9
19th Fane's H.	—	4	5	41	3rd Gurkhas ..	—	—	—	—

A few days later a second skirmish took place, but the march was not further interrupted, and by the end of the month Sir Donald Stewart had assumed the command in Northern Afghanistan.

His successor in the south now experienced a series of mishaps. At the Battle of Maiwand a British force was totally defeated, and Kandahar closely invested by the Afghans. A sortie, gallantly led by Brigadier Brooke, in which that officer lost his life, resulted in the siege being prosecuted by the Afghans with greater vigour.

CASUALTIES AT THE BATTLE OF MAIWAND, JULY 27, 1880.

Regiments.	Officers.		Men.		Regiments.	Officers.		Men.	
	K.	W.	K.	W.		K.	W.	K.	W.
Staff	1	1	—	—	3rd Scinde H.	1	—	14	5
Royal Artillery	2	1	12	12	3rd Sappers and				
Roy. Engineers	1	—	2	3	Miners ..	1	—	15	6
66th Roy. Berks	10	2	276	30	101st Grenadiers	10	6	356	55
33rd Q.O. Light					130th P.W.O.				
Cavalry ..	1	—	26	18	Baluchis ..	6	7	235	25

CASUALTIES AT THE SORTIE FROM KANDAHAR, AUGUST 16, 1880.

Regiments.	Officers.		Men.		Regiments.	Officers.		Men.	
	K.	W.	K.	W.		K.	W.	K.	W.
Staff	3	3	—	—	34th P.W.O.				
Royal Fusiliers	2	2	22	28	Light Cav.	1	1	—	4
59th E. Lanca-					3rd Sappers and				
shire ..	—	—	2	2	Miners ..	—	1	6	7
33rd Q.O. Light					119th Multan I.	2	1	20	24
Cavalry ..	—	1	6	2	128th Pioneers	1	1	30	22

The precarious situation at Kandahar demanded immediate measures, and once more Sir Frederick Roberts was chosen to vindicate British honour and to teach the

Afghans that they were powerless in the face of well-led and well-handled British troops ; and he was placed in command of the following compact force, with instructions to march to Kandahar with all possible despatch, and crush the anti - British movement in Southern Afghanistan.

DETAILS OF THE KABUL-KANDAHAR FIELD FORCE.

Commander-in-Chief : Lieutenant-General Sir Frederick Roberts, K.C.B.

Cavalry Brigade—Brigadier-General Hugh Gough, V.C., C.B. : 9th Lancers, 3rd and 23rd Regiments of Cavalry, and Central India Horse.

Artillery Brigade—Colonel Alured Johnson : Three mountain batteries.

Infantry Division : Major-General Sir John Ross, K.C.B.

First Brigade—Brigadier-General H. Macpherson, V.C., C.B. : 92nd (Gordon Highlanders), 23rd Pioneers, 24th Punjabis, and 2nd Gurkhas.

Second Brigade—Brigadier-General T. D. Baker, C.B. : 72nd (Seaforth Highlanders), 52nd and 53rd Sikhs, and 5th Gurkhas.

Third Brigade — Brigadier-General C. M. Macgregor, C.B., 2nd Battalion King's Royal Rifles, 15th Sikhs, 25th Punjabis, 4th Gurkhas.

The total strength being 2,562 British and 7,151 native troops, with eighteen guns.

On August 11 the Kabul-Kandahar Force commenced its march to the south, and on the 31st of the month reached Kandahar—a distance of 313 miles. No opposition was experienced on the march. The garrison of Kandahar was found in a state of extreme dejection. In order not to attract the enemy's fire the General in command had given instructions that even the British flag should not be hoisted on the walls. Neither Sir Frederick Roberts nor his force were the men to delay when a fight was in prospect, and as the army of Ayub Khan was still encamped in the vicinity, flushed with their victory over General Burroughs at Maiwand, Sir Frederick determined on at once attacking the Afghans, and on the very day of his arrival the Chief sent out General Hugh Gough to reconnoitre the enemy's position.

KANDAHAR, SEPTEMBER 1, 1880.

This honour is borne by the

9th Lancers.	Royal Fusiliers.
Royal Berkshires.	King's Royal Rifles.
Seaforth Highlanders.	Gordon Highlanders.
3rd Sappers and Miners.	3rd Skinner's Horse.
23rd Cavalry.	33rd Q.O. Light Cavalry.
34th Poona Horse.	38th Central India Horse.
39th Central India Horse.	15th Sikhs.
23rd Pioneers.	24th Punjabis.
25th Punjabis.	52nd Sikhs.
53rd Sikhs.	101st Grenadiers.
104th Wellesley's Rifles.	119th Multan.
128th Pioneers.	129th Baluchis.
2nd Gurkhas.	4th Gurkhas.

5th Gurkhas.

Sir Frederick adopted the same tactics here as in his earlier actions : making a wide sweeping movement with a portion of his infantry and his cavalry, he pressed home the frontal attack with the two Highland regiments, and in an hour the Afghan army was in full retreat. The only troops actually engaged were those who had marched down with General Roberts from Kabul.

CASUALTIES AT THE BATTLE OF KANDAHAR,
SEPTEMBER 1, 1880.

Regiments.	Officers. K.	W.	Men. K.	W.	Regiments.	Officers. K.	W.	Men. K.	W.
Staff	1	—	—	—	15th Sikhs ..	—	—	2	4
Royal Artillery	—	—	—	6	23rd Pioneers	—	1	2	13
60th Roy. Rifles	—	—	—	2	24th Punjabis	—	1	1	10
72nd Seaforths	2	2	11	20	25th Punjabis	—	1	—	1
92nd Gordons	—	2	19	69	52nd Sikhs P.F.F. ..	—	1	3	23
3rd Skinner's H.	—	1	—	1	53rd Sikhs P.F.F. ..	—	—	—	6
23rd Cavalry P.F.F. ..	—	1	—	6	129th D.C.O. Baluchis ..	—	—	—	1
33rd Q.O. Light Cavalry ..	—	1	—	1	2nd Gurkhas ..	—	2	8	21
3rd Scinde Horse ..	—	—	—	1	4th Gurkhas ..	—	2	1	4
38th C.I. Horse	1	—	—	5	5th Gurkhas ..	—	—	1	2

CHAPTER XXV

BATTLE HONOURS FOR OPERATIONS ON THE NORTH-WEST INDIAN FRONTIER, 1895-1897

Defence of Chitral—Chitral—Malakand—Samana—Punjab Frontier—Tirah.

DEFENCE OF CHITRAL, 1895.

THIS battle honour is borne by one regiment—the 14th Prince of Wales's Own Ferozepore Sikhs.

It commemorates one of those gallant but little-remembered occurrences where a handful of British officers, at the head of sepoys no less brave than themselves, have upheld the honour of our flag against overwhelming odds, and thus belied the oft-repeated cry of the decadence of the present generation of Englishmen. There are few episodes in our military history which can vie with the defence of Chitral, none which excel it in sublime heroism.

A few words are necessary in retrospect. Chitral is a small State perched up in the almost inaccessible Himalayas, on the main route between Hindustan and the Pamirs. In the year 1876 the ruler of this State, which hitherto had been independent, placed himself under the protection of the Maharajah of Kashmir, and so became one of our vassals.

Matters marched smoothly for some years, but in the early part of 1895 intertribal disputes arose, the ruler was murdered, and his throne seized by a usurper, who possessed the support of all the neighbouring clans, and was, it was shrewdly suspected, receiving the moral, if not the material, support of the Amir of Afghanistan. The Chief Political Agent in those regions was Surgeon-Major George

Robertson, a medical officer who had studied the languages and customs of the Upper Himalayan tribes, and who was trusted as implicitly by them as by our own Government.   He hurried from his headquarters at Gilgit to Chitral in the hope of allaying the excitement, but he found himself in the face of a determined effort on the part of the usurper and his supporters—all fanatical Moslems—to free themselves from the yoke of the Kafir. All that Robertson could do was to throw himself into the little native fort of Chitral, and there to hold out until help arrived from India.   The few scattered garrisons in the Upper Himalayas were isolated, and all were in equal danger.   In one case a detachment of Sikhs was practically annihilated, its surviving officers being taken prisoners.

Robertson had with him in Chitral five young officers, a company of the 14th Sikhs, numbering 88 men, and 300 Kashmiri levies—these last all untrained in the use of the rifle with which they were armed.   The story of the defence of Chitral has been told in all too modest language by one of the principal actors, and I can cordially recommend " The Story of a Minor Siege," by Sir George Robertson, to the attention of those who talk of the deterioration of our race.   For seven long weeks did that heroic garrison hold out, and when at last relieved, the relief was effected by a force entirely composed of native soldiers—the 32nd Pioneers—who, under their indomitable Colonel, had traversed the gigantic passes of the Himalayas, swept aside all opposition, and shown the world that the Indian army contains in its midst, men who are not to be equalled by any soldiers in the world.

The losses sustained by that one company of the 14th Sikhs during the defence of Chitral were 1 officer and 17 men killed, 1 officer and 53 men wounded.

CHITRAL, 1895.

This distinction, which was granted to commemorate the services of the troops which relieved the beleaguered garrison of Chitral, is borne by the following regiments :

Buffs.	Bedfords.
K.O. Scottish Borderers.	East Lancashire.
King's Royal Rifles.	Gordon Highlanders.
Seaforth Highlanders.	Q.O. Corps of Guides.
9th Hodson's Horse.	11th Probyn's Lancers.
1st P.W.O. Sappers and	13th Rajputs.
Miners.	15th Sikhs.
23rd Pioneers.	25th Punjabis.
29th Punjabis.	30th Punjabis.
32nd Pioneers.	34th Pioneers.
37th Dogras.	54th Sikhs.

4th Gurkhas.

The General in command was General Sir Robert Low, K.C.B., and his force was distributed as under :

First Brigade—Brigadier-General A. A. A. Kinloch, C.B. : 1st Battalion Bedfords, 1st Battalion King's Royal Rifles, 15th Sikhs, and 37th Dogras.

Second Brigade—Brigadier-General Waterfield : 2nd Battalion King's Own Scottish Borderers, 1st Battalion Gordon Highlanders, 54th Sikhs, and the infantry of the Corps of Guides.

Third Infantry Brigade—Brigadier-General Gatacre : 1st Battalion Buffs, 2nd Battalion Seaforth Highlanders, 25th Punjabis, and 4th Gurkhas.

On the line of communication and in reserve were the 1st Battalion East Lancashires, the Guides Cavalry, the 11th (Probyn's) Lancers, the 13th Rajputs, the 23rd Pioneers, and the 30th Punjabis.

Whilst this force was being hastily mobilized, messages had been despatched to Colonel Kelly, commanding the 32nd Pioneers at Gilgit, far away to the west of Chitral, advising him of the critical position of the garrison. Kelly was one of the few officers in the Indian army who had attained the command of a regiment without having participated in any great campaign. He was known to be a good and a keen soldier, but luck had been against him. Now his turn had come. In the depth of winter, the passes covered with snow, often waist deep, mountain torrents unbridged, paths over which even the mules picked their way with difficulty, every ounce of food to be carried for the whole long march of 200 miles, and a formidable rising of all the fanatical Moslem tribes in his front—these were some of the difficulties that Kelly had to face. The story of that march vies with the story of the defence. It was a war against Nature, and the British-led force won.

Sir Robert Low, with the main army pushing up over the Malakand Pass, easily dispersed the gathering of the tribes which endeavoured to bar his advance on Chitral, and so relieved the pressure which otherwise might have militated against Kelly's success. In these engagements the relieving force suffered the following casualties :

Regiments.	Officers.				Men.	
	British.		Native.			
	K.	W.	K.	W.	K.	W.
16th (Bedford)	—	—	—	—	1	2
25th (K.O. Scottish Borderers)	—	2	—	—	2	15
60th (King's Royal Rifles) ..	—	—	—	—	—	4
78th (Seaforth Highlanders) ..	—	—	—	—	—	—
75th (Gordon Highlanders) ..	—	3	—	—	3	9
11th (Probyn's) Lancers ..	1	—	—	—	1	10
37th Dogras	—	—	1	—	2	16
54th Sikhs	—	2	—	2	3	7
4th Gurkhas	—	—	—	—	—	3

PUNJAB FRONTIER.

This honour, which was sanctioned by the Viceroy of India, is borne by the following regiments of the Indian army :

3rd Skinner's Horse.
9th Hodson's Horse.
13th Watson's Horse.
38th Central India Horse.
Q.O. Corps of Guides.
12th Khelat-i-Ghilzai.
15th Ludhiana Sikhs.
22nd Punjabis.
30th Punjabis.
34th Pioneers.
36th Sikhs.
38th Dogras.

6th K.E. Cavalry.
11th Probyn's Lancers.
18th Tiwana Lancers.
39th Central India Horse.
1st P.W.O. Sappers and
    Miners.
20th Brownlow's Punjabis.
24th Punjabis.
31st Punjabis.
35th Sikhs.
37th Dogras.
39th Gharwal Rifles.

45th Rattray's Sikhs.	53rd Sikhs.
56th Punjabi Rifles.	81st Pioneers.
128th Pioneers.	1st Gurkhas.
2nd Gurkhas.	3rd Gurkhas.
4th Gurkhas.	5th Gurkhas.
9th Gurkhas.	

In the year 1897 Greece, in defiance of the warnings of the Great Powers, threw down the gauntlet to Turkey, and at the end of a brief fortnight's campaign was compelled to sue for peace. Through the good offices of the same Powers she was permitted to escape the just punishment she had incurred. The victory of the Turks was greatly exaggerated throughout the Moslem world, and there is no doubt that emissaries of the Sultan were sent through all Moslem countries to expatiate on the greatness of the Ottoman Power and the invincibility of her armies.

About this time the Amir of Afghanistan published a work appealing to the faithful, and a fanatical priest perambulated the mountains along our frontier preaching a war against the infidel. All these causes tended to a great feeling of restlessness—a restlessness not confined to one clan, but showing clearly all down the frontier, from the Black Mountain to the Waziri Hills.

A brief explanation of the condition of affairs on our Punjab frontier is here necessary. That frontier extends up to and impinges on that great mountain-range which interposes between the Indian Empire and the kingdom of Afghanistan. This range is peopled by wild warlike tribes, who own allegiance to no man. Their names are more or less familiar to the British public by reason of the many punitory expeditions we have been compelled to undertake into their hills. Intertribal jealousies have generally been our strongest ally, and never until the year 1897 have we found such a serious combination of tribes against us.

The campaign commemorated by this battle honour— " Punjab Frontier "—commenced by a most treacherous attack on a detachment of troops in the Tochi Valley. It was followed up by a most determined attack on our garrison at Malakand by the Swatis—a tribe who for many years had given us no trouble. Then came an incursion of the Mohmands into the Peshawar Valley, and finally came the attack on the garrisons in the Khyber Pass by the Afridis, that great clan which furnishes some of the very best soldiers to the Indian army. For the operations against the Afridis a separate battle honour—" Tirah "—was granted.

The casualties suffered by our troops in the various expeditions for which the battle honour " Punjab Frontier " was awarded to native regiments are tabulated on p. 402. It must be remembered that this distinction has not been conferred on the British regiments engaged.

MALAKAND, 1897.

This battle honour has been awarded to the under-mentioned regiments of the Indian army by the Viceroy in Council, in recognition of the gallant services rendered in the defence of the Malakand Pass on the North-West Frontier of India at the outset of the great rising of the tribes in 1897 :

11th K.E.O. Lancers (Probyn's Horse).	Q.O. Corps of Guides.
	24th Punjabis.
31st Punjabis.	35th Sikhs.
38th Dogras.	

The Chitral campaign of 1895 had taught us the necessity, not merely of constructing good gun-roads from our Punjab frontier stations to the remoter garrisons in the Upper Himalayas, but also of keeping garrisons on those roads in order to overawe the frontier tribes. The Malakand Pass lies some thirty miles beyond Hoti Mardan, the cantonment which for more than half a century has been the home of the Guides, the most famous of all our frontier regiments. The pass was held in strength. Its commander, Brigadier-General W. Meiklejohn, was a soldier who had a considerable experience of Frontier Wars, and who had received his early training under one of the most accomplished masters of the art of mountain warfare that the Indian army has ever produced—Field-Marshal Sir Charles Brownlow. Meiklejohn had with him some of the pick of the Indian army—a squadron of the 11th (Probyn's) Horse, the 24th and 31st Regiments of Punjab Infantry, and the 45th Sikhs. Within thirty-two miles were the Guides, and twenty-six miles farther south, at Nowshera, lay a brigade which comprised a battalion of British troops.

There had been ominous murmurings in the mountains to the north of Peshawar. As I have shown on p. 397, a fanatical Moslem priest had been preaching a religious war, and this spirit of fanaticism had been fanned into a flame by exaggerated accounts of the success of the Turks over the Greeks in Thessaly. Although nominally at peace with his neighbours, Meiklejohn was not a man to take any risks. On more than one occasion frontier camps had been rushed by fanatics, and when on the evening of July 26, 1897, the Swatis of Malakand endeavoured to rush the camp on the Malakand Pass, they were met by men who had studied hill warfare in the best of all schools—that of the Punjab frontier. When dawn broke the little garrison had lost 50 killed and wounded, but this they knew was but the commencement of their troubles. A telegram had been got through to Hoti Mardan before sundown. It reached that place at half-past eight in the evening. It must be here remembered that this was the month of July, the leave season, and that the cry of " Wolf, wolf ! " has so often been heard on the Punjab frontier that its repetition is never considered sufficient to stop leave. At that moment the temporary command of the Guides was in the hands of a Lieutenant, Lockhart. As I have said, he received the message at 8.30 p.m. ; five hours later—at 1.30 a.m.—the Guides were on the march for Malakand ; at half-past six the following evening they swung up the Pass, having covered thirty-two miles in the hottest season of the year in just seventeen hours, thus rivalling the marvellous march they made in the Mutiny from Mardan to Delhi. It is related by an officer who was present that so little affected were the Guides by this trying march that company after company, as it swung by the main guard of the Malakand Force, came to the shoulder with all the accuracy of a battalion of the Guards.

That night the garrison had to meet a second attack, in which the Guides fought with all their accustomed *élan*. The same day the Brigadier at Nowshera, in response to the messages from Malakand, despatched the headquarters and two squadrons of the 11th (Probyn's) Horse, two mountain batteries, and two battalions (the 35th Sikhs and 38th Dogras), to the relief of Malakand. Some idea of the severity of the weather may be gathered from the fact that the 35th Sikhs lost 21 men from heat apoplexy in that march from Nowshera to the foot of the Pass.

With the arrival of these reinforcements all danger had passed, but the attitude of the tribes made it abundantly clear that we were face to face with the greatest frontier upheaval since Sir Walter Gilbert had driven the Afghans through the Khyber Pass in the spring of 1849.

The first step was to chastise the tribes in the immediate vicinity of Malakand, and orders were at once issued for the mobilization of the following force, under the command of a distinguished officer of the Royal Engineers, Major-General Sir Bindon Blood, K.C.B., who had acted as Chief of the Staff to Sir Robert Low in the Chitral Expedition in 1895.   This force was brigaded as follows :

First Brigade—Brigadier-General W. Meiklejohn, C.B., C.M.G.: 1st Battalion Royal West Kent, 24th Punjabis, 31st Punjabis, and 45th Sikhs.

Second Brigade—Brigadier-General P. de Jeffreys : 1st Battalion Buffs, the 35th and 36th Sikhs, and the Infantry of the Guides.

Third Brigade—Brigadier-General J. H. Wodehouse, C.B., C.M.G. : 1st Battalion Highland Light Infantry, 1st Battalion Gordon Highlanders, 21st Punjabis, and the 2nd Battalion 1st Gurkhas.

The divisional troops consisted of the 10th Hodson's Horse, 11th Probyn's Horse, four mountain batteries, and the 22nd Punjabis.

The losses sustained in the defence of the position prior

to the operations of the army acting under Sir Bindon
Blood amounted to—

Regiments.	Officers.		Men.		Regiments.	Officers.		Men.	
	K.	W.	K.	W.		K.	W.	K.	W.
Q.O. Guides ..	—	3	3	27	31st Punjabis	—	2	12	32
24th Punjabis	1	2	8	24	45th Sikhs ..	1	—	4	28

No account of the defence of Malakand would be complete without an allusion to the gallant action of a
company of the 45th Sikhs, under a subaltern, in holding
on to the outpost of Chakdarra, a few miles farther up
the pass. So sudden was the outburst that Lieutenant
Rattray, the officer in command, was actually playing
polo with the officers at Malakand when he heard of the
threatened attack. He at once galloped back to the
outpost, passing *en route* groups of the tribesmen, who
made no attempt to hinder him. He arrived to find
that his brother subaltern had commenced to prepare for
the fray. That night they were attacked, and from
July 25 until August 2 were continuously under fire.
When they were relieved by the advance of a force from
Malakand, the casualties in the company of the 45th
Sikhs at Chakdarra amounted to 5 killed and 18 wounded,
whilst the sergeant's party of the 11th Bengal Lancers
lost 3 men.

While yet the force was being mobilized for the punishment of the Swatis for the attack on Malakand, the Mohmands raided some villages in the Peshawar Valley. The
raiders were promptly punished by the Peshawar Division,
under General Elles ; but this was not deemed sufficient,
and in the month of September Sir Bindon Blood, having
dealt with the Swatis, advanced against the Mohmands
from the north, the while that General Elles, with a well-
equipped brigade, moved up from Peshawar.

DISTRIBUTION OF THE MOHMAND FIELD FORCE.

First Division : Major-General Sir Bindon Blood, K.C.B.

First Brigade—Brigadier-General Jeffreys, C.B. : The Buffs, 35th Sikhs, and 38th Dogras.

Second Brigade—Brigadier-General Wodehouse, C.B. : The Queen's, 22nd Punjabis, and the 39th Punjabis.

Second Division : Major-General Edmond Elles, C.B.

Third Brigade : Somerset Light Infantry, 20th Brownlow's Punjabis, and 2nd Battalion 1st Gurkhas.

Fourth Brigade : 2nd Battalion Oxford Light Infantry, 37th Dogras, and the 9th Gurkhas.

After inflicting considerable punishment on the clans in the lower valleys, the Peshawar Division was withdrawn to take part in the Tirah Expedition (p. 404), whilst Sir Bindon Blood remained in occupation of the country. The Mohmand Expedition was productive of some sharp fighting, as the subjoined list of casualties prove :

CASUALTIES IN THE SWAT, MOHMAND, AND KURAM VALLEY
EXPEDITIONS IN 1897.

Regiments.	Officers.				Men.	
	British.		Native.			
	K.	W.	K.	W.	K.	W.
2nd (Queen's)	—	—	—	—	3	6
3rd (Buffs)	—	—	—	—	7	19
11th (Devons)	—	—	—	—	—	—
52nd (Oxford Light Infantry)	—	3	—	—	3	11
50th (Royal West Kent)	1	5	—	—	3	24
107th (Royal Sussex)	—	1	—	—	4	7
6th K.E.O. Cavalry	1	1	—	—	—	5
9th Hodson's Horse	—	—	1	—	3	4
18th Lancers	—	1	—	—	—	2
12th Pioneers	—	—	—	—	3	3
20th Brownlow's Punjabis	—	—	—	—	7	47
22nd Punjabis	—	—	—	—	—	3
34th Pioneers	1	—	—	—	—	2
51st Sikhs	1	2	—	1	13	15
55th Coke's Rifles	1	2	—	—	7	4
9th Gurkhas	—	—	—	—	2	2

SAMANA, SEPTEMBER 12-14, 1897.

This distinction was conferred on the 36th Sikhs by the Viceroy of India as a recognition of the gallant conduct of a detachment of that regiment at the defence of Fort Gulistan against a very superior force.

The attack on Fort Gulistan was one of the incidents which led to the expedition against the Afridis, and which is commemorated on the colours of our army under the title " Tirah." This fort, which is situated on the Samana Range, to the west of the frontier station of Kohat, dominates one of the main roads into the Afridi Hills, and is held by a detachment of native troops furnished from the garrison of Kohat. Almost simultaneously with the attack on the garrison of Malakand (see p. 398) symptoms of unrest displayed themselves amongst all the tribes along our North-West Frontier. The forts on the Khyber Road were attacked, the Mohmands made their descent into the Peshawar Valley, and the Afridis, not content with the attacks on the Khyber line, endeavoured to turn us out of the position on the Samana Ridge.

The garrison of Fort Gulistan consisted of two companies of the 36th Sikhs, under Major Des Vœux, and hard by was a little detached work, with a garrison of but twenty men, under a native officer. The conduct of this detachment must for ever remain one of the brightest pages in the history of our Indian army, and yet the history of that army abounds with instances of the self-devotion and heroism of our native soldiery.

Cut off from all communication with any senior officer, the Subadar[1] in command of the Saragai post was left entirely to his own devices. Gallantly did he carry out his orders. Surrounded by 10,000 Afridis, he not only repelled all attacks for three days, but when offered terms and a safe conduct to Kohat, his reply was that until he

[1] A native officer holding a rank equivalent to that of Captain commanding a company.

received instructions from his Colonel he could not abandon the post committed to his care ; and so the brave old Sikh and his gallant men stayed on and died, true to the last to their trust. When the Fort Gulistan was relieved, on September 14, it was found that Saragai was in the hands of the Afridis, and that every man of the garrison had died at his post. To commemorate the heroism of its garrison the Government of India erected a monument, on which the names of that heroic band are inscribed, within the walls of the great Sikh cathedral, the Golden Temple at Umritsar.

The losses sustained by the two companies of the 36th Sikhs in the defence of the Samana Ridge were 22 killed and 48 wounded out of a total of 166 combatants.

TIRAH, 1897-98

This battle honour, sanctioned by Army Order No. 23 of 1900, is borne by the following regiments :

Queen's.
Yorkshire.
K.O. Scottish Borderers.
Northamptons.
18th Tiwana Lancers.
15th Sikhs.
30th Punjabis.
53rd Sikhs.
128th Pioneers.
2nd Gurkhas.

Devons.
Royal Scots Fusiliers.
Sherwood Foresters.
Gordon Highlanders.
1st P.W.O. Sappers and Miners.
36th Sikhs.
56th Rifles.
1st Gurkhas.
3rd Gurkhas.

4th Gurkhas.

It was granted in recognition of one of the most arduous campaigns we have been called upon to wage on the Indian frontier. Our opponents were the great tribe of Afridis, who people the mountains to the west of the cantonment of Peshawar, and who furnish some of the best soldiers in our Punjab regiments. The Afridis are subdivided into a number of clans, all antagonistic to each other. Intertribal wars are of frequent occurrence, and although on many occasions we have been compelled to undertake punitory expeditions against certain of these, it has never been our lot to find such a unanimity of feeling against us as on this occasion.

It was thoroughly realized that we had a foe well worthy of our steel. The Afridis were well armed, and they counted some thousands of men who had been through the mill of discipline in our own regiments. Many of the very best regiments of the Indian army contained a large number of Afridis, and though these men have never hesitated to fight bravely against their own co-religionists in our border wars and in Afghanistan, there was more than a possibility that their loyalty would be too severely tried were we to employ them against their own fellow-tribesmen.

The chief command was entrusted to General Sir William Lockhart, an officer well versed in frontier warfare, one who understood the Afridi character thoroughly, and who was well known and well respected by the tribesmen. His army was the most powerful that we had ever mobilized for frontier war. It numbered close on 35,000 men, of whom 10,900 were British, and was distributed as under :

First Division : Major-General W. Penn Symons, C.B.

First Infantry Brigade—Brigadier-General R. C. Hart, V.C., C.B : 1st Battalion Devonshires, 2nd Battalion Sherwood Foresters, 2nd Battalion 1st Gurkhas, and the 30th Punjabis.

Second Infantry Brigade—Brigadier-General Alfred Gaselee, C.B. : 1st Battalion Queen's, 2nd Battalion Yorkshire Regiment, 2nd Battalion 4th Gurkhas, and the 53rd Sikhs.

Second Division : Major-General Yeatman Biggs.

Third Brigade—Brigadier-General F. J. Kempster, D.S.O. : 1st Battalion Dorsets, 1st Battalion Gordon Highlanders, 1st Battalion 2nd Gurkhas, and the 15th Sikhs.

Fourth Brigade—Brigadier-General R. Westmacott, C.B., D.S.O. : 2nd Battalion King's Own Scottish Borderers, 1st Battalion Northamptons, 1st Battalion 3rd Gurkhas, and the 36th Sikhs.

The divisional troops at the disposal of the Commander-in-Chief comprised the 18th Tiwana Lancers, three mountain batteries, and the 128th Pioneers.

A second column was organized to act from Peshawar, and was placed under the command of Brigadier-General

A. G. Hammond, V.C., an officer who had served in the
famous Corps of Guides for twenty years, and who was
a master in the art of mountain warfare, having won the
Victoria Cross during the Afghan War of 1879, under the
eyes of Lord Roberts.   His force comprised the 2nd Battalion Royal Inniskilling Fusiliers, the 2nd Battalion
Oxford Light Infantry, the 9th Gurkhas, the 32nd
Pioneers, and the 45th Sikhs, with the 9th Hodson's
Horse, one field and one mounted battery.

A third column, under Colonel Hill, of the Indian army,
was assembled in the Kuram Valley.   It consisted of the
6th King Edward's Own Cavalry, the 38th and 39th
Central India Horse, the 12th Pioneers, and the 1st Battalion of the 5th Gurkhas, the total force amounting
to 34,880 fighting men, British and native, with no less
than 20,000 followers.

No white man had ever penetrated the upper valleys of
Tirah, and our knowledge was based on the information
of the Afridi officers and men, who for forty years had
formed the backbone of so many of our Punjab regiments.
The frontier town of Kohat formed the base of operations, which had of necessity, owing to the absence of
roads, to be carried on in one single line.   The advance
took place on October 18, and two days later the Dargai
Heights, which commanded the entrance to the valley,
were stormed, with a loss of 200 killed and wounded.
The Afridis were too wise to risk a general engagement.
They had been trained in our own school, had studied
under our officers, and had well learned their lesson.
Instead of wasting life in futile attacks on our troops
when in mass, they waged a ceaseless war against convoys
or survey parties.   Sir William Lockhart remained in
occupation of the Afridi country until the middle of
December, when negotiations for peace were opened ; but
it was not until the commencement of April, 1898, that
the Afridis consented to pay the fines imposed or to give
up the rifles demanded.

Our casualties, which are set out in detail in the sub-

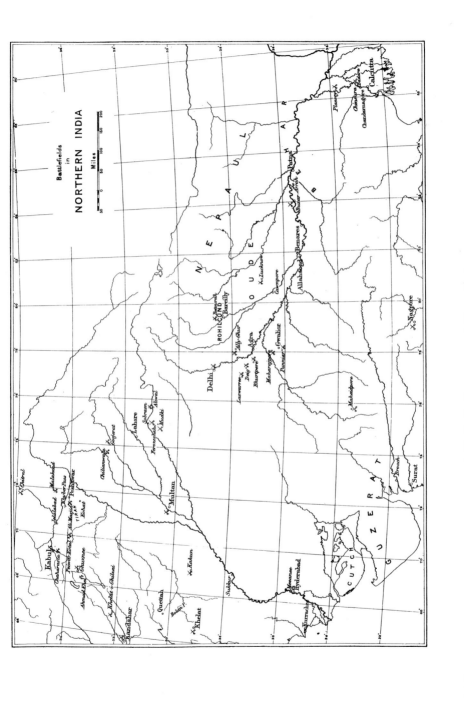

Battlefields
in
NORTHERN INDIA

Miles

joined return, amounted to 23 British officers, 4 native officers, and 287 other ranks killed ; 56 British officers, 16 native officers, and 853 of all ranks wounded—a tribute to the gallantry of our foe and to the musketry training of the British officers who had taught them how to shoot.

CASUALTIES IN THE TIRAH EXPEDITION.

Regiments.	Officers.		Men.		Regiments.	Officers.		Men.	
	K.	W.	K.	W.		K.	W.	K.	W.
Royal Artillery	1	2	4	21	Roy. Engineers	1	1	3	14
2nd Queen's ..	—	2	10	29	18th Bengal				
11th Devons ..	—	—	—	9	Lancers ..	—	1	2	6
19th Yorkshire	1	3	6	33	15th Sikhs ..	2	7	11	35
21st Roy. Scots					30th Punjabis	—	—	3	8
Fusiliers ..	—	1	2	13	36th Sikhs ..	—	5	15	50
25th K.O. Scot-					53rd Sikhs ..	—	4	8	28
tish Borderers	—	3	7	34	56th Punjab R.	2	—	5	27
39th Dorsets	4	4	19	65	121st Pioneers	—	1	2	13
48th N'amptons	3	1	23	41	128th Pioneers	—	1	9	24
75th Gordon H.	2	8	9	63	2nd Gurkhas	4	4	23	75
95th Derbyshire	1	1	8	33	3rd Gurkhas ..	1	3	13	43

CHAPTER XXVI

BATTLE HONOURS FOR SOUTH AFRICA, 1899-1902

Modder River—Defence of Ladysmith—Defence of Kimberley—
Relief of Kimberley—Paardeburg—Relief of Ladysmith—
Medals granted for the campaign—Decorations won regi-
mentally—Casualties by regiments.

SOUTH AFRICA, 1899-1902.

THIS battle honour is borne on the colours and appointments of practically every infantry regiment in the army,
in the cavalry the only regiments which were so unfortunate as not to participate in the campaign being the
4th Dragoon Guards, the 4th, 11th, and 15th Hussars,
which were in India, and the 21st Lancers, which were
at home. The following long list of regiments shows
those which are authorized to bear this honour :

1st Life Guards.	2nd Life Guards.
Royal Horse Guards.	King's Dragoon Guards.
Queen's Bays.	3rd Dragoon Guards.
5th Dragoon Guards.	Carabiniers.
7th Dragoon Guards.	Royal Dragoons.
Scots Greys.	3rd Hussars.
5th Lancers.	Inniskillings.
7th Hussars.	8th Hussars.
9th Lancers.	10th Hussars.
12th Lancers.	13th Hussars.
14th Hussars.	16th Lancers.
17th Lancers.	18th Hussars.
19th Hussars.	20th Hussars.
Grenadier Guards.	Coldstream Guards.
Scots Guards.	Royal Scots.
Queen's.	Buffs.
King's Own.	Northumberland Fusiliers.
Royal Warwicks.	Royal Fusiliers.
King's Liverpools.	Norfolks.
Lincolns.	Devons.

Suffolks.
West Yorks.
Bedfordshire.
Royal Irish.
Lancashire Fusiliers.
Cheshire.
South Wales Borderers.
Scottish Rifles.
Gloucesters.
East Lancashire.
Cornwall Light Infantry.
Border.
Hampshires.
Dorsets.
Welsh.
Oxford Light Infantry.
Derbyshire.
Northamptons.
Royal West Kent.
Shropshire L.I.
King's Royal Rifles.
North Staffords.
Durham L.I.
Seaforth Highlanders.
Cameron Highlanders.
Royal Irish Fusiliers.
Argyll and Sutherland
  Highlanders.
Royal Dublin Fusiliers.

Somerset Light Infantry.
East Yorks.
Leicesters.
Yorkshire.
Royal Scots Fusiliers.
Royal Welsh Fusiliers.
K.O. Scottish Borderers.
Royal Inniskilling Fusiliers.
Worcesters.
East Surrey.
West Riding.
Royal Sussex.
South Staffords.
East Lancashires.
Black Watch.
Essex.
Loyal North Lancashire.
Royal Berkshires.
K.O. Yorkshire L.I.
Middlesex.
Wiltshire.
York and Lancaster.
Highland L.I.
Gordon Highlanders.
Royal Irish Rifles.
Connaught Rangers.
Leinster.
Royal Munster Fusiliers.
Rifle Brigade.

YEOMANRY REGIMENTS.

Ayrshire.
Buckinghamshire.
Denbighshire.
1st Royal Devon.
Dorset.
Fife.
Hampshire.
Royal East Kent.
Lanarkshire.
Lancashire Hussars.
Leicestershire.
1st County of London.
3rd County of London.
Lovat's Scouts.
Northumberland.
South Nottingham Hussars.
Pembroke.
Shropshire.
West Somerset.
Warwickshire.
Worcestershire.
Yorkshire Dragoons.

Berks.
Cheshire.
Derbyshire.
Royal North Devon.
Essex.
Gloucestershire.
Herts.
West Kent.
Royal Lanarkshire.
Duke of Lancaster's.
City of London.
2nd County of London.
Lothian and Border Horse.
Montgomeryshire.
Nottingham Rangers.
Oxford.
Scottish Horse.
North Somerset.
Suffolk.
Westmorland and Cumber-
  land.
Yorkshire Hussars.

MILITIA REGIMENTS.

3rd Royal Scots.	3rd Queen's (West Surrey).
3rd Buffs.	3rd King's Own (Lancaster).
3rd Royal Warwicks.	4th Royal Warwicks.
5th Royal Fusiliers.	4th King's Liverpool.
3rd Norfolks.	4th Norfolks.
3rd Lincolns.	4th West Yorkshire.
3rd East Yorkshire.	4th Bedfords.
3rd Leicester.	3rd Yorkshire.
3rd Lancashire Fusiliers.	4th Lancashire Fusiliers.
3rd Cheshire.	3rd South Wales Borderers.
3rd Scottish Borderers.	3rd Scottish Rifles.
4th Scottish Rifles.	6th Worcester.
3rd East Lancashire.	3rd East Surrey.
3rd West Riding.	3rd Royal Sussex.
3rd South Stafford.	3rd South Lancashire.
3rd Welsh.	3rd Essex.
4th Derbyshire.	3rd Loyal North Lancashire.
3rd Northampton.	5th Middlesex.
6th Middlesex.	3rd Manchester.
4th Manchester.	3rd North Stafford.
3rd York and Lancaster.	3rd Durham L.I.
3rd Highland L.I.	5th Royal Irish Rifles.
3rd Argyll Highlanders.	4th Argyll Highlanders.
4th Royal Munster Fusiliers.	4th Royal Dublin Fusiliers.
5th Royal Dublin Fusiliers.	5th Rifle Brigade.

St. Helena.

One militia battalion was deputed to carry out the thankless but onerous task of guarding the Boer prisoners at this island, and so it comes about that the distinction " St. Helena " is borne on the colours of the 3rd Battalion of the Wiltshire Regiment.

Medals granted for the War in South Africa.

Two medals were given for this campaign—the one with the head of Queen Victoria, to which a number of clasps were appended ; the other with the head of His Majesty King Edward VII., to which were attached two clasps — " South Africa, 1901," and " South Africa, 1902."

The following were the clasps issued with the medal known as the Queen's Medal.

BATTLE CLASPS.

1. " Talana," for the action on October 20, 1899.
2. " Elandslaagte," for the action on October 21, 1899.
3. " Belmont," for the action on November 23, 1899.
4. " Modder River," for the action on November 28, 1899.
5. " Tugela Heights," for a series of engagements fought by Sir Redvers Buller in his first endeavours to force his way into Ladysmith in February, 1900.
6. " Relief of Kimberley," on February 15, 1900.
7. " Relief of Ladysmith," February 26, 1900.
8. " Paardeburg," for the action fought between February 27 and 28, 1900.
9. " Driefontein," for the action on March 10, 1900.
10. " Wepener," for the defence of that position between April 5 and 25, 1900.
11. " Johannesburg," for the operations leading to the seizure of that city, ending on May 31, 1900.
12. " Laing's Nek," for the operations by Sir Redvers Buller's army, ending June 12, 1900.
13. " Diamond Hill," for the action at that place on June 12, 1900.
14. " Witterburgen," for the operations in that district at the end of July, 1900.
15. " Belfast," for the defence of that position on January 7, 1900.

There were clasps given inscribed :

16. " Defence of Kimberley."
17. " Defence of Ladysmith."
18. " Defence of Mafeking."

Clasps were also issued bearing only the names of the various Colonies to those troops which had not been engaged in any of the above-mentioned engagements ; these Colony clasps were in number :

19. " Cape Colony."
20. " Natal."
21. " Orange River Colony."
22. " Rhodesia."
23. " Transvaal."

And there were also two date clasps inscribed :

24. " South Africa, 1901."
25. " South Africa, 1902."

BATTLE HONOURS FOR THE CAMPAIGN.

Whilst medals and clasps were distributed with a free hand, a different policy was enacted with reference to the names that were inscribed on the colours and appointments of the regiments which took part in the campaign. Only six battle honours were authorized for the two and a half years' fighting—" South Africa " (with a date indicating the period that the corps remained in the

country), " Modder River," " Defence of Kimberley,"[1]
" Relief of Kimberley," " Defence of Ladysmith," " Relief of Ladysmith," and " Paardeburg "—and no regiment
obtained more than four of these battle honours. Few were
able to add more than two honours for the campaign.

The relations between the British Government and the
Boers had never been marked by any cordiality. Their
hostility was not confined to ourselves. They had rebelled
against the Dutch East India Company prior to our conquest of the Cape of Good Hope, and from the earliest
days of the Dutch settlement there had been constant
friction between the Boers and the natives. It is not my
province to enter into the causes of the war, or whether
it might have been avoided, suffice to say that on
October 9, 1899, an ultimatum was handed to our Agent
in Pretoria, couched in such terms as to render hostilities
inevitable. On the 12th the first shot was fired, and
England embarked on a campaign of far greater magni-
tude than any in which we had ever been engaged. Our
forces were all too weak to cope with the situation, and
they were widely scattered.

The Boers from the outset assumed the offensive, whilst
we, owing to our numerical inferiority, were compelled to
act strictly on the defensive until the arrival of reinforcements, which were already on the way from England.
Within a very few days of the outbreak of hostilities it
became apparent that we had, as usual, grievously under-
rated the strength of our opponents. Sir George White,
with the bulk of the troops in South Africa, was shut up
in Ladysmith, where he made a gallant defence. Colonel
Kekewich, with a half-battalion of the Loyal North Lancashire Regiment and some artillery, kept the flag flying
at Kimberley, the headquarters of the diamond-fields ;
whilst Colonel Baden-Powell, with irregular troops only,
earned a world-wide reputation for his brilliant defence
of Mafeking. Not content with enveloping our forces in
this way, the Boers carried on a series of daring raids into

[1] The Loyal North Lancashire Regiment alone bears the
Distinction " Defence of Kimberley." See Appendix 2.

Cape Colony. In this they were to a great extent assisted by the disloyal conduct of many of the Dutch Colonials, who were actively hostile to our cause.

In justice to the General Officers who were in command during the earlier and less successful stages of the war, a brief description of the military resources of the Empire is desirable. As Lord Salisbury, the Prime Minister, had stated in the House of Lords that no Indian troops would be employed, I may eliminate the magnificent fighting material that we possess in our Indian army. Approximately we had the following forces to draw on from our fellow-subjects beyond the seas, who at once let it be known that they looked on the quarrels of the Mother Country as their own, and that they were ready to place at the disposal of the War Office the manhood of their peoples. Our resources may be thus summarized :

Regular troops in the United Kingdom		..		108,000	
,,	,,	in India	..	..	68,000
,,	,,	in other garrisons	..	..	30,000
,,	,,	in South Africa	..	..	22,000
Army Reserve in the United Kingdom			..	83,000	
					311,000
Auxiliary forces in the United Kingdom		..		344,000	
,,	,,	in Canada	..	..	33,000
,,	,,	in Australia		..	29,000
,,	,,	in New Zealand	..	..	7,700
,,	,,	in Tasmania		..	2,000
					415,700
			Total	..	726,700

Of this grand total of upwards of 700,000 men it was clear that large numbers would never be available. India could only be denuded of a small portion of the British garrison, and of the auxiliary forces in the United Kingdom a very large proportion were by no means fit to take their places in the field ; yet before the war was brought to a close the troops actually sent to the front were not far short of 400,000 men. Of these were despatched :

From the United Kingdom and the Mediterranean		338,000
From India	.. ..	19,500
From our Dominions beyond the seas	.. ..	30,000

For transport purposes and to supply the wastage in our mounted troops 470,000 horses and 150,000 mules and donkeys were purchased ; for the conveyance of the troops and animals to the seat of war no fewer than 1,057 ships were taken up, and 1,374,000 tons of stores were from first to last shipped to South Africa. Unfortunately, all this energy was delayed until after the actual declaration of war. So far back as the month of June the Commander-in-Chief had unsuccessfully applied for permission to mobilize an army corps on Salisbury Plain and to convert the existing transport waggons to mule draught. It was not until October 8 that the order for the mobilization was sanctioned, and the first reinforcements did not leave the country until the third week in that month, war having been declared on the 11th.[1]

Our forces at the outset of hostilities were scattered necessarily over a wide area. The frontiers of the two Republics ran conterminously with our own for a distance of 1,000 miles. To defend this with 22,000 men was a manifest impossibility. Sir Forestier Walker, who was in command in Cape Colony, determined to hold the most important positions on that long line of frontier ; whilst Sir George White in Natal, against his better judgment, deferred to the views of the Governor of Natal, and divided his forces, thus paving the way to defeat.

In addition to Kimberley, Sir Forestier Walker had weak detachments guarding the principal railway junctions of De Aar, Nauwpoort, and Stormberg. White had a brigade, under Sir Penn Symons, at Dundee, in the North of Natal ; the remainder of his force was at Ladysmith. On October 20 the Dundee column fought an action at Talana, and the following day White's troops, under General French, defeated the Boers at Elandslaagte ; but the arrival of strong Boer reinforcements and the death of Penn Symons compelled the retreat of the Dundee brigade, and on the 30th White suffered a severe check at Lombard's Kop. It was now clear that the army in South Africa was powerless until the arrival of

[1] On the score of expense the Secretary of State for War had refused to propose a credit for the re-armament of our Field Artillery with modern quick-firing weapons, with the result that throughout the campaign our guns were completely outranged and outclassed.

reinforcements from home, and these, late in the day as it was, were being hurried forward as fast as circumstances would permit. The Viceroy of India had been requested to despatch with all haste a cavalry brigade, one of infantry, and three batteries of artillery. Some of these, as well as the battalion from the Mauritius, were already in South Africa, and battalions from Malta, Cyprus, and Egypt were *en route*. The army corps asked for in June was now despatched, with Sir Redvers Buller to hold the chief command in South Africa. It was composed as follows :

First Division : Lieutenant-General Lord Methuen.

Guards' Brigade—Brig.-Gen. Paget : 3rd Battalion Grenadiers, 1st Battalion Coldstream, 2nd Battalion Coldstream, 1st Battalion Scots Guards.

Second Brigade—Brig.-Gen. Hildyard : 2nd Battalion Queen's, 2nd Battalion Devons, 2nd Battalion West Yorks, 2nd Battalion East Surrey.

One squadron 1st Life Guards and three batteries Field Artillery.

Second Division : Lieutenant-General Clery.

Highland Brigade—Brig.-Gen. Wauchope : 2nd Battalion Royal Highlanders, 1st Battalion Highland Light Infantry, 2nd Battalion Seaforths, 1st Battalion Argylls.

Fourth Brigade—Major-Gen. Lyttelton : 2nd Battalion Scottish Rifles, 3rd Battalion King's Royal Rifles, 1st Battalion Durham Light Infantry, 1st Battalion Rifle Brigade.

One squadron Royal Horse Guards and three batteries Field Artillery.

Third Division : Lieutenant-General Gatacre.

Fifth Brigade—Brig.-Gen. Hart : 1st Battalion Inniskilling Fusiliers, 2nd Battalion Royal Irish Rifles, 1st Battalion Connaught Rangers, 1st Battalion Royal Dublin Fusiliers.

Sixth Brigade—Brig.-Gen. Barton : 2nd Battalion Royal Fusiliers, 2nd Battalion Royal Scots Fusiliers, 1st Battalion Royal Welsh Fusiliers, 2nd Battalion Royal Irish Fusiliers.

One squadron 2nd Life Guards and three batteries Field Artillery.

Cavalry Division : Lieutenant-General French.

First Brigade : Carabiniers, 10th Hussars, 12th Lancers, one battery Royal Horse Artillery.

Second Brigade : Royal Dragoons, Scots Greys, Inniskilling Dragoons, one battery Royal Horse Artillery.

Lines of Communication : 2nd Battalion Northumberland Fusiliers, 2nd Battalion Somerset Light Infantry, 2nd Battalion Cornwall Light Infantry, 1st Battalion Welsh Regiment, 2nd Battalion Northamptons, 2nd K.O. Yorkshire Light Infantry, 2nd Battalion Shropshire Light Infantry, 1st Battalion Gordons, Highland Light Infantry.

Until the arrival of these reinforcements we were holding on to our own frontiers with but 15,000 men in Natal, 10,000 in the Cape Colony, and some 1,500 in Rhodesia, inclusive of colonial forces. Opposed to us the Boers had at the least 53,000 men. Of these, it was estimated that 23,000 men were before White in Ladysmith, 7,500 had been despatched against Baden-Powell in Mafeking, a slightly larger force was enveloping Kekewich in Kimberley, and the remainder were being mobilized for the defence of the two Republics.

The original plan of campaign decided on before the departure of Sir Redvers Buller from England was to invade the Republics from the south with the army corps, the composition of which I have just given, whilst making such diversions as might be possible from Natal. On Buller's arrival all this had to be changed. The relief of Ladysmith was now the primary object of our Commander-in-Chief, all question of an invasion of the Republics being for the present out of the question. So soon as the reinforcements commenced to arrive, Methuen, with the Brigade of Guards, was pushed up to relieve Kimberley ; the Second, Fifth, and Sixth Brigades were at once directed to Natal, where Buller quickly followed. To replace the Second Brigade in the First Division a Ninth Brigade, made up from regiments intended for the line of communications, was formed, and Wauchope's brigade of the Second Division advanced to the support of Methuen, and to strengthen our hold on the line of railway. Generals French and Gatacre were entrusted with the command of the railway running parallel with the frontiers of the Republics, and were stationed respectively at Nauwpoort and Stormberg, whilst Wauchope was posted at De Aar.

Buller expressed himself optimistic as to the relief of Kimberley, which was closely invested by the Boers, and by the middle of November Methuen commenced his advance. His force consisted of the Brigade of Guards, the Ninth Brigade (1st Loyal North Lancashire, 2nd

King's Own Yorkshire Light Infantry, 1st Northumberland Fusiliers, and 2nd Northamptons), the 9th Lancers, three squadrons of mounted infantry, three field batteries, a naval brigade 360 strong, with four long 12-pounder quick-firers, and the New South Wales Lancers. On October 23 he defeated the Boers at Belmont, his casualties being 3 officers and 51 men killed, 23 officers and 220 men wounded. On the 25th he fought a second successful action at Enslin, losing 3 officers and 15 men killed, 6 officers and 137 men wounded ; and on October 28 he again defeated the Boers on the Riet River. The action, however, is officially known as that of the Modder River.

MODDER RIVER, NOVEMBER 28, 1899.

This battle honour is borne on the colours and appointments of the following regiments :

9th Lancers	Grenadier Guards.
Coldstream Guards.	Scots Guards.
Northumberland Fusiliers.	Northamptons.
K.O. Yorkshire L.I.	Highland Light Infantry.
Argyll and Sutherland Highlanders.	

It commemorates the third of the three successful actions fought by Lord Methuen in the early stage of the South African War in his attempt to relieve Kimberley. A clasp, inscribed " Modder River," was given for this engagement, in which the casualties were as follows :

CASUALTIES AT THE ACTION ON THE MODDER RIVER.

Corps or Regiments.	Officers.		Men.		Regiments.	Officers.		Men.	
	K.	W.	K.	W.		K.	W.	K.	W.
9th Lancers ..	—	—	—	1	N'umberland F.	—	—	11	34
Royal Artillery	—	4	3	22	Loyal N. Lancs	—	1	3	16
Naval Brigade	—	—	—	—	Northamptons	—	—	—	—
Grenadier Gds.	—	3	8	40	K.O. Yorks L.I.	1	3	8	46
Coldstream Gds.	2	1	10	77	Highland L.I.	—	—	—	—
Scots Guards	—	2	10	37	Argyll Highl.	—	2	15	95

The Boer forces covering the Siege of Kimberley were under the command of General Cronje, and he, falling back after his third reverse at the Modder River, took up a strong position at Magersfontein, entrenching his whole front for a distance of nine miles. To hasten the relief of Kimberley, Wauchope was now pushed up to reinforce Methuen, and on December 11 that General attacked Cronje, but met with a most serious reverse, losing 22 officers and 188 men killed, 46 officers and 629 men wounded, the bulk of the casualties falling on the Highland Brigade, which also lost its gallant leader, Wauchope, the second of his name to fall at the head of English troops in an unsuccessful action, for Andrew Wauchope's uncle fell at Rosetta in our little-remembered, but unfortunate, expedition to Egypt in 1807.

In the meantime Buller had proceeded to Durban, and was concerting his plans for the relief of Ladysmith. He had at his disposal 18,000 men and thirty field guns, besides a naval brigade with fourteen long-range quick-firers. On December 15 he made his first effort, and was badly defeated at Colenso, losing, in addition to 7 officers and 136 men killed, 47 officers and 709 men wounded, and ten guns. The superior mobility of the Boers, and the fact that White had with him four regiments of cavalry shut up in Ladysmith, induced Buller to make the most earnest representations for a large force of mounted reinforcements, and the War Office responded to the call by mobilizing three more divisions, and taking steps to raise a force of 4,000 Yeomanry.

These repeated disasters had aroused the nation—temporarily, at any rate—to a proper sense of its responsibilities, and all ranks and all classes responded to the call for volunteers. The veteran Field-Marshal Lord Roberts, who had served his apprenticeship at the Siege of Delhi just two-and-forty years before, accepted the chief command, and at once embarked for the seat of war. On his arrival the situation was no clearer. Methuen, with the First Division, lay immobile twelve miles south of Kimberley, with a Boer army strongly entrenched in his front ; Gatacre, at Stormberg, had met with a serious reverse ; Sir George White was closely besieged in Ladysmith ; and Buller was gathering together his forces for a second attempt to carry the strong position before him. Lord Roberts landed in South Africa on January 10, and his first care was to organize his transport, so as to have all in readiness for an advance so soon as the reinforcements now on the seas should arrive. As his Chief of the Staff he had Lord Kitchener, fresh from his successful campaign in Egypt, where he had shown himself a master in the matter of organization.

It was not until the commencement of February that the Field-Marshal felt himself able to move. His plan of campaign was first the relief of Kimberley with the Cavalry Division, under French, then an advance on the capital of the Orange Free State. This advance, he felt sure, would relieve the pressure in Natal, and so enable Buller to join hands with Ladysmith. Approximately, Lord Roberts had now in the Cape Colony 52,000 men, and in Natal 40,000, of whom some 9,000 or 10,000 were shut up in Ladysmith. Even now he felt that he would need heavy reinforcements to meet the wastage of war, and he requested that 8,000 Imperial Yeomanry and thirty battalions of Militia might be despatched to the seat of war as soon as they could be mobilized. Then, and not till then, did Lord Roberts feel justified in his advance. His transport was in an effective condition, and he had received assurance from home that the reinforcements asked for would be sent without delay. On February 6 he left Cape Town for the front, and on the 15th French set forth for the relief of Kimberley.

The troops actually at Lord Roberts's disposal at this period consisted of four divisions of infantry and one of cavalry. The composition of the Cavalry Division is given on p. 422 ; that of the four infantry divisions was as follows :

First Division : Lieutenant-General Lord Methuen.

Brigade of Guards—Major-General Paget : 3rd Battalion Grenadier Guards, 1st Battalion Coldstream Guards, 2nd Battalion Coldstream Guards, 1st Battalion Scots Guards.

Ninth Brigade—Brigadier-General Pole-Carew : 1st Battalion Northumberland Fusiliers, half a battalion of the North Lancashire, 2nd Battalion Northamptons, 2nd Battalion King's Own Yorkshire Light Infantry.

Sixth Division : Lieutenant-General Sir Kelly-Kenny.

Thirteenth Brigade—Major-Gener 1 C. E. Knox : 2nd Battalion Buffs, 2nd Battalion Gloucesters, 1st Battalion West Ridings, 1st Battalion Oxford Light Infantry.

Eighteenth Brigade—Brigadier-General T. E. Stephenson : 2nd Battalion Royal Warwicks, 1st Battalion Yorkshire Regiment, 1st Battalion Essex, 1st Battalion Wiltshires. Three field batteries and two naval 12-pounders.

Seventh Division : Lieutenant-General Sir Charles Tucker.

Fourteenth Brigade—Major-General Chermside : 2nd Battalion Norfolks, 2nd Battalion Lincolns, 1st Battalion King's Own Scottish Borderers, 2nd Battalion Hampshires.

Fifteenth Brigade—Brigadier-General Wavell : 2nd Battalion Cheshires, 1st Battalion East Lancashire, 2nd Battalion South Wales Borderers, 2nd Battalion North Staffords. Three field batteries.

Ninth Division : Lieutenant-General Sir H. Colville, K.C.B.

Highland Brigade—Brigadier-General MacDonald : 2nd Battalion Black Watch, 1st Battalion Highland Light Infantry, 2nd Battalion Seaforth Highlanders, 1st Battalion Argyll and Sutherland Highlanders.

Nineteenth Brigade—Brigadier-General Smith-Dorrien : 2nd Battalion Cornwall Light Infantry, 2nd Battalion Shropshire Light Infantry, 1st Battalion Gordon Highlanders, Royal Canadian Infantry. Three field batteries and one of 5-inch howitzer.

At Sterkstrom, General Gatacre had the remains of the Third Division, consisting of the 1st Royal Scots, 2nd Northumberland Fusiliers, 1st Derbyshire, 2nd Royal Berkshire, 2nd Royal Irish Rifles, and a Militia battalion—the 3rd Durham Light Infantry—with three field batteries and a couple of naval guns.

At Nauwpoort, General Clements had the 2nd Bedfords, 1st Royal Irish, 2nd Worcester, 2nd Wiltshire, a Militia battalion—the 4th Derbyshire—with one horse and three field batteries.

The Second Division was with Sir George White in Ladysmith, and comprised a cavalry brigade, consisting of the 5th Dragoon Guards, 5th Lancers, 18th and 19th Hussars.

Seventh Brigade—Brigadier-General Ian Hamilton : 1st Battalion Manchesters, 2nd Battalion Gordons, 1st Battalion Royal Irish Fusiliers : and 2nd Battalion Rifle Brigade.

Eighth Brigade—Brigadier-General F. Howard : 1st Leicesters, 2nd Battalion King's Royal Rifles, 1st Battalion King's Liverpools, and a company of the Rifle Brigade.

White also had the following divisional troops, brigaded under Brigadier-General Knox : 1st Devons, 1st Gloucesters, and 1st King's Royal Rifles. There were also six field, one mountain battery, two 6-inch howitzers, and a naval brigade of 280 men, with five long-range quick-firing guns.

Sir Redvers Buller at the time of Lord Roberts's arrival had upwards of 30,000 men, thus detailed :

Second Division : General Lyttelton.

Second Brigade—Brigadier-General Hildyard : 2nd Battalion Queen's, 2nd Battalion Devons, 2nd Battalion West Yorks, and 2nd Battalion East Surrey.

Fourth Brigade — Brigadier - General Norcott : 2nd Battalion Scottish Rifles, 3rd Battalion King's Royal Rifles, 1st Battalion Durham Light Infantry, and 1st Battalion Rifle Brigade, with three field batteries.

Fifth Division : Sir Charles Warren.

Tenth Brigade — Major-General Coke : 2nd Battalion Somerset Light Infantry, 2nd Battalion Dorset, 2nd Battalion Middlesex.

Eleventh Brigade — Brigadier-General A. S. Wynne : 1st Battalion King's Own, 1st Battalion East Lancashire, and the Rifle reserve battalion, with three batteries of field artillery.

Third Division : Clery.

Fifth Brigade—Major-General Hart : 1st Battalion Inniskilling Fusiliers, 1st Battalion Border Regiment, 1st Battalion Connaught Rangers, 2nd Battalion Royal Dublin Fusiliers.

Sixth Brigade—Major-General Barton : 2nd Battalion Royal Fusiliers, 2nd Battalion Royal Scots Fusiliers, 1st Battalion Royal Welsh Fusiliers, and 2nd Battalion Royal Irish Fusiliers, with three field batteries.

Buller's cavalry consisted of the Royal Dragoons, 13th Hussars, and a large number of colonial troops, who were of the most effective service. He also had a naval brigade of 400 men, with a number of 4·7 and 12-pounder long-range guns.

Such was the position of the army commanded by Lord Roberts when, on February 12, General French was sent forward with the Cavalry Division (Kelly-Kenny, with the Sixth Division, following in support) for the relief of Kimberley.

RELIEF OF KIMBERLEY, FEBRUARY 15, 1900.

This battle honour has been conferred on the following regiments :

1st Life Guards.	2nd Life Guards.
Royal Horse Guards.	Carabiniers.
Scots Greys.	9th Lancers.
10th Hussars.	12th Lancers.
16th Lancers.	Buffs.
Yorkshire.	Gloucesters.
West Riding.	Welsh.
Oxford Light Infantry.	Essex.

There were many reasons why the Boers should have made great endeavours to seize this town. Cecil Rhodes, their arch-enemy, was shut up in the place, and the garrison was certainly none too large for the task confided to its commander. Lord Methuen had been checked by two serious reverses in his advance on Kimberley, and his division now lay a few miles to the south of the town, with the Boer army under Cronje facing him. Lord Roberts pushed up the Sixth Division, under General Kelly-Kenny, to Randam, hard by the Modder River. The Sixth was followed by the Seventh Division, under General Tucker ; and the Seventh by the Ninth, under Sir Henry Colville. The Cavalry Division, under Lieutenant-General French, was also moved westwards towards the line of railway leading up from the Cape to Kimberley. With this division Lord Roberts intended to effect the relief of the Diamond City.

French's division was composed of three brigades of cavalry, with a strong force of mounted infantry, and was brigaded as follows :

First Brigade—Brigadier-General Porter : The Scots Greys, the Carabiniers, one squadron each of the Inniskillings, 14th Hussars, and New South Wales Horse, and three batteries of Royal Horse Artillery.

Second Brigade—Brigadier-General Broadwood : Composite regiment of Household Cavalry, 10th Hussars, 12th Lancers, and three batteries of Royal Horse Artillery.

Third Brigade—Brigadier-General Gordon : 9th and 16th Lancers, with two batteries of Royal Horse Artillery.

Mounted Infantry Division—Colonel Alderson : Three battalions of mounted infantry, Roberts's Horse, Kitchener's Horse, the Queensland and New Zealand Mounted Infantry.

In the very early morning of February 12 French left
the line of railway, and, bearing to the eastward, crossed the
Riet River between Cronje's camp and the capital. He was
followed by the Sixth (Kelly-Kenny's) Division. Sweeping round through Watervaal and Klip's Drift, French
found the Boers astride his road. They were not in great
strength, and he made no attempt to bandy words with
them. The road to his objective lay between two hills,
on which the enemy were posted, and French, mindful of
the urgency of his mission, determined to ignore the
enemy, and, putting his men at the gallop, he forced his
way past the Boers with astonishingly little loss. His
way was now clear, and, pushing ahead as fast as the condition of his horses would allow, he swept round to the
north of the town, and at 6 p.m. had effected the task
before him. Leaving Colonel Porter in command, French
now retraced his steps, in order to take a part in the im-
pending attack on the position held by General Cronje
near Paardeburg.

CASUALTIES DURING FRENCH'S RELIEF OF KIMBERLEY.

Regiments.	Officers.		Men.		Regiments.	Officers.		Men.	
	K.	W.	K.	W.		K.	W.	K.	W.
Scots Greys ..	1	2	3	6	12th Lancers	—	—	—	1
Inniskillings ..	—	1	—	2	14th Hussars	—	—	—	1
9th Lancers ..	—	3	1	17	16th Lancers	1	1	3	18
10th Hussars	—	—	—	1	R.H. Artillery	1	3	—	24
Buffs ..	—	1	—	4	West Riding ..	—	—	—	19
Yorkshires ..	—	—	—	—	Hampshires ..	—	—	1	1
Gloucesters ..	—	1	2	8	Oxford L.I. ..	—	1	11	38
Cornwall L.I.	—	—	—	3	Roberts's Horse	—	1	—	5

PAARDEBURG, FEBRUARY 18 TO 27, 1900.

This battle honour was conferred on the following
regiments for the operation which resulted in the sur-

render of the Boer Commander-in-Chief in the war in the
Transvaal :

1st Life Guards.	2nd Life Guards.	Royal Horse Guards.
Carabiniers.	Scots Greys.	9th Lancers.
10th Hussars.	12th Lancers.	16th Lancers.
Buffs.	Norfolks.	Lincolns.
Yorkshires.	K.O. Scot. Borderers.	Gloucesters.
Cornwall L.I.	West Riding.	Hampshires.
Welsh.	Black Watch.	Oxford L.I.
Essex.	Shropshire L.I.	Seaforth Highlanders.
Gordon Highlanders.	Argyll and Sutherland Highlanders.	

By the brilliant relief of Kimberley Lord Roberts had
scored the first real success of the campaign, and had
opened the way for an advance on the capital of the Boer
Republics. General Cronje realized this, and, breaking
up his camp on the Modder River, commenced a hurried
retreat towards Bloemfontein. But Lord Roberts was
already practically athwart his path. French, returning
from Kimberley, threw himself across the head of Cronje's
army, and General Kelly-Kenny, with the Sixth Division,
clung to his rear. The Seventh and Ninth Divisions were
now closing up, and Lord Roberts was free to assault the
strong position which Cronje had taken up at Paardeburg.

Despite the large force at the disposal of the Commander-in-Chief, the operation was none too simple.
Cronje had with him a large number of women and
children, and, from motives of humanity, Lord Roberts
was averse to resorting to the usual methods of war.
Our first attack on the Boer position at Paardeburg was
met in the most gallant manner, our losses being very
heavy. Little by little we neared the Boer defences, our
troops actually sapping up to the cleverly-devised works ;
but it was not until February 27 that General Cronje
decided to surrender.

The road was now open for an advance on Bloemfontein,
the capital of the Orange Free State, and as soon as Lord
Roberts had filled up his convoys with provisions he
recommenced his forward march, and on March 12 the
Field-Marshal hoisted the British flag in Bloemfontein.

THE COLOURS OF THE QUEEN'S ROYAL WEST SURREY REGIMENT, 1902.

(Formerly the Tangier Regiment.)

CASUALTIES DURING THE OPERATIONS AT PAARDEBURG,
FEBRUARY 18 TO 27, 1900.

Regiments.	Officers.		Men.		Regiments.	Officers.		Men.	
	K.	W.	K.	W.		K.	W.	K.	W.
1st Life Guards	—	—	—	—	K.O. Scottish Borderers ..	—	1	—	15
2nd Life Guards	—	—	—	5	Gloucesters ..	—	1	5	19
Roy. H. Guards	—	—	—	4	Cornwall Light				
Carabiniers ..	—	—	—	1	Infantry ..	3	4	25	56
Scots Greys ..	—	—	—	2	West Ridings	1	2	22	104
9th Lancers ..	—	1	—	5	Hampshire ..	—	—	1	4
10th Hussars	—	—	2	10	Welsh ..	1	5	18	63
12th Lancers	—	—	—	1	Black Watch	1	3	19	79
16th Lancers	—	—	—	1	Oxford L.I. ..	3	4	6	30
Royal Artillery	—	—	3	21	Essex ..	—	3	15	47
Roy. Canadian	1	3	34	90	K.O. Shrop. L.I.	—	4	8	35
Buffs	1	1	2	7	Seaforth Highl.	2	6	45	103
Norfolks ..	1	1	—	—	Gordon Highl.	—	2	3	15
Lincolns ..	—	2	2	18	Argyll Highl.	1	6	19	66
Yorkshire ..	1	7	49	103					

RELIEF OF LADYSMITH.[1]

I have already alluded to the reverse that Buller met
with at Colenso on December 15. On January 24 a
second attempt by Sir Redvers Buller met with no better
success, our losses amounting to 1,700 killed and wounded.
The advance of Lord Roberts to the eastward had the
effect that the experienced Field-Marshal anticipated.
The pressure in Natal was lessened, and on the day that
Cronje surrendered to Lord Roberts Buller's mounted
brigade entered Ladysmith, after a series of well-fought
actions, in which, if our men upheld the traditions of the
British army, the Boers showed themselves gallant foemen.

[1] The regiments which have been authorized to bear this battle
honour are—The Royal Dragoons. 13th Hussars. 14th Hussars.
The Queens. The King's Own. Royal Fusiliers. Devons.
Somerset Light Infantry. West Yorkshire. Lancashire Fusiliers.
Royal Scots Fusiliers. Royal Welsh Fusiliers. Scottish Rifles.
Inniskilling Fusiliers. East Surrey. Border. Dorsets. South
Lancashire. Middlesex. King's Royal Rifles. York and
Lancaster. Durham Light Infantry. Royal Irish Fusiliers.
Connaught Rangers. Royal Dublin Fusiliers. Rifle Brigade.

CASUALTIES AT THE RELIEF OF LADYSMITH.

Regiments.	Officers.		Men.		Regiments.	Officers.		Men.	
	K.	W.	K.	W.		K.	W.	K.	W.
Royal Dragoons	—	—	2	6	Scottish Rifles	6	10	49	102
13th Hussars	—	—	—	—	Royal Inniskil-				
Royal Artillery	3	10	18	98	ling Fusiliers	5	14	98	248
Roy. Engineers	—	—	—	—	East Surrey ..	1	6	27	176
Queen's West					Border ..	1	6	14	20
Surrey ..	3	10	30	245	Dorsets ..	—	1	3	27
K.O. Lancs ..	3	4	107	225	South Lancs ..	2	4	26	121
Royal Fusiliers	—	—	5	69	Middlesex ..	—	—	20	71
King's Liverpl.	—	—	—	—	K. Roy. Rifles	3	9	47	143
Devons ..	—	7	16	189	York and Lanc.	—	4	13	137
Somerset L.I.	3	1	16	63	Durham L.I.	2	6	20	118
West Yorkshire	2	5	27	173	Roy. Irish Fus.	—	—	14	88
Lancashire Fus.	6	12	85	247	Connaught R.	—	7	56	177
Royal Welsh					R. Dublin Fus.	5	12	89	348
Fusiliers ..	2	2	10	54	Rifle Brigade	—	12	30	151

THE DEFENCE OF LADYSMITH,[1] OCTOBER 29, 1899, TO FEBRUARY 27, 1900.

The actual siege of Ladysmith commenced when Sir George White met with the reverse at Lombards' Kop on October 30, and lasted for four months. With the large force at his disposal there was but small chance of the place being carried by assault, but there was always the possibility of its being compelled to surrender by famine. Fortunately, in White we had a commander whose reputation for personal bravery was proverbial, and he had with him senior officers whose names were almost as well known for their gallantry. In his garrison were seasoned regiments of old soldiers who had but recently arrived from India. The Boers had experienced the metal of White's men at Talana and at Elandslaagte, and cared little to come again to close quarters with them.

[1] The following regiments bear this distinction : 5th Dragoon Guards. 5th Lancers. 18th Hussars. 19th Hussars. King's Liverpool. Devons. Leicester. Gloucester. King's Royal Rifles. Manchester. Gordon Highlanders. Rifle Brigade.

During that long siege of four months the Boers made but one attempt to attack the place. This action, known as Cæsar's Camp (January 6), was one of the hardest-fought actions of the war, our losses amounting to 18 officers and 158 men killed, 29 officers and 221 men wounded, whereas the total casualties for the rest of the siege only reached the total of 6 officers and 62 men killed, 33 officers and 262 men wounded. The losses by sickness were not unusually heavy. That they were not heavier was due to the cheerful face put on the situation by the brave commander and the self-devotion of the officers of the Royal Army Medical Corps, who, as ever, showed themselves as careless of their own lives as they were tenderly careful of those of the men committed to their charge.[1]

CASUALTIES AT THE DEFENCE OF LADYSMITH.

Regiments.	Officers.		Men.		Regiments.	Officers.		Men.	
	K.	W.	K.	W.		K.	W.	K.	W.
5th Dragoon Guards	—	4	1	9	Devons	3	4	25	50
5th Lancers	1	7	2	14	Leicesters	2	1	5	26
18th Hussars	—	1	9	19	Gloucesters	—	—	8	9
19th Hussars	—	—	6	16	K. Roy. Rifles	3	—	42	58
Royal Artillery	—	—	—	—	Manchesters	1	10	49	90
Roy. Engineers	2	1	7	7	Gordon Highl.	2	3	16	25
					Rifle Brigade	2	9	32	43

With the surrender of Cronje's army, the relief of Ladysmith, and the entry of our army into Bloemfontein, it was hoped that the back of the enemy was broken. The war, however, dragged on for close on two years, the principal incidents being the relief of Mafeking by Brigadier-General Mahon on May 15, the occupation of Johannesburg by Lord Roberts on the 31st of the same month, and the entry into Pretoria, the capital of the Transvaal, on June 5. The Boers showed marvellous powers of

[1] The strength of the garrison on November 2, 1899, was 13,496 of all ranks, the deaths up to the date of the Relief being exactly 600. Of these, 59 died from wounds and 541 from disease.

recuperation, and many hard actions were fought ere they were subdued. In the month of October the aged President Kruger deserted his fellow-countrymen, and embarked for Europe, and on the 25th of that month Lord Roberts formally proclaimed the annexation of the two Republics to the Empire, and in the following month Lord Roberts handed over the command to General Lord Kitchener. Then we entered on a long period of guerilla warfare, for which our troops were little prepared. More reinforcements were called for, and by the close of the year 30,000 men were sent out to South Africa. It was not until the month of March, 1902, that the Boer commanders consented to treat, although the hopelessness of the struggle must have been long apparent to the meanest understanding, and on May 31, 1902, the conditions of surrender were signed. Never was an enemy treated with more consideration.

The war in the Transvaal was noteworthy in many ways. It is true that in the campaign in Egypt a small body of Canadian Voyageurs had volunteered for service up the Nile, and that the Government of New South Wales had despatched a contingent to our assistance at Suakin in 1885 ; but during the war in South Africa contingents were despatched from all our dominions beyond the seas. Canada, Australia, India, New Zealand, and Tasmania all had their forces in the field ; whilst in the regiments of Yeomanry were to be found men drawn from all ranks of society and from all parts of our Empire —from the islands of the West Indies to Hong-Kong. Then, again, it was the first occasion in which men from our Volunteer corps had been permitted to strengthen the ranks of their line battalions, and the first in which the Yeomanry and Militia had been pushed forward into the fighting-line. There were two great lessons taught by the war—the one that our military organization was not adapted to modern warfare, and the second that the Mother Country could count on the warm-hearted support of her children beyond the seas.

DECORATIONS FOR THE WAR IN SOUTH AFRICA, 1899-1902.

Regiments.	V.C.	C.B.	C.M.G.	D.S.O.	D.C.M.[1]	Regiments.	V.C.	C.B.	C.M.G.	D.S.O.	D.C.M.[1]
1st Life Guards	—	1	—	3	3	West Yorks ..	2	1	—	8	15
2nd Life Guards	—	1	—	4	2	East Yorks ..	—	1	—	5	10
Roy. H. Guards	—	1	—	4	2	Bedfords ..	—	—	—	6	9
K. Drag. Guards	—	1	—	2	1	Leicesters ..	—	—	1	3	8
Queen's Bays ..	—	—	—	—	1	Royal Irish ..	—	1	—	6	12
3rd Drag. Gds.	—	—	—	3	1	Yorkshire ..	1	1	—	5	17
5th Drag. Gds.	1	2	—	2	6	Lancs Fusiliers	—	—	—	8	21
Carabiniers ..	—	2	—	5	6	Roy. Scots Fus.	1	2	1	3	10
7th Drag. Gds.	—	—	—	3	5	Cheshires ..	—	2	—	2	11
Royal Dragoons	—	2	—	2	6	Roy. Welsh Fus.	—	1	—	8	17
Scots Greys ..	—	—	—	4	5	S. Wales Bord.	1	1	—	4	11
3rd Hussars ..	—	—	—	1	1	K.O. Scot. Bord.	1	1	—	7	13
5th Lancers ..	1	—	—	3	5	Scottish Rifles	—	—	—	3	15
Inniskill. Drag.	—	1	—	2	7	Inniskilling Fus.	—	—	—	5	13
7th Hussars ..	—	3	—	6	1	Gloucesters ..	—	1	—	5	12
8th Hussars ..	—	3	—	1	4	Worcester ..	—	2	—	10	21
9th Lancers ..	—	1	—	6	10	E. Lancashire	—	1	—	8	10
10th Hussars ..	2	1	—	2	5	East Surrey ..	1	1	—	9	12
11th Hussars ..	—	—	—	—	—	Cornwall L.I.	1	—	—	3	11
12th Lancers ..	—	2	—	6	6	West Ridings	1	1	—	5	13
13th Hussars ..	—	1	—	4	5	Border ..	—	1	—	6	10
14th Hussars ..	1	—	—	2	5	Royal Sussex ..	—	1	—	6	15
16th Lancers ..	—	—	—	4	6	Hampshire ..	—	1	—	3	11
17th Lancers ..	—	—	—	3	3	South Staffords	—	1	1	4	8
18th Hussars ..	1	1	—	6	10	Dorsets ..	—	1	—	5	14
19th Hussars ..	—	1	—	3	8	S. Lancashire	—	1	—	5	6
Royal Artillery	9	27	11	95	261	Welsh ..	—	2	—	6	12
Roy. Engineers	1	8	5	35	76	Roy. Highl. ..	—	2	—	8	13
Grenadier Gds.	—	4	—	9	16	Oxford L.I. ..	—	1	—	7	13
Coldstream Gds.	—	4	—	13	19	Essex ..	1	3	—	8	13
Scots Guards ..	—	2	—	7	19	Derbyshire ..	2	2	—	6	20
Royal Scots ..	—	—	—	10	16	Loy. N. Lancs	—	2	1	8	15
Queen's ..	—	1	1	10	17	Northamptons	—	1	—	5	8
Buffs	—	2	—	10	16	Royal Berkshire	1	1	—	7	14
King's Own ..	—	1	—	10	16	Royal W. Kent	—	3	—	2	9
N'umberland F.	—	2	—	8	31	K.O. Yorks L.I.	1	1	—	5	15
Royal Warwicks	—	—	—	6	13	Shropshire L.I.	—	1	—	7	8
Royal Fusiliers	1	1	—	6	13	Middlesex ..	—	2	—	6	10
K. Liverpool ..	2	1	1	5	11	K. Royal Rifles	2	2	1	21	38
Norfolks ..	—	1	—	10	16	Wiltshire ..	—	1	—	3	9
Lincolns ..	—	1	—	2	15	Manchesters ..	2	1	—	14	23
Devons ..	1	2	—	11	32	N. Staffords ..	—	—	—	5	8
Suffolks ..	—	1	—	5	12	York and Lanc.	—	2	—	3	8
Somerset L.I.	—	1	—	3	11	Durham L.I. ..	—	3	—	9	16

[1] D.C.M., medal for distinguished conduct in the field.

DECORATIONS FOR THE WAR IN SOUTH AFRICA—*Continued*.

Regiments.	V.C.	C.B.	C.M.G.	D.S.O.	D.C.M.[1]	Regiments.	V.C.	C.B.	C.M.G.	D.S.O.	D.C.M.[1]
Highland L.I.	1	1	—	5	9	Connaught R.	—	2	—	4	12
Seaforth Highl.	—	2	—	3	14	Leinster	—	1	—	3	6
Gordon Highl.	6	3	1	10	32	R. Munster Fus.	—	2	—	5	14
Cameron Highl.	1	2	—	5	13	Roy. Dublin F.	—	2	—	10	18
Roy. Irish Rifles	—	1	—	4	15	Rifle Brigade ..	2	2	1	14	35
Roy. Irish Fus.	—	1	—	4	9	Army Med. C.	5	12	27	27	38
Argyll Highl.	—	2	1	5	10	Army Service C.	—	7	—	9	3

MILITIA BATTALIONS.

Regiments.	V.C.	C.B.	C.M.G.	D.S.O.	D.C.M.[1]	Regiments.	V.C.	C.B.	C.M.G.	D.S.O.	D.C.M.[1]
Royal Scots ..	—	1	—	2	3	Royal Sussex	—	1	—	—	1
Queen's W. Sur.	—	—	1	2	3	South Staffords	—	—	—	1	4
East Kent ..	—	1	—	1	3	South Lancs ..	—	—	—	2	2
K.O. R. Lancs	—	—	1	4	7	Welsh	—	1	—	2	3
Roy. Warwicks	—	1	—	1	3	Oxford L.I. ..	—	—	—	1	—
Norfolk ..	—	1	1	1	3	Derbyshire ..	—	—	—	2	2
Devon ..	—	—	1	—	—	Loy. N. Lancs	—	—	—	1	1
Somerset L.I.	—	—	1	—	3	Middlesex ..	—	—	1	2	3
West York ..	—	—	—	2	3	K. Roy. Rifles	—	—	1	1	2
Bedford ..	—	1	—	3	3	Manchester ..	—	—	—	—	1
Leicesters ..	—	—	—	1	—	North Stafford	—	—	1	1	2
Yorkshire ..	—	—	1	1	3	Durham L.I.	—	—	1	1	2
Lancashire F.	—	1	1	2	2	Roy. Irish R.	—	1	—	1	1
Cheshire ..	—	—	—	3	3	Argyll and					
S. Wales Bord.	—	—	1	1	3	Sutherland H.	—	1	—	1	2
Scottish Bord.	—	—	1	2	3	Leinster ..	—	—	—	2	3
Scottish Rifles	—	1	—	2	3	R. Munster Fus.	—	—	1	—	2
Worcesters ..	—	—	—	—	1	Roy. Dublin F.	—	—	—	2	3
East Lancs ..	—	—	1	1	3	Antrim Artill.	—	—	1	—	1
East Surrey ..	—	—	1	—	—	Donegal Artill.	—	—	—	—	1
West Riding	—	1	—	1	3	Londonderry A.	—	—	—	—	1
City Imp. Vol.	—	2	1	5	17	Imperial Yeom.	1	10	1	96	113
Engineer Vol.	—	1	—	—	4	Elswick Art. V.	—	—	—	2	1
Lovat's Scouts	—	1	—	2	4	Scottish Horse	1	1	—	3	6

CONTINGENTS FROM OUR DOMINIONS BEYOND THE SEAS.

Regiments.	V.C.	C.B.	C.M.G.	D.S.O.	D.C.M.[1]	Regiments.	V.C.	C.B.	C.M.G.	D.S.O.	D.C.M.[1]
Canadian troops	4	5	6	19	18	Tasmania ..	2	3	—	4	4
New South						Victoria ..	1	2	2	7	6
Wales ..	—	7	1	23	15	West Australia	1	2	—	6	8
New Zealand ..	1	5	2	10	11	South Africa ..	10	12	34	125	191
Queensland ..	—	6	1	8	11	Lumsden's Horse					
South Australia	—	3	1	9	10	(India) ..	—	1	1	2	6

[1] D.C.M., medal for distinguished conduct in the field.

TOTAL CASUALTIES DURING THE WAR IN SOUTH AFRICA, 1899-1902.

Regiments.	Officers.		Men.		Regiments.	Officers.		Men.	
	K.	W.	K.	W.		K.	W.	K.	W.
1st Life Guards	—	—	2	9	3rd Roy. Warw.	—	2	10	25
2nd Life Guards	I	I	3	14	2nd Roy. Fus.	4	4	17	92
Roy. H. Guards	2	I	19	15	1st K. L'pools	I	2	50	190
1st K.D. Gds.	4	8	9	30	2nd Norfolks	4	5	11	39
Queen's Bays	3	5	23	51	2nd Lincolns	I	8	34	68
3rd Drag. Gds.	I	2	5	15	1st Devons ..	5	10	36	92
5th Drag. Gds.	—	5	9	27	2nd Devons ..	—	9	36	203
Carabiniers ..	5	4	25	57	1st Suffolks ..	6	7	36	103
7th Drag. Gds.	3	8	21	57	2nd Somer. L.I.	8	4	21	78
1st Roy. Drag.	2	2	10	27	2nd W. Yorks	5	15	74	251
Scots Greys ..	6	6	34	103	2nd E. Yorks	2	3	9	55
3rd Hussars ..	I	—	4	10	2nd Bedfords	5	4	20	65
5th Lancers ..	I	9	19	74	1st Leicesters	2	4	15	71
Inniskillings ..	5	12	37	79	1st Royal Irish	5	8	39	87
7th Hussars ..	—	3	2	3	1st Yorkshire	I	10	73	132
8th Hussars ..	3	8	13	42	2nd Lancs Fus.	6	17	110	266
9th Lancers ..	5	15	40	130	2nd R. Scots F.	5	12	54	145
10th Hussars	4	8	61	57	2nd Cheshires	I	I	5	53
12th Lancers	3	8	25	79	1st R. Welsh F.	5	17	67	187
13th Hussars	—	4	17	45	2nd S. Wales B.	2	4	32	94
14th Hussars	I	I	23	30	1st K.O.S.B. ...	7	5	45	90
16th Lancers	7	12	29	95	27th Innis. Fus.	10	17	119	261
17th Lancers	7	9	58	100	28th Gloucesters	I	9	65	107
18th Hussars	3	10	37	85	29th Worcesters	—	4	12	33
19th Hussars	I	2	25	70	30th E. Lancs	I	I	19	39
20th Hussars	I	I	I	2	33rd W. Ridings	3	13	55	188
Royal Artillery	30	96	178	807	34th Border ..	2	9	27	199
Roy. Engineers	4	16	27	65	35th R. Sussex	2	7	31	94
2nd Gren. Gds.	2	7	40	132	36th Worcesters	4	4	38	88
3rd Gren. Gds.	5	11	53	183	38th S. Staffords	4	4	16	56
1st Coldst. Gds.	—	8	27	99	40th S. Lancs	4	4	45	130
2nd Coldst. Gds.	5	5	29	108	41st Welsh ..	5	12	67	187
1st Scots Gds.	—	6	33	75	42nd B. Watch	—	—	5	2
2nd Scots Gds.	I	5	15	55	43rd Oxf. L.I.	3	8	29	96
1st Royal Scots	2	4	17	32	44th Essex ..	2	7	51	170
2nd Queen's ..	4	12	38	294	45th Derbys ..	2	13	57	137
2nd Buffs ..	4	11	61	184	46th Corn. L.I.	4	6	32	49
2nd King's Own	13	12	128	249	47th Loyal N. Lancashire	4	8	27	107
1st N'umberland Fusiliers	9	15	85	189	51st K.O.Y.L.I.	I	5	—	4
2nd N'umberland Fusiliers	3	6	37	103	54th Dorsets ..	—	3	24	92
					56th Essex ..	—	4	3	15
2nd Roy. Warw.	I	5	11	44	58th N'amptons	—	6	8	32

Casualties in the South African War—*Continued.*

Regiments.	Officers. K.	Officers. W.	Men. K.	Men. W.	Regiments.	Officers. K.	Officers. W.	Men. K.	Men. W.
1st K.R.R.	11	11	72	234	97th Royal W. Kent	2	1	18	46
2nd K.R.R.	4	4	29	78	98th N. Staf.	1	1	9	1
3rd K.R.R.	6	14	61	216	99th Wiltsh.	2	6	33	79
4th K.R.R.	3	8	9	39	100th Roy. Canadns.	1	2	9	39
61st Glouc.	1	4	27	91	101st Royal Munsters	5	3	19	74
63rd Manch.	5	16	75	145	102nd Royal Dublins	2	5	78	124
65th York & Lancaster	1	5	30	162	103rd Royal Dublins	5	19	63	281
66th R. Brk.	1	5	23	93	104th Roy. Munsters	—	—	2	2
67th Hamp.	3	4	50	60	105th K.O. York. L.I.	6	11	56	151
68th Durh. L.I.	4	8	38	147	108th Inniskilling F.	1	—	3	5
70th E. Sur.	1	10	50	206	109th Leins.	—	1	—	9
71st H.L.I.	4	9	30	161	Rifle Brig. (1st Batt.)	6	16	48	291
73rd Royal Highl.	12	17	119	347	Rifle Brig. (2nd Bat.)	8	14	75	165
75th Gordon Highl.	8	16	50	181	Rifle Brig. (4th Bat.)	—	2	5	30
77th Middl.	5	6	47	76	R.A.M.C.	7	23	—	—
78th Ross. B.	10	23	122	276	C.I.V.'s	1	1	10	51
79th Camer. Highl.	4	8	22	65	Imp. Yeom.	67	131	470	1,236
85th Shrop. L.I.	—	12	44	105	Militia	15	34	160	368
86th Royal Irish R.	3	11	31	106	Volunteers	2	12	29	117
87th Royal Irish Fus.	2	11	40	96	Gen. Staff	11	30	—	—
88th Con. R.	—	16	58	242	Australian contingts.	29	77	222	658
89th Royal Irish Fus.	4	9	36	148	Canadian contingts.	7	23	87	255
90th Scottish Rifles	10	10	56	134	New Zealand cont.	7	26	78	176
91st Argyll Highl.	4	14	85	208	S. African contingt.	119	328	1,354	3,005
92nd Gords.	9	14	65	173					
94th Con. R.	—	16	58	252					
95th Derby	1	3	12	33					
96th Manch.	2	4	7	19					

Total casualties, including all departmental corps, killed, died of wounds, or wounded in action, irrespective of those who died from disease : Officers, 701 killed, 1,668 wounded ; men, 7,091 killed, 19,143 wounded.

CHAPTER XXVII

MISSING BATTLE HONOURS

Sir A. Alison's Committee—General Ewart's Committee—Marlborough's forgotten victories—Wellington's minor successes —Losses at Douai—Peninsula, 1705—Gibraltar, 1727— Peninsula, 1762—Belleisle—Dominica—Manilla—Cape of Good Hope, 1795—Indian honours—Pondicherry—Tanjore —Madras troops—An unrewarded Bombay column—The Indian Mutiny—Punjab frontier force—Umbeyla—Naval honours.

UNTIL some thirty years ago, the names inscribed on the colours and appointments of our regiments were mainly in recognition of services between the years 1793 and 1815, or for campaigns in India. It so happened that many regiments which had done good service in the wars of the Austrian or Spanish Succession were debarred from sharing in the honours so generously distributed for the Peninsular campaign, owing to the fact that they were at the time employed in garrisoning our distant dependencies, or in holding threatened points in other quarters of the globe. Several regiments had no names on their colours, although they had borne their share in the important victories won by Marlborough, or had fought in the no less arduous wars later in the eighteenth century. It was felt that such names as Blenheim and Malplaquet were as deserving of recognition as, let me say, Bushire or Surinam. In the year 1881 a Committee, under the presidency of the late General Sir Archibald Alison, was appointed to consider the subject, and, after much deliberation, came to the conclusion that " the names of such victories only should be retained as either in themselves or by their results have left a mark in history which render their names familiar, not only to the British army, but also to every educated gentleman."

The result of Sir Archibald Alison's Committee was that four of Marlborough's victories were added to the battle honours of the army—Blenheim, Oudenarde, Ramillies, and Malplaquet. What led to the selection of two out of these four names will ever remain a mystery. At Oudenarde the twenty-two regiments present lost but 168 officers and men killed and wounded. At Ramillies the casualties were only slightly heavier. On the other hand, during the same campaign we had lost far more heavily at Ath, Douai, Liége, Lille, Maestricht, Menin, and Namur. Until the present year (1910), the 18th (Royal Irish) was the only regiment which bore any reference to Namur on its colours, and the other names are still lacking.

Within the last few months another Committee, under the able presidency of the Adjutant-General, has been adjudicating on the same subject. To this Committee the regiments of the army owe a deep debt of gratitude. Its labours are confessedly incomplete. It has rescued from oblivion some long-forgotten campaigns in the West Indies ; it has given due credit to the regiments which participated in the costly capture of Namur by William III. ; it has to a certain extent satisfied the *amour propre* of our cavalry regiments by adding to their appointments three somewhat unimportant actions, and has placed on the colours of a few distinguished corps the names of battles in Flanders and the Peninsula to which they were justly entitled. The task of such a Committee is by no means a light one. The haphazard way in which battle honours have hitherto been granted, and the difficulties of obtaining accurate records of many of the earlier campaigns, have added not a little to its labours. It would appear that the Committee has been guided by two main principles in the selection of fresh battle honours—the one that no distinction should be

granted unless the headquarters of the regiment had been
present in the engagement, and that honours should only
be conferred on regiments with a continuous history from
the date of the action, a break in the direct genealogical
succession invalidating the claim.

These decisions rule out many regiments otherwise
eligible, and hitherto they have never been enforced.
Indeed, in one case, at any rate, General Ewart's Committee has evaded its own ruling. " Gibraltar, 1704-05,"
has been awarded to both the Grenadier and to the
Coldstream Guards; yet it was a composite battalion,
only 600 strong, made up from the two regiments, which
was sent from Lisbon to assist Prince George of Hesse
in the defence of the Rock. In earlier days battle honours
were not seldom bestowed on regiments which had been
represented in actions by single troops or companies.
A troop of the 11th Hussars acted as personal escort to
the Commander-in-Chief during the Egyptian campaign
of 1801, yet the battle honour was conferred on the regiment. The three regiments of Household Cavalry bear
the honours " Egypt, 1882," and " South Africa, 1899-
1900 "; yet it was a composite regiment, made up of a
squadron from each regiment, which earned the battle
honour. The headquarters of the 35th were not present
at Maida, nor of the 69th at St. Vincent, yet the Royal
Sussex and the Welsh have been awarded these battle
honours.

When we come to the question of direct representation,
the same anomalies crop up. A regiment, which I need not
further particularize, affords, perhaps, the most striking
instance. It was disbanded at the close of the eighteenth
century for acts of alleged disloyalty and indiscipline.
The order for disbandment was read at the head of every
troop and company in the army. That order contained
such strong expressions as " seditious and outrageous pro-
ceedings," " atrocious acts of disobedience," " insub-
ordination," " indelible stigma," and generally com-
mented on the conduct of the regiment in the strongest

possible terms.   Half a century later a new corps bearing
the same number sprang into existence, and was permitted to bear the battle honours that would have accrued
to its predecessor.   A similar privilege was conferred on
the 19th and 20th Hussars, when they were taken over
from the East India Company, and on the 18th Hussars
and 100th Royal Canadians when they were resuscitated
some fifty years ago.   But there is a long list of regiments
to whom this privilege will now be denied, amongst them
the 76th (Middlesex), 90th (Scottish Rifles), and 98th
(North Staffords), which accompanied General Ruffane
from Belleisle, and were present at the capture of Martinique and Havana.   The 79th, which was with Draper
at Wandewash, Pondicherry, and the capture of Manilla ;
the 84th—Eyre Coote's famous regiment—which took
part in all the earlier battles in India, and which, with the
78th and 91st, captured the Cape of Good Hope in 1795 ;
the 103rd and 104th, which were granted the battle
honour " Niagara " at the same time as the 19th Hussars
and the 100th Regiment.   This list could be added to
almost indefinitely.   I give these few instances to show
how regiments will be affected by the strict application
of the ruling of General Ewart's Committee.

The halo that surrounds the name of the great Duke
of Wellington has led many to suppose that the battles
fought in the Peninsula were combats of giants.   When
we come down to hard facts, and study the casualty
returns, and then reflect on the result of many of these
actions which are inscribed on our colours, it is clear that
they can hardly be described as " having by their results
left their mark on history."   In no less than ten engagements in the Peninsular War for which battle honours
have been granted our losses were less than those at
Oudenarde, the least costly of all Marlborough's battles,
whilst in three, the aggregate of killed only reached
sixteen men.

The following table is, I venture to think, instructive
as showing the scanty recognition accorded to the regi-

ments which fought under Marlborough, the generous
recognition of those which fought under Wellington :

MARLBOROUGH'S BATTLES FOR WHICH NO BATTLE HONOURS HAVE BEEN GRANTED.					WELLINGTON'S BATTLES FOR WHICH BATTLE HONOURS HAVE BEEN GRANTED.				
Engagements.	Officers.		Men.		Engagements.	Officers.		Men.	
	K.	W.	K.	W.		K.	W.	K.	W.
Schellenburg	32	85	638	1,419	Sahagun ..	—	—	2	18
Liége ..	11	20	142	365	The Douro ..	—	10	23	86
Menin ..	34	80	551	1,994	Almaraz ..	2	12	32	101
Lille ..	17	43	447	1,093	Arroyos dos	—	7	7	51
Douai ..	13	61	638	1,093	Molinos ..				
					Tarifa ..	2	3	7	24

On p. 16 I have given the list of regiments that fought
at Schellenburg, with a return of their individual losses.
At Menin we had four, at Liége and Lille five, and at
Douai eight, battalions engaged, so the severity of the
fighting may be gauged.

It may be urged that, as Schellenburg preceded Blenheim by only one month, and that as practically the same
regiments were present at both engagements, such a distinction would merely have the effect of granting two
battle honours to a few specially favoured regiments.
Four days intervened between Roleia and Vimiera—
actions which neither in their severity nor in their results
can be compared to the two victories of Marlborough ;
indeed, several regiments which escaped scathless in
Wellington's two earliest fights bear two battle honours
on their colours. The campaign in Persia lasted
exactly two months, and three insignificant skirmishes
brought four battle honours to the fortunate regiments
present.

I have been unable to trace the casualty returns for
Liége, Menin, and Lille. Those of Douai I give in the

following table, as I do not remember having seen them
in any recent publication :

CASUALTIES AT THE SIEGE AND ASSAULT OF DOUAI.

Regiments.	Officers.		Men.		Regiments.	Officers.		Men.	
	K.	W.	K.	W.		K.	W.	K.	W.
Roy. Artillery	—	—	34	96	24th S. Wales				
Roy. Engineers	—	—	35	45	Borderers ..	1	9	35	148
19th Yorkshire	—	11	94	207	26th Camer'ians	1	6	50	186
21st Roy. Scots					34th Border ..	1	5	81	125
Fusiliers ..	1	7	49	182	Sutton's Regt.	5	8	110	113
23rd R. Welsh					Honeywood's				
Fusiliers ..	2	9	54	147	Regt. ..	2	6	86	170

Surely these figures are eloquent enough to justify the
award of a battle honour to the regiments engaged !

Whilst Marlborough was fighting in Northern Europe,
another British army was engaged in the South, where a
century later our troops under Wellington were to earn
undying fame.   It is true the campaign was tinged with
more than one disaster, owing to the lack of support on
the part of our allies, but it was also relieved by many
gallant actions well worthy of recognition.   The storming
and capture of Valenza by the 33rd (West Riding), the
heroic defence of Alicante, Peterborough's daring capture
of Barcelona, are all feats of arms well worthy of being
emblazoned on colours which already bear such names as
Roleia, Douro, and Tarifa.   The regiments entitled to
share in the honours that might well be awarded for our
earliest campaign in the Peninsula are :

2nd Queen's Bays.	1st Royal Dragoons.
Royal Scots.	8th Royal Irish Hussars.
Royal Warwicks.	Queen's (Royal West Surrey).
King's Own (Lancaster).	Norfolks.
Leicester.	Somerset Light Infantry.
Cornwall Light Infantry.	East Surrey.
Border.	West Riding.
Worcesters.	Royal Sussex.

On p. 8 I have alluded to the gallant defence of Gibraltar by Lord Portmore in 1727 as an instance of a missing battle honour, and have given the losses sustained by the regiments which formed the garrison in that memorable defence. Should " Gibraltar, 1727," be added to the battle honours of the army, as well indeed it may be, the regiments which would be entitled to the distinction are the

Grenadier Guards.	Northumberland Fusiliers.
Somerset Light Infantry.	West Yorkshire.
Royal Irish.	Lancashire Fusiliers.
K.O. Scottish Borderers.	Cameronians.
Worcester.	East Lancashire.
Border.	Dorsets.

Five-and-thirty years later, when our armies, under Prince Ferdinand, were earning the battle honours " Minden," " Warburg," and " Wilhelmstahl," a second army, under Lord Tyrawley, was fighting on the historic battle-fields of Spain. In the year 1910 the 16th Lancers were authorized to wear a special cap plate in recognition of their services at Valencia di Alcantara in the campaign of 1762. On this occasion the Red Lancers made a forced march of forty-five miles, surprised the Spaniards, taking the General in command prisoner, and returning with three stand of colours. This is the only recognition yet accorded for the campaign in the middle of the eighteenth century.

As dates have been added to differentiate between our various campaigns in the West Indies, South Africa, and Gibraltar, it would be a graceful act, and one of strict justice, to add the dates 1727 to the battle honour " Gibraltar," and 1705-06 and 1762 to the battle honour " Peninsula." The following regiments would be entitled to this last distinction—" Peninsula, 1762 " :

16th Lancers.	Buffs.
Hampshire.	Gordon Highlanders.
Royal Irish Rifles.	Shropshire Light Infantry.
	Argyll Highlanders.

These represent the 3rd Buffs, 67th, 75th, 83rd, 85th, 91st, and 92nd Regiments of those far-off days.

Another name that might well be rescued from oblivion is Belleisle. A combined naval and military expedition, under Admiral the Hon. Sir A. Keppel and Major-General Studholme Hodgson, was despatched to that island in the spring of 1761. The troops comprised twelve battalions of infantry, the 16th Light Dragoons, and a strong body of artillery. As usual, we opened the campaign by despising our enemy, and on April 6 met with a sharp reverse. Additional troops were sent out from home, and two months later the French Governor surrendered. Our total losses in the campaign amounted to 13 officers and 271 men killed, 21 officers and 476 men wounded.

The regiments that would be entitled to bear the battle honour " Belleisle " are the

16th Lancers.	Buffs.
Norfolks.	Yorkshire.
Royal Scots Fusiliers.	East Lancashire.
Worcesters.	Hampshire.
Gordon Highlanders.	Middlesex.
Shropshire Light Infantry.	Scottish Rifles.
Welsh.	West Kent.
North Staffords.	

Immediately on the capitulation of the island General Ruffane, who had commanded a brigade throughout the operations, was despatched to the West Indies with the 69th (Welsh), 76th (Middlesex), 90th Light Infantry, and 98th Regiment, to assist in the reduction of Martinique and Havana. These operations have been rewarded with battle honours, and are fully described in Chapter VIII. Ruffane's brigade, however, with the exception of the Welsh, have been denied the honour.

Before leaving the West Indies, I would wish to draw attention to the fact that, whilst the defence of the Island of Dominica in 1805 is inscribed on the colours of the Cornwall Light Infantry, no recognition is made of the capture of that island by the troops under Lord Rollo in 1762, yet surely the one feat is as worthy of remembrance as the other. The appended table may not be without interest to the regiments concerned in the two transactions :

CAPTURE OF DOMINICA, 1762, FOR WHICH NO BATTLE HONOUR HAS BEEN GRANTED.					DEFENCE OF DOMINICA, 1805, FOR WHICH A BATTLE HONOUR HAS BEEN GRANTED.				
	Officers.		*Men.*			*Officers.*		*Men.*	
Regiment.					*Regiment.*				
	K.	W.	K.	W.		K.	W.	K.	W.
42nd Royal Highlanders	2	10	19	74	46th Cornwall L.I.	—	1	11	7

Guadeloupe, 1702, 1794, and 1815, are also battle honours well worthy of remembrance.

Simultaneously with the expedition against Havana, which is alluded to above, and set forth in detail in Chapter VIII., a force was despatched from Madras for the reduction of the Spanish settlement in Manilla, thus forestalling by 150 years the memorable exploits of Admiral Dewey on the same spot. This was under the command of General Draper, who, at the head of his own regiment (then the 79th), had done good service in Southern India. The Spaniards were utterly unprepared, and though the troops with Draper amounted to but one battalion of the line, a naval brigade 1,000 strong, and a brigade of Madras sepoys, the little army was thrown ashore, and after one week's bombardment the forts surrendered, our losses amounting to 5 officers and 28 men killed, 5 officers and 106 men wounded.

The prize-money must have been some slight compensation to the troops for the hardships endured. Field Officers received £1,500, Captains £900, whilst the privates received £6. The Spanish colours captured were presented by General Draper to King's College, Cambridge, and he raised a monument to the memory of the officers and men who fell in the grounds of his private residence, still known as Manilla Hall, Clifton. Under the present ruling of the Army Council there would appear to be no prospect of the word " Manilla " being added to the battle honours of the army.

Another missing distinction is " Cape of Good Hope, 1796." There would appear to be no reason why the first capture of the Cape should not be commemorated equally with the second. In connection with this later expedition there is one unaccountable omission, as I have explained on p. 351. Sir David Baird detached the 20th Light Dragoons and the 38th Regiment (South Staffords), under Brigadier, afterwards Field-Marshal, the Lord Beresford, to Saldanha Bay. The consequence was that they were not actually present at the operations on January 8, and so it comes about that, although they participated in the hardships of the campaign, and contributed to its results, the 20th Hussars and South Staffords have been debarred from bearing the battle honour.

The battle honours for our campaigns in India have been awarded in the same unequal manner : hard-fought battles are unrecognized, paltry skirmishes are emblazoned on our colours. This is partly due to the fact that in the case of those regiments which were in the service of the East India Company the Governor - General or the Governor of the Presidency authorized the distinction, whereas in the case of " King's regiments " the Sovereign alone was the fountain of honour. So it comes about that the Royal Munster and Royal Dublin Fusiliers, the direct representatives of the old European regiments of John Company, bear on their colours battle honours which have not been awarded to the King's regiments which fought by their side, and which, strangely enough, have also been denied to the Indian regiments which took part in the same operations. " Nundy Droog " is on the colours of the Dublins, but the 36th (Worcesters) and 71st (Highland Light Infantry) are still without the honour. The British troops which captured Pondicherry in 1793 comprised the 36th (Worcesters), 52nd (Oxford Light

Infantry), 71st (Highland Light Infantry), and 72nd (Seaforths), with the Madras European Regiment, but the Royal Dublin Fusiliers alone bear the honour.

In some cases a single battle honour, such as "Carnatic," "Mysore," and "Ava," covers a campaign which included in its operations a number of general actions, and had for its results the addition of a province to the Empire. Other campaigns of less severity, and which have had negative results, such as the two wars in Afghanistan and that in Persia, have been rewarded with a profusion of honours, some, indeed, representing the paltriest skirmishes. Battles in which we have lost hundreds are left unnoticed, whilst affairs in which the casualties may be counted on the fingers receive undue recognition.

The old regiments of the Madras native army have suffered under this lack of system. They are much in the same position that Marlborough's regiments occupied until Sir Archibald Alison's Committee gave them relief. They were excluded from any share in the eighteen battle honours awarded for the Afghan and Persian wars, and yet received no recognition of their presence in battles which have been inscribed on the colours of the Madras European regiment—battles which resulted in the overthrow of the Mysorean usurper and the expulsion of the French from India. Surely such battles as these, both in their severity and by their results, may be deemed of sufficient historic interest to warrant their being placed on the colours of the Indian troops which bore their share in the fighting.

At the siege and capture of Pondicherry in 1778 (a battle for which an honour was granted to the Madras Europeans, and which appears on the colours of the Dublins) the Indian regiments of the Madras army lost 19 officers and 646 of other ranks.

At the third capture of the French fortress by General Braithwaite in 1793, for which the Dublins also wear the honour, a strong force of Indian troops was present, and suffered severe loss. The following Madras regiments would become entitled to the missing battle honour, " Pondicherry, 1778-1793 ":

2nd Q.O. Sappers and Miners.	62nd Punjabis.
61st Pioneers.	66th Punjabis.
63rd Palamcottah Light Infantry.	69th Punjabis.
	76th Punjabis.
67th Punjabis.	80th Carnatic Infantry.
	73rd Carnatic Infantry.

Another campaign well worthy of recognition is that which led to the capture of Tanjore in 1771. In this the Indian regiments lost 8 officers and 297 men—a far heavier casualty roll than that which earned *four* battle honours in Persia. The following table shows the regiments that would be entitled to adopt the missing battle honour, " Tanjore, 1771 " :

TANJORE, 1771.

Regiments.	Officers.		Men.		Regiments.	Officers.		Men.	
	K.	W.	K.	W.		K.	W.	K.	W.
Royal Dublin Fusiliers ..	2	3	27	83	66th Punjabis	—	1	17	49
64th Pioneers	—	3	14	22	67th Punjabis	1	—	29	60
					69th Punjabis	—	—	6	21

The earlier Indian battles, which were fraught with great results, but which, fortunately, were not attended with any serious losses, such as Arcot, Plassey, Condore, Masulipatam, Badara, and Buxar, are well deserving of perpetual remembrance, for are they not the foundation-stones of our Indian Empire ? But there are other battles, no less momentous in their results, and which were attended with far heavier loss of life, which have been left unrecorded. Macleod's defeat of Tippoo Sultan at Paniani, Munro's capture of Negapatam from the Dutch, Stuart's victory at Cuddalore, were more far-reaching in their results, and entailed far harder fighting and far more severe privations, than, let us say, Koosh-ab or Charasia. "Seringapatam" can be read on the colours of the regiments which stormed the fortress under Lord Harris, but the distinction has never been granted to those which carried the place by assault under Lord Cornwallis seven years earlier. "Guzerat" was awarded to the Bengal troops which, under Goddard, marched to the relief of the Bombay army in 1779, but the services of the Bombay column which marched across the continent to the assistance of Lord Lake in the First Mahratta War have never yet been recorded. The 65th (York and Lancaster), 86th (Irish Rifles), 102nd Bombay Grenadiers, 104th Wellesley's Rifles, 105th Mahratta Light Infantry, and 117th Mahrattas, did right good and gallant work in that campaign, for which they have no distinction. In the same war the 22nd (Cheshires) played a conspicuous rôle, but their services in Cuttack, as well as at Bhurtpore, have been forgotten.

"Bourbon" is borne on the colours of the 69th (Welsh) and 86th (Royal Irish Rifles). Surely the honour should also be accorded to the 56th (Essex), which were present at both attacks on the island. If the capture of Bourbon, which was restored to France on the conclusion of peace, is deemed worthy of an honour, the taking of the Mauritius, still a British possession, is no less deserving of one. The regiments which formed General J. Abercromby's force included the 12th (Suffolk), 14th (West Yorks), 22nd (Cheshires), 33rd (West Riding), 56th (Essex), 59th (East Lancashire), 84th (York and Lancaster), 87th and 89th (Royal Irish Fusiliers), and 104th Wellesley's Rifles. From the Mauritius many of these regiments went on to the conquest of Java, for which they received a battle honour. It is true that the subjugation of that island cost us many lives, but it has never been the custom to take into consideration casualties in awarding battle honours. It seems difficult to understand why Bourbon and Java should be deemed worthy of distinction, whilst Mauritius and Ceylon remain unnoticed.

Another noticeable omission in the list of India battle honours is " Nepaul." If we except the two campaigns of 1846 and 1849 against the Sikhs, that against the Gurkhas entailed the hardest fighting we have ever experienced in India. At the outset we met with more than one reverse, and suffered enormous losses, the casualties of the 53rd (Shropshire Light Infantry) alone totalling 21 officers and 428 of other ranks killed and wounded. A dismounted detachment of the 8th Hussars, 100 strong, lost 5 officers and 57 men. The result of the war was a lasting alliance with the kingdom of Nepaul, and the opening up to our Indian army of a field of recruits unsurpassed for heroism, discipline, and loyalty. The troops entitled to such a distinction would be the 8th Hussars, 17th (Leicesters), 24th (South Wales Borderers), 53rd (Shropshire Light Infantry), 87th (Royal Irish Fusiliers), and the 2nd Queen's Own Rajput Light Infantry.

The 55th (Border Regiment) have no distinction to record the loss of upwards of 100 men in the campaign in Coorg in 1834 ; nor the Leicesters for their still heavier losses at the siege and assault of the fort of Kamounah twenty-five years previously.

A reference to the chapter on the Indian Mutiny will show that there were but three battle honours (if I except the two given to the 45th Sikhs) granted for the three years' campaign—" Delhi," " Lucknow," and " Central India." Yet there were many regiments whose task was no less arduous, and whose services were as valuable, as those performed by the regiments which took part in the final capture of Lucknow. Hunting down bands of rebels during the hot weather was not the easiest part of the campaign, and the disarmament of disaffected native troops in the Punjab was a task of the heaviest responsibility. The services of the 13th (Somerset Light Infantry) at Azimghur, of the 24th (South Wales Borderers) at Jhelum, of the 27th (Inniskilling Fusiliers) at Peshawar, of the 81st (Loyal North Lancashire) at Lahore, brought decorations to the commanders and medals to the men, but to the regiments nothing to show the part they played in holding fast to our Indian Empire in the day of our darkest trouble. Another fact in connection with the battle honours for the Mutiny is deserving of remark. The 32nd (Cornwall Light Infantry) have no special distinction to differentiate them from those regiments which shared in Sir Colin Campbell's final and comparatively bloodless capture of the city in March, 1858. The defence of Lucknow stands out as a feat apart, and must for ever remain one of the grandest episodes in our military history. A special clasp was granted with the medal, but no special battle honour. The regiments which were with Sir George White bear the distinction " Defence of Ladysmith "; the Loyal North Lancashire, " Defence of Kimberley "; the 13th (Somerset) have a mural crown, with the word " Jelalabad "; and the regiments that were with Eliott at Gibraltar have the castle and key, with a distinctive motto, as emblematic of its defence ; but the Cornwall Light Infantry bear the single word, " Lucknow," with no emblem commemorative of that heroic defence which thrilled our country half a century ago, and which made the name of Havelock a household word wherever the English language is spoken.

I have alluded to the two special honours awarded to the 45th Rattray's Sikhs for the Mutiny—" Defence of Arrah " and " Behar." The gallant defence of Arrah by a handful of Sikhs, under the leadership of a Bengal civilian, Wake, was a striking episode in a campaign in which heroic actions were of daily occurrence ; but the award of this battle honour to the 45th Sikhs brings out into strong relief the omission to grant a like honour to the 2nd Queen's Own Rajput Light Infantry for the no less heroic defence of Saugor. Saugor was in the centre of a district seething with revolt. The garrison of Jubbulpore, the nearest cantonment, had fallen away, murdering their officers, and the other sepoy battalion in Saugor also joined the mutineers ; but the 31st Bengal

Infantry (now the 2nd Queen's Own Light Infantry) stood firm. They had every inducement to abandon their trust. The neighbouring Princes had thrown in their lot with the rebels, and offered tempting rewards for the rupees that lay in the treasury and the ammunition that was stored in the arsenal. There was a large number of Christian women and children in the fort, whose surrender was demanded. The 31st not merely defended these, but on more than one occasion sallied out and attacked the rebels, and on one memorable day returned with a couple of guns. This was not a defence of a week, as at Arrah. The Saugor garrison was isolated from the month of July, 1857, when the Mutiny reached its head, until its relief by the Central India Field Force, under the command of Sir Hugh Rose, in January, 1858.

I am well aware that the 32nd (Cornwalls) and the 31st Bengal Native Infantry were respectively made Light Infantry regiments for the defence—the one of Lucknow, the other of Saugor ; but memories are short. Few outside their own ranks know whence their bugles came ; indeed, in this very year (1910) a leading Service paper, in answer to a correspondent, asserted that the 32nd were made light infantry in the year 1832 ! In addition to the special battle honours, " Defence of Lucknow " and " Defence of Saugor," all regiments which took part in the suppression of the great rebellion in India should be awarded the battle honour " India, 1857-58."

For upwards of half a century a picked body of native troops kept watch and ward over the North-West Frontier of our Indian Empire, waging numberless campaigns against the independent tribes who people the borderland between our frontiers and those of Afghanistan. In many of these border wars the fighting has been hard, the losses very severe, but until the year 1897 no battle honour was awarded for these services. Three medals have been issued, with clasps for close on fifty different expeditions, but the regiments of the old Punjab Frontier Force, which held that border for fifty years, and which in so doing lost upwards of 2,000 officers and men, have never been authorized to add to their colours the first two names of their old and well-known title.

The distinction " Punjab Frontier " was subsequently conferred on a number of regiments which were present in one of the more recent campaigns. In the Umbeyla Expedition of 1863 the total casualties were 36 officers and 1,080 men killed and wounded, the heaviest falling on the 71st (Highland Light Infantry) and 101st (now Munster Fusiliers), and the three magnificent Punjab regiments commanded by Majors Ross, Brownlow, and Keyes. At Umbeyla the Highland Light Infantry suffered more heavily than in the Crimea and Mutiny combined, but it bears no battle honours to remind it that it lost five officers killed in the Boneyr Hills.

Here it may not be out of place to call attention to the marvellous success that attended the Punjab Frontier Force as a training-school for officers of the Indian army. It was formed immediately after the conquest of the Punjab in 1849, the first commander being Brigadier Hodgson, a grandson of the Studholme Hodgson who took Belleisle in 1761. It was raised partly from the tribes beyond our border, partly from the disbanded soldiers of the Sikh army, partly from men of the Punjab, and was officered by selected Captains and subalterns from the three presidencies of Bengal, Madras, and Bombay. It was composed of five regiments of cavalry, two mountain and two field batteries, ten battalions of infantry, and the famous Corps of Guides. Not only did it bear the brunt of every expedition on the Punjab Frontier, but its regiments fought in Burmah in 1852 and in the Mutiny with rare distinction. In the half-century of its existence it has seen three of its members reach the highest rank in the army—that of Field-Marshal—fifteen have been raised to the dignity of Grand Cross of the Bath, and sixteen have won the Victoria Cross. The young officers of the Punjab Force were taught to act on their own responsibility. There was a total absence of red tape

29

from the first, and the result was the upgrowth of a school which did not a little to the saving of our Indian Empire in the dark days of 1857. Subalterns had found themselves in command of regiments, Captains at the head of brigades of all arms, and when the Mutiny broke out John Lawrence had at his hand a body of youngsters whom he employed to raise regiments on a nucleus of their own corps. The squadrons that Probyn and Watson (both these officers won the Victoria Cross, and have lived to wear the Grand Cross of the Bath) took down to Delhi expanded into regiments. As with the cavalry, so with the infantry. In the China War of 1860 practically the whole of the native troops employed at the front had been raised by officers of the Punjab Irregular Force, and in the Abyssinian War, seven years later, the Bengal Brigade was composed of regiments raised in the same manner. The regiments which served under the great Duke in Spain were authorized to bear the word " Peninsula " on their colours and appointments, even though they had not been present at any of the general actions for which a special distinction was conferred. It would be a graceful act to recognize the service of the Punjab Force by granting the battle honour " Punjab Frontier, 1849-1897," to each regiment of the old Frontier Force which for that long fifty years bore the brunt of the fighting from Cashmere to Baluchistan.

Honours to regiments for participation in naval actions appear also to have been bestowed with the same lack of system. When we remember that for many years prior to the Napoleonic wars, as well as throughout the period 1793 to 1814, detachments of troops were regularly employed in the fleet, it is certainly somewhat invidious that only three regiments should bear the naval crown on their colours and appointments. The Welsh is doubly honoured in having the words " St. Vincent," as well as the naval crown, with the date " April 12, 1782." The Queen's and Worcesters bear the crown, with the date " June 1, 1794." I make no pretence of giving an exhaustive list of the engagements in which soldiers have fought in the fleet. I merely wish to emphasize the fact that many regiments are entitled to the distinction conferred on the Queen's, the Worcesters, and the Welsh.

The headquarters of the 39th (Dorsets) was with Admiral Watson at the destruction of the nest of pirates at Gheriah, and subsequently accompanied him to the relief of Calcutta and the capture of Chandernagore. The 4th King's Own and 46th (Cornwall) were with Lord Byron in the action off Granada in 1779, the 14th (West Yorks) with Rodney at the Relief of Gibraltar. The 5th Fusiliers, 17th (Leicester), and 87th (Royal Irish Fusiliers) were with the same Admiral when he defeated De Grasse two years later. The headquarters of the 98th and a strong detachment of the 78th were in Sir E. Hughes's fleet in the five actions with Suffren in the Bay of Bengal in 1782-83. In his despatch Sir Edward alludes to the valuable services afforded by Colonel Fullerton, of the 98th. In the engagement of July 9, 1782, both regiments suffered severely.

Long prior to this the Grenadier and the Coldstream Guards were at the Battle of Solebay, in 1672, and the Royal Fusiliers were with Byng in the action off Minorca. The services of the Berkshires and of the Rifle Brigade in Nelson's fleet brought the battle honour " Copenhagen " to these distinguished corps, but they are without the crown to show that it was won for naval services.

I think I have written enough on " missing battle honours " to show that these distinctions are bestowed on no definite plan. Abyssinia represents a marvellous triumph of military organization, which gave the lie to the most ominous prophecies of disaster. Detroit, Reshire, and Charasiah record skirmishes rather than historic battles. Amboyna, Banda, and Ternate recall but minor deeds of glory. Martinique and Guadeloupe remind us of conquests oft repeated, with no permanent benefit to the Empire. Roleia and Vimiera are associated more with the humiliating Convention of Cintra than with military triumphs. On the other hand, the regiments which brought Ceylon, Dominica, and Mauritius under our flag are still unrewarded ; for Marlborough's victories but four honours have been granted, four-and-twenty for those of Wellington.

When Reshire and Hafir find a place on our colours, surely room might be found for Schellenberg and Douai, for Menin, Nepaul, and Umbeyla. Minorca and its gallant defence might be embroidered side by side with Tarifa, El-bodon and Lerena with Sahagun, Ramnuggur with Aliwal, and Barcelona with St. Sebastian.

The names on our colours do indeed testify to our " far-flung battle-line." From Niagara to Pekin, from Copenhagen to the Cape of Good Hope, the British soldier has fought, and bled, and conquered. To record all the gallant deeds of the British army would be impossible. In this chapter it has been my endeavour to recall a few which have as yet found no place on our colours. There is still room for the names of many such victories which " by their results have left a mark in history, and which are familiar not only to the British army, but to every educated gentleman."

The names inscribed on our colours should be familiarized to every schoolboy, and, at the risk of being accused of militarism, I would suggest that in every Board school should be hung the facsimile of the colours of the county regiment, and that every lad should be taught the part that regiment has played in the building of our Empire— an Empire which is the heritage of every son of Britain. Under the territorial system the nation and the army are being drawn closer to each other. Battle honours are now no longer the peculiar property of the regiment which earned them, but are proudly borne by corps which have never seen a shot fired in anger, and thus they become a source of pride to the county to which those regiments belong. The men of territorial regiments and the boys of cadet corps all have their share in the battle honours of their county regiments.

History, we are told, is but a record of crimes. Those crimes cannot be laid to the charge of the men who, in obedience to orders, went forth to face death in the battles which are inscribed on the colours of our army. Those dead heroes lie in long-forgotten graves, but the humblest private among them was an empire-builder—a member of that advance guard of civilization which Great Britain has sent forth to the uttermost ends of the earth. Hateful though war be, few are the wars we have waged that have not ultimately brought peace and prosperity in their train, and there are still fewer names on our colours from which other lessons than those of tactics and strategy may not be learnt.

"England expects that every man will do his duty " was the last signal of the immortal Nelson—one which he kept flying to the end. That, too, is the signal held before every soldier when the colours are uncased. The names embroidered in their letters of gold are a perpetual reminder to him that those who have gone before him, and whose privilege it has been to die under those standards, have ever acted up to Nelson's signal and to the immemorial traditions of the British army,

DULCE ET DECORUM EST PRO PATRIA MORI.

APPENDIX I

EGYPT, 1884

THIS distinction has been conferred on the

10th Hussars.	19th Hussars.
Royal Highlanders.	King's Royal Rifles.
York and Lancaster Regiment.	Royal Irish Fusiliers.
Gordon Highlanders.	

It commemorates a short campaign which entailed some hard fighting in the neighbourhood of Suakin, on the Red Sea, in the early part of the year 1884. The campaign of 1884 in Egypt was primarily due to the action of the mutinous Egyptian army, but it was soon found that the evil was far more deeply seated. The British occupation struck at the root of the prosperity of Upper Egypt, where thousands depended on the slave trade, and serious risings against the authority of the Khedive took place throughout the Soudan. The forces despatched to restore order were signally defeated. As these were under the command of English officers, lent to the Egyptian Government, we at once became involved. One of these armies, commanded by Hicks Pasha, which had been sent from Khartoum towards the Equatorial provinces, was annihilated. A second, under Valentine Baker Pasha, was cut to pieces in the near neighbourhood of Suakin. It was to wipe out the stain of this defeat that General Sir Gerald Graham was despatched with the above force in February, 1884. The 10th Hussars and 89th (Royal Irish Fusiliers) had been stopped on their way home from India ; the other regiments formed a portion of the army of occupation. Sir

454

Gerald fought two general actions—the one at El Teb on February 24, the other at Tamai on March 14. The Egyptian medal of 1882 was conferred on the troops present in the campaign, with clasps for the two actions, those present in both receiving one clasp with the two names engraved on it. The regiments received but one battle honour—" Egypt, 1884."

CASUALTIES AT EL TEB, FEBRUARY 24, 1884.

Forces employed.	Officers.		Men.		Forces employed.	Officers.		Men.	
	K.	W.	K.	W.		K.	W.	K.	W.
Royal Artillery	—	1	1	—	Roy. Engineers	—	1	1	—
10th Hussars	2	1	4	—	19th Hussars	1	2	13	20
Royal Highlanders ..	—	3	3	—	King's Royal Rifles ..	1	—	—	—
York and Lancaster ..	—	3	7	—	Royal Irish Fusiliers ..	—	1	—	7
Gordon Highlanders ..	—	—	—	—	Royal Marines	—	2	3	—
					Naval Brigade	1	2	2	9

CASUALTIES AT TAMAI, MARCH 14, 1884.

Forces employed.	Officers.		Men.		Forces employed.	Officers.		Men.	
	K.	W.	K.	W.		K.	W.	K.	W.
10th Hussars	—	—	—	—	19th Hussars	—	—	—	—
Royal Highlanders ..	1	4	60	29	King's Royal Rifles ..	—	—	—	5
York and Lancaster ..	1	1	30	23	Royal Irish Fusiliers ..	—	1	—	5
Gordon Highlanders ..	—	1	1	8	Royal Marines	—	—	3	15
					Naval Brigade	3	—	6	7

APPENDIX II

DEFENCE OF KIMBERLEY, 1899-1900

THIS battle honour is borne only by the Loyal North Lancashire Regiment. The importance of holding fast to Kimberley, the headquarters of the diamond industry in South Africa, was, of course, early recognized by the authorities at the Cape ; but, owing to the extent of territory we had to guard and the paucity of the troops at his disposal, Sir Forestier Walker was only able to spare a half-battalion of regulars for the garrison of this extremely valuable centre. Its command was entrusted to Colonel Kekewich, of the old 47th Foot. His position was one of great delicacy, for the uncrowned King of South Africa, the Right Honourable Cecil Rhodes, judged it his duty to undergo the perils of the siege. The gigantic intellect of Mr. Rhodes and his independence of character did not lend itself to a due appreciation of the military situation. He fretted at the action of the officers in supreme command. At the same time, he showed unexampled generosity in assisting the civilians who were beleaguered with him, and spent money like water in furthering all plans for the defence of the town which met with his approval. The population of the place was upwards of 40,000, of whom no less than 35,000 were natives. To feed these and to guard the long perimeter from attack taxed the slender resources of the brave commander to the uttermost. The force at his disposal consisted of one company of Garrison Artillery, four companies North Lancashire Regiment, Diamond Field Artillery (six guns), Kimberley Infantry,

Diamond Field Horse, Kimberley ¡Horse, numbering in all some 1,200 men. From the declaration of war on October 12, 1899, until the relief by General French on February 16, 1900, the town was closely besieged. The civilian element suffered but little from the desultory bombardment, nor were the casualties amongst the garrison abnormally heavy.

CASUALTIES AT THE DEFENCE OF KIMBERLEY.

Forces employed.	Officers.		Men.	
	K.	W.	K.	W.
North Lancashire Regiment ..	1	3	4	10
Other military details	1	7	13	43
Civilian population	—	—	5	24

APPENDIX III

AMBOOR

THE distinction commemorates the gallant defence of the Fort of Amboor, in the Carnatic, by a force under the command of Captain Calvert, of the Madras army, when closely besieged by Hyder Ali's army in the year 1767. Calvert's garrison consisted of a sergeant's party of the old 1st Madras European Regiment, now the Royal Dublin Fusiliers, one company of the 4th Madras Infantry, and the headquarters of the 10th Madras Infantry, some 500 strong. On November 15, five days after Hyder Ali's batteries opened fire, Calvert was compelled to abandon the lower fort, owing to the severity of the bombardment and the fact that the siege batteries commanded his outworks. He held the upper fort until the advance of the main army, under Colonel Smith, on December 10, compelled Hyder Ali to withdraw. In recognition of the steady gallantry displayed by the 10th Madras Infantry, it was officially designated the Amboor Regiment, and was authorized to carry a third colour, recording the defence of Amboor. Its casualties during the siege amounted to a native officer and 11 men killed and 23 men wounded. The 10th Gurkhas, which is the lineal descendant of the old 10th Madras Native Infantry, has not yet been authorized to assume this battle honour.

APPENDIX IV

WAR MEDALS

IN the reign of Queen Anne medals were struck to commemorate military operations, though it does not appear that these were actually bestowed on the officers who assisted at them. In Boyer's "History of the Reign of Queen Anne" excellent facsimiles are given of the medals enumerated below :

1. The Capture of Kaiserwart, Venloo, and Liége, 1702.
2. The Destruction of the Spanish Fleet in Vigo, 1702.
3. The Battle of Blenheim, 1704.
4. The Capture of Gibraltar, 1704.
5. The Battle of Ramillies, 1706.
6. The Relief of Barcelona, 1706.
7. The Battle of Oudenarde, 1708.
8. The Capture of Lille, 1708.
9. The Capture of Sardinia and Minorca, 1708.
10. The Capture of Tournay, 1709.
11. The Battle of Malplaquet, 1709.
12. The Capture of Mons.
13. The Capture of Douay.
14. The Capture of Bethune, St. Venant, and Aire, 1710.
15. The Battle of Almancara, in Spain, July 16, 1710.
16. The Battle of Saragossa, August 9, 1710.
17. The Capture of Bouchain, 1711.

The East India Company had for many years been in the habit of granting medals or other rewards to officers and men employed in military operations under the orders of the Governor-General. These had been conferred on officers of the King's as well as on those of the Honourable Company's Services, but in the case of King's officers permission was rarely granted for such medals to be worn outside the Company's dominions. It was not until the year 1815 that the Prince Regent, following the example of the East India Company, suggested the bestowal of a silver medal on all officers and men who had been present at the Battle of Waterloo or the engagements of the two previous days.

Prior to this the East India Company had granted gold medals to the British officers and silver to native officers present in the following campaigns :

1. The Campaign in Guzerat in 1778-1782. All ranks.
2. The War in Mysore, 1791-1794. Officers only.
3. The Expedition to Ceylon, 1796. Officers only.
4. The Capture of Seringapatam, 1799. Officers only.
5. The Expedition to Egypt in 1801. Officers only.
6. The Expeditions to Rodriguez, Bourbon, and the Mauritius, in the years 1809-10. Officers only.
7. The Expedition to Java in 1811. Officers only.

Then came the issue of the Waterloo Medal by the Prince Regent, subsequently to which the East India Company continued the issue of medals at the close of any important campaign. The medals now took a different form, being assimilated to that issued for Waterloo. These smaller medals were granted for—

8. The War in Nepaul, 1814-1817.
9. The First Burmese War, 1824-1826.
10. The Capture of Ghuznee.
11. The Defence of Jelalabad, 1842.
12. The Defence of Khelat-i-Ghilzai, 1842.
13. A medal for the War in Afghanistan, inscribed with one or more of the following names : Candahar, 1842 ; Ghuznee, 1842 ; or Cabool, 1842.

Queen Victoria, on being applied to, gave her consent to this medal being worn by officers and men in uniform beyond the dominions of the East India Company. At the same time the young Queen expressed her opinion that there should be but one fountain of honour, and that it should not be left to a company of merchants to award decorations to soldiers of the Crown.

The next occasion on which the East India Company bestowed a medal was for—

14. Sir Charles Napier's Expedition in Scinde, when a medal, inscribed " Meeanee " or " Hyderabad," or, in the case of those present at both battles, with both names, to all ranks who fought in Scinde.

15. For the Gwalior Campaign a bronze five-pointed star was issued ; and
16. The First Sikh War of 1846 saw the last issue of a medal by the East India Company.
17. The Medal for the Punjab Campaign of 1848 being authorized by Queen Victoria.

The Duke of Richmond, who had served on the Staff of the Duke of Wellington in the Peninsular War, now moved in Parliament that a medal be bestowed on the survivors of the campaigns fought under the Great Duke. The Duke himself, if he did not actually oppose the motion, at any rate threw cold water upon it. The young Queen, however, was a warm supporter of the idea of rewarding the men who had fought for England long years before, and, after lengthy discussions, it was decided that a silver medal should be bestowed on all survivors, officers and men, of the following battles :

Roleia, August 17, 1808.
Vimiera, August 21, 1808.
Sahagun, December 21, 1808.
Benevente, January 3, 1809.
Corunna, January 16, 1809.
The Douro, May 24, 1809.
Talavera, July 27, 1809.
Busaco, September 27, 1810.
Barrosa, March 4, 1811.
Fuentes d'Onor, May 5, 1811.
Albuera, May 16, 1811.
Ciudad Rodrigo, January, 1812.
Badajoz, March and April, 1812.
Salamanca, July 22, 1812.
Vittoria, June 21, 1813.
Pyrenees, July 28 to August 2, 1813.
St. Sebastian, August and September, 1813.
Nivelle, November 10, 1813.
Nive, December 9-13, 1813.
Orthes, February 27, 1814.
Toulouse, April 10, 1814.

Subsequently the issue of the medal was sanctioned to the survivors of the following operations :

Egypt, 1801.
Maida, 1806.
Martinique, 1809.
Guadeloupe, 1810.

Java, 1811.
Fort Detroit, August, 1812.
Chateaugay, October, 1813.
Chrystler's Farm, November 1, 1813.

Efforts were made, but unsuccessfully, to extend the medal so as to include the capture of the Cape of Good Hope, of Mauritius, and the war in Nepaul. It will be noticed that the medal was granted for services extending from the Egyptian campaign of 1801 to the Battle of Toulouse in 1814 ; yet the medal bears the dates 1794-1814, and is graced with the head of the young Queen Victoria, who was not born until five years after Toulouse was fought.

In February, 1851, a similar medal was granted to the survivors of the many campaigns waged in India between the years 1798 and 1826 ; with it were issued the following clasps :

Seringapatam.	Alli Ghur.	Delhi, 1803.
Assaye.	Assurghur.	Laswarree.
Argaum.	Gawalghur.	Delhi, 1804.
Deig.	Nepaul.	Kirkee.
Seetabuldee.	Nagpore.	Maheidpore.
Corygaum.	Ava.	Bhurtpore.

The issue of the Peninsular Medal inaugurated a new system with regard to the rewards for military services, and henceforth the officers and men of the navy and army have been rewarded with a medal for practically every campaign in which they have been engaged. Times have indeed changed. In the early days of the Peninsular War the Duke of Wellington refused to recommend the issue of the gold medal (which was only granted to field officers) except to those who had been actually under the *musketry* fire of the enemy. Ninety years later we have seen a medal granted for garrison service in Malta and St. Helena the while a war was in progress in South Africa.

INDEX

THE END